W9-BLT-987

Red Sox Heroes
of Yesteryear

OTHER BOOKS BY HERB CREHAN
Lightning in a Bottle: The Sox of '67
*Boston Red Sox *100 Years* The Official Retrospective*
(contributing author)

Red Sox Heroes of Yesteryear

Herb Crehan

Rounder Books

Cambridge, Massachusetts

Copyright © 2005 by Herb Crehan

Published by Rounder Books

an imprint of:
Rounder Records Corp.
One Camp Street
Cambridge, MA 02140

All rights reserved. No part of this book may be reproduced in whole or in part
without written permission from the publisher, except by reviewers who may quote
brief excerpts in connection with a review in a newspaper, magazine, or electronic
publication; nor may any part of this book be reproduced, stored in a retrieval system, or transmitted in any form or by any means electronic, mechanical, photo-
copying, recording, or other, without written permission from the publisher.

ISBN: 1-57940-118-X

Cover design by Sarah Lainie Smith
Interior design and typesetting by Swordsmith Productions

Crehan, Herb, 1943-
Red Sox Heroes of Yesteryear

1. Boston Red Sox (Baseball team). Biography. 2. Baseball Players. Biography. I
Title.

First Edition
2004117464
796.357
ISBN: 1-57940-118-X

9 8 7 6 5 4 3 2 1

For Janet

and

Soxer & Emma

Contents

Acknowledgments

All of these profiles of former players appeared in their original form in *Red Sox Magazine*, the official program of the Boston Red Sox. I am deeply indebted to the Boston Red Sox for allowing me to update, expand, and publish this material. I also want to acknowledge the approval of Major League Baseball to move forward with this project.

In particular at the Boston Red Sox, I want to thank Dick Bresciani, Vice President of Publications and Archives, and Debbie Matson who is the Director of Publications. Their encouragement and assistance during the 10 seasons that I have been associated with *Red Sox Magazine* has meant the world to me.

Debbie Matson has dealt with deadline challenges and misspellings with unfailing good humor. I especially appreciate her work in assembling the photographs that are contained in this book.

I also want to thank Bill Nowlin of Rounder Books, who conceived of this project and brought it to fruition. His commitment to quality and his knowledge of baseball has been invaluable.

A very special thank you is due to my lovely wife, Janet Salsman, who is my biggest fan and my toughest critic. She has improved every feature that I have ever written, and I can count on her to tell me if I have missed the mark in any way.

Most of all, I want to thank the 39 former players, and Billy and Richie Conigliaro, for the time that they spent with me. They have all been thoughtful with their responses and generous with their memories. To thank them, I am contributing a portion of any income I receive from this book to the Jimmy Fund, in their names.

Finally, I want to thank Mr. Red Sox, Johnny Pesky, for writing the foreword to this book, and for his considerable help over the years. His insights on these players and his colorful quotes have enriched my stories.

Writing for *Red Sox Magazine* and publishing this book have been wonderful experiences. But the best part has been the relationships that have been formed. I am especially thankful for each of those relationships.

—HERB CREHAN

Photographs on page 133 are courtesy of Gene Conley
Photograph on page 227 is courtesy of Richard Johnson and the
Sports Museum. All other photographs are courtesy of the Boston Red Sox.

Red Sox Heroes
of Yesteryear

FOREWORD

It's no secret I have a great love for this ball club. Everybody knows that. When I got involved with the Red Sox, they treated me like a king. The Red Sox have done a lot for me over the years and I have never forgotten that.

Every player has some rough spots in their career, but baseball has never disappointed me, and I have the same affection for the Red Sox that I had when I was a young player.

Is there something about Red Sox fans that makes them appreciate the past players more than fans of other teams? When Dom and Bobby and I went out on the field during the World Series, we got a pretty good ovation. When they've introduced me on the field, the fans are always extremely generous. It makes me feel good.

John Harrington treated us well. He is a fine man. These new owners have shown a lot of respect for tradition, too, and it's flattering.

The fans of today, the younger group, they never saw us play and they only know about us from what they might have read about players of our era. People are responding. I never got this attention when I was a player!

We have players today who impress me. I got to talking with Mr. Lucchino recently and I told him how much I appreciated Curt Schilling. I never saw a guy study the opposition—the hitters—like he does. The day he pitches, he comes to the ballpark at 2 o'clock and he'd open that book he keeps and study it for an hour. He'd get loose, he'd start the game, and I'd still see him going to that book in the dugout in the fourth or fifth inning. I admire that. Ted Williams was like that about hitting—prepared and thorough.

I always enjoy talking with Herb Crehan. When I mention players from the forties and fifties, he always knows who they are and what they did.

Herb's series of articles about Red Sox players of yesteryear has run in the

Red Sox magazine for years and years. I played with some guys and I've coached other guys. He'll call me from time to time and ask me about one of these players, and I'm always glad to help. Herb is an awful nice man.

I enjoy reading the stories and I look forward to each issue. I am sure that any true Red Sox fan will treasure this collection.

—JOHNNY PESKY

PROLOGUE

This book is written for Red Sox fans by a lifelong fan of the team. Before each interview with the former player I asked myself: what would the typical fan sitting in Fenway Park like to know about this man?

I began many of my interviews by saying: "I sat in the bleachers watching you play for many years, and there are a couple of questions I always wanted to ask you." The players always responded positively to these words. In many cases they volunteered their own special memories of the fans.

As I wrote each chapter I pictured three types of fans. First, I imagined a long-time fan with strong memories of the player. I wanted to provide that fan with a credible profile and a fresh perspective.

I also pictured the younger fans and thought back to my first game at Fenway Park in the early fifties. I want them to enjoy the colorful history of the team and its many outstanding former players. It would be nice if they grow up to love baseball and the Boston Red Sox as much as I do.

And I visualized the casual fan who gets to Fenway Park once or twice each season and who was swept up in the historic 2004 World Championship. I wanted them to know more of the team's past so that the World Series victory was even sweeter.

One of the best things about our long-awaited World Championship is that it changes our perspective on the players included in this book. Those *were* the good old days, and these former players are our nostalgic heroes now.

Johnny Pesky *did not* hold the ball in the 1946 World Series. You can learn what really happened through the words of former teammates Bobby Doerr and Dom DiMaggio. And you may think you have read everything there is to know about Ted Williams, but this book includes the only history of Ted's spring training experiences.

The team didn't win much to speak of in the fifties and early sixties, but some wonderful ballplayers played for the Red Sox during that era. Frank Malzone, Bill Monbouquette, and Dick Radatz are profiled here among others.

The Red Sox are the premier franchise in major league baseball and New England fans are the best, but you should know that the 1967 Impossible Dream Team made it all possible. The average attendance at Fenway Park in 1966 was 10,000 fans per game and interest in the team was waning.

But in 1967 more than 1.7 million fans crowded Fenway Park and the region's passion for baseball was reborn. Yaz, Jim Lonborg, and Tony Conigliaro are just three of the eight great players from that team who are included in these pages.

The Big Red Machine from Cincinnati was heavily favored to win the 1975 World Championship, but the Red Sox extended them to seven games in one of the most exciting World Series ever played. Pudge Fisk and Bernie Carbo describe their historic Game Six home runs in their profiles.

When you mention the Red Sox-Yankees playoff in 1978, the knee-jerk response is "Bucky Bleeping Dent." But Don Zimmer, Fred Lynn, and Butch Hobson all remember a team that wouldn't quit in the last two weeks of the season, forcing the historic confrontation.

Bob Stanley and Rich Gedman recall their personal disappointment at the heartbreaking loss to the Mets in the 1986 World Series. But Stanley shares a subsequent personal experience that puts that loss in its proper perspective.

These profiles provide rich insights into the players' lives once their active careers were over. Many of these former players continued in baseball after their playing days were over. In fact, nine of these former players went on to manage at the big league level.

After managing or coaching baseball, the next most popular "second career" is broadcasting. In addition to Jerry Remy, who comes into our homes on a regular basis, twelve of these former players have been actively involved in radio or television at some point.

Also, Jim Lonborg went on to a career in dentistry, Mike Andrews is the long-time Executive Director of the Jimmy Fund, and Bernie Carbo speaks to groups throughout the country as part of his spiritual ministry. Although many of these former players are retired, they are all still active and they are greeted warmly whenever they return to Fenway Park.

Two of the players featured here have passed away. Tony Conigliaro died in 1990, but his brothers Billy and Richie contributed their loving memories of Tony C's storybook career. I interviewed Maurice "Mickey" McDermott in May 2003, and sadly Mickey passed away on August 8, 2003.

Each of these profiles originally appeared in a similar form in *Red Sox Magazine*, the official program of the Boston Red Sox. However, every chapter has been updated and in most cases, substantially expanded. You will see in the introduction to each chapter, that every profile was preceded by a personal interview with the former player.

There is often a "disconnect" between what the fans are really interested in and what the media chooses to cover. The classic example is the so-called "Curse." I have never met a thoughtful Red Sox fan who considered the Curse to be a serious subject.

I am confident that every Red Sox fan will feel connected to these profiles.

1.
Bobby Doerr Interview
January 2001

Hall of Famer Bobby Doerr was the obvious choice as the first player to be featured in the Red Sox program for 2001. That season marked the team's one-hundredth anniversary and Bobby Doerr was clearly the greatest second baseman in Red Sox history.

I spoke by telephone to Bobby at his Junction City, Oregon, home on the banks of the Rogue River. An avid outdoorsman, he paused several times during our conversation to describe the wildlife that he could see through his living room window.

I knew that Bobby Doerr had put together a number of wonderful seasons for the Red Sox between 1937 and 1951. But I didn't appreciate how great he was until I did the research for this profile.

I first met Bobby Doerr at the 1988 Red Sox fantasy camp in Winter Haven, Florida. I have been fortunate enough to meet him several times since. You have probably read that Bobby Doerr is a very nice man and a real gentleman. In my experience, that understates the case.

Robert Pershing Doerr is number "1" on the façade of the right-field grandstand, and he is number one in my book.

BOBBY DOERR
THE GREATEST SECOND BASEMAN IN
RED SOX HISTORY

Bobby Doerr is the greatest second baseman in the history of the Boston Red Sox. In a 1969 poll of Red Sox fans, Doerr was named as the best second baseman, joining such former stars as fellow Hall of Famers Ted Williams, Carl Yastrzemski, and Jimmie Foxx on the Red Sox All-Time Team. When the poll was repeated in 1982 only Doerr, Williams, Yaz, and Foxx retained their spot as the very best at their positions.

Red Sox stalwart Johnny Pesky is eminently qualified to assess Bobby Doerr's place in Red Sox history. Pesky has been associated with the team for over 60 years, and he played in the same infield with Doerr for seven seasons.

"Bobby Doerr was as good a second baseman as I have ever seen. He was so steady in the field that you had to see it to believe it. Heck, if he hadn't retired at age 33 we would be considering him for the best second baseman in baseball history."

Bobby Doerr joined the Boston Red Sox in 1937. Chronic back problems forced him to retire following the 1951 season. He ranks among the top six on Red Sox all-time lists in eleven career-batting categories. He was elected to baseball's Hall of Fame in 1986 and his number "1" was retired by the Boston Red Sox in 1988. More importantly, when you speak with anyone who knows Bobby, the first thing they say is, "He is as nice a man as I have ever met."

L. A. BORN AND RAISED

Bobby Doerr was born in Los Angeles, California, on April 7, 1918. Growing up in Los Angeles in the 1920s was a very different experience from today. "We had plenty of places to play baseball. The weather was good and it seemed to me we played ball almost every day."

Bobby quickly earned a reputation as a fine young infielder. His American Legion team, which included future major leaguer catcher Mickey Owen, won the state championship in 1932. In 1934 the Hollywood Stars of the top-flight Pacific Coast League offered Bobby his first professional contract.

"I was only 16-years old, so my father had to sign for me. This was the middle of the depression and if a fellow was lucky enough to have a job, he made maybe $18-$20 a week. The Stars were offering me $200 a month. My father told me he would sign for me if I promised to finish high school between baseball seasons. It took me a couple of winters, but I did eventually get my high school diploma."

Despite his tender years, Doerr played well for the Stars. When the club moved to San Diego for the 1936 season, renamed the Padres, Doerr moved along with them as the starting second baseman and a bona fide major league prospect.

THE WEST COAST CONNECTION

Bobby Doerr was actually the first person connected with the Red Sox to meet Ted Williams. "We were taking batting practice before a game when our manager came over to us and said, 'Let this kid take a few swings.' There was a lot of grumbling from the veterans about giving up batting time to a skinny high school kid. But that kid was 17-year old Ted Williams and when he took a couple of cuts you just knew he was going to be a good one."

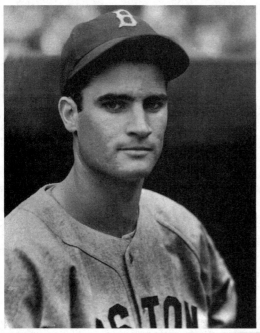

Red Sox General Manager Eddie Collins traveled to San Diego to check out the Padres' shortstop George Myatt during the 1936 season. He went to see Myatt but the two players who caught his eye were Doerr and Williams.

Doerr recalls, "One day I heard that Eddie Collins was in the stands and I was so nervous, I made three errors. Mr. Collins came down to the clubhouse between games of our double-header and told me to relax, he was going to sign me anyway.

Mr. Collins told our owner that he wanted to sign me and he also 'wanted to sign that skinny kid.' Mr. Bill Lane, our owner, told Collins that Ted Williams was a great young talent, but he wasn't ready to sign. Collins said that was okay, but 'I will leave only if you will promise to give me the first chance to sign the kid next year for the Red Sox.' So, in some small way I played a role in Ted coming to the Red Sox."

Bobby Doerr and Ted Williams were close friends for over 65 years. But Doerr has known Johnny Pesky even longer. "I first met Johnny in 1934. He was the clubhouse boy in Portland, Oregon. He was a hard working guy even then.

"I didn't meet Dominic DiMaggio until he came to the Red Sox in 1940. I did play with his brother Vince on the Hollywood Stars though."

Dom DiMaggio treasures the relationship between Doerr, Williams, Pesky and himself. "It is really amazing. There we were, four guys from the other coast, ranging from Portland in the north to San Diego in the south, and we all end up in Boston together. We all broke into professional baseball in the 1930s and sixty-plus years later we were all still close. It is extraordinary."

FOURTEEN SEASONS AT FENWAY PARK

When the 1937 Red Sox broke training camp in Sarasota, Florida, 19-year old rookie Bobby Doerr was headed to Boston for the first time. "The East Coast was so different after having grown up on the West Coast. Boston always fascinated me. I remember the first time I saw Fenway Park. My reaction was, 'Wow. What a beautiful ballpark.' I always loved playing in Boston."

Bobby was the backup second baseman in 1937, but in 1938 he took over as the regular at second. The year 1938 was important in another way; he married his wife Monica. "I first met Monica in 1936 on a fishing trip to the Rogue River in Oregon. She was a teacher in a one-room schoolhouse. It is a beautiful part of the country and it's where we made our home."

In 1939 Bobby batted .318, and continued his near-flawless fielding. In 1940 he knocked in 105 runs, the first of six seasons in which he would exceed the 100 RBI level. In 1941 he was named to the first of nine American League All-Star teams. Typical of Bobby Doerr, he lists Ted Williams's game-winning home run in that 1941 game as his greatest thrill.

All-Star honors followed in 1942 when he drove in 102 runs and in 1943 when he led all American League second baseman with a .990 fielding average. In the 1943 All-Star Game, Bobby's three-run home run led the American League to a 5-3 victory. In 1944 Bobby batted a career high .325 and he was named *The Sporting News* American League Player of the Year.

He enlisted in the Army Infantry Corps in September of 1944, missing the 1945 season, but when the 1946 season rolled around Bobby and his teammates were back from the military and ready to put together one of the best seasons in Red Sox history.

PERENNIAL ALL-STAR

The 1946 Red Sox broke out of the gate fast and stayed in first place for almost the entire season. They won 15 games in a row from the end of April to mid-May, and 41 of their first 50 games. Bobby Doerr was one of eight Red Sox representatives on an American League All-Star team that was victorious 12-0 in the first All-Star Game ever played at Fenway Park. The team clinched the 1946 American League pennant on September 13th in Cleveland.

How important was Bobby Doerr to the success of the 1946 team? Ted Williams has said, "We never could have won the 1946 pennant without Bobby Doerr." Johnny Pesky echoes Ted's sentiments. "Bobby was a leader on the field and in the clubhouse. In a clutch situation you would want Bobby at the plate or you would want the batter to hit the ball to Bobby. He was quiet, but you would see that he would never get rattled and that helped give you confidence."

The Red Sox took a three games to two lead over the St. Louis Cardinals in the 1946 World Series, but the Cardinals won the last two games in St. Louis to emerge as the Series victors. Bobby Doerr had a hit in each World Series game and batted .409 for the Series. In the ninth inning of game seven, with the Sox down by one run, he singled to put the tying run on second, but the Red Sox fell just short.

CLOSE CALLS

The 1947 season was another All-Star year for Bobby, but the Red Sox were never seriously in contention, finishing a distant third. The following season was another close call for the Red Sox. The team finished the 1948 season in a tie for first place with the Cleveland Indians and the first American League playoff game was held at Fenway Park.

Denny Galehouse was the surprise playoff starter for the Red Sox, but he was gone by the fourth inning and the Indians coasted to an 8-3 victory. Doerr hit a home run in a losing effort and he remembers the disappointment. "We wanted to win it for the Boston fans and for Tom Yawkey who was a great owner. And it would have been nice to play the Boston Braves in the World Series. We used to play them in the City Series before the season started, and facing them in the World Series would have been tremendous."

The 1949 Red Sox held a one game lead over the New York Yankees as they

Ted Williams, Dom DiMaggio, Bobby Doerr and Johnny Pesky during their playing days. The four remained lifelong friends.

headed into the Stadium for the two final games of that season. Doerr had a clutch triple off Vic Raschi in the final game but the Yankees swept both games to win the pennant.

Bobby Doerr's best year may have been 1950. He had hit around .350 in the second half of 1949, and his hot bat carried over to the following season. In 1950 he scored 103 runs, batted in a career-high 120 runs, and matched a career best with 27 home runs. He also led the American League with 11 triples and a fielding average of .988. But, despite a team batting average of .302, the 1950 Red Sox finished four games behind the Yankees in third place.

When the 1951 season began, Bobby Doerr was at the peak of his baseball skills. He had just turned 33 on April 7, he was a nine time All-Star, and he was a recognized leader on one of the strongest teams in baseball. Then, abruptly, misfortune struck in the form of a bad back. "I woke up one day and my back hurt so much I couldn't get out of bed. I went to see the doctors at the Lahey Clinic, and they said the only solution was an operation. But there was no guarantee that I would be able to play again, and it was a very serious operation. I decided the only thing I could do was retire."

The statistics Bobby Doerr compiled in 14 seasons give us some sense of his greatness. But to understand how truly great he was, you have to listen to his teammates. Joe Cronin, who was Bobby's first double-play partner and first manager once said, "I consider him as fine a player to ever put on a spiked shoe."

Dom DiMaggio played in center field behind Bobby Doerr at second base for nine seasons. "He was absolutely amazing. Time after time I would see a ball headed up the middle and I would come charging in ready to field it. But Bobby would move smoothly to his right, backhand the ball, and throw the runner out at first. It was really pretty to watch. You never saw Bobby leave his feet; there was nothing showy about him. He had such sure hands. He was a fabulous fielder."

LIFE AFTER RETIREMENT

Following Bobby's retirement from baseball, the Doerrs made Junction City, Oregon, their year-round home. Bobby tried his hand at cattle ranching for a number of years. "I found out just how hard you have to work to make any kind of living in that business. It was interesting, but you had to have a large herd to make any money."

In 1957 he accepted the Red Sox' offer to become a roving instructor in their minor league system. For the next ten seasons he traveled from the low minors to Triple A ball coaching Red Sox prospects on their hitting and fielding.

Mike Andrews is now the Executive Director of the Jimmy Fund, but in the early to mid-1960s he was working his way through the Red Sox farm system. "Bobby was really my mentor all the way to the big leagues. The first thing that struck you was what a nice man he was. If Bobby told me to move my left foot three inches to the left in the batter's box, I would do it and go out and get four hits. That's how much I believed in him."

In 1967, new Red Sox manager Dick Williams asked Bobby to move to the big leagues with him as a coach. Bobby agreed and he played an important role in the success of "The Impossible Dream Team."

Mike Andrews was a direct beneficiary of Bobby Doerr's presence in 1967. "There I was, a rookie second baseman, and I'm getting advice from the best second baseman in Red Sox history. And he never talked about himself, he only gave you examples of situations. Dick Williams was pretty flamboyant, but Bobby always kept his cool. He was a real positive influence on that team."

Bobby remained a coach with the Red Sox until Dick Williams was fired at the end of the 1969 season. He later returned to the big leagues as a coach with the Toronto Blue Jays from 1977 to 1981.

HALL OF FAMER

In 1986 the Hall of Fame Veterans Committee voted Bobby Doerr into baseball's Hall of Fame. Bobby responds with typical humility when talking about his Hall of Fame designation. "To be honest, I never thought of myself as a Hall of Famer. When I got the call, it was my ultimate thrill in baseball."

Bobby's long-time friend and teammate, Ted Williams, was a member of the Veterans Committee that gave Doerr his long due recognition. "I didn't have to do much lobbying for him," Williams said at the time. "Bobby did all the work on the field.

"I'll tell you what kind of guy Bobby was," Ted added in his 1986 interview, "When we played for the Red Sox we didn't have a captain, but Bobby was the silent captain. He was the guy everybody likes, the guy everybody wants to be around. He was just an all-around great player."

With good buddy Ted Williams.

Bobby's induction into the Hall of Fame in August of 1986 was an important event for the Doerr family. Bobby, his 90-year old mother, and his lovely wife Monica had the biggest smiles for miles around. It was also a great thrill for then National League President Bart Giamatti. Giamatti, who had previously been the President of Yale, had grown up as a diehard Red Sox fan. And among the Red Sox of his youth, Bobby Doerr was his greatest hero.

Giamatti sought out the Doerrs after the formal induction ceremony and said, "Mr. Doerr, you are my lifelong hero." The Doerrs were overwhelmed by his words. After a poignant silence Monica Doerr responded, "Mr. Giamatti, you are the former President of Yale. You are a hero to people like us."

Bart Giamatti later told friends that meeting Bobby Doerr was one of his great moments. First, because he had finally met his hero, but also because he was the person that Giamatti wanted him to be.

The Boston Red Sox retired Bobby Doerr's number "1" in a moving ceremony in May of 1988. His was the third number retired by the Red Sox, following Joe Cronin's "4" and Ted Williams' "9" in May of 1984.

"In my rookie year, I actually had number nine," Doerr chuckles. "Then the following year they gave me number six. In 1939 they gave me number one, and I wore it until I retired in 1951."

Today Doerr lives in a beautiful spot on the Rogue River in central Oregon. His beloved wife Monica passed away in December 2003. Bobby has one son, Don, a grandson Brad, and a granddaughter Mischel.

Doerr, who turned age 87 on April 7, 2005, continues to follow baseball closely. "There is a lot that is different about the game today. We didn't have the designated hitter when we played and the role of the closer didn't exist. The biggest difference is in the wide range of player backgrounds. Jackie Robinson didn't integrate baseball until 1947 and I retired in 1951, so we didn't have the diversity you have today."

NUMBER ONE FOR ALL-TIME

It is often said that Red Sox hero Ted Williams was John Wayne come to life. If that is so, then Bobby Doerr is Gary Cooper: the quiet, handsome gentleman, who always does the right thing.

Perhaps Bobby's friend of over 60 years, Johnny Pesky, says it best. "When I think about the definition of the word 'gentleman' to me it is Bobby Doerr."

Bobby Doerr: he's number "1."

CATEGORY	CAREER TOTALS	ALL-TIME BOSTON RED SOX RANK
Bobby Doerr's Rank in Red Sox History		
Games	1,865	5th
At-Bats	7,093	5th
Hits	2,042	6th
Walks	809	6th
Runs	1,094	5th
RBI	1,247	5th
Doubles	381	5th
Triples	89	4th
Total Bases	3,270	5th
Home Runs	223	6th
Home Runs at Fenway Park	145	5th
Grand Slam Home Runs	8	3rd

Source: 2004 *Boston Red Sox Media Guide*

2.

Interviews for Ted Williams

January–February, 2004

Nothing warms a cold New England winter day for a real Red Sox fan like some good baseball talk. And when that talk includes conversations about Ted Williams with former team greats like Bobby Doerr, Dom DiMaggio, and Johnny Pesky, it really doesn't matter what the temperature is, or how many inches of snow there are on the front walk.

More than ten books have been written on Ted Williams' baseball career and his colorful life, and hundreds of thousands of words have been devoted to the Splendid Splinter. But nothing has been written focusing exclusively on Ted Williams at spring training.

My story about Ted and his experiences at spring training is based on interviews with eight of his former teammates, and a great deal of reading alongside the hot stove. All of his former teammates delighted in recounting their relationship with Ted.

Charlie Wagner, who at age ninety-two has been associated with the Red Sox for seventy years, and Hall of Famer second baseman Bobby Doerr both preceded Ted with the team. They remember Ted's first spring training camp in Sarasota, Florida, as if it were yesterday.

Dom DiMaggio first reported to the Red Sox spring training camp in 1940, one year after Ted's rookie season with the team. Dom and his wife were packing to leave on a cruise when I called, but he made time to reminisce about Ted. Johnny Pesky joined the Red Sox two years after Dom, and he still loves to tell the story of Ted welcoming him to the team in the dining room of the Sarasota Terrace Hotel.

Mel Parnell pointed out that it was fifty degrees warmer in his native New Orleans when our conversation began, and he laughed at the memory of being tongue-tied when he was introduced to the great Ted Williams. Sam Mele was a particular favorite of Ted Williams. But Ted only took him fishing once. You will understand why when you read Sam's recollection of deep-sea fishing with Teddy Ballgame.

Frank Malzone trained with Ted in Sarasota and in Scottsdale. He confirmed that Ted didn't particularly care for Arizona. There isn't a lot of fishing in the Scottsdale area, and golf was one of the few activities where Ted did not excel.

Billy Monbouquette is a Medford, Massachusetts, native and he was a great fan of the Splendid Splinter growing up. His joy at forming a friendship with someone he had idolized is still apparent.

I was lucky enough to meet Ted Williams in February 1988. Like Mel Parnell, I was tongue-tied when I was introduced. I always thought that the description of Ted Williams in person as "larger then life," was overused. But I can't improve on it.

It became clear when I started this article that I couldn't limit it to Ted's time during spring training. I have included a few highlights from each of Ted's nineteen regular seasons with the Red Sox. As a young fan it was my great, good fortune to witness the last ten of those seasons.

TED WILLIAMS
MEMORIES OF TED AT
SPRING TRAINING

When 19-year-old Ted Williams arrived at his first spring training camp in Sarasota, Florida, Bobby Doerr took him to the Red Sox clubhouse to meet manager Joe Cronin. "I remember it like it was yesterday," Hall of Famer Doerr recalls from his Oregon home, "I introduced him and Ted's greeting to Cronin was, 'Hi, sport!' I think I knew at that moment that Ted would spend the 1938 season at Triple A in Minneapolis."

That was the official beginning of Theodore Samuel Williams's relationship with the Boston Red Sox and major league baseball. It was an association that would last for over sixty years and an affiliation that would define the man and the sport. For all or parts of eight decades, Ted Williams was often the biggest story of spring training.

THE GREATEST HITTER WHO EVER LIVED

Ted Williams and Bobby Doerr were 17-year-old teammates on the 1936 San Diego Padres. Ted was a San Diego native who had grown up telling anyone who

would listen, "When I walk down the street people are going to say, 'There goes Ted Williams, the greatest hitter who ever lived.'" When Red Sox General Manager Eddie Collins traveled to the west coast to sign Doerr to a major league contract, young Ted Williams caught his eye and Collins negotiated an option on his contract with Padres' owner Bill Lane.

In 1937 Doerr spent the year with the Red Sox, showing great promise, while Ted confirmed the wisdom of Collins's judgment by pounding Pacific Coast League pitching. Eddie Collins asked Doerr to accompany Ted on the cross-country trip from California to spring training in 1938. Collins apparently recognized that the well-grounded Doerr would be a good balance for the exuberant Williams.

"Ted and I had trouble hooking up for the train trip because of heavy rains in California and throughout the south," Doerr remembers. "I finally caught up with him in El Paso, Texas, and we took the train from there to Florida. I remember saying to Ted, 'Wait until you see Jimmie Foxx hit the ball.' His response was, 'Wait until those guys see me hit the ball.'"

Asked if he had any inkling during that first trip that he and Ted would go on to Hall of Fame careers and a life-long friendship, Bobby Doerr laughs. "We were just a couple of teenagers who were serious about our baseball careers. And we both enjoyed going to the movies to watch westerns. The rest of it never occurred to me."

In his autobiography *My Turn at Bat*, written with John Underwood (Simon & Schuster, 1969), Ted remembers his first visit to the locker room at old Payne Field to suit up for practice. "When I finally got into the dressing room in Sarasota, everybody else was on the field and Johnny Orlando, the clubhouse boy says, 'Who are you? Ted Williams. Oh, well, The Kid has arrived, eh. You dress over there with the rookies, Kid.' " Ted Williams would retain his nickname of "The Kid" for the rest of his life.

A lot has been written about the ribbing that Ted took from his veteran teammates during this first training camp. Bobby Doerr doesn't remember it as being particularly vicious. "The veterans gave Ted a hard time. But all of the young players took some riding from the older players. That's the way it was in those days. They were rough on him but it was mostly good-natured. And let me tell you, Ted gave it back as good as he got."

Former Red Sox pitcher Charlie Wagner was Ted Williams's first roommate and they continued to room together through Charlie's final season with the team in 1946. Wagner remembers every detail of his first meeting with Ted.

"I was sitting in the clubhouse between Lefty Grove and Jimmie Foxx, right next to manager Joe Cronin's office. Ted marched into Cronin's office and asked in that big, booming voice of his, 'Do you have anybody around here who doesn't drink, doesn't smoke, goes to bed early, and gets up early?' Cronin pointed at me and said, 'He's sitting right there.' Ted looked at me and said, 'Will you be my roommate?' I answered, 'Of course I will.' Ted said, "Good.' And we roomed together for seven years and were friends for life."

Ted showed a lot of promise during his first training camp but he learned that major league pitching was tougher than the Pacific Coast League. On March 21, the Red Sox optioned him to their farm club in Minneapolis. The proud Williams was crushed by his demotion. He told clubhouse attendant Johnny Orlando, "Someday I'm going to come back and earn more money than those three put together," referring to regular Red Sox outfielders Joe Vosmik, Doc Cramer, and Ben Chapman.

Ted Williams may not have been prepared for the big leagues but he certainly was ready for the International League. In 1938 with the Minneapolis Millers he led the league with a batting average of .366, and finished second in the balloting for league MVP. Williams, who celebrated his twentieth birthday in August that season, also topped the league with 43 home runs and 142 RBI to earn his first Triple Crown.

FUTURE ALL-STAR

Bobby Doerr knew that Ted Williams would stick with the Red Sox following training camp in 1939. "We had traded Ben Chapman for Denny Galehouse, so there was an opening in the outfield. And after his great season in Minneapolis, everybody knew he was ready for the majors."

Williams had spent the off-season in his hometown of San Diego. Ted and his long-time friend Les Cassie, Sr., started the 3,000-mile drive to Sarasota with plenty of time to arrive on schedule for camp. Unfortunately, Ted came down with a serious bout of the flu and the pair stopped for medical assistance in New Orleans, Louisiana. He arrived in Sarasota one week after the opening of camp, looking positively skeletal.

"That's when he picked up the nickname 'The Splendid Splinter,' " Doerr reminisces. "Ted was really thin as a young man and when he arrived in camp right after getting over the flu, he was as thin as a rail. But it didn't affect his hitting at all."

Ted hit a game-winning home run in his first exhibition game that spring and continued in top form throughout the camp. He had yet to play a major league game, but already he was gaining a national reputation. The front page of the April 19, 1939, edition of *The Sporting News* featured a story on leading candidates for "rookie of the year." The first name mentioned was Ted Williams, "The kid outfielder, who, in addition to being a great hitter, has the allure that goes with screwball tendencies." The article concludes by nominating Williams and the Yankees' Charlie Keller as the leading candidates for the honor.

When the 1939 regular season began, the greatest left fielder in Red Sox history took his place in the starting lineup: in *right* field. "He played behind me all season," former All-Star second baseman Bobby Doerr recalls. "The thing I remember best is how much the fans in the right-field grandstand loved him. He would have a great at-bat, and when he ran back out to his position they would all stand up and cheer for him. Then he would take his hat, grab it by the button, and lift it as high over his head as he could. Everything changed later when he moved over to left field, but that season he tipped his hat as much as any player I ever saw."

Ted Williams made *The Sporting News* prophecy look good, batting .327 and leading the American League with a rookie record 145 RBI. His 31 home runs served notice that he could hit with power to go along with a high batting average. The official Rookie of the Year Award hadn't been created by 1939, but Ted was certainly the rookie sensation of that year.

The big stories in spring training in 1940 revolved around Ted Williams and the outfield. During the off-season, the Red Sox had added bullpens in right-center, and constructed new seating in right field to improve Ted's home run chances at Fenway Park. The Boston press quickly dubbed the new area "Williamsburg".

The other change was manager Joe Cronin's plan to shift Ted from right to left field. On March 14, 1940, a front-page story in *The Sporting News* was headlined "Cronin Has His Mind on Williams' Eyes." The article pointed out that Babe Ruth played right field in Yankee Stadium because left field was the "sun field." But he was shifted to left field on the road when the team played in parks where right was the sun field. The article concluded, "The better Williams gets, the more the Red Sox will benefit in many ways. So why keep him in the sun field if it is not necessary?"

Another reason to shift Ted from right field was the arrival of outstanding defensive outfielder Dominic DiMaggio. Dom joined the Red Sox from the San Francisco Seals in 1940 to begin a major league career that would span eleven seasons and include seven All-Star selections. It was also the beginning of a friendship with Ted Williams that would endure for over sixty years.

"I remember when they took me around the clubhouse to introduce me in spring training that Ted was very welcoming, very friendly. We had played against one another in the Pacific Coast League and he knew who I was."

"I can remember during batting practice that spring we would crowd around the cage to watch him hit. It reminded me of an incident that took place in 1937 when he was playing for San Diego. Our manager, Lefty O'Doul, went over to speak to Ted. That never happened in those days. When Lefty got back to the bench we all wanted to know what he said. 'I told him, whatever you do, don't ever let anybody change that swing of yours.' "

THE LAST .400 HITTER

By the standards applied to a mere mortal, Ted Williams's second season with the Red Sox would be judged a tremendous success. In 1940 he raised his batting average 17 points to .344, good enough for third place in the American League. But the Boston press and Red Sox fans held Ted to a higher standard. His home run total dropped from 31 to 23 despite the easier target in right field, and Ted came in for his first round of criticism. Always thin-skinned, he told a Cleveland newspaper writer that he would rather be a fireman than a baseball player.

For the second year in a row, Ted spent the off-season in Minneapolis to be near friends he had made during his season with the Millers. He enjoyed the hunting and fishing and it gave him a chance to be near his future wife, Doris Soule. But when the first day of spring training arrived, Ted was nowhere to be found.

Ted was not pleased with the contract that the Red Sox had sent him for 1941 and he had not responded to the team. On March 1, 1941, baseball writer Mel Webb updated fans on Ted's whereabouts with this item in *The Boston Globe*: "There's no more news about Williams except the Red Sox now know that he is in the land of the living. Also, he wants to talk things over with Eddie Collins."

Ted quickly reached agreement with the Red Sox but he arrived at training camp one week late. James C. O'Leary described Ted's arrival for *Globe* readers: "Ted Williams, the hard-hitting outfielder of the Red Sox, arrived in camp last night after a 1,600 mile drive over the road from Minneapolis. It was a hard trip through snow, hail and rain from start to finish."

"I'm perfectly satisfied," Williams told reporters, "and am well pleased to be back to work. You may be sure that I will do my best to show my appreciation, and that's all I can do."

Ted quickly got in shape and appeared to be in regular season form until he injured his ankle in an exhibition game on March 19. He was treated for a sprained ankle, but X-rays taken during a stopover in Birmingham, Alabama, revealed that he had a chipped anklebone.

Bobby Doerr has an interesting theory on the affect the ankle injury had on Ted's hitting. "Ted didn't play much early in 1941, but he adjusted quickly and got back in the lineup. I watched him closely that year and I was sure that he was waiting on the pitch until the very last second because he was conscious of his ankle. It was probably his best year and I really thought he waited on the pitch better than he ever had."

Clearly Ted did most things right in 1941. While the baseball world focused on Joe DiMaggio's 56-game hitting streak, Williams quietly crept over .400 and stayed there until the next-to-last day of the season. Williams brought a .39955 average into a doubleheader against the Philadelphia Athletics. He managed six hits in eight at-bats for the two games to finish at .406. Ted had become the first American Leaguer to finish over .400 since Harry Heilmann had batted .403 for the Detroit Tigers in 1923.

A new face was added to the Red Sox roster for spring training in 1942: shortstop Johnny Pesky. But Johnny was no stranger to Ted, Bobby Doerr, and Dom DiMaggio. All three of them had met Pesky years earlier when he was the visiting clubhouse assistant for Portland in the Pacific Coast League.

Johnny Pesky will never forget the first time he met Ted Williams as a Red Sox teammate. "I was having dinner with Bobby Doerr in the dining room of the Sarasota Terrace Hotel. Bobby and I had finished dinner and we were talking and all of a sudden Ted appeared. He sat down and started talking to Bobby. I was kind of in awe. Here I was a rookie sitting with Ted Williams, who hit .406 the year before.

"Eventually he turned to me and said in his great, booming voice, 'Are you the kid from Louisville?' I told him that I was, and he said, 'If you can hit .280 you'll help us.' I told him that I could run .280, and Ted kind of laughed. I got to know Ted, Bobby and Dom that spring and we stayed friends for all these years. Ted and Bobby are in the Hall of Fame, of course, and Dominic should be. Me? I just sort of tagged along with the three of them."

The four teammates would remain fast friends for 60 years. Their relationship is wonderfully captured in David Halbertam's *The Teammates* (Hyperion, 2003).

WORLD WAR II

There was a cloud hanging over spring training for all major league teams in 1942. Pearl Harbor had preceded the opening of camp by less than three months. A number of big leaguers were already in the armed services including Cleveland's Bob Feller and the Tigers' Hank Greenberg. Ted's draft status had been reclassified as 3A since he was the sole support of his mother back in San Diego, but the nation was clearly gearing up for the war effort.

Charlie Wagner remembers talking with Ted about enlisting in the armed services. "It was on both our minds. We both wanted to do the right thing. We knew we were going to enlist. The only question was when."

Ted played in 150 games in 1942, enlisting in the Navy Air Corps during that season with a delayed reporting date. He also took night school aviation classes on a regular basis while the season was in progress. Ted won the first of his two American League Triple Crowns in 1942, and registered a league-leading on-base percentage of .499.

When spring training camps opened in 1943, Ted was in preflight training in Chapel Hill, North Carolina. In 1944, Ted was in Florida, but it was Pensacola for advanced flight training. After his training was completed, Ted married his first wife, Doris Soule, whom he had met during his 1938 season with the Minneapolis Millers. Following his advanced training, Williams was stationed in Jacksonville, Florida, where he was being readied for combat while spring training took place in 1945. He was in San Francisco, en route to assignment in the Pacific Theatre, when World War II came to an end.

AMERICAN LEAGUE CHAMPIONS

Spring training camp in 1946 holds a special place in Johnny Pesky's heart. "The war was over and you got to see guys you hadn't seen for three years. We had all been in the service and you had some concerns for one another. It was like a reunion, we were so happy to see one another. And we knew we had a great team that year.

"Ted had hardly held a bat in his hand for three years, but when he stepped into the batting cage for the first time, you could see that his swing was exactly the same. Sure, he had to get his timing back, but from the first swing you could see he hadn't lost a thing. Ted had that great, graceful swing and he picked up right where he had left off."

When spring training began Ted had only played four seasons in the big leagues. But an article in *The Sporting News* by the dean of American sports-

Ted with manager Joe Cronin and teammate Charlie Wagner in spring training 1946. Both Williams and Wagner had just returned from serving in World War II.

writers at the time, Grantland Rice, left little doubt of the impression that he had made. "Someone asked me to name the most interesting personality I met in the six-week invasion of spring training that included over seven hundred players. I can give you his name—Ted Williams of the Red Sox, the greatest hitter in baseball today. He is probably one of the greatest hitters of all time, and possibly the greatest hitter of all times."

Charlie Wagner remembers seeing his old roommate for the first time in three years. "It was so great to see him. He said, 'Are you going to try me again?' I told him of course I was. And we picked back up like there had never been a break."

Questioned about stories that he had asked the Red Sox to find him a new roommate early in his career because Ted wouldn't stop talking about hitting, Charlie Wagner chuckles.

"Those stories just aren't true. We always got along great. But I'll tell you another funny story. Ted got a new shipment of Louisville Sluggers. We're in our room, and I'm lying down on an old four-poster bed. Ted is looking in the mirror, getting a feel for his new bat. He takes a swing, whacks the bed with his bat, and the whole thing collapses. Ted looks at the bed lying on the floor, and all he said was, 'Call downstairs and have them send up a new bed. I've got to get some more of these bats. They're great.'

"Ted was just a terrific fellow. I remember one time we were having breakfast and a woman came over to our table with her ten-year old son looking for Ted to give him some batting tips. Ted rolls up his newspaper and tells the youngster to take a swing. Ted says, 'That's not much of a swing. Remember, you have to go back before you go forward. Take a good swing, don't push the ball' and the kid went off beaming with a good batting tip from the great Ted Williams."

Spring training in 1946 included a trip to Cuba to play a series of exhibition games against the Washington Senators. In *My Turn at Bat,* Ted recalled his outfield adventures in one game. "I remember we played in a nice little park in Havana where the outfield sloped up, the main part of the field was down in a gully, and early in the game I came running down the slope to catch a fly ball and I dropped it. In Latin America they don't boo you for a bad play, they whistle, and I heard those whistles for the first time. It was a new thrill. I had been blasted by experts in every imaginable way. This was art in a new form."

In 1946 the Red Sox jumped out ahead of the field in the American League and clinched the pennant in mid-September. Ted led the league in runs scored and total bases, and he was named the American League's Most Valuable Player. But the Red Sox lost a heart-breaking, seven game World Series to the St. Louis Cardinals as Ted batted a disappointing .200, with only five singles. It would turn out to be his only World Series appearance.

THE LATE 1940s

Sam Mele, who played the outfield for the Red Sox and spent over 30 years with the team as a scout and roving instructor, was a rookie in 1947. "For some reason

Ted took a liking to me. He wanted me to sit next to him on all the bus rides we took to exhibition games that spring and talk hitting. He used to say, 'Come on, Meal. Let's go.'

"And he would talk hitting the whole ride. 'Look for this. Look for that.' And he would quiz me about what I would do in a certain situation. When you finally got off the bus you thought you were the greatest hitter in the whole world."

Ted led the American League in batting average, home runs, and RBI in 1947, earning his second Triple Crown. He also led the league in runs scored, walks, slugging average, and extra base hits. He finished second in the balloting for the league's Most Valuable Player.

The big story of the 1948 spring training camp was the arrival of new manager Joe McCarthy. Long-time Red Sox manager Joe Cronin had moved up to General Manager and McCarthy, who had led the New York Yankees to seven American League pennants, was hired to get the Red Sox back to the World Series.

Joe McCarthy was known as a stern disciplinarian and a stickler for formal team rules. The Boston sportswriters, who feasted on any controversy involving Ted Williams, had a field day speculating on their potential clash. McCarthy, who was well aware of Ted's disdain for neckties, deflated the controversy by appearing for breakfast at the team's headquarters in the Sarasota Terrace Hotel in an open sports shirt. Asked if he thought he would clash with Williams, he answered, "I wouldn't be much of a manager if I couldn't get along with a .400 hitter, now would I?"

Johnny Pesky still marvels at Ted's dedication to hitting. "We would be playing in an exhibition game, and Ted would be up and down the dugout asking for insight on the pitcher. We would play a lot of National League clubs, pitchers we wouldn't ordinarily see, and he'd be saying, 'Who do we see in our league who reminds you of this guy? Where's his release point?' These were just exhibition games, but Ted would approach them just the way he would a regular season game."

Sam Mele laughs when he recalls the only time Ted Williams ever invited him fishing. "We would get a few days off during spring training, and this one time Ted invited me to come along on a fishing trip. I remember Mickey Harris (Red Sox pitcher) was along, and when we got out there I was seasick. I mean I was really seasick. We had to go back to shore to get me something to settle my stomach. I caught a huge king mackerel fish, the biggest fish we caught all day. I don't know if Ted was madder because I got seasick or because I caught the biggest fish. All I know is he never invited me fishing again.

"He worked harder than any player I ever saw. He had all sorts of contraptions he had rigged to build up the strength in his forearms. But he did love his fishing. I remember one time Joe McCarthy said to him, 'Ted, I wish some day you would catch a whale so you will stop talking about fishing.' "

The 1948 Red Sox tied Cleveland for first place in the American League but lost the one-game playoff game to the Indians at Fenway Park. Ted led the American League in batting with a .369 average that year, and he also led the league in on-base percentage and slugging average.

When spring training began in 1949, Ted's career batting average stood at .354. Only three players in major league history have ended their careers with a higher lifetime average: Ty Cobb, Rogers Hornsby, and Shoeless Joe Jackson.

Former Red Sox pitcher Mel Parnell has a very strong recollection of the first time he met Ted Williams. Parnell, who would go on to win more games in a Red Sox uniform than any other left-handed pitcher, remembers, "I was in the outfield and somebody introduced us. I was amazed and tongue-tied. I couldn't believe I was actually meeting the great Ted Williams. I managed to mumble something, and later we became great friends, but that first day I was just over-whelmed and practically speechless."

Mel remembers pitching batting practice to Ted in spring training. "I pitched a lot of batting practice to Ted over the years. He didn't face many left-ies at Fenway Park, so he wanted me to pitch to him like it was game conditions. I liked it, because I knew if I could figure out how to pitch to the great Ted Williams, I could pitch to anyone."

The 1949 season was a disappointing one for Ted and his Red Sox team-mates. The Red Sox held a one-game lead in the American League standings with two games to be played at Yankee Stadium to end the season. The Yankees swept both games and the Red Sox season was over. Williams led the American League in 10 major batting categories, and he was voted the Most Valuable Player in the American League, but a shot at another World Series appearance had eluded him.

THE EARLY 1950s

When training camp opened in 1950, Ted Williams, Bobby Doerr, Dom DiMaggio, and Johnny Pesky had formed the nucleus of the Red Sox for five full seasons. "We had some great teams those years," Johnny Pesky recalls. "We felt like we were the best team most of those years, but something always prevented us from winning it all. But we really looked forward to spring training that year. We knew we wouldn't stay together forever."

Ted Williams was at the height of his career that spring. "The Kid" was thir-ty-one years old when training camp began in 1950. He took spring training very seriously, and in *My Turn at Bat*, he describes his approach to the pre-season. "You start seeing the ball, really ripping it, within two to three weeks, but you need four to five to be really sharp. Maybe not at age 22, but certainly at age 31. Spring training does that for you. You can't just tape up an injury like they do in football and go out on the field. It's too exacting a game."

Mel Parnell looked forward to seeing Ted each year when spring training rolled around. "I remember him for the great hitter he was, but also because he was a wonderful teammate. He knew that if he stayed at the hotel with the rest of us, he wouldn't get a moments peace, so by that time he was living in an apartment by himself. We all understood that. But you couldn't ask for a better teammate in the clubhouse or on the field.

"He was a different guy when he was just with his teammates. He was loud, and he could be profane, but mostly he was just fun to be around. He was different around the writers, but with his teammates he was real good-natured, almost happy-go-lucky."

Ted suffered his first serious injury at the All-Star Game in Chicago that year. He made a nice catch against the wall on a long drive hit by Ralph Kiner, but he broke 13 bone chips in his left elbow in the process. Ted returned to the starting lineup in mid-August, but the Red Sox drive for the pennant ran out of gas in the last week of the season. Ted appeared in only 89 games that season and his batting average of .317 was his career-low to that point.

Training camp in 1951 would be the last spring that Ted, Bobby, Dom and Johnny would all be together. Ted liked to refer to his three pals as, "My guys." But Bobby Doerr's back was beginning to be a chronic problem. It would ultimately result in his premature retirement at age 33 following the 1951 season.

"Ted was such a smart hitter," Bobby Doerr remembers. "When he was in spring training he would use a 34-ounce bat. That's a pretty big bat, but Ted could handle it real well. When it got late in the season he would shift to a lighter bat and not miss a step."

Ted had another concern as he rounded into shape that spring training. In *My Turn at Bat,* he describes his elbow surgery after the All-Star Game and the prognosis at the time. "Doc Fadden (Red Sox trainer) told me later that neither doctor held out much hope for a complete recovery. One of them wanted to take the whole tip out, the radius. The other held out for the thirteen bones chips I'd broken off the bone. He said, 'Leave as much of the radius in as possible, this guy's a ballplayer, it's his only chance.'"

Gearing up for 1951 spring training with manager Steve O'Neill and teammate Lou Boudreau.

Ted had asked manager Steve O'Neill to limit his appearances in spring training games to give his elbow a chance to heal fully. But O'Neill, in an apparent effort to show who was in charge, played Ted in almost every game. The Splendid Splinter was not pleased.

Ted batted only .318 in 1951, but this was the fourth highest batting average in the American League. He finished first in the league in slugging average, walks, and on-base average.

CAPTAIN WILLIAMS, U.S.M.C.

Ted Williams reported on time for spring training in 1952, but getting in shape for the upcoming season was not his greatest concern. In January he had been notified that the U.S. Marine Corps would call him to active service in May. Ted had remained in the Marine Corps Reserve following World War II, and with hostilities heating up in Korea, the Marines were recalling 1,000 pilots.

Ted expressed mixed feelings about the handling of the conflict in Korea, and he questioned the fortitude of politicians. But he wrote in *My Turn at Bat*, "I was bitter about it, but I made up my mind that I wasn't going to bellyache about it." He would serve his country as he had in World War II.

Mel Parnell remembers the spring of 1952 as a tough time for Ted. "We all felt badly for him. He had already lost three years to World War II. But any time you wanted to find Ted Williams at night during spring training, you could go out and look on one of those bridges in Sarasota. He was on one of those bridges fishing somewhere. He was a master. He could tell you what the fish was doing in the water before it took your bait."

Ted made every effort to get into regular season shape in Sarasota because there was a possibility that his elbow injury would disqualify him from active military duty. After a cursory examination of his elbow, Marine doctors cleared Ted for service as a fighter pilot. He would play in only six games in April before his return to active duty.

Red Sox and Boston city officials declared April 30, 1952, as Ted Williams Day. Ted told the crowd of 25,000, "This is a day I'll always remember, and I want to thank you, fans, in particular, from the bottom of my heart." In what many thought would be his last at-bat in the major leagues, Ted Williams homered into the right-field grandstand.

When the Boston Red Sox reported for spring training in 1953, Captain Ted Williams, U.S.M.C., was 8,000 miles away serving as a combat pilot in P'ohang, South Korea. Charlie Wagner later spoke to John Glenn, former astronaut and U.S. Senator, who had flown with Williams in Korea. "John Glenn told me that Ted was as good a pilot as he ever saw. He said that very few pilots could have landed a flaming jet the way that Ted did and walk away from it. He flew 39 missions over there. It was a remarkable record."

The U.S. Marine Corps discharged Ted in July of 1953, about two months shy of his thirty-fifth birthday. He signed a contract with the Red Sox for the balance of the season in late July and established his own training regimen to get himself in shape. Whatever he did certainly worked since he batted .407 in 37 late season games. It was said that he had set back spring training by about 10 years.

THE SHORTEST SPRING TRAINING

Spring training in 1954 would last less than one hour for Ted Williams. In his book, *Ted Williams: 'Hey Kid, just get the ball over the plate!' former Red Sox pitcher Russ Kemmerer describes Ted's arrival at camp that year.*

"Spring training in 1954 began with high expectations; a sense of excitement prevailed. Williams' return and the changes in personnel gave a new look to the club. However, destiny often steps in to alter a team's course, as it did one morning during batting practice. Williams had just taken his turn in the batting cage, then pranced out to his position in left field to shag a few balls. A low line drive was hit in his direction. He attempted a shoestring catch. Suddenly, he tripped and lunged forward, falling on his shoulder as he hit the ground. Pop! "I think I broke my collarbone!" he exclaimed. He slowly raised himself from the turf and headed for the clubhouse. Trainer Jack Fadden confirmed the break. The injury changed the direction the Red Sox would take, and stalled, at least for the time being, the drive to the top of the standings."

After surgery to insert a four-inch, stainless steel pin, Ted worked out at Fenway Park to salvage what was left of the 1954 season. He returned to action in May, playing in 117 games while compiling a batting average of .345. But the combination of injuries and personal issues led Ted to announce that he would retire at the end of the season. In what was expected to be his final at-bat in his final game, Ted homered into the right-field grandstand in Fenway Park.

When spring training rolled around in 1955, Ted was in the Florida Keys fishing. On Opening Day at Fenway Park, Ted was still fishing. Eventually, the combination of inactivity and financial pressures resulted in a change of heart. On May 13, two days after his divorce from his first wife Doris was final, Ted returned to Boston and signed a contract covering the balance of the 1955 season.

By this time, Ted had mastered the art of individual conditioning. He returned to the lineup in late May and picked up right where he had left off, batting .356 for the season. Despite playing in only 98 games, he finished third in the American League with 28 home runs for the season.

THE LATE 1950s

When Ted Williams arrived at training camp in 1956, he was 37 years old and he had played in all, or parts, of 14 major league seasons. By this time Bobby Doerr, Dom DiMaggio, and Johnny Pesky had all retired as active players. Mel Parnell was one of the few players remaining from the great Red Sox teams of the late 1940s.

"I always looked forward to seeing Ted at spring training," Mel reflects from his home in New Orleans, Louisiana. "As a player, you always looked forward to spring training and seeing all of the players, but seeing Ted was special. He was a wonderful teammate.

"He and I would talk hitting all the time. As a pitcher, it was a big help to me. He was always very generous with his knowledge of hitting, sometimes to a fault from the pitcher's point of view. We would see him giving advice to a hitter from another team and we would just shake our heads. But he would help anyone who asked him."

Ted Williams had an outstanding season in 1956. His batting average of .345 ranked second in the American League and his on-base average of .479 led the league. Best of all, he stayed reasonably healthy and appeared in 132 games, his highest level since 1951.

Spring training in 1957 was a special time for Ted Williams. Recognizing the value of their best hitter, the Red Sox allowed Ted to set his own schedule. He didn't appear in an exhibition game until March 17.

Spring training in 1957 was also a special time for former Red Sox third baseman Frank Malzone. The eight-time American League All-Star followed training camp with an outstanding season, earning a Gold Glove as the best fielding third baseman in the American League. "I remember the first time I met Ted in spring training. I had been in the service and I had played a lot of ball in Hawaii. Ted was one of the first players to greet me. He said, 'I know who you are. I heard you were playing some great ball in Hawaii. You're really going to help us.' I thought to myself that this is a great guy. He goes out of his way to meet me, and he knows who I am."

THE KID HITS .388

The 1957 regular season was one of Ted's best seasons in the big leagues. He batted .388 in 132 games, his second highest average for a full season. If five more of his line drives had fallen in for hits, he would have batted an even .400 for the season. No one had achieved the .400 mark since his .406 average in 1941, and no one has reached it since. But at age 39, Ted came as close as anyone.

March 1958 was the twentieth anniversary of Ted Williams's first spring training camp in Sarasota with the Red Sox. He had come to camp as a teenager and now he was approaching his fortieth birthday in August. During his 16 seasons he had been named to 14 American League All-Star teams, he had led the league in batting average five times, and he had been named the Most Valuable Player in the American League twice. He had become a legend in the game.

"Ted was always the biggest story in spring training," Frank Malzone remembers. "All of us listened to every word he said about hitting. And during batting practice the players from other teams, especially the National League teams who never got to see Ted hit, would crowd around the batting cage to watch him hit. You would see the biggest stars in the game standing around like little kids. You could see how impressed they were."

Former Red Sox pitcher Bill Monbouquette grew up in Medford,

Massachusetts, and watched Ted as a fan in the late 1940s and early 1950s. "Ted was the biggest sports star in Boston. Growing up in Boston, you read about him all the time and every kid on the playground wanted to be Ted Williams when they grew up. I still remember the first time I met him in spring training. I was introduced to him, and he said, 'I know this guy. He can throw strikes.' When I signed with the team as a kid, I hung around Fenway and pitched batting practice until I was assigned to a minor league team. I was so happy that he remembered me in a good way."

Ted turned 40 on August 20, 1958, and he celebrated in September by winning his sixth American League batting title, edging out teammate Pete Runnels with a .328 average. Veteran sports writer Harold Kaese wrote in *The Boston Globe*, "Aladdin had his wonderful lamp, King Arthur had Excalibur. Ted Williams has his bat. If you are given a choice, take the bat. It is the magic wand of the century."

Spring training in 1959 required a major adjustment for Ted Williams. After nearly 20 years of training in Sarasota, Florida, he reported to the new Red Sox training camp in Arizona. Payne Field in Sarasota was beginning to show its age and the Red Sox elected to move 2,500 miles west to the then-sleepy little town of Scottsdale, Arizona.

"I remember playing golf with Ted out in Scottsdale," Frank Malzone reminisces. "I think he played more golf out there because he couldn't go fishing. He was a pretty good golfer, but not a great one. I remember I was paired up with Lu Clinton (former Red Sox outfielder) who was a terrific golfer. Ted was playing with Dick Stuart (former Red Sox first baseman, commonly known as "Dr. Strangeglove"), who could hit the ball a mile. After about 10 holes, we were beating them really badly. Ted turned to Stuart and said, 'I thought you could play this game.'"

Ted's biggest problem in spring training in 1959 was a neck injury. Ted wrote in *My Turn at Bat*, "I was at my home in the Florida Keys, telling an old friend what I thought I was going to do that season, how good I felt. I got up and started swinging the bat. I didn't realize it then, but I hurt my neck that day. I'm sure of it."

His spring training was cut short when the Red Sox sent him to the Lahey Clinic in Boston for treatment. Bothered by his neck injury throughout the regular season, Ted had his worst season in the major leagues, batting an embarrassing .254. Long-time Red Sox owner Tom Yawkey, who had been extremely close to Ted throughout his career, wanted him to retire. Yawkey felt that the years had caught up with Ted, and that playing at a diminished level would detract from his legacy.

THE LAST AT BAT

But Ted Williams was convinced that he had one more All-Star caliber year left. He was determined to finish his career on a high note, not with a .254 batting average. Remembering spring training in 1960, the 41-year-old Williams wrote,

"I felt good that spring. Not The Kid from San Diego any more, all full of spit and vinegar, but not old either."

When Bill Monbouquette thinks back on that spring he remembers Ted's good spirits. "He was full of energy that year. We would horse around in the outfield during batting practice. You could tell he was enthusiastic about his last year. What I remember most was playing against the San Francisco Giants and seeing Willie Mays and Willie McCovey, future Hall of Famers, and great hitters like the Alou brothers, all crowded around the batting cage. They couldn't wait to see Ted hit.

"Ted was a great teammate. He was loud, he had that great booming voice, and I think he intimidated a lot of the writers. But you couldn't ask for a better teammate. He was my friend, but I was in awe of him. I'm still in awe when I think about him."

It is fair to say of the 1960 season that Ted went out in a blaze of glory. One of a handful of players whose career spanned four decades, he hit home run number 512 in August to move into third place in career home runs, trailing only Babe Ruth and his former Red Sox teammate Jimmie Foxx. His batting average for the season was .318 in a year when teammate Pete Runnels won the American League batting title with a .320 average.

On September 26, 1960, the Red Sox announced that Ted would retire at the end of the season. His last major league game was at Fenway Park on September 28 against the Baltimore Orioles. Twice before, first when Ted was headed to combat duty in Korea and in 1954 after he had prematurely announced his retirement, Ted had homered in what was scheduled to be his last at-bat in the major leagues. In the eighth inning, in what would truly be his last at-bat, with the count 1-1, Ted drove a pitch from Jack Fisher deep into right-center field. The drive cleared the fence, struck the canopy over the bullpen seating area, and came to rest in the bullpen for career home run number 521.

SPRING TRAINING 2004

Ted Williams's lifetime batting average of .344 ranks fifth among all players in major league history, and his lifetime on-base percentage of .483 is the highest ever achieved by a major leaguer. He was inducted into baseball's Hall of Fame in 1966, and his acceptance speech was the catalyst for recognition of the stars of the Negro Leagues by the Hall of Fame. More than 40 years later, Ted still ranks either first or second on 11 categories of the Red Sox all-time career batting leaders list.

When spring training begins each year, Ted's long-time friends think back to their times together. "Of course I think about Ted every spring," Dom DiMaggio offers. "Those were terrific years. I have wonderful memories of Ted in spring training."

"I think of Ted all the time," Johnny Pesky adds, "especially when spring training rolls around. He was a dear friend. We had some great times together in the spring."

Ted's long-time roommate Charlie Wagner offers, "When spring training starts, he's the first person I think about. Spring training means Ted Williams to me."

Most Red Sox fans under the age of 50 never had the great pleasure of watching Ted Williams bat in person. If they had been able to see him play in only one game, they probably would have seen him get a base hit. Ted had 2,654 hits in 2,292 games.

But as impressive as his numbers are, Ted was a lot more than statistics. If they could have seen him stride to home plate just one time, they would have heard the same crowd murmur that accompanied Frank Sinatra's stage entrance, or the start of a Bobby Orr rink-length dash at the Boston Garden. And most importantly, they would have seen the greatest hitter who ever lived.

3.
Dom DiMaggio Interview
July 1998

I interviewed Dom DiMaggio in the reception area of the Dana-Farber Hospital in Boston. The setting seemed particularly appropriate since Dom has been a tremendous supporter of The Jimmy Fund for more than 50 years.

When I set up our meeting I told Dom that my typical interview lasted one hour, sometimes running as long as 90 minutes. He said, "What are you going to do, write a book? I'll give you 30 minutes. That should be plenty."

With that limitation in mind, I tried to move the questions along briskly. But Dom couldn't have been more gracious, answering every question thoughtfully and completely. Ninety minutes later we were still talking baseball as we rode down together on the elevator.

Dom DiMaggio was close to the ideal interview. He had a wonderful career, he is very articulate, and he has almost total recall. He is as bright as any CEO or board member I have ever spoken with.

I am always totally focused on getting all of the information that fans would like to read about. But I am first, and foremost, a baseball fan. It was a tremendous thrill to talk baseball with one of the great center fielders in Red Sox history, and a member of the legendary DiMaggio family.

DOM DIMAGGIO
"THE LITTLE PROFESSOR"

"Dom DiMaggio came as close to being the perfect ballplayer as anyone I have seen in all my years of baseball. He could do it all. He absolutely belongs in baseball's Hall of Fame."

These are the words of Johnny Pesky, who has done a little bit of everything for the Boston Red Sox since he joined the big league club in 1942. If anyone is an authority on the subject of Dom DiMaggio, it is Johnny. Pesky batted in the second position and Dom was the leadoff hitter during most of DiMaggio's distinguished Red Sox career.

Throughout his career Dom DiMaggio was regarded as one of the finest defensive outfielders in the major leagues. He achieved All-Star status in seven of his 10 full seasons with the Red Sox, and scored more than 100 runs in seven seasons. He still holds the Red Sox consecutive game hitting record with a standard of 34 set in 1949.

THE CITY BY THE BAY

Dominic Paul DiMaggio was the youngest of nine children born to Giuseppe and Rosalie DiMaggio. His parents had emigrated to the San Francisco, California, area from Palermo, Sicily, Italy, at the turn of the century. Giuseppe DiMaggio supported his large family as a crab fisherman sailing out of historic Fisherman's Wharf.

The Bay Area was a baseball hotbed and Dom's older brothers Mike and Tom were known as two of the finer players on the local sandlots. But their baseball careers were cut short because they were needed in the family fishing enterprise.

The next DiMaggio son was Vince who was two years older than future New York Yankee great, Joe, and four years older than Dom. Vince, who would break in with the Boston Braves in 1937, attracted the interest of the minor league San Francisco Seals and was signed to a contract in 1932.

Giuseppe DiMaggio wasn't too keen on Vince's choice of a career. But it was clear in Joe's case from his earliest days on the diamond that he was destined for greatness. The elder DiMaggio gave Joe permission to pursue a baseball career, and Giuseppe quickly became Joe's biggest fan.

"My father used to wake me up at 4 A.M. when the newspaper arrived, to go over the box score with him. He would be ready to head off for a day of fishing but he couldn't decipher the box scores and he had to know how Joe had done," Dom remembers.

Big brothers Vince and Joe had paved the way for Dom's baseball career, but he had more than a few obstacles to overcome. Not only was he the kid brother and the smallest of the three boys, but he wore glasses. In the 1930s, baseball players with glasses were almost unheard of.

"It was viewed as such a negative that I used to play a lot without my glasses. One day I wore my glasses and got four hits. I wore them every game after that.

"Today it's different, but back then there were safety concerns. And wearing glasses made you suspect as a prospect. It was almost a sign of weakness. Now you have glasses that won't shatter and a lot of players wear contacts."

Dom's big break in baseball came when he starred at a tryout camp run jointly by the Cincinnati Reds and the San Francisco Seals. The Seals signed him to a contract, but immediately moved him from his usual spot at shortstop. Seals owner Charley Graham reportedly said, "With those glasses we better get him in the outfield."

Dom's first manager was Lefty O'Doul who had batted .349 over an eleven-year big league career. DiMaggio flourished under O'Doul's tutelage and batted .306 in his first season with the Seals.

He played three seasons for the Seals, batting .361 in 1939, his final season with the team. Asked when he first knew that he was headed for the major leagues, Dom recalls, "There was a writer for the *San Francisco Daily News*

named Tom Laird. He used to write that my brother Joe was the greatest ballplayer he had ever seen, but that I was a poor player who was cashing in on Joe's name. When Laird changed his tune and started writing good things about me, I knew I had arrived."

BOSTON BOUND

The Red Sox purchased Dom's contract from the Seals following the 1939 season, and he reported to Sarasota, Florida, to play under manager Joe Cronin in February of 1940. Dom faced the challenge of trying to break into an outfield that already included Ted Williams, and 11-year veteran Doc Cramer. His outstanding play in the Grapefruit League earned him the starting position in right field on Opening Day in Washington, DC.

It should be noted that Dom DiMaggio is considered to be the first base-ball player ever to work his way through the minors, and go on to a successful career in the major leagues wearing glasses from the beginning. A number of earlier players had donned glasses after establishing themselves in the big leagues, but in the 1940s Dom DiMaggio was a real inspiration to many aspir-ing major leaguers.

The 23-year old DiMaggio immediately earned a spot as a Red Sox fixture, batting .301 in his rookie year. Early in the 1940 season, manager Cronin shifted Dom to center field to make better use of his defensive genius.

His shift to center meant that three of the sixteen major league center field-ers at that time shared the surname of DiMaggio. Joe led the way in 1936 with the Yankees, and in 1940 brother Vince was a regular with the Pittsburgh Pirates. The three brothers were known widely as "The Royal Family of Baseball." Five Delahanty brothers had actually made it to the major leagues just before and immediately after the turn of the century. However, the three DiMaggio broth-ers were the first to each play in over 100 games in a season, a feat they sustained from 1940 through 1942.

The 1941 season was a special one for Dom personally, and a very special year for baseball. On a personal level, he scored 117 runs for the Red Sox and he was selected for the American League All-Star team. In the tenth edition of the midsummer classic, played at the old Polo Grounds in New York, Dom played in the outfield alongside his brother Joe. He singled in the eighth inning to drive Joe in with an important run, and watched as teammate Ted Williams won the game for the American League with a three-run homer in the ninth inning.

In 1941 Dom watched with pride as his brother Joe set a major league record with base hits in 56 consecutive games. On a daily basis, he watched Ted Williams become the last major league hitter to reach .400.

"THE LITTLE PROFESSOR"

Early in his Red Sox career, the baseball writers took to referring to Dom as "The Little Professor." With his wire-rim glasses and relatively small stature at 5'9", it was said that he looked more like a college professor than a baseball player. But his nickname suited his intellect and thoughtful demeanor as well. According to legend, once when he was called out on strikes with a pitch that he felt was def-initely a ball, he returned to the dugout, stood on the top step and shouted back at the umpire, "I have never witnessed such incompetence in all my life!"

Johnny Pesky joined the Red Sox in 1942 as a 22-year-old rookie shortstop. "I was so impressed with Dominic as a ballplayer and as a person. He could hit, he could run, and he was as good in the outfield as anyone I have ever seen. Dom was the leadoff hitter, and I would follow him. He was the ideal player to hit behind. I don't think I ever saw him make a mistake on the bases. His instincts were uncanny."

Dom was named to the American League All-Star team again in 1942, but major league baseball players were heading off to the Armed Forces to serve in

World War II. Dom DiMaggio spent the 1943, 1944, and 1945 seasons in the U.S Navy.

The 1946 season was a great one for the Boston Red Sox and for Dom DiMaggio. Dom was returned to the American League All Star team in midseason and the Red Sox clinched the American League pennant in mid-September. He played well in a losing cause in the World Series against the St. Louis Cardinals. Dom scored the winning run in the fifth game, to give the Red Sox a 3-2 edge in the Series.

Dom DiMaggio still gets upset when he recalls Enos "Country" Slaughter's mad dash for home in the eighth inning of Game Seven, and the lingering accounts that Johnny Pesky "held the ball." He is anxious to set the record straight.

"I suppose that losing the seventh game and the World Series to the St. Louis Cardinals was my biggest disappointment in baseball. But what bothers me most is the way we lost it and the bad rap that Johnny Pesky has taken all of these years. And if I hadn't gotten hurt, I don't think it would have turned out that way.

"I had pulled a hamstring in our half of the eighth inning and Leon Culberson had to play my spot in center field. If I had been playing center field I would have shaded Harry Walker more towards left field. In fact, we were on the bench trying to get Culberson to move in that direction. And I would have charged Walker's hit and cut it off before it got deeper in the outfield.

"I would have come up firing to third base. I don't think I would have caught Slaughter because he had such a good jump, but I think I could have held him to third. Now this isn't a knock on Culberson, because he was a pretty good ballplayer, but I was a much better fielder than him.

The DiMaggio brothers: Vince, Dom and Joe during the 1986 Old-Timers' Game at Fenway Park.

"Johnny Pesky didn't hold that ball. He turned around, saw Slaughter round-ing third, and he was as surprised as everyone in the ballpark. But Johnny didn't hesitate. He followed through and made that throw. Give Slaughter credit for being an aggressive base runner, but for goodness sake, don't blame Johnny Pesky."

During the next several seasons, Dom emerged as one of the premier play-ers in the major leagues. In 1948, he scored 127 runs as the Red Sox tied the Cleveland Indians for the pennant, losing in a one game playoff at Fenway Park. In 1949, he scored 126 runs while his team came within one game of beating the Yankees for the American League pennant.

While Dom was recognized as a star in his own right, it was brother Joe who gathered most of the headlines with the New York Yankees. Asked how it felt to be in his brother's majestic shadow, he says, "I've always told people how very proud I am to be Joe's brother. And then I would remind them 'yes, he's my brother, and I'm *his brother, too.*' I also had a little more privacy, since he's the first DiMaggio they would approach for a special favor or appearance. I didn't have to deal with as many off the field distractions as he did."

PERENNIAL ALL STAR

Former Red Sox first baseman Walt Dropo grew up in Moosup, Connecticut, reading about DiMaggio, Williams, and Bobby Doerr. Dropo was named the American League Rookie of the Year in 1950 when he rapped out 144 RBI for the Red Sox, and he still marvels at Dom's skills.

"The thing that amazed me about Dom was his consistency. He played the game flawlessly day after day. Some players go hitless for three games and then go out and make a big splash with a four-hit game. Dom would go out every day and get a hit, draw a walk, run the bases to perfection, score a run, and field his position perfectly. I think he got overlooked sometimes simply because he was so consistent."

Dom DiMaggio celebrated his 33rd birthday just before reporting to spring training in 1950. Dom seemed to get better with age, putting up some of his best offensive numbers over the next three years. He led the league in triples and stolen bases in 1950. He led the American League in runs scored in both 1950 and 1951. He also continued his string of All-Star Game selections, which stretched consecutively from 1949 to 1952.

In the spring of 1953 new Red Sox manager Lou Boudreau instituted a "youth movement" which significantly reduced Dom's playing time. After con-siderable soul-searching, he decided to retire from baseball at the age of 36.

"I felt that I had several good years still in me, and I wasn't prepared to sit on the bench. I asked Red Sox General Manager Joe Cronin to trade me or release me, but the team declined. I decided I would rather retire than accept part-time play, my pride wouldn't let me, so that's what I did in April, 1953."

For the first time in 17 big league seasons, there were no DiMaggios playing major league baseball.

CAREER ACHIEVEMENTS

Dom DiMaggio's career statistics place him in the upper echelon of baseball players for all-time. During his 10 full years, he ranked first in number of hits, second in runs scored, and third in doubles [see box] when compared to all major leaguers during this period. He has three of the 15 longest hitting streaks in Red Sox history. On average, he scored 105 times each season; only two Hall of Fame members from the 20th century—Lou Gehrig and brother Jolting Joe DiMaggio—averaged over 100 runs scored per season.

Fielding statistics are less revealing than hitting, but he is one of only three American League outfielders to average three or more chances per game. And he is one of only five out-fielders to have over 500 putouts in a season.

"I took a great deal of pride in my fielding," Dom emphasizes today. "I practiced hard all the time and I studied the hitters. I think I worked as hard on my fielding as Ted (Williams) did on his hitting."

"Dom's numbers compare to anyone's," Johnny Pesky thinks. "But to truly appreciate him as a player and a man, you had to have seen him day after day, season after season. He was the complete baseball player and a real gentleman."

THE LATER YEARS

Dom DiMaggio went from the baseball diamond to the business world without missing a beat. For many years he owned and managed a plastics manufacturing company in Lawrence, Massachusetts. His success in business mirrored his achievements in baseball.

In his early years with the Red Sox, Dom returned to his native San Francisco during the off-season. That changed shortly after he married his wife

Emily in 1948. "Emily is a Boston girl, so New England became home for us. I still love to go back to San Francisco but our roots are firmly planted here."

The DiMaggios, who celebrated their 56th wedding anniversary in October 2004, have three grown children and six much-loved grandchildren. Dom and his wife divide their time between Marion, Massachusetts, and Delray Beach, Florida. For over 20 years, Dom has sponsored a golf tournament that raises money for the Jimmy Fund and a number of causes in the southeastern Massachusetts area.

"THE GREATEST FIELDER I EVER SAW"

When Joe DiMaggio retired from the New York Yankees in 1951, he was asked to name the greatest hitter, and the greatest fielder he had ever seen. "Ted Williams was the greatest hitter I ever saw, and my brother Dom was the greatest fielder."

Asked for his response to that quote, Dom answers, "My brother Joe never got to watch himself play center field." Dom DiMaggio is a very gracious individual.

In July 1998, Dr. Gene Budig, then President of the American League, came to Boston to appear at a press conference announcing the plans for the 1999 All-Star Game at Fenway Park. Dr. Budig said, "This is a great day for me. I finally got to meet my idol Dom DiMaggio. He has been my hero all these years, and it was a thrill to meet him."

Dom DiMaggio was the first baseball player this writer ever saw, and my first baseball hero. Based on his distinguished baseball and business careers, and his exemplary commitment to family and community, he is still a hero.

Ten-Year Offensive Statistics
1940-42 and 1946-52 Seasons

Player	Hits	Player	Runs	Player	Doubles
D. DiMaggio	1,679	Williams	1,144	Williams	322
Slaughter	1,619	D. DiMaggio	1,046	Musial	316
Musial	1,606	Musial	929	D. DiMaggio	308
Williams	1,582	Reese	894	Vernon	275
Reese	1,447	J. DiMaggio	870	Boudreau	269

Ranked #1-5 for all Major League Players for Time Period Indicated.

Source: *The Baseball Encyclopedia, Ninth Edition*

4.
Johnny Pesky Interview
March 1999

I interviewed Johnny Pesky in the Red Sox dugout at City of Palms Park in Fort Myers, Florida, one hour before their exhibition game against the Pittsburgh Pirates. I have enjoyed all of my interviews over the years, but this one was probably my favorite.

I spent 45 minutes interviewing Johnny and it was obvious that the players get a big kick out of him. I wasn't prepared for the good-natured bantering but Johnny gave as good as he got. Hanging around baseball dugouts for 70 years will do that for you, I guess.

As many Red Sox fans know, Johnny Pesky is the most approachable of all of the former Red Sox greats. Whenever I need a quote to enrich a player profile I call on Johnny. And he treats me as if I was calling from the New York Times.

I have to admit that I got a big kick out of the fact that 20 minutes before game time, Peter Gammons and I were the only media types in the Red Sox dugout. I think Peter is probably still trying to figure out who I was. As game time approached, manager Jimy Williams looked as if he wanted me out of his dugout. But Johnny answered all of my questions fully, providing a number of colorful anecdotes. Johnny Pesky is Mr. Red Sox.

JOHNNY PESKY
ALL-STAR MEMORIES

Johnny Pesky still clearly remembers the day he signed with the Boston Red Sox 60 years ago. "A number of teams had shown an interest in me, but the Red Sox scout, Ernie Johnson, had been following me for a couple of years. He used to come by our house and bring some pretty flowers for my mother, and a bottle of bourbon for my dad.

"I told my mother that I was thinking about signing with another team. She said, 'Johnny, you will sign with the Red Sox.' When she made that decision for me, she sent me to heaven. It has been a wonderful association with the team.

"I remember they gave me $500 to sign with them. I thought I was rich. I had never seen $500 all in one place in my life!"

FROM CLUBHOUSE BOY TO THE BIG LEAGUES

John Michael Paveskovich was born on September 27, 1919, in Portland, Oregon. The fifth child of six, his father had emigrated from Yugoslavia just before the outbreak of World War I. Friends and neighbors re-named the family "Pesky", and Johnny has always been known by that name ever since. The baseball bug bit him at an early age.

"Portland had a strong team in the Pacific Coast League, and I started hanging around their clubhouse shining shoes when I was 10 years old. Eventually I worked my way up to head clubhouse boy. It was great.

"That's how I first met Ted Williams and Bobby Doerr. Ted and Bobby were outstanding players for the San Diego ball club, but they were only a couple of years older than me. I got to know them back in the 1930s, and they remained my great friends for over 60 years."

Pesky began his Red Sox career in Rocky Mountain, North Carolina, in 1940. Playing under manager Heinie Manush, a Hall of Famer, he led the Piedmont League in base hits. His fine showing earned him a promotion to the top Red Sox farm club in Louisville, Kentucky, the following season. The young shortstop went on to lead the American Association in hits, and he was named the league's Most Valuable Player.

Pesky came to the Red Sox major league spring training camp in Sarasota, Florida, in 1942, with high hopes of winning the starting shortstop job. Red Sox manager Joe Cronin announced that he had played his last season as the regular shortstop, so that he could concentrate on managing the team. "I was competing with Eddie Pellagrini [Red Sox infielder from 1946 to 1947] for the job at short.

Joe Cronin gave us both a shot during the spring games, and I did a little bit better with the bat than Eddie. When the team headed North, I had won the job."

Johnny Pesky's first season with the Red Sox compares favorably with any rookie in the team's history. He batted .331 in 147 games and displayed a wide range at shortstop. Most impressively, he led the American League with 205 base hits. "I was very fortunate hitting in that lineup. Dom DiMaggio was the leadoff hitter, and I got to follow him. I had Ted Williams hitting after me, with Bobby Doerr right behind. When you're surrounded by guys like that, it is a lot easier to hit."

World War II interrupted Pesky's promising career from 1943 to 1945. He is philosophical about those three lost seasons. "I went into a Navy program along with Ted [Williams] and Johnny Sain [former Boston Braves pitching great]. It was a great experience. My own father thought when I was commissioned it was the greatest thing in his life—greater than my being a big league ballplayer."

THE 1946 ALL-STAR GAME

Fans who reveled in the exciting 2004 baseball season would have also loved the 1946 season. The outstanding players had all returned from the Armed Services, and their fans turned out in record numbers to welcome them back.

The 1946 season was a memorable one for the Boston Red Sox and for Johnny Pesky. The team got off to a great start, winning 41 of their first 50 con-

Johnny takes a turn at bat during a spring training game in Sarasota, FL.

tests. At the All-Star break, their American League rivals had all but conceded the pennant to the Red Sox and Pesky continued his league-leading hitting pace.

"We had a wonderful team that year. Ted, Bobby, and Dom were all at their peak. We got great pitching from Boo Ferriss [25-game winner], Tex Hughson, and Mickey Harris. We won 104 ball games in a 154-game season."

On July 9, 1946, the bunting was unfurled for the first All-Star Game ever hosted at Fenway Park. A crowd of 34,906 fans cheered the American League to a 12-0 trouncing of their National League rivals.

"One thing that stands out in my mind is that the Red Sox had eight players named to that American League team. I was lucky enough to be one of them, but I went 0-for-2 at the plate, and I made an error," Pesky laughs remembering the game. "But I guess I didn't hold us back too much since we won by twelve runs!"

"Another thing I remember is how proud Tom Yawkey [the late Red Sox owner] was that day. We were in first place, and he was playing host to everyone in baseball. He was always the perfect gentleman, and that was a very special event for him. But what I will always remember the most is the batting show that Ted Williams put on that day."

Coming into the game, the American League held an 8 to 4 edge in victories in the series, which had begun in Chicago's Comiskey Park in 1933. Following a Ted Williams single in the first inning, the Yankees' Charlie Keller homered to put the American League out ahead 2-0. In the fourth inning, Williams homered against the Brooklyn Dodgers' Kirby Higbe, a drive that was estimated to travel 450 feet into the center-field bleachers. He singled again in the seventh inning, coming around to score as the American League ran their advantage to 8-0.

THE LEGENDARY TED WILLIAMS

"When Ted came to bat against Pittsburgh Pirates pitching ace Rip Sewell in the eighth inning, everybody in the park knew that Sewell was going to throw Ted his blooper pitch. Rip had this pitch that he could throw 25-30 feet in the air and drop it right over home plate. He called it his 'eephus pitch' and it was awfully tough to hit because of the trajectory.

"He threw in a couple of eephus pitches to Ted, and you could see Ted taking the measure of that pitch. Remember, Ted Williams is the greatest student of hitting who ever lived. Well, Ted moved up in the box, Rip threw another pitch 30 or so feet in the air, and Williams timed his swing perfectly. He drove that ball right into the Red Sox bullpen, and the crowd went nuts. When you look at the film you can see that Ted was out of the batter's box when he hit the ball, but I guess that doesn't really matter 60 years later!"

Following the All-Star break, the Red Sox resumed the quest for their first American League pennant in 28 years. The team reached its goal with a 1-0 victory over the Cleveland Indians on September 13, 1946.

The Red Sox took a three-game-to-two lead in the World Series against the St. Louis Cardinals in the World Series, and flew to St. Louis for the deciding games with hopes high. Unfortunately, a ninth inning Red Sox rally in the seventh game fell short, and the Cardinals emerged as World Champions.

"That is the one disappointment I've had in my baseball career," Pesky says emotionally. "The fact that we've never won the World Series, especially for Tom Yawkey. I want a championship for this team so bad I can taste it."

OUTSTANDING CAREER

The ending to the 1946 season was a disappointment, but Pesky had rapped out 208 hits to lead the American League for the second year in a row. Remarkably, he accumulated 207 hits to top the American League again in 1947. This marked his third straight year of leading the American League in the number of hits.

Over the next five and one-half seasons he would continue his extraordinarily consistent hitting with the Red Sox. He batted over .300 in six of his seven full seasons with the team, and he averaged well over 100 runs scored each year.

"I batted in front of Ted Williams, and my job was to get on base even if it meant leaning in to get hit by a pitch. We never wanted him to lead off an inning with no one on to drive in."

The 1946 All-Star Game was Johnny's only appearance in the midsummer classic. With perennial All-Stars such as Phil Rizzuto of the Yankees and, when Johnny later moved to third base, George Kell of the Tigers, there simply wasn't enough room. But he still has fond memories of the annual All-Star Games during his career.

"There were so many great players at that time. To watch Joe DiMaggio on the same field with his brother Dom, and Ted [Williams], was a great thrill. And to look across at the National League dugout and see future Hall of Famers like Stan Musial, Ralph Kiner and Jackie Robinson. That was really something.

"My worst All-Star memory is Ted Williams fracturing his wrist catching a line drive in Comiskey Park in 1950. That ended our chances for the 1950 season. I ended up hitting third in the batting order for the only time in my career. I remember getting the 'hit' sign on 3-0 pitches, and thinking I was seeing things!"

On June 3, 1952, the Boston Red Sox traded Johnny Pesky, along with four other players, to the Detroit Tigers for four players, including future Hall of Famer George Kell. The *Boston Evening American* of the next day describes Red Sox fans as "amazed and shocked" at the Pesky trade. Rosemary Rohmer of Brookline is quoted as saying, "Johnny Pesky has been with the Sox so long, I thought he was part of the franchise." And that was over fifty years ago!

"I was disappointed to be traded," Johnny recalls, "but it is part of baseball. And the Detroit Tigers were a class organization. I enjoyed my time there.

"And you always have to remember that professional baseball is a business. This is a great game, but at the professional level it is still a business. I didn't like it when I was moved off the bench a few years back, but I understood it. It was just business."

Johnny Pesky retired following the 1954 season after compiling a lifetime batting average of .307. His 205 hits in 1942 remained the Red Sox record for a rookie until Nomar Garciaparra surpassed it in 1997. Johnny's accomplishments include a share of the major league record for scoring six runs in a single game [May 8, 1946], and an amazing streak of batting safely in 11 consecutive at-bats. But his 50-year off-the-field career in baseball was just beginning.

EVERYTHING BUT SELL THE TICKETS

Johnny Pesky "came home" to the Red Sox in 1961 after managing in the Detroit minor league system for six years. His first assignment was to manage the Red Sox Triple A farm club in Seattle, Washington. After two successful seasons in that role, he was named as manager of the Boston Red Sox for the 1963 season.

The 1963 Red Sox got off to a fast start under their new manager, challenging the Yankees into June. Pesky was named as an American League coach for that year's All-Star Game in Cleveland. But the 1963 team tailed off in midseason to finish seventh in the ten-team American League standings. In 1964, the team dropped to eighth place in the standings, and Billy Herman replaced Pesky as manager at the end of the season.

Outstanding Red Sox relief pitcher Dick Radatz remembers Johnny Pesky as a manager. "I had a lot of terrific managers, but Johnny Pesky was special. He was like a second father to me. I would do anything for Johnny Pesky."

Pesky's next move was to manage in the Pittsburgh Pirates farm system and to coach at the major league level during the next five years. The Red Sox brought him back as a radio-TV announcer from 1969 to 1974.

"I liked announcing," Pesky recalls, "but I was never totally comfortable in that role. I can remember hearing people criticize me as an announcer, and I would agree with them. To tell you the truth, I was best at rain-delays. I did have a lot of great stories to tell."

In 1975 Johnny put his Red Sox uniform back on, and joined manager Darrell Johnson's coaching staff. His return was certainly a good omen as the team won the American League pennant and forced the powerful Cincinnati Reds to a seventh game, before bowing in an epic World Series. He remained as a coach when Don Zimmer replaced Johnson in mid-1976, and served as the interim manager for the last five games of the 1980 season when Zimmer was replaced.

After four more years as a coach under Red Sox manager Ralph Houk, Pesky became a special assistant to General Manager Lou Gorman. In mid-1990, he stepped once more into the breach, taking over as manager of Pawtucket, the Red Sox Triple A entry in the International League for the balance of the season.

ADOPTED SON OF NEW ENGLAND

When Johnny Pesky arrived in Boston nearly 60 years ago, he was a long way from his birthplace in Portland, Oregon. Asked when he first decided to make Boston his new home, he answers, "The moment I arrived here. I took one look around, and I said to myself, 'This is where I was meant to be, and this is where I want to be.' "

Johnny Pesky met Ruth, his wife of 54 years, while both were serving in the U.S. Navy. The couple was married on January 10, 1945, and they have lived in Swampscott, Massachusetts, for many years. "She [Ruth] is the best thing that ever happened to me. It's not easy being married to a baseball guy, but she has been there for me every step of the way."

Johnny Pesky's eyes really light up when he talks about the couple's son, David. "He is a terrific young man. He's a college graduate, and we are so proud of that. Make sure you give my wife credit for how well he has turned out. She was the one who did all the good work raising him. She was the one who was always there for him."

Pesky was among the first Red Sox to be inducted into the Red Sox Hall of Fame in November 1995. He posed with fellow inductees: Bobby Doerr, Dom DiMaggio, Jim Rice, and Frank Malzone at the Induction Ceremonies.

EIGHTY-FIVE YEARS YOUNG

During the 2004 season, Johnny Pesky worked extensively with Red Sox infielders before most home games. In past years when the team was on the road he frequently worked with the younger players in Pawtucket, and with the Red Sox single A minor league team in Lowell.

Asked how many ground balls he hits with his ever-present fungo bat in a typical day, Pesky considers for a moment, and responds, "Oh, about 300, I suppose."

"I used to think I would keep after it until I turned 80. But now that 80 has come and gone, I think I'll take it one year at a time!"

Pesky laughs when it is pointed out that he is the only former major leaguer with a foul pole named after him. "Mel Parnell (former Red Sox pitching star, and Pesky's former broadcasting partner) named the right field foul pole 'Pesky's Pole.' I only had 17 home runs in the big leagues, but I managed to curl eight of them right around that pole."

Yes, Johnny Pesky, you are a Boston Red Sox legend.

5.
Dave "Boo" Ferriss
Interview

July 2004

I had two concerns when it came time to write a profile of Dave "Boo" Ferriss. My first concern was that his major league career was relatively brief. After his first two brilliant seasons, Boo suffered a shoulder injury and his playing career ended prematurely.

My second concern was that I had never seen Boo play. I have written more than 50 player profiles over the years, and I had seen all of the players in a game at Fenway Park. I can't claim a strong memory of Bobby Doerr, Dom DiMaggio, and Johnny Pesky, but I did see all of them in action.

After 10 minutes on the telephone with Boo at his Cleveland, Mississippi, home, any anxiety melted away. He is a very warm person, he has some wonderful anecdotes, and he has led a very rich life.

Boo Ferriss celebrated his eighty-fourth birthday on December 5, 2004, but he is gifted, seemingly, with almost total recall. He described his arrival in Brattleboro, Vermont, 64 years ago to play in a summer league with vivid detail.

When you look at his first two years in the major leagues, you have to wonder what he would have achieved if he hadn't been injured. But when you look at the positive impact that Boo had on hundreds of players over 26 years, you realize that coaching baseball at the college level was his true calling.

DAVE FERRISS
"BOO"

Dave "Boo" Ferriss began his pitching career with the Boston Red Sox with the radiance of a shooting star across the evening sky. In 1945, his rookie year, Boo won 21 games and was named to the American League All-Star team. His 25 wins the following season helped to propel the 1946 Boston Red Sox to their first American League pennant in 28 years.

But like a shooting star, his period of pitching brilliance was all too brief. In 1947 Boo injured his shoulder pitching a complete game shutout against the Cleveland Indians. For the balance of his major league career, Ferriss pitched credibly, relying primarily on his competive spirit and knowledge of the hitters. But his shoulder problems kept him from regaining his All Star form.

Speaking from his home in Cleveland, Mississippi, Boo is philosophical about what might have been. "I had two wonderful years, and I got to spend six seasons in the major leagues. I had some terrific teammates and I have lots of great memories. Sure, I wish my arm had responded and come around, but I have had a wonderful life in baseball."

Johnny Pesky, who has been associated with the Boston Red Sox for 52 seasons, was Boo Ferriss' teammate in 1946. "We were all in the service in 1945, but we kept hearing about this rookie pitcher and how great he was. When I saw him in spring training I knew they were right.

"It seemed like right after the war every team had a couple of great pitchers. Guys like Bob Feller with the Indians, Hal Newhouser with the Tigers. And I can tell you this. In 1946 Boo Ferriss was as good as any of them."

THE PRIDE OF SHAW, MISSISSIPPI

Boo Ferriss has warm memories of coming of age in Mississippi. "Shaw, Mississippi, is a little town in the Delta region and it was a wonderful place to grow up. When I was just learning to talk, I tried to say "brother" and it came out "Boo." I have been Boo ever since. I can't think of anyone who calls me Dave.

"My father was the biggest influence in my life. I got my love of baseball from him. He had been a semi-pro player and he did a lot of managing after his ball playing days were over. We were big fans of the St. Louis Cardinals. I can remember listening to their games being broadcast by KMOX on our old Atwater Kent Radio.

"Dizzy Dean [Hall of Fame pitcher] was my hero growing up. And my dad would take us over to Memphis to see the Memphis Chicks play in the higher minor leagues and to Greenville to see their Class C team. I can remember playing catch off our five front steps and throwing the ball against the side of our house, dreaming of becoming a baseball player.

"I had a fine high school career. I was 19-2 combined in my junior and senior years. And I was a good hitter as well. There were some major league scouts watching me, but my Dad said, 'You are going to college.'

"I ended up with a full baseball scholarship to Mississippi State. It was the first one they had ever given. I played under coach Dudy Noble there. He was a great coach. I really learned a lot during my three seasons under him."

WELCOME TO NEW ENGLAND

In 1941 Boo Ferriss made the long trip from Mississippi to Brattleboro, Vermont, to play in one of the best summer baseball leagues in the country. "I made the whole trip by train, and I think it took me the better part of two days. The train dropped me off at the Brattleboro station at about three in the morning. I took a look around and I knew I was a long way from home. I'll tell you, if a train came along heading the other way, I would have hopped right on it.

"But once I got settled in, I really liked it up there. There were some great college players in the league. I think there were 50 or so who eventually went on to play in the major leagues. I remember my friend, Sam Mele, played for Burlington. It was something like the Cape Cod League is today.

"But the best part of the experience is that we got to go down to Fenway

Park. Our manager, Bill Barrett, said, 'Some of you southern boys have never seen a big league baseball game, so I'm going to take you down to Boston.' I ended up pitching some batting practice for the Red Sox. They even took me on a road trip, and I can remember walking down the street in New York City with Ted Williams, who was very good to me. It was quite an experience for a 19-year-old kid from Shaw, Mississippi."

The following season the Boston Red Sox signed Ferriss and he spent the 1942 season with their Class B team in Greensboro, North Carolina. The first-year professional pitched 130 innings and compiled an impressive ERA of 2.21. Manager Heinie Manush, a former major league star and Hall of Famer, passed on a glowing report to the Red Sox.

In December 1942, Ferriss was drafted into the Armed Services. "I was looking forward to going in the service, to serving my country. There was some debate whether they were going to take me because I had severe asthma as a teenager, but I wanted to do my part.

"Eventually I ended up at Randolph Field in San Antonio, Texas. I was a physical training instructor and I also got a lot of chances to play ball. They had an eight-team league with a lot of former major leaguers on the rosters. There were guys like Enos Slaughter and Howie Pollet of the St. Louis Cardinals. I was very fortunate because it gave me a chance to play at a very high level of ball."

In early 1945 his asthmatic condition worsened and he was hospitalized for over six weeks. The doctors finally concluded that his condition would not improve to the standards of the Armed Services, and Boo received his honorable discharge. The Red Sox then assigned him to their top farm club in Louisville, Kentucky.

ROOKIE PHENOM

"I had a couple of good outings in exhibition games against the Cincinnati Reds and their manager, Bill McKechnie, called Joe Cronin [Red Sox manager] to tell him that I was a real prospect. But I remember when the Louisville manager called me in; I thought 'Uh oh, they're going to send me to the lower minors.' I was on cloud nine when I found out I was headed to the big leagues.

"I figured I would start out with some relief work but on April 29 I walked in and found the game ball in my locker. I went over to Del Baker and asked him if there was some mistake. He said, 'Kid, you're the pitcher today.'

"It was against the Philadelphia Athletics and I can remember looking into their dugout and there's Connie Mack [legendary Athletics manager] sitting in there in a suit. And I saw Al Simmons [Hall of Famer], one their coaches. These were guys I had only read about, men I had idolized.

"I think 15 of my first 17 pitches were balls and I walked the bases loaded. But I settled down after that and I did okay." Okay as in pitching a 2-0 complete game shutout in his first major league game. Okay as in going three-for-three as a hitter.

Rookie Ferriss followed that with a 5-0 whitewashing of the Yankees in his next start. It wasn't until the fifth inning of his third major league start, facing a Detroit Tigers team that would go on to win the 1945 World Series, that he finally gave up a run. His 22-inning scoreless streak to begin his career established a new American League record. The merely mortal Mr. Ferriss defeated the Tigers 6-2 that day.

Two weeks later, against the Chicago White Sox, he pitched a one-hitter, giving up only a second-inning single to Tony Cuccinello. His 7-0 victory was his sixth straight win and his fourth shutout. It wasn't until mid-June that he lost his first decision, a tough 3-2 loss to the Yankees. At that time the American League consisted of eight teams. And the 23-year-old Ferriss defeated all seven of the other teams the first time he faced them.

His amazing start earned him a selection to the American League All-Star team, an unusual honor for a rookie. On August 26, he defeated the Philadelphia Athletics for his twentieth win. His double in the tenth inning provided the margin of victory. These 20 victories in his first 30 games is the major league record for the fewest games required to reach 20 wins, a record he shares with three other major league pitchers.

The Rookie of the Year award didn't exist in 1945, but Boo Ferriss clearly was the rookie standout of that season. His final record of 21-5 (.677) placed him second in the American

League in wins, and fifth in winning percentage. His complete game total of 26 was second best in the league and his sparkling ERA of 2.96 ranked ninth. He finished fourth in the balloting for the American League's Most Valuable Player award.

AMERICAN LEAGUE PENNANT WINNERS

When Boo Ferriss reported to the Red Sox spring training headquarters in Sarasota, Florida, for the 1946 season, he was introduced to returning veteran teammates including Ted Williams, Bobby Doerr, Dom DiMaggio, and Tex Hughson. The team was counting on him to be an important member of the rotation. But baseball writers questioned whether he would be as dominating against the great players who had returned from World War II, as he was in 1945. The answer was somewhat surprising: he turned out to be even better in 1946.

Boo answered the skeptics by winning his first 10 decisions in 1946. On June 11 the Red Sox defeated the Cleveland Indians to improve their record to an extraordinary 41-9. Boo's 10-0 record was a major factor in the team's spectacular start. "We had a great team that year, I had a lot of hitting support," Boo modestly observes. "Ted [Williams] was amazing all year long, Bobby Doerr had a great year, along with Dom DiMaggio and Johnny [Pesky]. And Tex Hughson and Mickey Harris pitched great also."

His outstanding start earned him All-Star honors for the second straight year. He joined seven of his teammates on the American League squad that routed the National League 12-0 at Fenway Park. Boo suffered a few defeats between mid-June and mid-July, but then he went on to start an even-longer winning streak.

Johnny Pesky remembers what a pleasure it was to play behind Boo Ferriss in 1946. "Looking in from shortstop I had a real good view of how he was pitching. Every pitch he threw had movement on it. He was almost unhittable. He wasn't overpowering like Feller and some of those guys, but he had this great sinker. And it seemed like every pitch he threw was at the knees or below. Man, he was really something."

Boo Ferriss was in a zone and he was practically untouchable at Fenway Park. When he defeated the St. Louis Browns on August 21, the Red Sox had won 50-out-of 60 games at home. "At one point that season I won 13 in a row at Fenway Park," Boo acknowledges.

On September 13 the Red Sox clinched the American League pennant with a 1-0 victory over the Indians in Cleveland. Ted Williams provided the margin of victory with an inside-the-park home run. It was the only inside-the-park home run that he would hit in his long and storied career.

Boo Ferriss' second winning streak eventually reached 12 games. Walter "The Big Train" Johnson [Hall of Famer] and outstanding Brooklyn Dodgers' pitcher Preacher Roe are the only other pitchers in major league history who have put together two winning streaks of 10 or more wins in one season.

When the 1946 regular season came to an end, Boo Ferriss had topped the Red Sox pitching staff with an eye-popping record of 25-6, for a winning percentage of .806. That winning percentage easily paced the American League, he was second in games pitched (40) and games started (35), and his 26 complete games ranked third in the league standings.

WORLD SERIES

When Boo Ferriss took the mound at Fenway Park to start Game Three of the historic 1946 World Series between the Boston Red Sox and St. Louis Cardinals, both teams had won one game. The Red Sox had won the Series opener in St. Louis 3-2 in ten innings on a Rudy York home run. But Harry Brecheen had held the Red Sox to four singles the following day, and the Cardinals evened the Series with a 3-0 victory.

"Pitching in the World Series was like a dream come true for me," Ferriss recalls. "Playing in the World Series was my childhood dream. I can remember following the Cardinals in the World Series back in the 1930s.

"I remember I met my boyhood hero, Dizzy Dean, standing around the batting cage before that third game. I think he could tell I was a little nervous and he told me I would be fine. And I did all right."

Doing "all right" is a Boo Ferriss understatement for pitching sensationally. He held the Cardinals to six scattered hits while pitching the fiftieth shutout in World Series history. The Red Sox 4-0 victory gave them a two-games-to-one lead in the Series.

With the Series tied at three games apiece, Boo Ferriss took the mound for the Red Sox for Game Seven at Sportsmans Park in St. Louis. He held the Cardinals to three runs, but with Red Sox manager Joe Cronin pulling out every stop, Boo was relieved by Joe Dobson in the fifth inning. Enos Slaughter's aggressive base running in the eighth inning produced the winning run in a 4-3 squeaker, and the Cardinals were World Champions.

"That loss was heartbreaking for all of us," Ferriss remembers. "For me personally, winning Game Three was my biggest thrill in baseball. And losing Game Seven was my biggest disappointment."

PITCHING IN PAIN

The defending American League pennant winners got off to a slow start in 1947. On Memorial Day the Red Sox were languishing in fourth place with a record of 19-18. At the All-Star break they were in third place, eight games out of first. But they were in the midst of a five-game winning streak and there was still plenty of time for this star-studded team to make its move.

On July 14, Boo Ferriss pitched his finest game of the year against the Indians at Cleveland Stadium. The Red Sox defeated Cleveland 1-0 behind his complete game masterpiece. But immediately following the game, Boo knew something was wrong.

"I knew right away there was something wrong with my shoulder. I tried to soft toss the next day but I couldn't throw overhand at all. We did all of the things you did at the time for an injury, but nothing seemed to help."

Ferriss finished 1947 with a respectable record of 12-11, but his shoulder never improved. Ferriss and the Red Sox hoped that the shoulder would respond to rest during the off-season, but there was no sign of recovery in 1948. He pitched mainly in relief that season and managed to put together a 7-3 record. "I finished out the last game of the season, when we beat the Yankees to force the one-game playoff against the Indians. I contributed where I could that season."

His shoulder never responded in 1949 and he appeared in only four games that season. In 1950, his last season in the major leagues, he was able to pitch in only one game for the Boston Red Sox. "If I had that injury today, they would probably do Tommy John surgery. It's amazing what they can do with arm and shoulder problems in this day and age. But we didn't have anything like that back then. I'm sorry my arm injury came along, but that's baseball. There was nothing to be done about it."

Boo Ferriss went back to the minor leagues in 1951 and 1952, attempting to pitch his way through his shoulder problems. By 1953, he had gravitated to his ultimate calling: coaching and teaching baseball. That year, and the following season, he was a coach with the Red Sox top farm club in Louisville, Kentucky.

RED SOX PITCHING COACH

In 1955, Boo Ferriss returned to Boston as the pitching coach under new manager Mike "Pinky" Higgins. "It was great to be back in Boston. I remember we lived in Needham during the season and we really enjoyed that town. Our kids were young and they liked it there a lot."

Boo continued in his role as pitching coach through the 1959 season. "We had some good teams. We had some good seasons during that time. And I had some great pitchers to work with. Guys like Tommy Brewer, Frank Sullivan, and Mel Parnell who was my former teammate and great friend to this day."

Frank Sullivan, who won 90 games for the Red Sox between 1953 and 1960, remembers Boo warmly. "He was never negative and always there with sound advice. He had a gift shared by very few. He could keep nine or ten pitching personalities in line and on track with never a hint of favoritism.

"His obvious delight when I won made each victory even sweeter. But his immediate caring when things went bad was like a warm blanket in a cold world."

The Ferriss family enjoyed their time in Boston but their roots in Mississippi were even deeper. "In 1958 I met the President of Delta State University, and he asked me to think about the job of athletic director and baseball coach. I thought about his offer and after the 1959 Red Sox season I accepted that position. My wife Miriam and I were getting tired of the traveling and our children were getting older. It seemed like it was time to settle down. It turned out to be a wonderful decision. We've been right here in Cleveland, Mississippi, ever since."

Boo went on to coach baseball at Delta State University for 26 seasons. His 639 victories and .622 winning percentage place him in the top 40 among all-time Division II coaches. "I really loved coaching here. I had some chances to move up to bigger jobs, but my heart is right here in Mississippi. We're only about 10 miles from where I grew up in Shaw."

The state-of-the-art baseball facility at Delta State University was named in his honor following his retirement in 1988. He is justifiably proud of his team's successes and of the 25 players who signed professional baseball contracts. But he seems proudest of his many former players who followed in his footsteps and now coach baseball.

"At various times while I was still coaching I had as many as 55 former players coaching at the high school or college level. Even today, after being retired since 1988, there are still 25 of my former players coaching. I continue to follow their teams and watch them play when I can. It has been very meaningful to me."

GOOD WRITE, NO HIT

Ironically, the best-known celebrity associated with Delta State baseball never made the team. Best selling author John Grisham was cut from the squad in 1974. Grisham recently told *American Profile* that getting cut wasn't the worst day of his life. "The day before, we had an inter-squad game and the opposing pitcher was throwing 90 miles an hour. I had never seen that before and have never seen it since on the field. I said to myself, 'I would really like to go back to the dugout. It's over. I don't want to do this again.' "

Boo Ferriss remembers giving Grisham the news that his career was over almost before it started. "I remember saying, 'Have you given any thought to spending more time with the books?' He told me that all he really wanted to do was play baseball, but I think we both knew it wasn't going to work out.

"He sends me an autographed copy of all his books inscribed, 'Thanks for pointing me in the right direction.' When I see him, I kid him. I tell him, 'Why didn't you let me know you were going to turn out to be famous? I could have found something for you. Heck, you could have been my assistant. We would have a domed stadium by now.' "

Boo Ferriss loves baseball, his former teammates, and his former players. But his strongest emotions are reserved for his family. "My wife Miriam and I were married in 1948. She was a schoolteacher in Shaw. She has been a great support to me for all these years.

"We have two wonderful children. Our son, Dave, Jr., is a doctor and Senior Medical Executive for CIGNA Healthcare in Brentwood, Tennessee. He has two

Boo caught up with his former teammate, Ted Williams, during the 1984 Old-Timers' Game at Fenway Park.

children. His daughter Miriam went to Vanderbilt University and Law School at Ole Miss. Dave, III, went to Delta State and now he's with the Brentwood YMCA.

"Our daughter Margaret is the Administrator of the Mississippi Sports Hall of Fame & Museum. That is over in Jackson and she has been there since 1995. We are so proud of both our children and our grandchildren."

THE LEGENDARY BOO FERRISS

In 2002 Dave "Boo" Ferriss was inducted into the Boston Red Sox Hall of Fame. This recognition acknowledges the importance of his place in Boston Red Sox history. "It was one of the great honors of my life, and it was wonderful to see so many of my former teammates and friends. But what really stands out in my memory is that 18 of my former players went to the trouble of traveling all the way to Boston to see me receive that honor. That really meant so very much to me."

Nobody calls him Dave in Mississippi and some of Boo's acquaintances may think his real first name is "Legend." Every story in his native state seems to begin, "Legend Boo Ferriss . . . " And in his case it is deserved. The Mississippi Sports Hall of Fame & Museum has established the Ferriss Award to be given annually to the state's best college baseball player for the regular season. The winner receives an original work of bronze sculptured by noted artist, Dr. Kim Sessums.

"They had a banquet over in Jackson to acknowledge the award and there were over 400 people in attendance. I was both overwhelmed and humbled. It is nice to get any sort of recognition, but when your local friends honor you, that really means a lot."

When Boo was inducted into the Boston Red Sox Hall of Fame, his friend and former teammate, Mel Parnell, told *GoGreenMagazine*, "Everyone liked 'Boo,' and he got along with everybody. He was not a braggadocio and always played down his accomplishments . . . he was very modest. Players used to try to get him to use a cuss word, but he just wouldn't do it. He was a perfect gentleman."

Johnny Pesky remembers Boo the same way. "What a gentlemen. One of the nicest men you would ever want to meet. I always enjoyed being around him."

Former pitcher Frank Sullivan adds an exclamation point. "If there is any person on this planet who dislikes Boo Ferriss, they ought to be institutionalized."

Boo Ferriss is obviously both a legend and a gentleman. And that is quite an extraordinary combination.

6.
Sam Mele Interview
July 2003

I interviewed Sam Mele by telephone at his Quincy, Massachusetts, home on four separate occasions. Each conversation lasted from 20 to 30 minutes. Sam was attending to important family business and he was nice to find the time to talk to me.

One of the great things about the Red Sox players from the 1940s is that they have stayed in touch with one another for all these years. Sam Mele met his wife Connie through Johnny Pesky. More than 50 years later Sam and Johnny still argue over whether that was a favor on Pesky's part.

Sam Mele was connected with professional baseball for almost 60 years. And his uncles Tony and Al Cuccinello both played major league baseball. As you can imagine, Sam has as many great baseball stories as any player I have ever interviewed.

Over the years 24 major league baseball players have also appeared in the NCAA basketball tournament. Sam Mele was the first. He offers an interesting perspective on "March Madness," then and now.

Red Sox fans hold a special place in their hearts for players who adopt the Boston area as their home. And that's especially true for players who grew up in New York and embrace our region. Sam Mele is an adopted son of New England's team.

SABATH ANTHONY MELE
"SAM"

Sam Mele was born into a baseball family and spent almost 60 years in professional baseball. Mele, who had two tours of duty in the Boston Red Sox outfield, is the nephew of Tony Cuccinello who played for 15 seasons in the major leagues and Al Cuccinello who was with the New York Giants and St. Louis Cardinals. After his 10-year big league career, Sam Mele went on to manage the Minnesota Twins and then served as a Red Sox scout and roving instructor for more than 30 years.

NEW YORK NATIVE

Sabath Anthony Mele was born in Astoria, New York, on January 21, 1923. The middle child of seven, he has fond memories of growing up in a warm family in a tight-knit neighborhood in Queens.

"My mother was born in Avelina, Italy, and she came to the United States with her mother when she was a little girl," Sam reflects. "Nobody remembers how she was able to do it, but she managed to buy an apartment building in Astoria. She was the family matriarch, a very special lady.

"We were a very close family. I still remember the woodstove and baths in the kitchen, the wine cellar in the basement. What great memories. My father, who was also born in Italy, worked for ConEdison. He made $14 a week and since it was the depression he was happy to have a job. He walked two miles to get to work every day and he never owned a car."

Baseball was a strong presence in Sam Mele's life from an early age. "My mother's two younger brothers were both professional ballplayers. My uncle Tony Cuccinello was a terrific second baseman. He played in the first All-Star game in 1933. He was away playing when I was growing up, but I would write to him all the time. He would send me gloves, balls, anything I asked him for.

"My Uncle Al was younger, so he was around a lot when I was a kid. He was great to me. He took me everywhere with him, and made me into a ballplayer. He was my mentor. I talked to him the other night, and I told him, 'Uncle Al, everything I have I owe to you. My career in baseball, this house, my pension, everything is because of you.' He said, 'Well, why don't you mention me in your will?' I had to laugh, but everything I said to him is true."

"My uncle Al would take me down to the park and hit balls to me. He noticed that I handled balls in the air better than grounders. He made me into an outfielder where I played my whole professional career."

HOOP STAR

But it was on the basketball court that Mele first made his mark as an athlete. "For some reason we only had a baseball team for one season at my high school. But we had a good basketball team and I played the game every chance I got. I used to play three games a day. My Uncle Al took me to the 67th Street YMCA to play. He was awfully good to me."

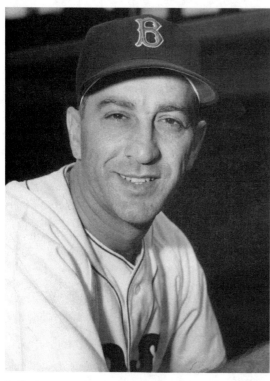

Mele starred for the Blessed Sacrament CYO team in Jackson Heights and at William Cullen Bryant High School. His basketball talents earned him a scholarship at New York University where he played baseball as well. His collegiate accomplishments earned him election to the NYU Sports Hall of Fame for basketball and baseball. Mele and former Brooklyn Dodgers pitcher Ralph Branca are two of only seven graduates who are enshrined for both sports.

Twenty-four former major league baseball players have also played in the NCAA postseason basketball tournament. The answer to the trivia question: Who was the first major league baseball player to play in the NCAA tournament? Sam Mele.

"I remember we beat the University of Wyoming in the first round at the Garden and then we lost in the second round. It was very exciting. People forget that in those days the NIT [National Invitation Tournament] was much bigger than the NCAA tournament."

While Mele was better known for his basketball exploits, he was starting to make a name for himself on the baseball diamond as well. "I was a good hitter and Uncle Al had taught me so much about the game that it gave me a big edge. At every level I knew more about baseball fundamentals than anyone I played with or against. It really helped."

Sam remembers working out at Fenway Park as a collegian in 1940. "I was in awe of all the big leaguers on the field. But I knew how to play the game so I was okay," Mele emphasizes. "I remember Ted Williams talking to me when I came out of the batting cage. Ted took a liking to me for some reason. It was the beginning of a friendship that would last for 60 years.

"I worked out with the Boston Braves at the Polo Grounds also. But that was more as a courtesy to my Uncle Tony who was playing for the Braves at the time. They didn't have the money to sign me."

Sam Mele signed his first baseball contract in 1942 with the Red Sox. "I'll never forget it. I met with Mr. Yawkey and Neil Mahoney who was the director of the farm system at the Commodore Hotel in Manhattan. They knew I was going into the service but they wanted to sign me. Mr. Yawkey said, 'How much will it take to sign you?' I told him at least $5,000 and he said 'Fine, we'll give you $2,500 now and the other $2,500 when you get out of the service.' I took that first check for $2,500 and turned it right over to my mother."

BOSTON BOUND

Like most baseball players of his generation, Sam Mele spent 1942-45 in the service of his country during World War II. "I started out in the V-12 program. I got to play some baseball and Red Rolfe [former Yankee third baseman] was our manager. Eventually I ended up on a small aircraft carrier. We were the first carrier to go up the Mississippi River, and later we went through the Panama Canal. It was quite an experience.

"I was discharged in early 1946. Shortly after my discharge, I got on a train in Grand Central Station and headed for spring training in Sarasota, Florida. Johnny Pesky was also on that train and another lifelong friendship began. Johnny is one of the best guys in baseball.

"The Red Sox actually took me north after spring training. I sat on the bench for the first three games and then they sent me down to the minors. I ended up in Scranton, Pennsylvania, where I played on one of the great minor league teams of all time. We won the league by about 18 games and eight of us went on to play in the major leagues. I hit .342 and I was the MVP of the Eastern League."

Sam Mele cracked the starting lineup for the 1947 Boston Red Sox and put together a wonderful rookie season. Appearing in 123 games in right field, he batted .302 for the year. His slugging average of .448 placed him sixth in the American League and his eight triples ranked tenth in the league.

Sam Mele's first trip to Yankee Stadium in a Red Sox uniform is one of his favorite big league memories. "I got tickets for my mother and father right behind the Red Sox dugout. It was their first time in a major league ballpark, and I was fortunate enough to hit a home run. I could see their faces all the way around the bases. They weren't cheering like everyone else behind our dugout, but I could tell from the smiles on their faces that they knew I had done something special. Tom Dowd, our traveling secretary, tracked down the home run ball for me, and I gave it to my mother."

Mele is quick to credit Ted Williams for his hitting success as a rookie. "I talked hitting with Ted every chance I got. I sat next to him on trains, on buses, every chance I got. And he was very good to me. He told me to study the pitchers, to look for their patterns. Anticipate how they were going to handle me. He made me a much better hitter.

"I remember one time I said to him, 'Ted, I'm having a little trouble on fly balls hit over my head. He stopped me, and pointed to Dom DiMaggio in centerfield. 'Any questions on fielding, you go to that guy. Questions on hitting, you come to me.' Ted was a wonderful guy."

THE 1948 BOSTON RED SOX

After his great rookie season, Sam Mele was looking forward to the 1948 season with one of the stronger Red Sox teams in the franchise's storied history. The Red Sox had finished third in Joe Cronin's last year as manager the previous season, but they had improved the roster with the addition of slugging shortstop Vern Stephens and veteran pitcher Ellis Kinder. And the legendary Joe McCarthy, who had managed the New York Yankees to seven world championships, had replaced Cronin as manger.

"The 1948 season was a disappointment for me," Mele recalls. "I had a wide-open stance at the plate, similar to Joe DiMaggio's, not that I was ever the hitter that Joe was. McCarthy watched me hit in spring training and told me to close up my stance. The man had won all those championships and I had been taught to listen to my manager, so I tried it. It might have been good advice for most players, but it didn't work for me. I went from hitting in the low .300s to hitting in the low .200s."

Sam Mele and the Red Sox both got off to slow starts in 1948. Mele shared playing time in right field with the light-hitting Sam Spence, and in early June the team was mired in seventh place, nine games out of first place. Although Mele's season-long slump continued, the Red Sox picked up the pace during the month before the All Star game, improving their position to fourth place.

The team continued its winning ways in the second half behind the strong pitching of Kinder and rookie Mel Parnell, and a balanced offense led by Ted Williams. After the All-Star break, the Red Sox won 70 percent of their games. A win over the Yankees on the last day of the season created the first playoff game in American League history.

There was every reason for optimism as the Red Sox prepared to meet the Cleveland Indians in their historic one-game face-off. They had gone 55-22 at Fenway that season and the Indians had traveled by train overnight from Cleveland following a disappointing loss to the Detroit Tigers.

"I really thought we were going to win that game," Sam remembers. "I had been hurt and missed the last part of the season, but I expected Mel Parnell to pitch and to pitch well. I was surprised when Denny Galehouse got the start. I think we all were," is Mele's recollection of the 8-3 Red Sox loss.

VETERAN BALLPLAYER

Sam Mele struggled to regain his hitting stroke with the Red Sox in 1949 and manager Joe McCarthy used him sparingly in right field. In mid-June he was traded from the pennant-contending Red Sox to the last place Washington Senators for side-arming pitcher Walt Masterson. "I hated to leave the Red Sox and Boston but I knew I would get to play in Washington and get back on track," Mele reflects.

He got into 78 games with the Senators in 1949. Playing regularly in 1950, his offense returned to its rookie year levels with 12 home runs and 86 RBI. By 1951 Mele was firmly established in the Senators' lineup and he led the American League with 36 doubles. Showing surprising speed, his seven triples ranked seventh in the league.

"I had good speed, but not great speed. I got my share of triples during my career because I knew how to run the bases. Again, I'm back to the fundamentals that my Uncle Al taught me. You turn doubles into triples by reading the situation."

In early May of 1952 the Senators traded Mele to the Chicago White Sox. His home run total of 16 for the season was his career best. "One of the best things about going to Chicago was playing under manager Paul Richards. He really knew the game and I learned a lot from him."

In 1952 he had a game against the Red Sox that major league players only dream about. The first time he came up in the fourth inning of an early June game, Mele hit a three-run home run. The White Sox bats were hot that day and he came up later in the same inning with the bases loaded. Mele cleared the bases with a triple bringing his RBI total for the inning to six. "My teammates were all over me in the dugout. Of course everybody is in a good mood when you win 15-2."

In 1953 Mele hit a solid .274 to go along with 12 home runs and 82 RBI. That winter he was traded from the White Sox to the Browns who were moving from St. Louis to Baltimore for the 1954 season. Much in demand, his stay in Baltimore was relatively brief, as the Red Sox reacquired him in July.

"It was great to be back with the Red Sox. We had settled in Quincy and we had a young family. I was hoping to be there for awhile."

Mele compiled his career-high batting average of .318 in 42 games with the Red Sox in 1954. But after a slow start in 1955, he ended up with the Cincinnati Reds for his first stop in the National League. In Cincinnati he played under former Red Sox teammate Birdie Tebbetts. Mele remembers getting one of only two hits off a young southpaw with the Brooklyn Dodgers by the name of Sandy Koufax.

He played his last major league season with the Cleveland Indians in 1956. "That was a great year because my Uncle Tony was a coach with the Indians and Al Lopez was a terrific manager. It was also the season I got a summer vacation.

The Indians had a roster problem, and they told me to disappear. I came home to Quincy, did some work on the house and spent time with my family. About 10 days later they told me to come back. I may be the only major leaguer who ever got a summer vacation."

BORN TO MANAGE

Sam Mele played Triple A ball in 1957 and 1958 and joined the Washington Senators major league coaching staff in 1959. "I scouted for the Senators for a couple of months and then I joined the big league team as a first base coach under Cookie Lavagetto. Eventually Cookie made me his third base coach, and when the team moved to Minnesota to become the Twins I moved along with them.

"In midseason 1961, Calvin Griffith the Twins owner asked me to come to his office and be sure to wear a tie. When I got there he told me they were going to make a change and that I was going to replace Cookie as manager. He introduced me at a news conference as the new manager of the Twins."

The rookie manager brought the Twins near to .500 baseball over the balance of the 1961 season and in 1962 the Twins improved to second place in the American League. Mele began to change the style of the Twins over the next two seasons. "We were built around power and I knew we had to introduce more speed into the lineup."

Mele was honored by the Knights of Columbus at Fenway Park in 1966 for leading the Twins to a 102-60 record, the American League Pennant and a World Series appearance in 1965.

In 1965, Mele's retooled offense took hold and the Twins won 102 games to take the American League pennant. Mele looks back at a moment in spring training that made all the difference in the Twins' 1965 season.

"Zoilo Versailles had a ball hit three feet from him at shortstop and he didn't even move for it. I pulled him out of the game immediately. He started to talk back to me and I got all over him. Billy Martin, who was one of my coaches, got all over him, too. We told him in no uncertain terms that he had to go all out on every play.

"Billy made Zoilo a special project. Took him out to eat, watched his every move on the field. Zoilo went on to have an outstanding season. He was voted the Most Valuable Player in the American League that year and he deserved it. When the season was over, he came to me and said, 'Thank you for making me a ballplayer.' "

The Twins took the Los Angeles Dodgers to seven games in the 1965 World Series. Sam Mele identifies the Twins' loss in the seventh game of the 1965 World Series as his toughest loss in baseball.

"Sandy Koufax beat us 2-0 to win the series for the Dodgers. I thought we (the Twins) had a chance, but I'll tell you, in his prime Sandy Koufax was the greatest pitcher I ever saw. He beat us in Game Five, 7-0, and he was standing in the doorway of their clubhouse when I walked by. He looked at me and said, 'You got a hit off me 10 years ago.' I doubled off him in 1955 playing for the Cincinnati Reds and 10 years later he still remembered it. He was serious about his pitching."

HEY THERE: YOU'RE AN ALL-STAR

Sam Mele certainly remembers managing the American League All-Star team in 1966. In characteristic style he manages to convert a moment of high drama into humor.

"Since I managed the Twins to the pennant in 1965, I was the manager of the American League All-Star team for 1966. Mickey Mantle was on the team but he called me a few days before the game to say his knees were bothering him and he would rather use the three day break to rest them. I told him I understood and named White Sox outfielder Tommy Agee to replace him.

"I was in my hotel room and I got a phone call from a guy who was furious that I replaced Mantle with Agee. He told me that he was coming to the game and he was going to shoot the Twins' Tony Oliva and me. He sounded pretty serious and I thought well, if he's going to shoot Oliva he might as well shoot me too, since Tony was my star. I had to notify the police because there was no way of knowing if the guy meant it or not.

"The police took all sorts of security precautions, and thankfully there were no incidents. When it was time to exchange lineup cards before the game I got right in the middle of the umpires. I said, 'If anyone is going to get shot, it may as well be one of you guys.' "

Sam Mele's 1966 Twins finished second in the American League, eight games behind the Baltimore Orioles. In early June of 1967, Calvin Griffith informed Mele that he was being replaced as manager of the Twins.

"It was tough because he couldn't really give me a reason. He said they had just decided to make a change. We were playing .500 ball and we were in the race. It would have been easier if he could have given me a reason."

Sam Mele found himself out of baseball for the first time in 20 years and living in the Boston area while the Red Sox battled his former team for the American League pennant. Asked if would have done anything differently when the Red Sox swept the Twins on the final weekend of the 1967 season, he limits his comments to "Oh yeah." He adds, "In his book, Tony Oliva said that the Twins would have won if I was still managing them. He didn't have to say that. It was nice of him."

SPANNING FOUR DECADES WITH THE RED SOX

"Tom Yawkey had said to me, 'If you ever need a job, Sam, you call me.' And since the Twins had let me go and I had a wife and five kids, that's exactly what I did. I got together with Mr. Yawkey and Dick O'Connell, who was the general manager at the time, and Mr. Yawkey told Dick, 'I want him working for us.' I

Serving as a Red Sox spring training instructor.

went to work for the club at the beginning of 1968 and stayed with the team for over 30 years. It's a great organization.

"I did a lot of scouting for the team, but mostly I worked as kind of a roving instructor. I worked in the instructional league in the fall and I got around to the minor league teams all over the country during the season.

"One of my prize pupils was Jim Rice. He would grab me every chance he got and I would hit him fly balls, ground balls and line drives. He was a natural hitter, but he worked as hard on his fielding as anyone I have ever seen. He made himself into a darned good outfielder. He used to call me 'Mr. Mele.' He still does."

Former Red Sox star right fielder Dwight Evans is another favorite of Sam Mele's. "I remember when Dewey was struggling at Louisville, hitting in the low .200s. They asked me to go work with him and together we got him back on track. He brought his average into the .300s and he went on to have a great major league career. Several people said I made him into a hitter. I don't believe that's true, but it's nice to hear."

When Sam Mele thinks back on his baseball career, he focuses on the friends he has made. "I had some good games as a player and it was a thrill to manage in the World Series, but mostly I think about the relationships I have established. Ted Williams was one of my great friends. And Dom DiMaggio is one of the best guys I have ever known. Dom is one of the smartest guys I have ever met, both on and off the field.

"And Johnny Pesky has been my good friend over all these years. You'll never find a finer guy than Johnny. He introduced me to my wife Connie. John was doing a promotion at Jordan Marsh where she worked. When I saw Johnny at the Baseball Writers' Dinner in 1948, he said, 'I've got just the girl for you.' Connie and I dated and we have been happily married for over 50 years. I kid Johnny about playing matchmaker all the time, but he was right."

Connie Clemens was a native of the Merrymount section of Quincy and the Meles have made their home in the City of Presidents for over 50 years. Sam Mele's focus these days is on his family and he is eager to talk about them. "We have five great kids. Sherry Ann is our oldest. Our daughter Marilyn has two children and our son Steven has one boy. Our daughter Marsha has a daughter and our son Scott has two boys. They all live nearby or down the Cape, so we get together all the time."

Looking back on his career in baseball, Mele selects a compliment from baseball veteran Don Zimmer as one of his favorite memories. "The Red Sox had flown a whole bunch of us out to the west coast and Don Zimmer was holding court with the baseball writers before a game. He has a million stories and the writers love to interview him. He paused, pointed at me and said to the writers, 'Now that man is a professional.' That meant a lot to me, especially coming from a baseball guy like Don Zimmer."

Today, Sam Mele's family is his top priority. But for nearly 60 years he was widely recognized as the consummate baseball professional.

7.
Mel Parnell Interview
February 2003

When I heard Marvelous Mel Parnell's voice over the telephone from his native New Orleans, Louisiana, the first thing I thought of was the Impossible Dream team of 1967. Mel spent that season in the broadcast booth with Ken Coleman and Ned Martin describing the wonderful year that ushered in the "Golden Age" of Red Sox history.

As a young fan I learned the meaning of the term "stylish southpaw" by watching Mel Parnell on the mound every fourth game. My strongest memory of Mel is watching on television as he pitched a no-hitter against the Chicago White Sox.

Sometimes, no matter how many great anecdotes you collect, you simply run out of space to include them all. I had always read that Mel was so tough to hit because a broken finger that didn't heal properly caused his fastball to sink. Mel told me that the story was a fabrication.

"I knew I needed something extra at Fenway, so I taught myself to throw a slider. Don Newcombe [former Brooklyn Dodger star pitcher] was introducing the slider in the National League at the same time. It gave me a big advantage because the hitters couldn't recognize it. I would be asked about it and I would say, 'Oh, I broke my finger, so I have a funny grip on the ball.' It was a small lie that has been perpetuated all these years. But a pitcher needs every edge he can get."

Mel also punctured another myth during his interview. Since time immemorial we have been told that catcher Birdie Tebbetts talked to all of the Red Sox pitchers before the 1948 playoff game, and reported to manager Joe McCarthy that Denny Galehouse was the only one who wanted the ball. Mel Parnell tells us what really happened.

MEL PARNELL
"MARVELOUS MEL"

Mel Parnell is one of the great left-handed pitchers in Red Sox history. His 123 lifetime wins sets the standard for all Red Sox southpaws, and he holds the club career record for innings pitched and games started by a lefty. Only two right-handed Red Sox pitchers, Roger Clemens who won three Cy Young awards in a Red Sox uniform and Cy Young himself, have won more games for the Red Sox than Mel Parnell.

The 1948 season was Mel Parnell's first full season in the major leagues. "Marvelous Mel" as fans knew him, won 15 games that season and led the Red Sox pitching staff with an era of 3.14. The 1948 Boston Red Sox started slowly and found themselves in seventh place, more than 10 games out of first place on June 1. But the team rallied to an 81-36 record over the next four months. Their dramatic 10-5 victory over the New York Yankees on the last day of the season set the stage for the first playoff in American League history.

THE 1948 BOSTON RED SOX

The Red Sox were considered to be serious pennant contenders as the 1948 season got under way. The nucleus of the 1946 team that had come within one game of a World Championship was still intact, and renowned manager Joe McCarthy had succeeded Joe Cronin at the helm. Veteran pitcher Ellis Kinder joined young Mel Parnell in the starting pitching rotation and slugger Vern Stephens, acquired along with Kinder from the St. Louis Browns during the off-season, added power at the shortstop position.

Despite this multitude of talent, at the end of May the team was nine games under .500 with a record of 14-23. Parnell had pitched well, but had little to show for it due to poor run support.

"I remember that Maxine Dobson [pitcher Joe Dobson's wife] brought me some old nylon stockings with runs in them. She said she wanted to get me some runs. But I was pitching well, and feeling more confident."

The team caught fire in June. Led by the slugging of Ted Williams, the team won three-quarters of their games that month and moved up to fourth place. The team set a team record with 25 wins in July and claimed first place at the end of the month.

On August 31 Mel Parnell was a complete game winner over the Detroit Tigers, while Ted Williams contributed two hits, scored two runs, and stole a base. At that point the team held a one game lead over the Yankees.

The 1948 season was the high-water mark for Boston as a two-team major league city. The combined home attendance for the Red Sox and the Braves during the 1948 regular season was 3,014,237. The attendance for the three-game "City Series" between the Red Sox and the Braves prior to Opening Day, plus the 120,000 fans who crowded Braves Field for the World Series, brought total attendance for the year to almost 3.2 million fans.

"We were looking forward to playing the Braves in the 1948 World Series. We had a good rivalry with them. We always played them in spring training and the City Series was very intense," Parnell remembers. "Playing in the same city, we were very aware of how they were doing and we really wanted to beat them in the World Series."

By mid-September the American League pennant race was a three-way affair among the Red Sox, Yankees and the Cleveland Indians. Based on a mid-September coin toss, the Red Sox were named as the home team in the event of a tie with the Indians.

Entering the final weekend of the season, the Red Sox and Yankees were tied for second place, each one game behind the first-place Indians. A two-game sweep of the Yankees, coupled with the Indians loss to the Detroit Tigers on the final day of the season, set the stage for a one-game playoff at Fenway Park on Monday, October 4.

THE FIRST AMERICAN LEAGUE PLAYOFF GAME

With less than 24-hours notice, 33,957 Red Sox fans bought tickets for the historic contest against the Indians. The cool temperatures and brisk wind did not put off baseball-mad Boston fans, but weather conditions would play a key role in the day's events.

The random coin-toss placing the playoff game at Fenway Park put the Indians at a serious disadvantage. After their disappointing loss to the Tigers on Sunday the team was forced to board a 9 P.M. train from Cleveland that would arrive in Back Bay station at 10 A.M. Monday.

When the Indians finally arrived at the visitors clubhouse, player-manager Lou Boudreau informed the press that he was starting either Bob Feller, Bob Lemon, or rookie pitcher Gene Bearden. All three pitchers played their parts in the charade designed to keep the Red Sox off balance.

The Red Sox selection of a starting pitcher against the Indians is one of the great controversies in Red Sox history, and Mel Parnell was a central character. Parnell was the logical choice to start the playoff game. He was well rested and he had been the team's most reliable pitcher down the stretch. Over the years a number of theories have been advanced regarding manager Joe McCarthy's selection of a starting pitcher. Mel Parnell was there, and he knows what really happened.

"My family had come to town to watch me pitch the big game. We went out to dinner the night before but I was in bed by 9 P.M. because I wanted to be well rested. When I arrived at the clubhouse the next day the ball was under my cap, which was how they let you know you were going to start.

"I was getting myself mentally prepared when Joe McCarthy came out of his office and approached me. He put his hand on my shoulder and said, 'Kid, I've changed my mind. The elements are against a left-hander, the wind is blowing out to left field. I'm going with a right-hander.' With that, he told our clubhouse boy to run out on the field and call Denny Galehouse in."

Fifty-five years later the emotion in Mel Parnell's voice is evident when he says, "My biggest disappointment in baseball was not getting to pitch in that playoff game against Cleveland. I was ready to pitch that game and I wanted to pitch that game. It would have been the biggest game of my life and I wanted to win it for my teammates."

Asked if he thought Joe McCarthy sought advice from others on his pitching choice, Parnell responds emphatically, "Anyone who knew Joe McCarthy, particularly anyone who played for him, knows that he was his own man. I am certain that he made the decision on his own. And every teammate I've discussed this with agrees with me."

McCarthy was right about one thing: the wind was definitely blowing out to left. And the Indians' Boudreau took advantage of it with a first-inning home run over the Green Monster to give the Indians an early lead. The Red Sox countered with a first-inning run against Gene Bearden, who Boudreau had intended to start all along. The Indians drove Galehouse from the mound with four runs in the fourth inning.

Lou Boudreau's four hits led the Indians to an 8-3 victory for the American League pennant. Boston had missed out on its one chance for a streetcar series to determine baseball's world champion.

THE "BIG EASY"

Melvin Lloyd Parnell was born in New Orleans, Louisiana, on June 13, 1922. He credits his father with directing him to baseball as a youngster and encouraging him throughout his career.

"My dad had played semi-pro baseball and he encouraged me in that direction. He always told me to play as much as I could and to work on my weaknesses.

"I played as much ball as I could. I played every day even though the heat in New Orleans in the summer was terrible. We just got used to it. My mother was always after me to come home for lunch. I would tell her, 'Mama, I don't have time to eat lunch. I'm playing ball.'"

Parnell would develop into one of the best pitchers in Red Sox history but his original position was first base. "I loved to bat," Parnell recalls. "I would pitch batting practice, but first base was my position. That's where I always played as a youngster."

"The Cleveland Indians trained in New Orleans when I was growing up, and I loved to watch the Giants' Carl Hubbell pitch against Bob Feller. Feller would be grunting and groaning, throwing his fastball, but Hubbell made it look so easy. I loved his style and I would like to think that some of it rubbed off on me."

But Giants' first baseman and future Hall of Famer Mel Ott was his favorite. "Mel was a great hitter and a great person. He grew up just across the river from New Orleans, and I knew everything about him. When I got to meet him he took a liking to me and we became great friends."

When Parnell would pitch batting practice to his high school teammates, they would ask him to stop throwing breaking balls. "I was throwing them fastballs, but my pitches always had a lot of movement on them. One day we were short of pitchers and the coach asked if I would like to pitch. As it turned out, there were a lot of major league scouts there to see some of my teammates. I struck out 17 batters that day and I drew a lot of interest after that."

THE ROAD TO THE BIG LEAGUES

Red Sox scout Herb Pennock recognized the young lefthander's potential and, along with area scout Ed Montague, convinced Parnell to sign a minor league contract. "I signed for a $5,000 bonus and $125 a month in the minors. I thought I was rich. But mostly I remember how happy my dad was for me."

Parnell did not get off to an auspicious start in the Red Sox organization. "I was a 130-pound teenager. When I reported to the Red Sox farm team in

Owensburg, Kentucky, manager Hugh Wyatt looked at me and said, 'What are you supposed to do?' I said, 'Sir, I am supposed to pitch.' His response was, 'I have four left-handed pitchers, and I certainly don't need a fifth.'

"That turned out to be a big break for me. They sent me to Centerville, Maryland, where Eddie Popowski was the manager. He was great and I pitched well. Then I was sent to Canton, Ohio, where I led the league in earned run average."

His journey through the Red Sox minor league system was interrupted by a four-year tour of duty with the Air Force. In 1946, at age 23, Parnell was one of many young ballplayers returning from the service at the end of World War II. "The Red Sox had so many good young players, that they had to send half of them to Louisville in Triple A and half to Scranton, Pennsylvania, in the tough Double A Eastern League. I was sent to Scranton along with future Red Sox teammates Sam Mele and Maury McDermott. We finished first, 19 games up, and I led the league in earned run average."

TEN SEASONS AT FENWAY PARK

That outstanding season earned Parnell an invitation to the big league spring training camp in Sarasota, Florida. "There were two spots open on the pitching

Rival pitchers, Parnell and Allie Reynolds, of the Yankees, meet before they face off for the Fenway opener on April 18, 1950.

staff and I earned one of them. I was thrilled. Boston is a lot like New Orleans in that they both have a lot of history and they're not too big. Plus, I'm as Irish as they come, so I fit in right away. I was comfortable with the city and the fans from the beginning."

But Parnell was not as comfortable with the friendly confines of Fenway Park and the nearby wall in left-field. "The first time I saw that left field wall I thought maybe I made a mistake and went to the wrong ballpark. I had been a fastball pitcher in the minor leagues, but I knew right away that I would have to become more of a breaking ball pitcher.

"My next door neighbor in New Orleans was Howie Pollet, who pitched for the St. Louis Cardinals against the Red Sox in the 1946 World Series. Howie told me that I would have to keep the ball down to survive in Fenway. That wasn't hard for me. My high school coach had nicknamed me 'Dusty' because I threw so many pitches in the dirt."

Mel Parnell still remembers his first major league start in 1947. "It was April 20, 1947, against the Washington Senators. I lost that game to Walt Masterson, 3-2, on a passed ball. My first win was in Detroit against Hal Newhouser. He had won nine straight so I guess they thought they would toss a rookie out there to see what I could do. We ended up winning 4-1. That's still a great memory."

Parnell was sent down to Louisville in mid-season to get more work. But he took a ground ball off his pitching hand and sat out the balance of the season. Red Sox manager Joe McCarthy was not a big fan of young pitchers, but Mel Parnell earned a spot as a key member of the Red Sox pitching staff in 1948.

CLOSE CALLS

Following the disappointing end to the 1948 season, Parnell was determined to have a good season in 1949. And he exceeded everyone's expectations. In 1949, Parnell won 25 games. No Red Sox pitcher has equaled that mark in 55 seasons. The Red Sox and the Yankees staged an epic battle for the 1949 American League pennant. Parnell started the year strong and his outstanding pitching earned him a spot on the American League All-Star team. In early August he beat the Yankees for his seventeenth victory as the Red Sox whittled away at the Yankee's hold on first place.

As the race came down to the wire manager Joe McCarthy relied mainly on Parnell and right-hander Ellis Kinder. They each started on three days' rest and went to the bullpen between starts. During the Red Sox final 19 games the pair started 10 times and relieved seven times. The slender Parnell became practically gaunt, dropping from 185 to 160 pounds.

For the second year in a row, the Red Sox and the Yankees went head-to-head in the last two games of the season with the pennant on the line. In 1948 the final games were in Fenway and the Red Sox swept the pair. In 1949 the games were in Yankee Stadium and the Yankees won both games to win the American League pennant.

Mel Parnell led the American League in wins, complete games, and innings pitched in 1949. For the 1948 and 1949 seasons combined, the Boston Red Sox had more wins than any team in major league baseball. Despite all these accomplishments, Parnell and the Red Sox had fallen just short of their goal.

In 1950 Parnell went 18-10 to lead the Red Sox pitching staff. His win total ranked fourth in the American League and his 21 complete games was third in the league. In 1951 he won eighteen games again and his ERA of 3.26 ranked seventh in the league. His outstanding season earned him American League All-Star honors for the second time.

The 1952 season was an off year by Parnell standards: his record fell to 12-12. But it was the season of his one major league home run, and he still remembers every detail. "I hit it off Lew Kretlow who was a fastball pitcher. It was in old Comiskey Park in Chicago. I hit that ball over the fence in right-center, the deepest part of the ballpark. When I got back to the dugout my teammates gave me the silent treatment. But that was okay. I hit that ball a long way."

In 1953 he returned to form with a staff-leading record of 21-8. His 21 wins placed him second in the American League, and his sparkling winning percentage of .724 ranked fourth.

MARVELOUS MEL MEETS MICKEY MCDERMOTT

"Mickey McDermott had a terrific arm and a wonderful personality. He was a great teammate and a really good friend. We had been close since we were teammates at Scranton in 1946. I remember later when we were on the Red Sox they made us roommates and the front office said, 'We want you to be like a father to this kid.' But Mickey was a free spirit.

"After he was traded to the Washington Senators we remained friends. I remember we were scheduled to pitch against one another in Washington in late April of 1954. We had made plans to go out to dinner together that evening. I came to bat against Mickey in the third inning, and he threw me a pitch that took off and kept bearing in on me. I just couldn't get out of the way and it hit me on my left wrist.

"Mickey ran to the batter's box to see how I was. I said 'Mickey, I think it's broken.' I looked up and he had tears coming out of his eyes." Mel Parnell came back to pitch later that season, and he pitched for two more years in the big leagues, but he was never the same pitcher again.

"I tried to come back too soon. I wanted to pitch again so badly. But I wasn't ready and I injured my arm. I still knew how to pitch, but I had elbow problems. My arm was never quite right again."

NO-NO

By the 1956 season, Mel Parnell's major league pitching career was winding down. But on July 14 he pitched one of the most memorable games of his career. Facing the Chicago White Sox in a Saturday afternoon game at Fenway Park, Parnell looked like the 20-game winner of old. When former teammate Walt

Dropo stepped to the plate with two men out in the ninth inning, Parnell was one out away from the first no-hitter by a Red Sox pitcher in 33 years.

"I was really 'on' that day. My sinker was working and my slider was very sharp. I have to laugh when a pitcher says that he didn't realize he had a no-hitter going. As a pitcher, you're always reviewing in your mind what's gone on. What has worked for you, what they've hit. You have to know. I certainly knew. But I wasn't nervous because I didn't believe that it could possibly happen.

On July 14, 1956, Parnell pitched the first no-hitter for the Red Sox in 33 years.

"But when Dropo stepped in, I could feel the pressure. He was a good hitter and he loved to hit in Fenway. He hit a high hopper right back to me. I speared it and I ran all the way to first to make the play by myself. It was the only no-hitter to end in an unassisted putout by the pitcher. Our first baseman, Mickey Vernon said, 'What was the matter, didn't you trust me to make the play?' I told him that wasn't it at all. I didn't trust myself to make the throw."

Parnell finished the 1956 season with a record of 7-6, and decided it was time to retire. "I probably could have pitched a little longer, but I knew I would never get back to my previous level. It was time."

After his retirement he was associated with the baseball program at Tulane University and later served as the general manager of the minor league New Orleans Pelicans. The Red Sox coaxed Parnell back to their organization in 1960. "I managed at Alpine, Texas, and later out in Seattle, Washington. I enjoyed it, but I thought it was time to spend more time with my family.'

THE BROADCAST BOOTH

Parnell returned to Boston one more time, working with the Red Sox television crew from 1965 to 1969. "Curt Gowdy convinced me to give it a try. I enjoyed working with Curt until he left to join the national network and it was great working with Ned Martin and Ken Coleman. But I was never totally comfortable with the role. It did allow me to be a part of the 1967 season and that was one of my great years with the Red Sox."

Few people remember who coined the term "Pudge's Pole" to describe the left field foul pole in Fenway Park. But all serious Red Sox fans know that Mel Parnell named the right field foul pole as "Pesky's Pole." Parnell chuckles at the memory. "I think it was maybe in 1948 that John curled a home run right around the pole. It must have gone all of 310 feet. We were giving it to him pretty good in the dugout. I said, 'John, you wrapped it right around that pole of yours.' Twenty years later when I was doing the color for the Red Sox telecasts, someone hit a home run down the line in right field, and I said, 'We used to call that Pesky's Pole.' The fans just picked it up. It stuck," Parnell laughs.

RED SOX HALL OF FAME

Mel Parnell was honored with induction into the Boston Red Sox Hall of Fame in 1997. Mel Parnell's 123 victories give him the highest win total of any Red Sox left-handed pitcher. In addition, his 71-30 record at Fenway Park results in a winning percentage of .703, ranking him first among all left-handed pitchers with 75 or more decisions at Fenway. His last trip to Fenway Park was in 2001 as an honored guest at the celebration of the team's 100th anniversary.

Today Mel lives in his native New Orleans with his wife Velma. They celebrated their fifty-fifth wedding anniversary in 2002. Their four children all chose careers in the health care field. Mel Junior is an orthopedic surgeon, Barbara is a nutritionist, Sheryl is a nurse anesthesiologist, and Patty is a critical care nurse.

Mel Parnell has battled serious illness during recent years. After extensive treatment he is optimistic. "I'm hoping I've got one more win," Parnell declares.

All Red Sox fans, whether they had the pleasure of watching him in action, or have only read about his accomplishments, are rooting for one more victory for Marvelous Mel Parnell.

Mel Parnell's Rank in Red Sox History

CATEGORY	CAREER TOTALS	ALL-TIME BOSTON RED SOX RANK
Wins	123	3rd*
Games Started	232	4th*
Winning Percentage (100 Decisions)	.621	9th
Complete Games	113	6th
Shutouts	20	6th
Innings	1,752.2	4th*
Games	289	9th
Strikeouts	732	16th
ERA (1,000 Innings)	3.50	18th

* Ranks first among Red Sox left-handed pitchers

Source: 2004 *Boston Red Sox Media Guide*

8.

Maurice "Mickey" McDermott Interview

May 2003

Before I called Mickey McDermott for our interview, I read a pre-release copy of
A Funny Thing Happened On The Way to Cooperstown. *The book tells Mickey's life story with an emphasis on wine, women, and song.*

When Mickey answered the phone in his Phoenix home, the first thing I said to him was, "I just finished your book and I have only one question for you. How is it you are still alive?" Mickey laughed and answered, "God looks after little children and drunks."

We had a great time during our lengthy interview and vowed to get together the next time he came to Boston. I imagine that anyone who spent more than five minutes talking to Mickey would want to spend some more time with him.

I can still see Mickey on the mound at Fenway Park in my mind's eye. He looked the way a 10-year-old imagined that a pitcher should look. A review of his early career confirms that my judgment was accurate.

Mickey McDermott passed away about two months after our interview. I never got to meet him. I have thought about my first words to him many times since.

MAURICE McDERMOTT
"MICKEY"

Mickey McDermott, who pitched for the Boston Red Sox between 1948 and 1953, was blessed with the curse of unlimited potential. By the time he was 20 years old he had pitched three no-hitters for the Red Sox farm club in Scranton, Pennsylvania. One year later, pitching for the Louisville Colonels, he set an American Association record by striking out 20 St. Paul Saints in a nine-inning game. As a youngster he was considered at least as talented as teammate Mel Parnell, who would go on to win more games for the Red Sox than any lefthander in team history.

Mickey McDermott pitched his last game for the Red Sox in 1953. Most Red Sox fans never saw him in action, but many fans have seen a famous picture of him without realizing it. One of artist Norman Rockwell's best-known paintings is "The Rookie," which first appeared as a cover for the *Saturday Evening Post*. Mickey McDermott is the rookie captured in the painting.

A picture of McDermott arriving in the Red Sox locker room for spring training was published in *Life* magazine in 1948. Rockwell later used that picture as the basis for his painting. A reed-thin McDermott is portrayed in an ill-fitting suit, carrying a battered suitcase held together by an old belt. Other Red Sox players pictured include Ted Williams, Jackie Jensen, and Billy Goodman.

As another benchmark for younger Red Sox fans, the left-handed McDermott was Bill Lee before Bill Lee was even born. To say that Mickey was a character would be to understate the case. But Mickey was a free spirit who didn't have a mean bone in his body.

Johnny Pesky, who has seen a lot of players come and go during his long association with the Boston Red Sox, calls McDermott "as likeable a guy as you will ever meet. I got friendly with him in spring training in 1948 and he was such a good kid that my wife Ruthie and I invited him to live with us when we got back to Boston. He lived with us for about six weeks. Everybody loved Mickey."

THE NEXT LEFTY GROVE

When Maurice "Mickey" McDermott arrived in Boston, Red Sox General Manager Joe Cronin told the press, "Why, McDermott's just a baby, but he has all the natural requisites to become an outstanding and a most popular star . . . It's our belief that McDermott has a fine chance to come close to both Lefty Grove and Lefty Gomez when they were tops, and that stardom may catch up with Maurice overnight."

Respected baseball writer Al Hirshberg profiled McDermott in *Sport* magazine at the time, adding Cleveland Indians star pitcher Bob Feller to the comparison. Grove, Gomez and Feller are all respected members of baseball's Hall of Fame.

Johnny Pesky still shares their sentiments more than 55 years later. "Mickey's arm was so strong he could have thrown a strawberry through a battleship. He was as good a young pitcher as I have ever seen." Even allowing for hyperbole, that is quite an endorsement from a baseball professional with Pesky's experience.

In the 2003 book *A Funny Thing Happened On The Way to Cooperstown* (Triumph Books, Chicago, IL), written by McDermott with Howard Eisenberg, the focus is on a potential Hall of Fame pitcher who ended his career with a .500 record: 69 wins and an equal number of losses. But during his six seasons with the Boston Red Sox, Mickey McDermott never had a losing record.

Pitching in parts of two seasons and four full seasons, he won 48 games against 34 losses for the Red Sox. He led the American League in strikeouts per nine innings pitched in 1951 and 1952. His 18 wins in 1953 placed him fifth in the American League and his 3.01 ERA was sixth best.

But that is only a small part of the story. Baseball researchers have built a computer model that compares each player's record with the statistics of every player in baseball history. When you enter Mickey McDermott's statistics from his six years with the Red Sox, his closest match among more than 7,000 major league pitchers is Dodgers Hall of Famer Sandy Koufax.

"I'm not that surprised to hear that," was Mickey's response to the result. "You need three good pitches to succeed in the majors. And it took Koufax five or six seasons to perfect his three pitches. I've talked to Sandy about it. I had a great fastball and a terrific curve, but I was having too much fun with those pitches to truly master the changeup and use it consistently."

Instead of taking the express lane to Cooperstown with Koufax to join Grove, Gomez and Feller, Mickey spent a great deal of time in the breakdown lane. "If there was a Hell-Raisers Hall of Fame, I would definitely be in it. In fact, I'm sure they would put a statue of me in the lobby, just the way they have a statue of my pal Ted Williams in the lobby in Cooperstown."

THE 1948 BOSTON RED SOX

The 1948 Boston Red Sox featured the strongest offense in the American League. Dom DiMaggio and Johnny Pesky were the table setters. Sluggers Ted Williams, Bobby Doerr, and Vern Stephens combined for 375 RBI. This team produced an average of nearly six runs per game, tops in the American League.

Pitching would prove to be the Achilles heel for the 1948 team. The 1946 Red Sox World Series team had been led by pitchers Dave "Boo" Ferriss, Tex Hughson, and Mickey Harris. But this trio all had disappointing training camps in 1948. Veteran manager Joe McCarthy decided to take a chance on McDermott, and the 19-year-old headed north when the team broke camp.

How wild was the teenage southpaw with the electrifying fastball? To answer, Mickey referred to a tape of legendary baseball announcer Gordon McClendon calling McDermott's first pitch in an early game at Sarasota, Florida, in 1948.

"McClendon was announcing the game from a booth high above the backstop, and he started out, 'Spring training is about to begin on a beautiful sunny day here in Sarasota. And young left-hander Maurice McDermott is on the mound for the Red Sox. Here's the pitch . . . ' There's this pause and then you hear McClendon shout, 'Ohmygod!'

"I had thrown the ball as hard as I could and it went high over the backstop and right into McClendon's booth. He was lucky I didn't kill him. On the next

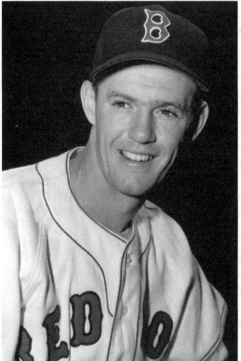

pitch I hit Clyde Vollmer square in the back with another fastball. He was one tough guy, so he got right up and trotted down to first. But his legs started to wobble as he was going down the line and he passed out right on the first base bag. Most batters didn't crowd the plate when I was pitching."

Mickey McDermott had a strong memory of his major league debut on April 24, 1948. "It was in Yankee stadium. I remember I struck out Charlie Keller who was one of the great Yankee hitters. After the game, Keller told everyone, 'If they've got any other young left-handers like this kid, I'm going home to my farm and raise horses.'"

Manager Joe McCarthy used McDermott sparingly in 1948 but Mickey did manage to tie a major league record. "It was around the middle of May in a game against Cleveland. Mickey Harris started for us, but he was wild so they brought me in for relief, if you could call it that. I walked eleven guys in a little over six innings. Between the two of us, we walked 18 men to tie the American League record.

"I can remember Harris was standing on the top step of the dugout shouting, 'Walk this guy. If you do, we break the record.' Joe McCarthy didn't think that was very funny. Eventually he had Harris traded to Washington."

While he wasn't a major factor for the Red Sox in 1948, he had fond memories of watching his teammates in action. "Ted Williams was unbelievable. He was the best hitter I ever saw. Ted took a liking to me. I think he recognized that we both came from modest backgrounds. But he would never take batting practice against me. He claimed I was too wild.

"I was just a kid, but I remember watching Bobby Doerr, Johnny Pesky, and Junior Stephens. I couldn't believe how good they were. And I got to watch my old teammate from Scranton, Mel Parnell, get established as a big leaguer. Mel was a great pitcher."

In June, the Red Sox sent McDermott back to Scranton so he could pitch regularly and work on his control. McDermott pitched well in his return to Scranton, averaging 13 strikeouts per game. He capped his season with a no-hitter in the playoffs.

"When the Eastern League playoffs ended, the Red Sox brought me back to Fenway. It was great watching them sweep the Yankees on the last weekend to tie the Indians for the pennant. I was as surprised as anyone when McCarthy [Red Sox manager] picked Denny Galehouse to pitch the one-game playoff. We all expected and wanted Parnell to pitch. I think it might have turned out differently."

TEENAGE SENSATION

In earlier years, McDermott's blazing fastball simply overwhelmed opponents as he established a name for himself pitching for St. Patrick's High School of Elizabeth, New Jersey. He moved his game up a notch pitching at the semi-pro level on Staten Island, New York, with equal success. Professional baseball scouts began to take notice.

The only roadblock to a professional career was the fact that McDermott was too young to sign a contract. His father, Maurice McDermott, Sr., solved that problem by taking a pen to Mickey's birth certificate and turning him into a 16-year-old. The Boston Red Sox signed him to a contract, adding a $5,000 bonus to clinch the deal.

"When it was time to head off to Scranton, my father's parting words were, 'Here's a new shirt and a $5 bill. Don't change either of them. And come back with money in your pockets.'"

Most young baseball players come of age starring for their local high school team. Mickey McDermott came of age pitching in Scranton, Pennsylvania, becoming a legend in the Eastern League. At age 16 he pitched his first professional no-hitter, striking out Albany's player-manager, former major leaguer Rip Collins, to end the game.

"Years later I ran into Collins, and he told me, 'I saw a 16-year-old out there on the mound, one out from a no-hitter. I grabbed a bat, put myself in, and made sure you got it.'"

At age 17, he pitched his second no-hitter, losing this one 1-0 when he threw a wild pitch in the ninth inning. His third no-hitter, after being sent down by the Red Sox in 1948, set a record for the Eastern League that is unlikely to be matched.

McDermott was assigned to Louisville in the Triple A American Association to start the 1949 season. His 20-strikeout game against the St. Paul Saints served notice on the Red Sox that his stay in the minors would be brief. When he followed that game with 73 strikeouts in his next four games, he was on his way back to Boston.

"McDERMOTT WINS FANS, OUTSHINES TED"

Red Sox great Ted Williams was mildly amused when the headline above appeared in a Boston paper. Mickey McDermott and the city of Boston were seemingly a match made in heaven. "I loved Boston right from the start. It's the best city in the world. It's big, but not too big. The crowds at Fenway were great, and the fans are terrific. I had a wonderful six years there."

The Boston fans loved Mickey back. His blazing fastball captivated the faithful and his struggle for control added to the drama. He could hit as well, and it turned out that he could sing. "My off-season job was as a recreation director at Grossinger's in the Catskills. The Red Sox got me the job, hoping I would gain weight and stay in shape. I struck up a friendship with singer Eddie Fisher and I got hooked on show business.

"During the off-season I sang at Steuben's, a popular night club on Boylston Street. I stole half of my act from Eddie Fisher. The crowd loved it. I loved it too."

After he was recalled from Louisville in 1949, McDermott started 12 games as the Red Sox battled the New York Yankees to the wire for the pennant. McDermott won five of his starts, pitching six complete games including two shutouts.

Mickey began the 1950 season in the bullpen for the Red Sox. But he got a big break when starter Ellis Kinder developed a hip problem before retiring a batter in the first inning of a game against the White Sox. McDermott's book tells a dif-

McDermott (left) with his 1952 Red Sox teammates, catcher Gus Niarhos and LHP Bill Wight.

ferent version of Kinder's ailment, but regardless, Mickey took full advantage of his opportunity. He pitched a four-hitter as the Red Sox defeated Chicago 12-0.

Manager Joe McCarthy resigned in the middle of the 1950 season. "He couldn't take watching us lose to the Yankees anymore," McDermott recalls. Mickey started 15 games in 1950 and recorded seven wins against only three defeats.

In 1951, McDermott turned in two of the great "iron man" performances in the history of the Boston Red Sox. On July 13, 1951, the Red Sox and White Sox waged an epic 19-inning battle. Amazingly, McDermott pitched the first 17 innings for Boston, limiting the White Sox to two runs. "I threw something like 240 pitches. It seems crazy now, but I was having a great time. I didn't want to come out."

But that is only half of the story. Two weeks, later McDermott pitched *all sixteen innings* in an 8-4 victory over the Indians. He struck out 15 Cleveland hitters and walked only one batter in a pitching masterpiece. "I think I threw about 230 pitches in that one. Cleveland manager Birdie Tebbetts was on the top step of their dugout, hollering, 'That's 202, Maurice . . . that's 203 . . . ' trying to rattle me. I was exhausted. Right after that I spent three days in the hospital recovering."

THE NEXT BABE RUTH?

When long-time Red Sox fans wax nostalgic for the days when pitchers took their turn at bat, they are probably remembering Mickey McDermott and not Ellis Kinder, who had a lifetime batting average of .144. McDermott was the best hitting Red Sox pitcher since Babe Ruth. In 1950 he hit .364 in 44 at-bats and in 1953 he hit .301 in 93 at-bats. The Red Sox used him frequently as a pinch-hitter and he often batted seventh or eighth in the batting order.

"One time Ted Williams asked me, 'Are you trying to copy my swing?' I told him I wasn't and he said, 'Well, you've got a pretty nice swing there.' I know Ted went upstairs to the front office and tried to convince them to make me into an everyday player. He told them they were wasting my bat playing only every four days. Of course, he also knew I would get into trouble if I had time on my hands during the three days between starts."

When the 1952 season began McDermott was only 23 years old. But he had already won 20 big league games and finished in the top ten for American League pitchers in ERA, strikeouts and fewest hits for nine innings pitched. On May 25, 1952, McDermott showed a flash of greatness, pitching a one-hit, 1-0 shutout over the Washington Senators. The lone hit was a bloop single in the ninth inning just beyond the reach of first baseman Walt Dropo. McDermott finished with 10 victories for the year and led all American League pitchers in strikeouts per nine innings pitched.

In 1953 Mickey McDermott finally reached his potential. In July, with an assist from Ellie Kinder in relief, he pitched a one hitter against the Cleveland Indians. One week later, he shut out the St. Louis Browns, 6-0, one of his four shutouts for the season. His 18 wins and 3.01 ERA ranked him fifth among

American League pitchers. But his colorful run in Boston was about to come to an end.

McDermott was devastated when the Red Sox traded him to the Washington Senators for outfielder Jackie Jensen the following December. But he was not surprised. "I had popped off to the writers. I had a lot to say about how much I should get paid. And one time after I had been knocked out of a game I was rushing to the players' parking lot when a woman offered me some words of consolation. I kind of pushed by her and muttered something under my breath. I found out later that the woman was Jean Yawkey. When my pal Ted Williams heard that story, he said, 'Bush, you're going to love it in Washington.' He was wrong."

"FIRST IN WAR, FIRST IN PEACE, AND LAST IN THE AMERICAN LEAGUE"

One of McDermott's first games for his new team was a start against the Red Sox facing old friend and former roommate Mel Parnell. And Mickey managed to hit Parnell with a sailing fastball that broke Mel's wrist.

"I felt terrible when that happened. I loved Mel. He was a great pitcher and an even greater person. If I could take back any pitch I ever threw, it would be that one. I ran to him at the plate, and I was yelling, 'Marvelous, Marvelous, are you all right?' He was in such pain he was losing his lunch, but he managed to stammer, 'Of course I'm not all right. I think you broke my wrist.' "

Things went so badly for McDermott in 1954 that President Dwight Eisenhower asked reporters, "What's wrong with McDermott?" Mickey was flattered that the President took time away from the affairs of state to follow his career. His response was, "What's wrong, Mr. President? Washington! That's what's wrong."

He ended that year with a woeful record of 7 wins and 15 losses for the lowly Senators. The following season Mickey improved his record to 10-10, but it was clear that his arm wasn't right. "My elbow was all full of chips and splinters. One time I was sitting at a bar and a splinter actually popped through the skin and blood squirted all over the woman sitting next to me. I thought she was going to pass out. It was around that time that my heavy-duty drinking started."

Mickey got a second chance when he was traded to the New York Yankees before the 1956 season. The outstanding Yankee teams of the 1950s played hard on, and off, the field. McDermott couldn't crack the starting rotation on the mound, but he made the first team off the field. His one season in New York resulted in life-long friendships with Mickey Mantle, Whitey Ford, and Billy Martin. He also gained a World Series ring, appearing in one game for the Yankees as they defeated the Brooklyn Dodgers in the seven-game Series.

The Yankees traded him to the Kansas City Athletics during the off-season. In Kansas City, he had more home runs than wins. The Athletics used him extensively as a pinch-hitter and played him at first base for two games. But he was relegated primarily to the bullpen and his four home runs easily outdistanced his one victory.

Following the 1957 season Kansas City traded him to the Detroit Tigers. McDermott had become an itinerant ballplayer, joining his fifth team in six years. In the off-season he played winter ball to make ends meet. He had played in Mexico, Venezuela, and in January 1959, he found himself in the midst of the Cuban revolution. "There were soldiers at the ballpark carrying weapons. Then Castro came to Havana to make a fiery speech. When he got to the 'Yanqui go home!' part, I did."

After pitching two games for Detroit in 1958, Mickey decided to leave the team and go home to Miami Beach to see if he could get his life in order. He had limited success in that department, but he did find himself back in the minor leagues pitching for Miami in the International League.

The St. Louis Cardinals decided to take a chance on McDermott in 1961. Even years later there was always the hope that "The Fenway Rifle" would return to form. He pitched 19 games in relief for the Cards before the team released him. Kansas City then picked him up again, but after appearing in four games for the Athletics, Mickey McDermott's big league career was over.

WITH A LITTLE BIT OF HELP FROM HIS FRIENDS

Over the next 30 years Mickey did a little bit of everything in a number of different locations. Billy Martin gave him a job as a scout. At one point he was an agent for professional athletes, and he even worked as a security guard. He was a ticket taker at a racetrack when he met Bill Lee for the first time. "It was one of my many low points," McDermott recalls. "The best job I could find was taking tickets at the Santa Anita Raceway. Rod Dedeaux [legendary USC baseball coach] asked me to play with a squad of former major leaguers against his kids. I hit a long home run against one of their lefthanders. I had no idea who the pitcher was, but it turned out to be Bill Lee.

"Lee went crazy after I hit my homer. He was ranting and raving, saying, 'How could I give up a home run to a broken-down, old ticket taker?' It turned out he had been to Santa Anita and he recognized me from the track, but he had no idea that I had been a player. I had an old baseball card so I wrote a note on it that said, 'I've hit a lot of home runs off pitchers who were a lot better than you'll ever be.' I had a USC coach give it to Lee."

Over the years Mickey McDermott spent time with Frank Sinatra, Jack Kerouac, Jimmy Cagney, and former President George H. Bush. But the one constant for Mickey was a series of loyal friends who were quick to lend him a helping hand. Mickey named former Red Sox first baseman Walt Dropo as one of his great supporters.

"Walt has been my good friend since we played together in Scranton over 55 years ago. There was one time I had no place else to go, and of course Walter took me in. But he had his own issues to deal with. He kept telling people I would drive him crazy if I stayed much longer.

"Walt lived in a high rise where you could see right down into Fenway Park. One morning he took me out on his terrace and I looked over into the park.

There on the scoreboard were three big words: 'MICKEY, GO HOME.' He said, 'That cost me $500.' I said, 'You wasted your money. I was about to leave anyway.' "

SAFE AT HOME

In June 2003, McDermott lived in Phoenix, Arizona, with his wife Stevie. "She's a terrific lady. She takes really good care of me," he said at the time. He had four daughters from prior marriages and two grandchildren.

It is often said that Mickey McDermott was one of the funniest ballplayers ever. A one-hour telephone interview with McDermott confirmed that. He was even able to joke about his near-death experience during triple bypass surgery. "I saw a guy in a red suit with a pitchfork beckoning me in. I told him, 'Hell no, I'm not going. Not with all those umpires down there.' "

Throwing out the first pitch before the Red Sox-Rangers game at Fenway.

Mickey McDermott had reached what he described as "one of the lowest points in my life," in 1991. Then an incredible stroke of good fortune changed his life. "I had been on a two-day bender and my wife at the time, Betty, burst into the bedroom and tells me, 'Wake up, you drunken Irishman.' I told her, 'All I want is a cup of coffee and a cigarette.' Then she tells me we've won the Arizona Lottery for $7 million. I said, 'Betty, you're the most beautiful woman I ever met. Let's go to the Lincoln-Mercury dealer.'"

In McDermott's book, *A Funny Thing Happened on the Way to Cooperstown*, former Yankee pitcher and Hall-of-Famer Whitey Ford recalls McDermott's phone call with the good news. "A few years ago our ringing phone woke me up at 5 A.M., and I figured it was one of two Mickeys: Mantle or McDermott. My wife, who is less trusting, wondered if it was a woman. 'Listen for yourself,' I said, handing her the phone. 'You can tell it's McDermott. He's so drunk he thinks he won $7 million in the Arizona lottery.' "

McDermott remembered that his old pal Mickey Mantle was even less impressed. "He just shrugged when I told him. Then he said, 'Hell, I *owe* more than that.' "

While his big win didn't impress his former Yankee buddies, it had a profound impact on McDermott's life. "If I hadn't won the lottery I probably would have been on the side of the road with a sign saying, 'will pitch for food.' Of course, I probably wouldn't have used the money for food."

Despite his good fortune, Mickey had one more wild pitch in his repertoire. He followed his big break with three weeks of celebration, an inevitable DWI, and a 60-day sentence in the Durango County Jail.

"That's when I got down on my knees and asked God to help me. I said if He helped me I would never take another drink. He did, and I haven't. It's been over ten years since I had my last drink, and I could care less about ever having another one."

It was a seat-squirmer that came down to the bottom of the ninth with two men out, but at long last, Maurice "Mickey" McDermott was safe at home.

9.
Frank Sullivan Interview
March 2004

The toughest part of the Frank Sullivan profile was determining the time difference between Natick, Massachusetts, and Kauai in the Hawaiian Islands. Apparently a lot of folks have trouble with this and Frank gets a lot of calls at odd hours.

Legendary Dodger broadcaster Vin Scully told Frank's lovely wife Marilyn that Sullivan is the funniest ballplayer he has ever met. I haven't interviewed even a fraction of the ballplayers that Scully has, but Frank is as funny as anyone I have ever talked to.

Frank pitched for a number of uninspired, but colorful, Red Sox teams between 1953 and 1960. Any time that Frank took the mound you knew the Red Sox had a shot at a win. From 1954 to 1958, Frank Sullivan was one of the top ten pitchers in the American League.

Sullivan and former Red Sox catcher Sam White moved to Kauai in 1964, and that seemed pretty radical at the time. About every ten years a Boston sportswriter would check in with them and report that they were enjoying a life of leisure. The reality was quite different, as you will learn.

Frank has written a number of vignettes about his career and his life after baseball. After reading some of them, I suggested that he write his own profile. Frank declined, but I managed to work some of his material into the story. I'm sure you will enjoy his prose.

FRANK SULLIVAN
"THE BOSTON SKYSCRAPER"

To say that former Red Sox pitcher Frank Sullivan has led an interesting life would be an understatement. He has traveled the world, practiced with the Boston Celtics, graced the cover of *The Saturday Evening Post*, and played the Old Course at St. Andrews. Forty years ago, he moved to Kauai in the Hawaiian Islands with his great pal, former Red Sox catcher Sammy White. Neither Sullivan nor White had ever set foot on Kauai before in their lives.

And Frank had a very adventuresome career in the major leagues. His first full year in the majors was spent with a 1954 Boston Red Sox team that won only 69 games. The team had lost Hall of Fame leftfielder Ted Williams when he separated his shoulder in the first hour of spring training. Sullivan earned his spot in the starting rotation when All-Star pitcher Mel Parnell had his wrist broken by a pitch thrown by former teammate Mickey McDermott. Frank achieved a very respectable 15-12 record for a Red Sox team that had a winning percentage of .448.

Frank had another excellent adventure with the 1961 Philadelphia Phillies. "I shudder whenever I think of that team," Sullivan offers from his home in Liheu, Kauai. "We had lost 11 straight games and then we went out and won one. Right after that we lost 22 games in a row. That one win broke up an amazing losing streak."

A STAR IS BORN

Franklin Leal Sullivan was born in Hollywood, California, on January 23, 1930, and grew up in nearby Burbank. "I grew up during the Depression, but my father always had a good job and he was always encouraging me to play sports. He had been a pretty good athlete and he wanted me to compete.

"I remember one time I got a job at a service station and he showed up there and said, 'Go play ball.' He didn't want me working. I was a big kid, but I was coordinated, so I did well. Actually basketball was my first love then, and baseball was kind of filler.

"I had an offer of a basketball scholarship to Stanford, and I was leaning in that direction, but Red Sox scout Jack Corbett saw me pitch and he wanted to sign me. Jack saw me pitching American Legion ball, but there was another left-handed pitcher named Frank Sullivan, and I think he showed up thinking he would see him. I went to Boston with Jack to talk about signing a contract."

Sullivan still remembers that fateful trip to Boston. "We flew to Boston for a tryout at Fenway Park. We were staying at the Somerset Hotel in Kenmore

Square, and we ran into Red Sox pitchers Mickey McDermott and Chuck Stobbs. They invited me to join them. I took my first cab ride ever, to downtown Boston, and I followed Mickey into the Arrow shirt store. Mickey bought a dozen new shirts, put one of them on, and left the one he was wearing in the store. That's when I made the decision to sign a pro baseball contract if it was offered."

CLASS A BALL TO THE MAJORS

Sullivan's early days in the minor league were painful. "I didn't have a lot of success, and to tell you the truth, I was homesick. I had to do some growing up fast."

His nascent professional baseball career was interrupted by two years of service with the Army in the Korean War. During his tour of duty he spent four and one-half months on the front line in combat. It was an experience that made a lasting impression on him. He was awarded a Combat Infantry Badge and was honorably discharged as a Staff Sergeant in 1952.

"I didn't really become a pitcher until 1953, when I was with the Red Sox farm club in Albany, New York, in Class A ball. That was also the year I discovered I wasn't considered a prospect. I had experienced a little arm trouble and I went to our manager, Jack Burns, to tell him I was fine and that I wanted to pitch. He said, 'I know you're fine, and I want to get you in there, but the Red Sox told me I have to pitch the prospects.' But he did work me in and I pitched pretty well.

"It was around that time that my catcher Len Okrie came out to the mound and said, 'Stop worrying about what you are doing out here, and start worrying about what is happening at home plate.' It was as if a light went on for me. From that point on I was a different pitcher.

"Later that season Jack Burns was in Boston attending a meeting at Fenway Park. Red Sox manager Lou Boudreau said, 'Don't we have anyone in our organization who can throw strikes?' Jack said, 'I've got a guy who can throw strikes.' And I was on my way to Boston."

THE BOSTON SKYSCRAPER

Baseball writers often referred to Frank Sullivan as the "Boston Skyscraper," because at 6'7" he was one of the tallest pitchers in major league history. "My father was 6'0" and my mother was 5'5", but I was always tall. I found it to be a big advantage as a pitcher, especially coming in sidearm the way I usually did."

Sullivan made his debut on July 31, 1953, and pitched well in 14 relief appearances. "The best thing for a pitcher is to come up as an unknown. I had made the jump all the way from "A ball" so the hitters didn't know anything about me. And I could throw my slider for strikes. They would be looking for a fastball and I would come in with a slider for my out pitch."

Frank started the 1954 season in the bullpen for the Red Sox, but in mid-April, a teammate's misfortune created a spot for Sullivan in the starting rotation. The Red Sox had traded pitcher Mickey McDermott to the Washington Senators in the off-season, and his errant pitch broke Red Sox pitching ace Mel Parnell's left wrist. The 24-year-old Sullivan took advantage of this opportunity, putting together 15 wins, tops among Red Sox pitchers.

Sullivan pitched well at the beginning of the following season, and his strong start earned him a spot on the 1955 American League All-Star team. The American League jumped out to an early lead in the first All-Star Game played in Milwaukee, but Sullivan was called in to squelch a National League rally in the eighth inning. "When I was walking in from the bullpen in center field, Mickey Mantle said, 'Sully, you better shut them down or we're going to miss the cocktail hour.' I was too nervous to reply. I got the first batter to hit a ground ball but Al Rosen booted it, and they tied the score.

"I got out of the inning and then I shut them down in the ninth, the tenth and eleventh. I was pitching to guys like Musial, Mays, and Aaron, but I managed to hold them. Then Musial comes up for the second time and hits a ball into the right field stands. My catcher, Yogi Berra, comes up to me later in the locker room and says, 'I should have told you he was a high fastball hitter.' "

Frank continued his winning ways in the second half of the season, and the Red Sox nipped at the Yankees' heels in the American League pennant race before running out of gas in mid-September. He led the American League in games started, innings pitched, and his earned run average of 2.91 was fifth in the league. His 18 wins tied for the American League lead and led the Red Sox staff for the second year in a row.

Like most pitchers before the era of the designated hitter, Frank Sullivan enjoys talking about his hitting prowess. In Frank's case, his favorite hitting memory is his triple in 1955. "The ball hit the top of the left field wall and bounced away. And I think the leftfielder fell down. I went sliding into third base and they almost threw me out. After I dusted myself off, our third base coach, Jack Burns, shook my hand and said, 'I want to introduce myself. I'm the third base coach. You haven't spent a lot of time here.' "

FRANK AND SAM

Frank Sullivan is quick to share credit for his pitching success with his battery mate and long-time friend, Sammy White. "Sam was my first roommate with the Red Sox and we hit it off right away. He was my close friend for almost 40 years and I never had a bad moment with Sam.

"We were so attuned that Sam would only give me signs for the first three innings of a game. By then we would have established our pattern and he didn't have to give me a sign. He knew what was coming and I knew he would be ready for the pitch I would throw. It was almost uncanny."

In 1956, Frank Sullivan compiled a career-best winning percentage of .667, which ranked seventh in the American League and first for the Red Sox. He also was named to the American League All-Star team for the second season in a row.

On an off day in 1956, Sullivan, Sam White, and Jackie Jensen were told to drive to Stockbridge, Massachusetts, and to bring their uniforms. "When we got there we were greeted warmly by a small, slim man, whose name meant nothing to me. He posed us and took a number of pictures, explaining that the background would be the locker room we used in Sarasota, Florida, for spring training. I remember ragging on Jackie Jensen on the way back, saying the trip was all his idea, and the photographer didn't seem to know what he was doing.

"The following March, I pick up *The Saturday Evening Post*, and there we were on the cover. The man was an illustrator, not a photographer, and if you look closely, you'll see we are wearing street shoes, not spikes. The cover was titled 'The Rookie' and the man's name turned out to be Norman Rockwell."

The 1956 Red Sox finished fourth in the American League for the fourth straight year. Frank Sullivan's earned run average of 3.42, and his 33 pitching starts led the Red Sox pitching staff. His 14 victories were second to teammate Tommy Brewer's 19 wins.

The break following the 1956 season is one of Frank's favorite memories. "In the past, I had always gone home to California to work or gone to Mexico to pitch winter ball. Sam convinced me to stick around and make personal appearances around New England. We were so in synch that we developed a pretty good presentation and I think we were making more than we did playing ball.

"This one time we were booked to speak way up in Presque Isle, Maine. We get there and they have us scheduled in a very large auditorium, before a huge audience. We were on between a tap dancer and a banjo player. I was a little overwhelmed since we usually appeared in a more intimate setting, but Sam assured me he would take care of everything.

"He stood before the microphone and announced, 'Ladies and gentlemen, my name is Sam White and I am a catcher for the Boston Red Sox. Normally I would be here to talk to you about baseball, but not tonight. Tonight I am here to introduce the funniest man I know. In fact, he is so entertaining that I am coming down to sit with you.' And with that, he left the stage. Fortunately winter in Presque Isle is pretty boring. Nobody threw anything."

RENAISSANCE MAN

Frank also made a significant contribution to a Boston sports team during this eventful off-season. "It was the season that Bill Russell joined the Celtics, and Jack Nichols was the other center. He was finishing up dental school and he told Red Auerbach that he could play in the games but he didn't have time to practice. Nichols had played college basketball with Sam White, and Jack asked me if I would replace him in practice.

"I said I would, and two things happened every practice. Every time I was chosen to be on one team for a scrimmage, the other team clapped, and I would end up trying to guard Tom Heinsohn, who was rookie of the year that season. Auerbach used me all pre-season and asked me to think about playing two sports, but I told him I was already maxed."

The 1957 Red Sox improved to third place in the American League, trailing the pennant-winning Yankees and the second place Chicago White Sox.

Apparently Frank Sullivan's winter training with the Celtics was offset by his time on the banquet circuit, as his personal win total held at 14. That win total ranked seventh in the American League, and his complete game total of 14 ranked fourth.

It was in this time period that Sullivan became a sailor. "I bought a 38' ketch rigged sailboat in Westerly, Rhode Island. Somehow I managed to sail it back to Winthrop. Looking back on it, it probably would have been good to take a lesson or read a book. I decided to sail down to spring training before the next season. I wish I could say I sailed down, but the truth is, we kind of bumped our way south.

"I finally made it to the Florida Keys, not without incident, and I docked at the marina in Islamorada. I called my teammate, Ted Williams, who came down to pick me up. We had a lot of laughs as I related my trip down. He had predicted that I would never make it.

"I spent one day helping Ted with a carpentry project and learned that the greatest hitter in baseball history didn't own a tape measure. He picked me up the next morning with a boat in tow when it was still pitch-black. The sun was just rising as we reached the launch ramp, and I jumped out of the car looking to buy a case of beer. The next thing I knew he had the boat in the water and he was hollering, 'Get over here, "Bush," or I'm fishing alone.'

"We fished all day and his concentration was unreal. All we had with us was an apple apiece and some water. Ted worked every minute we were out there and I have never been more exhausted after a day of fishing. But just think, I spent eight years watching the best hitter and even got to fish with the best fisherman."

The 1958 Red Sox finished third again, and Ted Williams won his sixth American League batting title, edging out teammate Pete Runnels for the honor. Frank Sullivan continued his consistent pitching ways with 13 wins. It was his fifth straight season of double-digit win totals for the Red Sox.

After the 1958 season, Sullivan agreed to deliver a 42-foot Chris Craft powerboat to Fort Lauderdale, Florida, for George Page, who owned the Colonial Country Club in Lynnfield. He selected Sam White as his crew. White was selected more for his pleasant company than for his seamanship.

"I was told that Red Sox owner Tom Yawkey owned an island off the South Carolina coast. The closer we got to South Carolina, the better the idea of stopping by to say hello to Mr. Yawkey sounded. I located Cat Island, and after a quick stop we called and we were graciously invited for a visit. We were met at a long pier by two World War II Jeeps and we were driven to the main complex. Mr. Yawkey personally showed us his private game preserve. They treated us to a great dinner and we all had many laughs. The evening came to an end shortly after Mr. Yawkey gave Sam some hitting advice, using a broom as a bat."

WINDING DOWN

The big change for the Red Sox in 1959 was a shift in their spring training headquarters. The team had trained in Sarasota, Florida, since 1933, but in 1959, spring training was shifted to Scottsdale, Arizona. "I hated training in Arizona," Sullivan recalls. "You couldn't raise a sweat, you couldn't get loose. And there was nothing to do in Scottsdale.

"I was pitching against the Cubs in Mesa, Arizona, and the mound was terrible. I just couldn't get comfortable. I felt a tweak in my back and I knew I was in trouble. I felt back spasms all the way back to Scottsdale. Then we broke camp, and flew to New York to open the season. It was raining there, but I wanted to get my running in. The next thing I knew I was very sick and I was diagnosed with pneumonia. They sent me back to Boston by train, and I stayed in Sancta Maria Hospital in Cambridge until I recovered."

Frank Sullivan never did 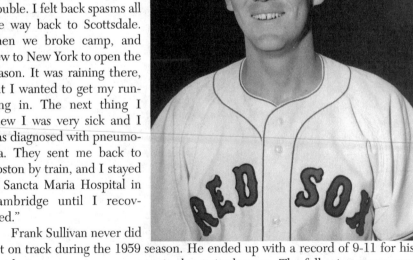 get on track during the 1959 season. He ended up with a record of 9-11 for his first losing season in seven years in the major leagues. The following season was worse, as his record fell to 6-16. On December 15, 1960, he was traded to the Philadelphia Phillies for 6'8" pitcher Gene Conley.

"The Red Sox sent me a telegram, 'You have been traded to the Phillies, good luck.' I remember saying to the telephone operator who read it to me, 'Honest?' I was destroyed. I talked to George Page, whom I considered my second father, and he advised me to tell the Phillies that I wasn't sure I wanted to play any more because I could make more money working for George.

"When Gene Mauch, who managed the Phillies called that evening, I told him I was going to call it quits and stick with my off season job. He said, 'How much do you need, Sully?' That's when I realized I wasn't prepared with an answer, and I told him $25,000. He replied, 'That's easy, Sully. You got it.' Now you now why most players have agents."

The 1961 season would turn out to be Frank Sullivan's worst in the major leagues. He won three games and lost 16, playing for a Phillies team that lost 107 ballgames in a 154 game season. "We were terrible," Sullivan recalls. "Our best hitter batted .277. I was awful, but Robin Roberts was 1-10, and he's in the Hall of Fame."

After starting the 1962 season with a 0-2 record, he was released by the Phillies and signed immediately by the Minnesota Twins. "I got to play for my great friend Sam Mele, who had been a teammate on the Red Sox. He was one of the best managers I ever had."

Sullivan rebounded nicely for the Twins, going 4-1 in 20 appearances during the balance of the 1962 season. But on June 19, 1963, the Twins released him. After 11 seasons in the major leagues, his professional baseball career was over.

"It's a big adjustment for a player when his career ends. All those years, for seven months each season, you walk into the clubhouse and there's a fresh uniform waiting for you. And then, just like that, it's over."

CHANGES IN ATTITUDES, CHANGES IN LATITUDES

"I did a number of different things over the next year or so. Then one day Sam White said, 'We ought to go someplace totally different and start over.' That appealed to me, and an island seemed to make sense to both of us. We thought a little bit about the Caribbean, but that didn't feel right. Finally, we settled on Kauai in the Hawaiian Islands."

Kauai is the oldest and northernmost of the main Hawaiian Islands. It is about a 20-minute flight from Honolulu. It is 550 square miles with a permanent population of a little over 50,000. It is also Frank Sullivan's vision of paradise.

"Sam and I had never been here, but we got a job with a helicopter company right away working construction. We built landing pads at different locations throughout the island. I had no idea what a hard worker Sam was. He would stick a cigar in his mouth and work all day."

Asked if there were many Red Sox fans on Kauai, Frank laughs heartily. "Shortly after we got here, Sam and I put on a clinic for a bunch of little leaguers. I was throwing to Sam behind the plate, and we were really humming. When I walked off the field, this little kid said, 'Who do you play for?' I said proudly, 'I played for the Red Sox.' He looked me over and replied, 'So do I.' I knew at that moment that I was a long way from Boston. It was very humbling.

"My wife to be, Marilyn, joined us after about three months and she got a job as an executive secretary at the Kauai Surf Hotel. After a year of working construction, I took over the beach concession for the Kauai Surf. A couple of years later, I became the assistant golf pro there, and eventually I became the head pro.

"In 1978, Sam and I got certified by the PGA, and I've been the Director of Golf for a number of courses here over the years. I've been a golf consultant to the Grove Farm Company for almost 10 years now."

Sadly, Sam White passed away on Kauai in 1991. "Sam was my close friend for almost 40 years. I enjoyed every minute I spent with him. He was like a brother to me."

Frank looks back fondly on his years in Boston. "Those were wonderful years. I loved that city and the fans were great. I got to play for eight years with Ted Williams, and watch the greatest hitter ply his craft. He could tell you if he hit one seam, or two seams, of a ball that was coming at him at 100 miles per hour."

He enjoys watching the games that are televised in Kauai, but gets mildly annoyed with the color commentators. "I'm amazed when I hear commentators

Frank with Washington Senators pitcher Pedro Ramos.

like Tim McCarver and Joe Morgan telling the viewers exactly what is going through the minds of the players. I can remember standing on the mound at Fenway and thinking, 'Damn, this is a nice day! What could be better? Here I am facing Mickey Mantle and he's smiling at me.' Of course I found out later that Mickey, and a bunch of his teammates, had spotted my VW Beetle behind the Kenmore Hotel, lifted it up on the sidewalk, and deposited it behind a telephone pole next to a brick wall. But there was no way that any announcer could have guessed what I was thinking."

Frank and his wife Marilyn celebrated their thirty-eighth wedding anniversary in March 2004. They have a son, Mike, and an eight year-old granddaughter, Kea, who beats Frank regularly at cards. Frank's son from his first marriage, Mark, lives in Maggie Valley, North Carolina, and he has three children, Summer, Lauren, and Kevin.

THE PEN OF A POET AND THE HEART OF A ROSE

Frank has been writing down his memories of baseball and his interesting life for the past several years. "When my father was 86 years old, I asked him to tell us some stories about what it was like for him growing up. He told us stories that I had never heard before for over three hours. I learned that he had been a very good athlete, that he had a number of fascinating experiences, and I learned that my great, great grandfather had been the sheriff of Virginia City. It motivated me to start writing things down."

The following is an excerpt from a tribute that Frank wrote upon the death of former teammate Willard Nixon, who pitched for the Red Sox from 1950 to 1958:

> "We leave the dock at 6:30 A.M. on this Sunday, December 10, 2000, which is the same time we have been leaving it for 20 years in one boat or another. As usual, I am busy helping out with the different chores required for departure. As we leave the harbor still in the dark, I can feel the heave of the boat, and here on Kauai, the moment you leave the harbor you can get a real read on what the day will be like. When we push out past the headlands, it is obvious that we are going to be treated to an incredible sunrise.
>
> I can't help reflecting that this sun that is rising so beautifully for me has just set on the life of my friend and teammate, Willard Nixon. I go down to the back deck and sit on one of the fish boxes alone and I don't deny crying. Here I am watching one of the most glorious sunrises while alive and healthy, and Willard's luck has just run out.
>
> My day remained glorious and we caught plenty of tuna, but I found it hard fishing with tears in my eyes."

Frank Sullivan started 201 games for the Boston Red Sox and he completed 72 of those starts. But in this case, we are going to use him as the closer.

"Simply put, I've had a hell of a good life. I've seen Niagara Falls bathed in floodlights and been to the Rock Islands of Palau. Watched the sunset in the lee of Niihau and pitched in a major league All-Star Game.

I sat in the company of Joe DiMaggio to hear Sinatra sing with the Tommy Dorsey Band at the Palladium and drank with Ralph Evinrude on his yacht. Been to the rain gauge at the wettest spot on earth and watched Ted Williams hit his last home run in his last at-bat in Fenway Park.

I've been to Hatchet Bay, Eleuthera, and taken the tube in London. Attended the Masters Golf Tournament in Augusta and flown to Kwajalein. Seen the Rock of Gibraltar and had my picture taken with Ed Sullivan. My hometown honored me with a parade and I got paid to play ball in Mexico.

With all of that said, the best thing I ever did was marry the girl with whom I live."

Frank Sullivan can write as well as he pitched. And as the record shows, he was a very fine pitcher.

Frank Sullivan's Rank in Red Sox History

CATEGORY	CAREER TOTALS	ALL-TIME BOSTON RED SOX RANK
Strikeouts	821	9th
Games Started	201	10th
Innings	1,505.1	12th
Wins	90	15th*
ERA (1,000 Innings)	3.47	16th
Shutouts	14	16th*
Games	252	18th
Complete Games	72	19th*

* Tied

Source: 2004 *Boston Red Sox Media Guide*

10.
Frank Malzone Interview
July 1998

When I interviewed Frank Malzone, he was in his Pittsburgh hotel room getting ready to watch the Pittsburgh Pirates at Three Rivers Stadium that evening. When you are a special assignment scout for a major league ball club, you spend a lot of time in hotel rooms.

During our conversation Frank told me that the Red Sox had re-acquired Mike Stanley from the Toronto Blue Jays. He also told me that I couldn't tell anyone because the trade wouldn't be announced for several hours. I enjoyed being an insider even for a very brief period of time.

I met Frank Malzone for the first time in 1992 and realized quickly that he is not as garrulous as many of his former teammates. But when he says something it is meaningful.

I remember asking him if a certain player was a potential "superstar." Frank's immediate response was, "I prefer the term 'elite player.'" The difference in terminology is subtle, but important.

Frank properly ranks in the top 20 among Red Sox players of the past 60 years. He is sometimes overlooked because his Red Sox teams never played in the postseason, and because the average annual attendance at Fenway Park during his career was less than one-half of today's sellout crowds.

Frank Malzone let his bat and his glove do his talking. And it is quite an impressive story.

FRANK MALZONE
ALL-TIME RED SOX THIRD BASEMAN

Frank Malzone, former Boston Red Sox All-Star third baseman, spent eight years working his way through the minors before making it to the big leagues to stay. Once he established himself at third base in 1957, you couldn't get him out of the lineup.

Between May 21, 1957, and June 7, 1960, Malzone played in 475 consecutive games for the Red Sox. This is the third-longest consecutive game streak in Red Sox history, and no other Red Sox player has equaled his iron man stint in over 40 seasons.

Frank Malzone was the Red Sox regular third baseman from 1957 to 1965. During that time he was an eight-time American League All-Star, and he won three Gold Gloves in recognition of his fielding prowess. He was inducted into the Red Sox Hall of Fame in 1995.

These achievements are certainly impressive, but to really put his career into perspective, listen to Johnny Pesky who has been associated with the team in virtually every phase of the game for more than 60 years. "Frank Malzone is the greatest third baseman I ever saw in a Red Sox uniform. He was outstanding in the field, and he was a terrific hitter. I played a lot of third base in the major leagues, but I'll tell you one thing, he was one heck of a lot better third baseman than I ever was!"

BRONX BORN

Frank Malzone was born and raised in the Bronx not far from Yankee Stadium. He played a lot of his sandlot ball in the ballpark directly across from "The House That Ruth Built."

"I'll admit to being a Yankees fan as a youngster. As a kid in the 1940s, the Yankee-New York Giants-Brooklyn Dodgers rivalry was really hot, and if you grew up in the Bronx, you had to be a Yankee fan. You didn't have much choice. But I was more of a player than a fan."

Asked when he first thought of a career in the big leagues, Frank responds, "I never gave it a thought until the summer of 1948 when I went into the local sporting goods store to replace my worn-out spikes. Cy Phillips was the owner and a 'bird-dog' for the Red Sox. He told me I should think about making baseball my career. He ended up signing me to a minor league contract with the Red Sox in October of 1948, and I've been in the game ever since."

"I was on the train with a bunch of other young players heading for the Red Sox minor league spring training camp in Melbourne, Florida, the following spring, and one of the guys said, 'I got a $1,500 bonus to sign my contract, how did you make out?' I didn't really answer him because that was the first time I ever heard you could get a bonus for signing!"

LONG ROAD TO THE MAJORS

Malzone started his professional baseball career in Milford, Delaware, in Class D ball. His .300 average and solid play earned him a promotion to Oneonta, New York, up one notch to Class C ball. Playing under long-time Red Sox minor league manager Eddie "Pop" Popowski, he hit .329 and produced 27 triples.

"Oneonta was where I learned what professional baseball was all about. More importantly, it was where I met my lovely wife Amy. Best thing that ever happened to me."

Amy Malzone was Amy Gennarino at the time, and she remembers her husband of fifty-three years as "very shy and very well-mannered." Amy was in her first year of college when she was introduced to Frank at an Oneonta restaurant. Frank asked if he could walk her home, but she "wasn't sure about this ballplay-er." Amy took a chance, and fol-lowing a proper courtship, the Malzones were married in August 1951.

His career appeared to be on a fast track after his terrific season at Oneonta when he was promoted another level to Scranton, Pennsylvania, for the 1950 season. Unfortunately, he dislocated his ankle in just the second game, and the season was lost.

"I'll never forget the doctor saying, 'I'm not sure you'll ever play baseball again.' Fortunately, he was wrong."

Malzone returned to Scranton in 1951, batting nearly .300 and continuing his outstanding play in the field. Following that season, his career went on hold once more when he was drafted into the U.S. Army.

"I spent two years (the 1952 and 1953 seasons) in the Army. But I spent most of it stationed in Hawaii, and I got to play a lot of baseball. I played mostly at shortstop, and that gave me a different perspective on playing third base."

Malzone spent the 1954 season with Louisville, Kentucky, at the Triple-A minor league level. His solid season contributed to his team's victory in the "Junior World Series." He was back in Louisville for the 1955 season, but he was clearly the Red Sox third baseman of the future. The parent team called him up to the majors in September of 1955, and he rewarded their confidence by going 6-for-10 in a doubleheader against the Baltimore Orioles.

The 1956 season should have been his first full season in the majors, but a personal family tragedy threw him totally off-stride. The Malzones had lost an infant and baseball was the last thing on Frank's mind at the time. The Red Sox sent him to their top farm team in San Francisco after 27 games in the majors.

Playing under manager Joe Gordon in San Francisco, Frank gradually adjusted to his terrible loss and eventually got his game back on track. Nearly nine years after signing his first contract with the Red Sox, he was ready for "The Show."

ROOKIE SENSATION

Frank Malzone was 27-years-old when he finally made it to Fenway Park for good. He started the season as if he was trying to make up for lost time, and never slowed down. His first half was so strong that he was named to the American League All Star team along with teammate Ted Williams. By the end of the season he had knocked in 103 runs, rapped out 15 home runs, and compiled the best fielding average of any American League third baseman.

How great was Frank Malzone's rookie year? He became the first player in modern baseball history to lead his position in games played, putouts, assists, double plays, and fielding percentage. And he finished seventh in the balloting to determine the American League's Most Valuable Player.

About the only way you could have kept Frank Malzone from winning the Rookie of the Year award for 1957 was to change the rules. And that is exactly what happened. Under new guidelines adopted by the Baseball Writers Association of America following the season, since he had more than 75 at-bats during his time with the Red Sox in 1955 and 1956, he was ineligible for the award.

The award went instead to Tony Kubek of the New York Yankees who had a nice rookie year, but not one that compared to Malzone's. The definition of "rookie" was liberalized in 1971, and under the current criteria, Malzone would have been a shoo-in as Rookie of the Year.

More than forty years later, Malzone is still miffed about the process. "I don't think there is any question that the New York writers got together and changed the rules. They wanted Kubek to win it. Not to take anything away from Kubek, but I had a much better season."

While the writers were busy drafting the "Malzone Amendment" to the Rookie of the Year award, the Rawling Sporting Goods Company was introducing a new award: the Gold Glove Award to recognize fielding excellence. Gold

Gloves were awarded for the first time following the 1957 season, and Frank Malzone was recognized as the best-fielding third baseman in the major leagues.

In 1958 Malzone played every one of the Red Sox' 155 games and virtually duplicated his outstanding first full year performance. He led the American League in games played and at-bats, he was second in hits, sixth in doubles, and his eighty-seven RBI ranked seventh in the junior circuit.

He made the American League All-Star team for the second straight season and he helped the Red Sox to a respectable third place finish in the eight team 1958 race. At the All-Star Game in Baltimore's Memorial Stadium, he contributed a key single and scored the deciding run as the American League prevailed 4-3. That year the Gold Glove Award was expanded to recognize a player at each position in both leagues, and he was voted the best fielding third baseman in the American League.

HOT CORNER STANDOUT

Malzone's consistency continued into 1959 as he once again appeared in all 154 Red Sox games, made the American League All-Star team for the third year in a row, and earned another Gold Glove at third base. In 1960, Malzone demonstrated that he was human as his 475 consecutive game streak came to an end.

Malzone in his prime.

"To be honest, I don't even remember the day my streak ended. In those days, the players and the media weren't as conscious of statistics as they are today. It may have been the second game of a doubleheader, and they decided to give me a rest. I never paid much attention to individual statistics anyway."

In 1960, his Gold Glove streak came to an end also, but it took a future Hall of Famer to do it. Baltimore's Brooks Robinson won his first of 16 consecutive Gold Gloves as the America League's best fielding third baseman. "Since I won the first Gold Glove Award and the only one they ever gave for all of major league baseball, I used to kid Brooksie and say, 'You're winning them all now, but I've got one fielding award you'll never win!' " laughs Malzone.

Over the next five years, Malzone would play in almost every game, contribute significantly to the offense, and field his position flawlessly. Frank enjoyed his best day at the plate as a major leaguer on August 15, 1961. That day he went 5-for-5 and belted a pair of home runs in an 8-0 defeat of the Cleveland Indians.

In 1962 he ranked tenth in the American League in both at-bats and RBI. His 95 RBI and 21 home runs led the Red Sox that year.

In 1963 he was named to the American League All-Star team for the fifth time. His .291 batting average placed him sixth in the American League that year. In 1964 he was named to the American League All-Star team once again, and he completed his seventh consecutive season in double figures, with 13 home runs.

TEAMMATES' FAVORITE

He was so consistent during his 11 seasons with the Red Sox, that his contributions were not always recognized. Former Sox pitcher Gene Conley calls Malzone one of his favorite ballplayers. "I first saw Frank Malzone when he batted against me in Scranton in 1951. We were just a couple of 20-year-old kids. I was pitching for Hartford and he hit my best pitch a ton. He impressed me then and he still impresses me."

"I think he sometimes got overlooked because he made the hard plays look easy. When I was pitching for the Red Sox he used to say 'If the ball is hit towards third base, you just duck down and stay out of the way. I'll take care of it.' And he always did."

Johnny Pesky recalls, "He was just about the perfect ballplayer. He went out every day and worked his butt off. And he played the game as well as any of them."

Following the 1965 season, General Manager Dick O'Connell told Malzone that he didn't fit in with the club's future plans, and gave him his release so he could catch on with another team. In 1966, Frank played in 82 games for the California Angels. "It was pretty strange coming into Fenway Park in a visitor's uniform," Frank reflects. "I remember doubling into the left-field corner and feeling a little funny standing on second base." And it was equally strange for Red Sox fans to see Frank Malzone standing on second base in an Angels' uniform.

MAJOR LEAGUE SCOUT

When the Red Sox released Frank Malzone following the 1965 season, General Manager Dick O'Connell had promised that there would be a place for him in the Red Sox organization when his playing days were over. In the fall of 1966 Malzone returned to the organization in the Scouting Department. For the next 27 years he served as an Advance Scout, providing the ball club with valuable information on their upcoming opponents.

In his last 10 years with the club he served as a Special Assignment Scout providing evaluations on players in the majors and the minors. "It's a part of the game the fans don't see," observes Johnny Pesky. "But I can assure you that Frank Malzone is as good at evaluating talent as anybody in the business."

Frank Malzone's two-week itinerary in late July and early August of 1998 represented a typical assignment. He started out in Milwaukee, moved on to Philadelphia for five days, and then headed off to Pittsburgh. "You like to stay five days in a city so you can get a look at all of a team's starting pitching. I stay out

Still showing his enthusiasm for the game during an Old-Timers' Game at Fenway in the 1980s.

for two weeks and then come home for a few days. If you stay at it much over two weeks, you start to lose your edge."

"All the big league clubs provide seats for the scouts right behind the back-stop. My job is to accumulate as much information about the player, both on the field and off the field, as I can. I summarize my findings for the front office, and they make the final decisions. I don't carry a radar gun to check the pitcher's speed; I can usually tell from the batter's reaction how fast the pitch was."

THE HOME FRONT

Frank Malzone is originally from New York City, and his wife Amy is from upstate New York, but Needham, Massachusetts, has been home for over 40 years. "We decided to stay in the area after the 1958 season, so my kids grew up there and went through school there. We've gotten to know a lot of people in Needham over the years. It's definitely our home."

Most major leaguers never return to their minor league "roots." But the Malzones make it back to Oneonta several times each year to visit Amy's family in the area.

Frank and Amy Malzone celebrated their fifty-third wedding anniversary in August 2004. Their five children Jimmy, Paul, Frankie Jr., Anne Susan, and John all live within an easy drive of the Malzone's Needham home. The children, six grandchildren, and one great grandchild are frequent visitors at the Malzone home.

"We are very family-oriented. It's great when the kids and grandkids come over for a visit."

LOOKING BACK

"I was fortunate to have so many great teammates during my eleven years on the field with the Red Sox. Ted Williams, Yaz, of course, Billy Monbouquette, Dick Radatz, and Gene Conley. I could fill your story with all of the names, but I would be afraid I would leave somebody out.

"One of my biggest thrills was flying to St. Louis with Ted Williams for the 1957 All- Star Game. Here I was in my first full year and I'm sitting with Ted on my way to play with Mickey Mantle and Al Kaline, and against Stan Musial and Willie Mays. What a great experience!"

Frank Malzone was inducted into the Red Sox Hall of Fame in 1995. His inclusion in the first group of former players to be selected to the Red Sox Hall of Fame is testimony to his proper place in Red Sox history.

The Boston Red Sox have been blessed with many outstanding players during their 104 exciting seasons. But if you had to pick one single player to make the crucial play in the field, or to bring the winning run home from third base, you couldn't make a better choice than Frank Malzone. Frank Malzone is a *very* dependable man.

Frank Malzone's Rank in Red Sox History

CATEGORY	CAREER TOTALS	ALL-TIME BOSTON RED SOX RANK
Hits	1,454	9th
Games	1,359	10th
At-Bats	5,273	10th
Total Bases	2,173	11th
RBI	716	12th
Home Runs	131	15th
Doubles	234	17th
Extra Base Hits	386	17th*

* tied

Source: 2004 *Boston Red Sox Media Guide*

11.
Bill Monbouquette Interview
March 1998

I have enjoyed every interview I have conducted with former Red Sox players. My interview of Bill Monbouquette is near to the top of my most enjoyable sessions.

I interviewed "Monbo" at Frank's Steakhouse, a Cambridge institution since 1938. There is nothing pretentious about Frank's and there is nothing pretentious about Bill Monbouquette. And I mean that in the very best way.

There was snow on the ground, and a chill the air, but Frank's was warmed with over 40 years of great baseball memories. And what a passion Bill has for the game, for playing it properly, and for respecting the game he loves.

When my wife, Janet, went to the Red Sox Fantasy Camp in 1992, I asked Monbo to keep an eye out for her since she didn't know anyone else. I thought he would cross paths with her a couple of times and ask how she was doing. Instead, he tracked her down every day between 5:30 and 6 P.M. to make sure she was doing okay. Bill Monbouquette is a gentleman of the old school.

We had a great conversation, an excellent meal, and Preacher Jack was playing boogie-woogie piano in the background. It really doesn't get much better than that.

BILL MONBOUQUETTE
"MONBO"

Bill Monbouquette left his Medford, Massachusetts, home on a June day in 1955 for a tryout with the Boston Red Sox at Fenway Park. Fifty seasons later, Monbouquette is still playing an important role in professional baseball.

"I remember Ted Williams watched me pitch, and he said to me afterwards, 'Hey, I like the way you throw strikes.' What a thrill that was for an 18-year-old local kid."

When you check the Red Sox record book for all-time pitching leaders you find Bill Monbouquette in the top 10 for eight pitching categories. Among them, he ranks fifth for games started, seventh for innings pitched, and eighth in strike-outs. While those statistics are impressive, they only begin to tell the story of a lifetime of commitment to the game he loves.

THE PRIDE OF MEDFORD, MASS

Bill Monbouquette was born and raised in Medford, Massachusetts, where he starred in baseball and hockey. His enthusiasm for both sports goes way back, and he thinks that hockey was probably his first choice as a youngster.

Monbouquette with another Sox pitching great, Smoky Joe Wood.

"I loved hockey," Monbouquette recalls, "but in those days there were only three rinks in the Boston area: the Boston Arena, the Boston Skating Club, and the Lynn Arena. I used to work out with the Bruins when I was pitching for the Red Sox, but they would be up one end of the rink, and I would be down in the other trying to catch up. Boy, did I pick the right sport!" he laughs.

Although his premier pitching seasons were with the Red Sox and he has continued a close relationship with the team even after leaving the organization, Monbouquette grew up as a fan of the Boston Braves. The Braves moved to Milwaukee before the 1953 season, but from 1901 to 1952 Boston was a two-team baseball town.

"The Braves had the 'Knothole Gang' for children, and you could get into Braves Field for next to nothing. Kids came from all over Greater Boston to watch the Braves. And I was always a big fan of Warren Spahn. He won more games than any left-hander in baseball history and I used to love to watch him pitch."

Monbouquette pitched for Medford High School, and played for the local CYO and American Legion baseball clubs. In the summer following his junior year, he was selected to appear in the Hearst All-Star game, featuring the nation's best high school ball players in New York's Polo Grounds. When he was named the game's MVP, he became a certified major league prospect.

Red Sox scout Fred Maguire got him his fateful tryout at Fenway Park. "The

funny part of the story is that I almost went to jail instead of to the Red Sox farm system. My mother and father were there to watch me, and a couple of toughs spilled beer all over my mother. I took one look at my father, and he gave me a nod, so we gave the two guys a pretty good going-over."

"The next thing I knew, we were both in handcuffs. I said to the cop, 'Could you call Mr. Murphy (Red Sox Minor League Director) upstairs? I'm with the team.' Thanks to his help, I headed off to the Red Sox farm team in Corning, New York, instead of the Charles Street Jail."

On May 12, 1961, Monbouquette struck out 17 Washington Senators to set a then-new Red Sox one-game strike out record that has since been surpassed twice by Roger Clemens' 20.

Monbouquette toiled for parts of four seasons in the Red Sox minor league system. Along the way he played for long-time Red Sox minor league manager Eddie Popowski in Albany, New York, and Gene Mauch at the Red Sox Triple-A farm club in Minneapolis, Minnesota.

LOCAL BOY MAKES GOOD

The pitching-poor Red Sox called up the 21-year-old right-hander in July of 1958. His ability to persevere against big league competition was tested in his first game in the major leagues. He served notice that he was here to stay with a purpose pitch to certified tough-guy Billy Martin.

"I remember my first game was against the Detroit Tigers, and they hammered me pretty good. They scored five runs off of me, and Billy Martin [former New York Yankee player, and later manager], stole home. The next time he came up, I unloaded on him. When he trotted by me on the mound, he said, 'I guess you owed me that one, Rook!'

The Boston Red Sox of the late 1950s through the mid-1960s bore little resemblance to today's Red Sox teams. Those teams spent most of the time in the second division of the American League standings, and more of the seats in Fenway Park were empty than occupied. He can remember Fenway Park when you could hear the vendors hawking their wares three sections away.

"We used to average 8,000-10,000 fans a game. Not only could I hear everything the fans yelled, I recognized a lot of the voices. I would hear a fan getting all over me and I would say to myself, 'Hey, that's Billy So-and-So from Medford Square.' "

"Monbo," as he was known to his teammates, established himself as one of the premier pitchers in the American League in 1960. His 14 wins for a seventh-place Red Sox team earned him a spot on the American League All-Star team. On May 7 that year he pitched a one-hitter at Fenway Park in a 5-0 win over the Detroit Tigers.

Not only was he selected to the American League All-Star team, but also he was named as their starting pitcher for the July 11 game in Kansas City. In five short years, he had gone from Playstead Park in West Medford, to throwing the first pitch in the mid-summer classic.

"I'll never forget that game. Willie Mays [former San Francisco Giants Hall of Famer] tripled off of me in the first inning. Then Ernie Banks [former Chicago Cubs Hall of Famer] hit a home run. Somebody said 'Del Crandall [former Milwaukee Braves catcher] isn't much of a curveball hitter.' Boom! He hits a home run off of me. I was shell-shocked.

"But what I really remember is the next night I was sitting all alone in the hotel lobby in New York, and along comes Stan Musial [former St. Louis Cardinals Hall of Famer.] He asked me if I had any plans, and when I said 'no', he said, 'Come on, let's go to dinner.' Years later I told him how much that invitation meant to me, and he responded, 'Hey Bill, we're all professionals.' I wish that all big leaguers had that same professional attitude today."

ACE OF THE STAFF

In 1961, he won 14 games again, and established a new Red Sox strikeout record, fanning 17 Washington Senators in May. The 17-strikeout-game was quite a feat for a pitcher who was better known for his pinpoint control.

"I wasn't a strikeout pitcher per se, but that night everything worked for me. The funny thing is I never struck out three of their nine hitters, so I was working the other six hitters pretty good. I struck out Willie Tasby four times, and he never even had a swing off of me!" Monbouquette's 17 strikeouts stood as the Red Sox standard for nearly 25 years, until Roger Clemens struck out 20 Seattle Mariners on April 29, 1986.

Monbo increased his win total to 15 for the eighth-place 1962 Red Sox, and he was selected once again for the American League All-Star team. He added a no-hitter to his growing list of achievements, defeating the Chicago White Sox 1-0 in a night game at old Comiskey Park.

"The funny part is that I hadn't been pitching that well before the no-hitter. And what stands out in my mind," he remembers, "is that we were flying to Chicago, and I was having trouble doing the crossword puzzle. The stewardess came over to see if she could help, and she said 'Don't worry about it. You're going to pitch a no-hitter tomorrow night.' I had never seen her before, and I never saw her again, but she predicted my no-hitter."

When the 1962 season came to an end, Monbo ranked fourth in the American League in games started and in shutouts. He led the Red Sox with 11 shutouts and his ERA of 3.33 topped the staff as well.

The 1963 season was the high point of his major league career as he entered the elite 20-game winners circle, achieving All-Star status for the third time. Remarkably, he walked only 42 batters in 258 innings of pitching.

"My control was always good. I always knew how to throw strikes. Of course that meant I got hit a lot, too. Monbo chuckles and adds, "In fact, when I was scheduled to pitch, they used to call the Mass Turnpike and tell them to shut down the Cambridge to Boston extension. They were afraid somebody would get killed by a home run ball I had thrown."

Good nature aside, Monbo's 1963 season was truly remarkable. He won 20 games for a Red Sox team that finished 26 games behind the pennant winning Yankees. And his win total accounted for more than one-quarter of the team's 76 wins.

Bill Monbouquette's win total dropped to 13 in 1964 as the Red Sox fell to eighth place in the American League. In 1965, he won ten games as the Red Sox continued their downward spiral to ninth place. But in both years, he logged well over 200 innings, and walked only 40 batters each season. His outstanding control placed him at the top of all American League pitchers in fewest walks per nine innings pitched in 1964, and second in the league for 1965. Always a workhorse, he led the Red Sox in complete games in both seasons.

TRADE WINDS BLOW

Two days after the close of the Red Sox 1965 season, Monbouquette received a call from then Red Sox General Manager Dick O'Connell telling him that he had been traded to the Detroit Tigers. "I told Dick that I understood completely. It was part of baseball. I had 11 wonderful years with the organization. Mr. Yawkey was the best owner in baseball."

Monbouquette spent the 1966 season with the Tigers where he split his time between starting and relieving. He began the 1967 season with Detroit, but soon found himself in the pinstripes of the New York Yankees. Asked if that was a strange experience for a Medford boy, he responds, "At first it was, but it was great to be a part of their wonderful baseball tradition. And Ralph Houk [former Yankees manager and Red Sox manager] was the best all-around manager I ever played under."

One game during the 1967 pennant race stands out in Monbo's mind. "We [the Yankees] were in ninth place and the Red Sox were fighting for the pennant. I pitched my best game of the season, and we beat them 5-2." Asked how he felt about beating his old team at Fenway Park in a crucial game, he responds with relish, "It felt *great*."

His Yankee career lasted through the middle of the 1968 season, when he was traded to the San Francisco Giants. "The Giants didn't use me much, but I got to play with Willie Mays, Willie McCovey, Gaylord Perry, and Juan Marichal: all Hall of Famers. It was great experience."

He tried to catch on with a major league team in the spring of 1969, but failed. After 11 major league seasons, and 114 victories, his pitching days were over.

Bill Monbouquette has an interesting perspective on longevity in the big leagues. "Everybody talks about how hard it is to get to the majors. And believe me, it is. But the really hard part is staying there. Because the minute you make it there, somebody else is waiting to take your job. You have to remember that every single day."

A SECOND CAREER

Bill Monbouquette's major league pitching career was over, but his career as a coach and instructor was just beginning. And this phase of his professional baseball career began with the New York Yankees.

"In the spring of 1969 Ralph Houk asked me to scout nationally for the Yankees to help them with the June draft, and then they sent me to Johnson City, Tennessee, to manage their rookie club."

In less than one year, Monbo had gone from the major leagues and top-shelf hotels, to the lowest level of the minors and long bus rides. "I had to do everything from ordering the bats, the balls, and the tape, to making the motel reservations. One year I'm doing all of my travel first class and the next thing I know, I'm back to riding in a bus. About the only thing I didn't do was drive that bus."

His role with the Yankees was the first of a 35-year career as scout, manager and coach at the minor and major league levels. During that time he has been with the Yankees (twice), the New York Mets, the Toronto Blue Jays, and most recently the Detroit Tigers for the past five years.

"I've done a little bit of everything over the years. I was a pitching coach at the major league level for the Mets in 1982-83. I was Billy Martin's pitching coach for the Yankees in 1985: now *that* was an experience!"

Monbo spent the 2004 season as the pitching coach for the Tigers' short season single-A team in Oneonta, New York. His young pitchers have access to 50 years of baseball experience, and lessons learned at the big league level.

"A couple of years ago, one of my pitchers got beat two nights in a row with his fourth-best pitch. I called him into my office after the second night when he gave up a 'walk-off' home run. To emphasize my point, I couldn't help adding, 'By the way, that home run sure went far into the night!' He got a little hot and came back with 'What do you know about home runs?' I looked at him and said 'Son, I gave up 211 home runs in the *big leagues*.' He came back the next day and apologized to me."

Asked what he tells his young pitchers during those conferences on the

Monbo returned to Fenway in 1984 to participate in the Old-Timers' Game.

mound, Monbo chuckles, "I learned from the master, Sal Maglie [former Brooklyn Dodgers pitching star, and Red Sox pitching coach of the 1960s.] Sal used to come out and say 'Skip doesn't like what he's seeing. And he suggests that you get your act together, or he's going to get somebody else!'"

TEAMMATES

When he talks about his baseball career, Bill Monbouquette always comes back to the many teammates he remembers. "Ted Williams was absolutely wonderful. We're all still in awe of him. Yaz was great. Gene Conley was terrific, and Pumpsie Green was a real pal."

One of his favorite Yaz stories goes back to the 1960s when the Red Sox used to train in Scottsdale, Arizona. "Willie Mays hit a rocket off me. I mean it cleared the outfield fence at the 350 mark, it soared over the parking lot behind the fence, and it landed beside a swimming pool which was at least 500 feet from home plate. When the ball left the bat, Yaz didn't even move. Just stood there with his head down, and his hands on his knees.

"I was waiting for him on the top step of the dugout when he came in, and I said, 'Don't you ever show me up like that again! You can at least make some effort to get back under it.' He looked me in the eye and said, 'Bill, I'm not going to play back at the swimming pool.'"

Asked to reflect on his lifetime association with baseball, Monbo answers, "Baseball has been a wonderful experience for me. In fact, it has been everything. I put my heart and soul into it. I had a dream and it came true for me. And nobody, but nobody, ever outworked me on the baseball diamond."

"All three of my sons are the same way. My oldest son, Marc, is a pilot in the Navy, my next son, Michel, is a captain in the Marines, and my youngest son, Merric, is a logger up in New Hampshire. Nobody outworks them either. They are *horses!*"

Johnny Pesky has been associated with the Boston Red Sox for almost 60 years. Asked to put Monbo's career with the Red Sox in perspective Johnny offers, "I would place Bill in the top five among all the Red Sox pitchers I have seen over the years, and that puts him in some very good company. I managed him in 1963 and 1964, and I still remember how hard he worked. He ran and ran between starts, and that gave him something to draw on in the late innings. He was a very good one."

BASEBALL PROFESSIONAL

In November of 1997, the City of Medford honored Monbouquette in a ceremony renaming Playstead Park, the baseball park of his youth, as "Bill Monbouquette Field." Many former Red Sox colleagues including Rico Petrocelli, Dick Radatz, Pesky and Conley were on hand for the dedication.

"It was really a great thrill. They had a nice stone placed there. I just wish I had a dollar for every hour I spent on that field!"

If you were a talented painter you would paint Bill Monbouquette on the pitcher's mound in Oneonta, New York, lecturing some 19-year-old pitcher on the virtue of first-pitch strikes. If you were a very talented artist, they would hang it in a nationally recognized museum and title it: "Baseball Professional."

Medford's own Bill Monbouquette: the consummate baseball professional.

Bill Monbouquette's Rank in Red Sox History

CATEGORY	CAREER TOTALS	ALL-TIME BOSTON RED SOX RANK
Games Started	228	5th
Innings	1,622	7th
Strikeouts	969	8th
10-K Games	6	10th
Wins	96	11th*
Shutouts	16	12th*
Games	254	17th
Complete Games	72	19th*

* tied

Source: 2004 *Boston Red Sox Media Guide*

12.
Pumpsie Green Interview
July 2004

I probably spent more time thinking about the best focus for the Pumpsie Green feature than any other profile I have written. Obviously Pumpsie was the first African American to play for the Boston Red Sox. And the Red Sox were the last major league baseball team to integrate. But that story has been told and retold.

I moved into my teenage years watching the Boston Celtics of Bill Russell and the Jones boys hoist World Championship banners to the rafters of Boston Garden. And while the Patriots were just a glimmer in Billy Sullivan's eye, we had all watched players of color in the NFL on television every Sunday.

Even the Bruins, in a league where the color of the players invariably matches the color of the ice, had integrated the NHL in 1958 with winger Willie O'Ree. And if you knew your baseball, you knew that Sam Jethroe had been the first African-American baseball player in Boston, playing with the Braves from 1950 to 1952.

For most of us the absence of an African American on the Red Sox was a mystery. Pumpsie arrived in Boston in July 1959 and his career with the Red Sox only lasted through 1962. We never really got to know Pumpsie Green.

I decided to ask Pumpsie Green to tell us who he really is. I learned that he is a warm, much-loved man, with a nice story to tell. I liked him a lot and wish I had gotten to meet him instead of spending 90 minutes talking to him by telephone at his El Cerrito, California, home. I think you will like him as well.

ELIJAH GREEN
"PUMPSIE"

Every story about Pumpsie Green begins the same way. Pumpsie Green was the first African American to play for the Boston Red Sox. He was "the bookend" to Jackie Robinson when the Red Sox became the last major league team to set aside the racial barrier.

But Pumpsie Green was, and is, more than just an important footnote in the history of the Boston Red Sox. He was a three-sport star in high school, a big brother to four younger siblings, and a capable professional baseball player. Today he is a devoted husband and father, who dotes on his granddaughter, and works out five-days a week at the local YMCA.

Elijah "Pumpsie" Green never set out to be a racial pioneer. "I just wanted to be a major league baseball player, to make the team. I really got tired of the writers asking me about the situation before I was brought up. People were asking me so many questions about things I had no control over."

Pumpsie never wanted to be placed in the spotlight that focused on Fenway Park. But he handled the pressure with grace and good nature. He is much more than just a footnote to the history of the Red Sox. He is an important part of who the Boston Red Sox are today.

BAY AREA NATIVE

Elijah Jerry Green was born on October 27, 1933, in Oakland, California. "I was named Elijah after my father, but my mother called me Pumpsie when I was a couple of years old. I used to ask her why she called me that but she never gave me a good explanation.

"Pumpsie is the only name I have ever known. I don't remember anyone calling me Elijah. Some of my friends today, even the ones I've known a long time, I'm not even sure if they know my real name."

Pumpsie grew up in Richmond, just outside of Oakland, where his father worked for the city. Pumpsie was followed by four brothers, including Cornell who was an All-Pro defensive back with the Dallas Cowboys, and Credell who played for the Green Bay Packers.

"When I was growing up, it seemed as if everyone was playing baseball, all the time. Baseball was a natural part of life where I grew up. All the kids in the area, the young and old, men and women, everybody played baseball.

"I never really played against my brothers, even though they were athletes. They were younger than me and I had my own crowd. I also played mostly against guys that were older than me. When I was 10, I played against guys who were 13 or 14 years old."

He still remembers his first baseball glove and the events leading up to it. "I must have been about eight or nine, and I still didn't have my own glove. It was at a time when the family really couldn't afford that kind of expense. But I talked my mother into it and I did work around the house every day. Finally she saved enough money, I think it was seven or eight dollars, and she bought me a brand new glove.

"My hero was Artie Wilson, who played shortstop for the Oakland Oaks, and he wore a three-fingered glove. My mother bought me a three-fingered glove, a

Caledonia, and I loved it. I tied the whole thing up into a neat package, oiled it and so forth. I used it, and used it, until I wore it out."

PACIFIC COAST LEAGUE

In the years immediately after World War II, the quality of baseball played in the Pacific Coast League was just a notch below the major league level. There were no major league teams west of the Mississippi River, and the eight-team PCL circuit stretched from Seattle in the north to San Diego in the south. Fans on the West Coast followed their teams with the passion of big league fans. The 1948 Oakland Oaks, who won their first PCL pennant in 21 years under manager Casey Stengel, were Pumpsie Green's team.

"The Pacific Coast League was really big. I listened to Bud Foster doing every Oakland Oaks game and followed a whole bunch of guys on that team. It was almost a daily ritual. Artie Wilson was the best thing I had ever seen at that point, but I loved to watch Jackie Jensen and Billy Martin also. When I got old enough to wish, I wished I could play for the Oakland Oaks."

Like most fans on the West Coast, Pumpsie didn't follow major league baseball closely as a youngster. "I can remember seeing a big billboard with a picture of Stan Musial on the highway. But that was the only association I had with major league baseball."

But he does remember hearing about Jackie Robinson integrating major league baseball with the Brooklyn Dodgers in 1947. "That was very exciting to hear about. After the 1948 season, he barnstormed with an All-Star team and they played in the Oakland Oaks ballpark. I scraped up every nickel and dime I could find. And I was there. I had to see that game with the Jackie Robinson All-Stars. I still remember how exciting it was."

Growing up he played all sports, but baseball was the most popular sport in his neighborhood. He made himself into a switch-hitter as a youngster for an unusual reason. "We played a team from another neighborhood that was cross-town and they beat us 44-0. But we had a rematch, and we said, 'Hey, let's do everything the opposite of what we normally do.'

"I was a right-handed hitter, so I turned around and batted left-handed. That moment in time is what began the switch-hitting for me. I had a heck of a day with the bat and we only lost 35-10. I was a switch-hitter from then on, but my natural side, the right side, was my stronger side. I always took batting practice left-handed because I knew that was where I needed the work."

THREE-SPORT STAR

Green was a three-sport star at El Cerrito High School in Richmond. "When the calendar changed, I moved on to whatever sport was in season. And we had some great high school sports teams in the area. I remember playing against Frank Robinson [Hall of Famer], Vada Pinson [former Cincinnati Reds star], and Curt Flood (former St. Louis Cards star) when we were all kids. You could see even then that they were going to be big leaguers.

"They all went to McClymonds High School in Oakland, where Bill Russell played basketball before going on to the University of San Francisco and the Celtics. McClymonds beat us in basketball, but we were better in baseball."

"My first love was actually basketball. And I think that may have been my best sport. But I was offered a baseball scholarship to Fresno State, so that's where I was headed after high school."

Looking back over 50 years, Pumpsie thinks the biggest influence in his baseball career was Gene Corr, who had been his first baseball coach at El Cerrito High. "I was all set to go to Fresno State, but Gene Corr had moved up to become the baseball coach at Contra Costa Junior College, and he wanted me to go there. He promised that I could play shortstop if I went there, so I changed my plans and went there. I'm glad I did."

Pumpsie polished his skills under Corr and after his final season at the junior college, his mentor helped him to advance to the next level. "In my senior year at Contra Costa, Gene Corr got me a tryout with the Oakland Oaks. It was like a dream coming true. I got into his car, and we drove to Oakland, which was seven or eight miles away. I tried out with the team for a week.

"My workout would take place before the regular team did its exercises. Then when the game started, Gene Corr and I would sit in the stands and watch the games. I'd talk to the Oakland third baseman, Spider Jorgensen. My favorite player was Piper Davis, who made it to the majors."

THE LONG ROAD TO FENWAY

"The people in charge of the Oaks finally came to a decision about me. It was just sign and go play ball. Oakland was an independent team, so there was no draft that applied to me. I got no bonus, just a regular salary of three or four hundred dollars a month."

Pumpsie Green got his start in professional baseball in 1953 with the Oaks' farm club at Wenatchee in the state of Washington. "It was an adjustment. I was only 19, away from home for the first time. It was a small town, the apple capital of the world," Green recalls with a chuckle.

"I did okay as a rookie. Then the next year at Wenatchee I hit almost .300 [.297], and scored a lot of runs. I had a good season, stole a bunch of bases."

His strong second season earned him a promotion to Stockton, the Oaks' top farm team in the California State League. "I was having a great year, we were in first place, and it was the middle of June. Then one day my manager Roy Partee told me, 'Hey, Pumps, the Red Sox bought your contract. You are going to their organization, to Montgomery, Alabama.'

"I was excited that a big league club had that kind of interest in me. But I did not want to go. I wasn't ready for it. They told me that Earl Wilson was there and I could be his roommate, but I don't think there was a black man in America who wanted to go to Montgomery, Alabama, in 1955."

Pumpsie was allowed to finish the season in Stockton and he was voted the league's most valuable player. He joined the Red Sox organization the following spring and spent the 1956 season with the Red Sox farm team in Albany, New York. The following season he was advanced to Oklahoma City in the Texas League, and his fine play earned him a promotion to the Red Sox top minor league team in San Francisco to finish the 1957 season.

"That was a big thrill," Pumpsie remembers. "Coming back to the Bay Area and playing in the Pacific Coast League after following the teams in that league as a kid. The team was in the pennant race and I hit well [.333], so it's a nice memory."

The following year the Red Sox Triple A franchise was moved to Minneapolis and Pumpsie spent that season playing shortstop for the Millers. After a full year at the top minor league level, he was invited to the Red Sox major league spring training camp to prepare for the 1959 season.

HISTORY IN THE MAKING

The 1959 Boston Red Sox spring training camp was the team's first in Scottsdale, Arizona, and Pumpsie Green was the focus of the media. In June 1958, Ozzie Virgil had become the first African American to play for the Detroit Tigers, and the Red Sox were on the verge of becoming the last team in the major leagues to integrate.

"I didn't think of myself as another Jackie Robinson, as a pioneer with the Red Sox. I just wanted to make the club. The press wanted to make a big deal out of it, but I just wanted to play. I met all the guys, including Ted Williams, and they were great to me.

"I had the best spring of anyone on the team, including Ted Williams. Everyone told me I was going to make the team, but when we were barnstorming back to Boston, I was sent back to Minneapolis. The writers all wanted to know what I thought, and I said, 'You are asking the wrong person.' I just put it in the perspective that there were only so many roster spots and I didn't have one of them."

Pumpsie Green went back to Minneapolis and batted .320 during his three months with the team. After scoring 77 runs in 98 games, and excelling at shortstop, he got a telephone call in the early morning hours of July 21, 1959.

"The phone rang at about 7 A.M. and I couldn't imagine who was calling at that hour. They told me to pack my bags and get to Chicago as quickly as I could to join the Red Sox. Just like that I was on my way to the big leagues."

Green joined the team in Chicago, and manager Billy Jurges sent him in to pinch run in the eighth inning of his first game. He stayed in the game to play shortstop in the ninth inning, but his clearest memory is of starting the next day against future Hall of Fame pitcher Early Wynn.

"I'll never forget my first at bat. I'm facing Early Wynn, who I had seen pitch on television in the World Series. I had two strikes on me before I knew it. I finally just flicked my bat and grounded out to second base. That was probably my worst at-bat in the major leagues."

WELCOME TO BOSTON

When the Red Sox returned to Boston for their upcoming homestand, the team was greeted by a large media contingent. "We're getting off the plane, and all of a sudden all these bright lights came on. I just thought that was what happened every time. It wasn't until later that I realized the cameras were there because of me."

Pumpsie did pick out one familiar face in the waiting crowd. "Bill Russell was there waiting to pick me up. I had known him since our high school days and it was nice of him to go the trouble. He drove me to my hotel and wished me luck. He was a big help during my time in Boston."

Fenway Park was sold out for Pumpsie Green's debut in a Red Sox uniform. "I guess a lot of people showed up to see me, but the team always drew well." When it is pointed out that the Red Sox attendance only averaged about 13,000 fans in 1959, the self-effacing Green acknowledges, "Yes, I guess most of them were there to see me. I remember it was so loud you could barely hear. It was a little nerve-racking."

Shortly after joining the team, Ted Williams approached him and said, "Come on, Pumpsie, let's go warm up." The pair warmed up before every game until Williams retired at the end of the 1960 season.

"I had gotten to know Ted in spring training and we got along well. He did-n't say anything beyond the invitation to play catch, and it surprised me a little bit. But I understood and appreciated the gesture. I respected and admired that man."

One week after Pumpsie joined the team, pitcher Earl Wilson was called up from Minneapolis and became the second African-American to play for the Boston Red Sox. Green chuckles when it is pointed out that *he* was almost the second African American to play for the team. "Things would have been a little different," he muses. "But you play with the hand they deal you," he reflects.

Pumpsie Green and Earl Wilson became roommates and their relationship continues 45 years later. "I saw Earl at a baseball card show in Sturbridge, Massachusetts, a few months ago. He's a good man. We spent a lot of time together coming up to the Red Sox through the minors and then in the majors."

SETTLING IN

The 1960 season was Pumpsie Green's first full season with the Red Sox and he appeared in 133 games, playing mostly at second base. He was less of a celebrity and more of a regular member of the team in his second season with the club. "I felt a little more comfortable that second year. You know, the baseball was always easy. It was the rest of it that was hard."

Green remembers many of his teammates with fondness. "Ted was special, and of course Earl and I were close, but there were a lot of good guys on those Red Sox teams. Frank Malzone was a real nice guy. Jackie Jensen was a great athlete and a terrif-ic teammate. I had watched him play football at the University of California, and play for the

Oakland Oaks because I was younger than him. It was great to have him as a teammate.

"Pete Runnels was another great guy. I remember him especially as a great teammate. We had a lot of good guys, but those are the ones who come to mind."

The Bay Area history was helpful to Green in adjusting to Boston. In addition to former basketball rival Bill Russell, Pumpsie connected with another University of San Francisco alumnus, K.C. Jones. "A lot of the Celtics players were a big help getting comfortable with the city. I remember that Bill Russell would have Earl Wilson and I out to his house for dinner at least once a month. It really meant a lot."

At spring training in 1961, it seemed that Pumpsie was poised to move his big league career up to the next level. He played well in pre-season and he was named as the starting shortstop when the team broke camp. On April 21, 1961, he doubled against the White Sox to tie the game, and his home run in the eleventh inning was the game winner, breaking a Red Sox losing streak. But a stomachache in Washington, D.C., in mid-May derailed his career advancement.

"The pain was so bad I called Win Green [Red Sox trainer], and he took me to the hospital. It turned out I had appendicitis and they operated on me. That set me back."

Green was out of the lineup for about four weeks, and it took him even longer to get his full strength back. But he does vividly remember a rare display of power later that season.

"We were in Anaheim and I hit two home runs in one game and then I hit another homer the following night. I remember it so clearly because one of the Los Angeles writers wrote something like, 'How can a weak hitter with a funny name like Pumpsie hit all those home runs, when Mickey Mantle and Roger Maris couldn't do anything like that when the Yankees were here last?'

"That really bothered me. It's one thing to criticize a player when he makes an error and plays badly, but I didn't think what he wrote was fair. So I sat down and wrote him a letter to tell him so. I showed it Vic Wertz, who was a good friend, and asked him what he thought. He agreed with me and told me he would deliver it and tell the writer what he thought as well.

"Well, the next day the writer apologized to me in the paper. I remember it so well because I thought he did the right thing and it meant a lot to me."

WINDING DOWN

By the 1962 season, Green had settled into a key role as a back-up infielder and frequent pinch-hitter. During his Red Sox career he had 22 base hits as a pinch-hitter, the tenth-best total in Red Sox history. But it was his fielding that Pumpsie remembers best.

"I always thought of myself as a better fielder than a hitter. I covered some ground and I had a pretty good arm. When I look back, my favorite memories are of turning a double play, not hitting a home run."

In December 1962, the Boston Red Sox traded Pumpsie Green to the New

York Mets. His career with the Red Sox was over. Today, Green looks back philosophically on his role with the team.

"People will sometimes ask me if I wished I had played for another team. I tell them, no. If I had it to do over, I wouldn't change a thing. I wanted to be a ballplayer and I was able to do it.

"It was tough there from time to time, but it was rough in lots of places in the United States at that time. I always told people I had enough trouble trying to hit a curveball. I wasn't going to worry about some loudmouths."

Green played 16 games at third base for the Mets in 1963. But most of his time during the next three seasons was spent in Buffalo, New York, with the Mets' top farm club. "It was tough adjusting to life back in the minors, but it was still professional ball. And I was playing with and against some good players. All I had ever wanted to be was a professional ballplayer."

Hobbled by injuries, Green decided to call it quits after the 1965 season. "My hip was really bothering me. It was time. I had spent 13 years playing the game I loved at the professional level."

BACK HOME IN THE BAY AREA

After he retired from baseball, Pumpsie went to work at Berkeley High School in Berkeley, California. "I was at Berkeley High until I retired after more than 30 years there. I was a counselor and I coached baseball for over 20 years. I even taught math in summer school. In a school system like that you do a little bit of everything.

"We had some good ballplayers come out of Berkeley. Claudell Washington (17-year major leaguer) played there. Rupert Jones played at Berkeley. We had some good players and a lot of good kids."

Pumpsie, with his wife, Marie, returned to Fenway for the Red Sox 100th anniversary commemoration in 2001 and met up with former teammate, Ted Lepcio, with his wife, Martha.

Pumpsie followed the football career of his younger brother Cornell closely. "He went to Utah State on a basketball scholarship. I remember he came to see me in Arizona during spring training one year. He was trying to decide whether to play pro basketball with the Chicago Bulls or football with the Dallas Cowboys. He wanted my advice.

"I asked him what he really wanted to do. He told me he was leaning towards football. I said, 'Then give it a try. If it doesn't work out, you can always go back to basketball.' It worked out pretty well for him," Green says of the five-time Pro-Bowl defensive back.

"My brother Credell played for the Green Bay Packers for a year. And my brothers Travis and Eddie Joe were good athletes, too. Somebody was always playing ball in our house."

Pumpsie and his wife Marie bought their present home in El Cerrito, California, seven years after his retirement from baseball. The Greens celebrate their forty-eighth wedding anniversary this year.

On the day of his interview, Pumpsie Green was getting ready to attend his daughter Heidi Keisha Green's graduation. "She's getting her Masters Degree from Mills College tomorrow. We're very proud of her. She's so busy it's hard to keep track of her."

Pumpsie is equally proud of his son Jerry who lives in Castro Valley, California. But the clear apple of his eye is Jerry's 14-year-old daughter Brittany. "I try to see her as often as I can. She's very special to us."

Asked if he is a Red Sox fan today, Pumpsie responds emphatically. "Of course I am. They're my team. I want them to beat Steinbrenner's guys and win the whole thing."

Like 99.9% of the athletes who play major league baseball, Pumpsie Green is not headed to the Baseball Hall of Fame in Cooperstown, New York. But if they establish a Good Guys Hall of Fame, he would be a charter member. Pumpsie Green is much more than just an important footnote in the history of the Boston Red Sox.

13.
Gene Conley Interview
April 1998

I met with Gene Conley at the Dedham Hilton Hotel over breakfast. When I called to schedule the interview with the 6'8" Conley, I told his wife Katie to make sure he looked down, because I am only 5'7." Her response was, "I wish I could be there. You're going to look just like Mutt and Jeff."

Fortunately Gene did look down, and we spent two hours talking about his fascinating, two-sports professional career. For six straight years, Gene would play a full season in the NBA, take a couple of weeks to get his arm in shape, and then pitch for a full season in the major leagues. Only an action-figure hero could duplicate that performance today.

I could fill three chapters with all of the great stories that Gene Conley has to tell. His profile includes the best of the lot. The balance of his tales will have to wait for another day.

When it came time to talk about his brief sabbatical from the Red Sox and his attempt to fly to Jerusalem, Gene asked, "Do we have to talk about that? I'm really tired of answering questions about that."

I told Gene that if we didn't address it, readers wouldn't find the story to be credible. I also promised to put it in perspective. I believe that I kept my promise.

In December, Gene Conley dropped me a note telling me about the new book on his life, One of a Kind *(www.advantagebookstore.com). He said that his wife Katie was inspired to write the book after reading my July 1998 profile on Gene in* Red Sox Magazine. *If that is true, even in a small way, it is a terrific outcome.*

GENE CONLEY
TWO-SPORTS STAR

Gene Conley, who pitched for the Boston Red Sox from 1961 to 1963, is the proud owner of one World Series Championship ring, and three NBA World Championship rings. No one else can make this claim, and it is highly unlikely that anyone will ever duplicate his feat.

Conley earned his World Series Championship ring pitching for the Milwaukee Braves in 1957. He earned his NBA World Championship rings during consecutive seasons with the Boston Celtics spanning 1958-1961.

Over the years, there have been a number of athletes who have combined two professional sports. Recently, Deion Sanders and Bo Jackson were able to mix baseball and football careers for several seasons. The late Chuck Connors is better known as the "Rifleman" for his TV series of that name, but he also put together three seasons with the Boston Celtics and a season for the Brooklyn Dodgers in 1951. Danny Ainge spent parts of three seasons as an infielder with the Toronto Blue Jays (1979-81), before deciding to concentrate on basketball with the Celtics.

Gene Conley is the only athlete in history to play two professional sports for *twelve* consecutive sports seasons during a *six-year* span.

OKIE FROM MUSKOGEE

Gene Conley was born in Muskogee, Oklahoma, in 1930, and lived there until his teenage years. "The Depression years were especially rough in Oklahoma. Folks had a tough time scratching out a living. But I was so busy playing every sort of ball game that came along to pay too much attention."

"In 1944 my dad headed out to Washington state to look for work, and the rest of us, my

mother, brother and sister, followed him by train. I don't know if we appreciated how difficult that must have been for him. We ended up in Pullman, Washington, where I went to high school."

Conley did a lot of pitching, but it was his prowess on the basketball court that earned him a scholarship to Washington State. He continued to play both basketball and baseball, and in 1948 he appeared in the Hearst All-Star Game in the old Polo Grounds in New York. His opposing pitcher in that game was Frank Torre, later Conley's teammate on the Milwaukee Braves, and brother of current New York Yankees' manager Joe Torre.

Conley's outstanding pitching at the College World Series in Omaha, Nebraska, in 1951 really caught the major league scouts' attention. This was long before the era of aggressive sports agents, but Gene was fortunate to have his father as an able advocate.

"The Boston Braves showed the most interest. And my father was pretty astute. The Braves offered me $5,000 to sign, and my dad said, 'He'll sign if you'll agree to bring him to spring training with the big leaguers from the beginning, and then when the Braves get into the World Series, the Braves will agree to fly my wife and I to the Series.' Bill Marshall [long-time Braves scout] got the approval from Boston and I signed on the dotted line."

FAST-TRACK TO BOSTON

In 1951 he was a 20-game winner with the Hartford (Connecticut) Chiefs in Class A ball. He was named Minor League Player of the Year and promoted to the major league club in 1952. "I really wasn't ready, but the Braves wanted to get a look at me at the highest level. The big leaguers hit me pretty good in the few games I pitched, and I got sent back down to the Triple A club in Milwaukee. But I did get to pitch at old Braves Field, and at 6'8", I was the tallest player to appear in the big leagues up to that time."

Following the 1952 season, Conley received a call from Boston Celtics coach and General Manager Red Auerbach asking if he was interested in playing for the team. "Bill Sharman [former Celtics great and Los Angeles Lakers coach and General Manager] had seen me play basketball in college, and recommended me to Red. To be honest, I wasn't even sure who the Celtics were. I made the team, but I didn't play a whole lot since I had limited college experience. I was pretty amazed by the high level of talent on that team and throughout the league."

The Braves left Conley with their top farm club in Toledo, Ohio, for the 1953 season. When he earned the Minor League Player of the Year honors for the second time, he was ticketed for the big leagues to stay. Since his future was clearly in baseball, Conley declined the Celtics' offer to return for the 1953-54 season.

His rookie season with the Braves, now relocated to Milwaukee, yielded a 14-9 record, and All-Star honors. He finished second in the Rookie of the Year balloting in the National League, losing out to Wally Moon of the St. Louis Cardinals, but finishing one slot ahead of teammate Hank Aaron, who would go on to establish the all-time major league home run record.

He started even stronger in 1955, running his record to 11-3 before the All-Star Game. "I was named to the National League All-Star team again, but I hurt my arm pitching in a game in early July. I felt something let go in my shoulder, and my catcher, Del Crandall, came running out because he could hear my shoulder pop from 60 feet away. I pitched eight more years in the big leagues but, to be honest, my arm was never the same again."

Sore shoulder and all, Conley was called upon to pitch the twelfth inning of the All-Star Game, which was held in Milwaukee that year. "That was probably the highlight of my big league career. I struck out the side and Stan Musial hit a home run in the bottom of the twelfth to win it, so I was the winning pitcher."

Arm troubles limited his pitching for the balance of the 1955 season, and his win total fell to eight in 1956. "I had lost about a yard off my fastball, and I got by with my high leg kick and pretty good control. I had to make the transition from a power pitcher to more of a finesse pitcher."

The 1957 season was a personal disappointment for Conley (he went 9-9), but it was a high-water mark for the Braves in Milwaukee. "We beat the Yankees in a seven-game World Series, and the people in that city couldn't do enough for us. Every time we turned around, they were doing something else to honor us. Those early years in Milwaukee, from the time we moved there in 1953, were really unique. People would drive up and leave a case of beer on your front porch because they were so happy you had come to their city."

DOUBLING-UP

In 1958, Conley's pitching career reached a new low. His arm had gotten worse instead of better, and he was only able to pitch 72 innings. At the end of the season, he called Red Auerbach and told him he wanted to come back to the Celtics. It is hard to comprehend in this era of multi-million dollar contracts, but Conley wanted to return to the hardwood courts because he needed to pay his mortgage.

"I had used my World Series share to start building a new house in Milwaukee. Before we finished it, I realized I was running out of money. I called Red and he said, 'Gene, you've been away from the game for five years, and I don't think you can make this team. But if you'll pay your own way to training camp, I'll give you a tryout.' I told my wife that I had to figure out a way to make the team because we needed the money!

"I wasn't that surprised that Red told me I had to pay my own way. He used to make us buy our own sneakers when the pair the Celtics gave us wore out. Red was pretty shrewd about money."

Conley did make the 1958-59 Celtics and he averaged 15 to 20 minutes of playing per game, mostly at forward. The Celtics reclaimed the World Championship that they had lost to the St. Louis Hawks the previous year, and Conley headed off to Florida for the first of several unique spring training sessions.

"By the time the basketball playoffs would end, my baseball teammates would be leaving spring training to start the regular season. Depending on the timing, I might overlap with them for a few days, but mostly I was on my own to get in baseball shape. I had to recruit players to practice with and against.

"I used to pitch to some of the old ballplayers like Hall of Famers Paul Waner and Edd Roush. It was a pretty unusual sight. They would wear their old-time uniforms—it was sort of like having my own '*Field of Dreams*.' The ball club would call after a week or so and ask me if I was ready. I would always tell them 'yes' because I didn't want to miss out on anything."

While Conley was busy contributing to the Celtics' NBA championship, the Braves traded him to the Philadelphia Phillies. The change in scenery seemed to agree with him as he posted a 12-7 record and was selected to his third National League All-Star team. As soon as the 1959 baseball season ended, Conley rejoined the Celtics in a successful quest for their second straight championship. "I remember when we went in to Philadelphia to play the Warriors [who moved to San Francisco after the 1962 season], some of my teammates from the Phillies like Robin Roberts and Richie Ashburn would sit behind our bench and give me the high sign. That was a lot of fun."

BACK TO BOSTON

He had pitched well for the 1960 Phillies, but at the end of the season, the team traded him to the Boston Red Sox. In what baseball humorists have called "the biggest two-man trade in baseball history," the Red Sox traded 6'7" pitcher Frank Sullivan to Philadelphia for the 6'8" Conley. When informed of the trade, Sullivan earned his place in Red Sox folklore by uttering the immortal words, "I am in the twilight of a mediocre career."

The two-sport athlete as a member of the Red Sox, 1961-3 (left) and the Celtics (1952-53, '58-61). Photos courtesy of Gene Conley.

By this time the Conley entourage consisted of Gene, his wife Katie, three young children, a station wagon, and a 60-foot trailer. As Boston's first two-team professional athlete, the Conley family sited the trailer in Foxboro, Massachusetts, beginning a relationship with that town that lasted for about 40 years. Today it is hard to visualize a player who is a starting pitcher for the Red Sox and an important backup for the Celtics living in a mobile home, but Gene remembers that it worked well for his family.

The 1960-61 Boston Celtics produced their third-straight NBA title, and Conley contributed coming off the bench again. "Red Auerbach used to say 'Gene Conley is a great back-up at center for Bill Russell.' Of course, Russell played 47 out of 48 minutes, and I was going in mostly for Tommy Heinsohn, but I didn't contradict Red very often."

The Celtics won their championship in early April 1961 and two weeks later Conley defeated the Washington Senators 6-1 in his first appearance at Fenway Park. The two-week turnaround in sports seems amazing, but Conley puts it in perspective.

"You have to remember that I was in excellent shape. After all, I had been running up and down a basketball court for six months. I wasn't a regular with the Celtics but Red ran a very strenuous practice. My challenge was simply to get my arm in shape."

Conley won 11 games for the 1961 Red Sox, and he remembers that team fondly. "We didn't do that well in the standings [sixth place], but we had some very good players. Frank Malzone was an outstanding third baseman. He used to say to me, 'If it's hit to the left side, all I want you to do is duck. I'll take care of everything hit over here.' And of course Yaz was a rookie, and we knew right away that he would be a great one."

The Celtics did not protect Conley in the 1961 expansion, and rather than join the new Chicago NBA entry that had selected him in the draft, he elected to play for New York in the fledgling American Basketball Association. "That was another great experience. They played wide-open basketball in that league. We would run down to our basket and let it fly."

The 1962 season was his best with the Red Sox, as he posted 15 wins for the eighth-place team. His win total matched teammate Bill Monbouquette's in victories and he led the Red Sox staff in innings pitched.

That season also featured his well-chronicled, unauthorized leave of absence from the team. The Red Sox bus was caught in a mid-Manhattan traffic jam, and he and teammate Pumpsie Green got off to search for a men's room. Conley was next heard from three days later when he surfaced at a New York airport attempting to buy a ticket for Jerusalem.

Asked what he remembers best about the incident Conley responds, "Tom Yawkey's understanding and kindness. He called me into his office and said, 'Gene, we would all like to do what you did. But we can't. Now I'm going to fine you $1,500, but if you stay in line for the rest of the year, I'll give it back.' I did, and he did. Good thing too: we really needed the money."

Conley has a thoughtful response to the question: why Jerusalem? "Religion has always been a very important part of my wife Katie's life. I honestly felt that if I spent some time in the Holy Land, I would have a better understanding of what religion means to her."

Following the 1962 baseball season, Conley returned to the NBA, this time with the New York Knicks. His stint with the Knicks represented his tenth back-to-back season over five years.

The next season would turn out to be his last in baseball. "My arm was sore from 1955 on, but it really hurt in 1963. The Red Sox were good to stick with me that whole year. A couple of my teammates had terrific years in 1963. My old roommate Billy Monbouquette won 20 games. He was an outstanding pitcher. And Dick Radatz pitched as well as any pitcher ever has. He threw what I call a 'small ball.' By the time it got to the plate it looked about as big as a pea to the hitters."

The 1963 season also featured an unusual mound matchup of NBA players. Gene Conley was the starting pitcher for the Red Sox on April 27 and in the fourth inning the Chicago White Sox brought in pitcher Dave DeBusschere as a relief pitcher. DeBusschere had just finished his rookie season with the NBA's Detroit Pistons. DeBusschere ultimately put his baseball career on hold, going on to stardom with the New York Knicks.

WINDING DOWN

Gene Conley played throughout the 1963-64 season with the New York Knicks, but the successive seasons were starting to take their toll on his body. When he could barely throw the following year, the Red Sox released him in spring training.

"I wasn't trained to do anything but play ball, so I called the Cleveland Indians to see if I could catch on with them. They let me pitch a couple of games in the lower minors to see if I had anything left. It was pretty obvious, even to me, that I just couldn't pitch any more.

"So here I am in this little town in the middle of nowhere, with no idea of what I was going to do next. I noticed there was a church service next to the hotel I was staying at, and I dropped in to think things through. Before I knew it I was crying my eyes out, I was so discouraged. A kindly gentleman slid over beside me and whispered, 'What's the matter son? Did you lose your dad or your mom?'

" 'No sir,' I sobbed. 'I lost my fastball!' "

After 13 years of earning his living as a professional athlete, Conley was faced with the prospect of having to find a regular job. "The late Paul Cohen, who was the president of Tuck Tape, had always told me to give him a call when I was through with sports. When I called him up, he said, 'I was wondering when you would call!' He set me up as his regional sales manager for this territory, and I spent the next year calling on companies all over the area."

"Then he advised me on how to set up my own operation as a manufactur-er's representative handling industrial packaging supplies. My wife Katie and I ran our little company, Foxboro Paper, for over 35 years."

LOOKING BACK

His eight combined seasons of professional baseball and basketball give him a unique perspective on the two sports. He acknowledges that basketball players are better all-around athletes, but he is adamant that baseball is much harder to play at the professional level.

"Baseball requires a much greater skill set to perform at the highest level. No knock on professional basketball players, because they are wonderful athletes, but basketball is a pretty basic game. In baseball you have to be able to throw, to run and hit, and you have to be aware of all of the game situations. The really great baseball players, Warren Spahn, Early Wynn, Hank Aaron, talked the game, studied the game, and learned everything they could about the game.

"When Michael Jordan tried his hand at baseball, I got a lot of calls from the media. I told them all that Michael didn't have a prayer. My wife said, 'Maybe you shouldn't say that. Maybe he'll be terrific.' I told her there is no way he is going to be able to hit a baseball.

"Why am I so sure that professional basketball is the easier game to play? Because I was able to play it."

Asked to name the greatest all-around athlete he saw during his career, Conley selects the late Dodger, Jackie Robinson. "I played with and against some marvelous athletes. But Jackie Robinson could do it all. He could hit and field,

The proud grandfather with his wife, Katie, and their seven grandchildren in a recent photo. Pictured left to right from the top: Gene, III, Patti, Kimberly, Katie, Stacey, James and Ryan.

but he really intimidated the other team running the bases. He was a great football player, and a track and field star. He stood out."

Today Conley's passion is his family. The Conleys have been married for over 50 years and they have three children and seven grandchildren. "My son Gene Jr. is a urologist in California. My daughters Kitty and Kelly are both nurses. All of our kids ended up in the healthcare field. We visit with our grandkids as often as possible."

A favorite trivia question for long-time Boston sports fans is: who played for the Red Sox, Celtics, and Bruins? The humorous answer is organist John Kiley.

But Gene Conley really did play for the Boston Braves, Red Sox and Celtics. And he played at a very high level throughout his professional sports career. We shall not see his like again.

Gene Conley's Major League Sports Career

Baseball		Basketball	
1952	Boston Braves Milwaukee Brewers	1952-53	Boston Celtics
1953	Hartford (Minor league Player of the Year)		
1954	Milwaukee Braves (All-Star)		
1955	Milwaukee Braves (All-Star)		
1956	Milwaukee Braves		
1957	Milwaukee Braves		
1958	Milwaukee Braves	1958-59	Boston Celtics
1959	Philadelphia Phillies (All-Star)	1959-60	Boston Celtics
1960	Philadelphia Phillies	1960-61	Boston Celtics
1961	Boston Red Sox	1961-62	New York (ABA)
1962	Boston Red Sox	1962-63	New York Knicks
1963	Boston Red Sox	1963-64	New York Knicks

14.
Carl Yastrzemski Interview
June 1999

My time with Carl Yastrzemski has to rank among my most unusual interview sessions. For openers, I sat with him in the visitors dugout at Fenway Park and I didn't have the presence of mind to ask him if he had ever been interviewed in that spot before.

Yaz had come to Boston a few weeks before the 1999 All-Star Game to film a commercial for the Fan Fest scheduled at the Hynes Auditorium as part of the celebration. Fenway Park was empty, except for the crew shooting the commercial, on a beautiful weekday morning. I was scheduled to interview Yaz during a break in the production.

I certainly enjoyed watching the activity on the field behind third base for the first 30 or 40 minutes. How often does a Red Sox fan get to sit in a nearly empty ballpark and watch one of the team's all-time greats up close and personal? But after about one hour the wait for Yaz began to get a little monotonous.

If anyone ever tells you that making a commercial is exciting, sit for two hours while they shoot a 30-second spot sometime. Even if it is in Fenway Park, even if it is Yaz, after a while it becomes like watching paint dry.

It appeared that the only person with less patience for the process was Yaz. Joe Mooney, the legendary Fenway groundskeeper, was watering the infield and asked Yaz if he was going to play golf that day. His response was, "Yeah. If we ever finish this." Mooney gradually edged closer and closer to the production unit with his hose. Fairly quickly, the producer announced that he had what he needed, and I had my time with Yaz.

I knew that Yaz had already missed his tee time, but he couldn't have been more gracious with his time and the thoughtfulness of his answers. I just wish I had asked him if he had ever been interviewed in the Fenway Park visitors dugout before.

CARL YASTRZEMSKI
ALL-STAR MEMORIES

Carl Yastrzemski was selected to his first American League All-Star team in 1963. Thirty-six years later he still clearly remembers walking into the locker room at Cleveland's old Municipal Stadium.

"Bill Monbouquette, Frank Malzone and Dick Radatz were all selected along with me. When we got to the park, the first player I saw was Al Kaline [Detroit Tigers future Hall of Famer]. I looked across the room and there was Brooks Robinson and Elston Howard. I was just a 23-year-old kid. I was in awe.

"When I got to our dugout, across the way I see Willie Mays and Roberto Clemente. Then I spotted Stan Musial, who was my idol growing up as a kid. I remember being a little overwhelmed."

Carl's other strong memory of his first All-Star selection involves the late Red Sox owner Tom Yawkey. "When [Bill Monbouquette], Frank [Malzone], Dick [Radatz] and I were picked for the 1963 team, Mr. Yawkey made it a point to stop by the locker room to congratulate us. He was a great person, and a great owner, but more than anything, he was a great baseball fan."

ALL TIME ALL-STAR

The term All-Star and the name Carl Yastrzemski are virtually synonymous. Yaz was selected for the American League All-Star team 18 times. He was the honorary Captain of the American League All-Star team in 1989. His batting accomplishments in 14 All-Star appearances place him among the elite in the history of the game. In Red Sox history, only the legendary Ted Williams with 18 appearances in 16 seasons (Williams played in both All-Star Games held in 1959 and 1960) has a comparable All-Star record.

The 1999 All-Star Game at Fenway Park brought Yaz back to Boston as one of one hundred players selected for the All Century team. Taking a break from his role as honorary chairman of the most successful "All-Star Fan Fests" in baseball history, he recalled his All-Star memories.

"Back when I was playing, it was really only a one-day event. Now it goes on for several days, and the fans have a lot more opportunity to get involved. My only regret is that we don't have a bigger ballpark here in Boston so more fans could see the games and the other activities."

THE EARLY YEARS

Carl Michael Yastrzemski succeeded Ted Williams as the Red Sox left fielder in 1961. Yastrzemski had been a three-sport standout at tiny Bridgehampton High School on Long Island, New York. He enrolled at Notre Dame University on a combination baseball and basketball scholarship in the fall of 1957. Yaz's college aspirations were put on hold when he signed with the Boston Red Sox during the Thanksgiving break of his sophomore year.

The first professional baseball stop for Yastrzemski was the Red Sox Class A team in Raleigh, North Carolina, for the 1959 season. His .377 batting average easily topped the league and earned him a promotion to the top Sox farm team in Minneapolis. His .337 batting average in Triple A, and the retirement of Ted Williams at the end of 1960 bought him a one-way ticket to Fenway Park. His career with the major league club was to last through 23 memorable seasons.

Replacing Ted Williams in left field and in the hearts of Boston Red Sox fans was a Herculean task for any player, let alone a 20-year-old with two years of professional baseball experience. Ted Williams was a larger-than-life figure on and off the field. It is often said, only partly in jest, that the late actor John Wayne only *wished* he could be Ted Williams.

Yaz in 1961, his rookie year.

Laboring under the lengthy shadow cast by the memory of Williams, Yaz batted .266 in his rookie year, and improved to .296 with 43 doubles in his second season in 1962. His All-Star selection in July of 1963 heralded his break-through season when he led the American League with a .321 batting average while playing outstanding defense in left-field.

Yaz's continued success earned him All-Star honors in 1965 and 1966. His first six seasons in the major leagues had established him as one of the star players in the game. But his 1967 season would propel Carl Yastrzemski to a place among the elite players in the history of the game.

THE IMPOSSIBLE DREAM TEAM

The 1967 Boston Red Sox assembled in Winter Haven, Florida, for Spring Training under rookie manager Dick Williams with little fanfare. The team had finished in ninth place the year before and the "experts" in Las Vegas had assigned them a 1-in-100 chance to win the American League pennant.

The first sign that things might be different appeared when rookie Pitcher Billy Rohr came within an Elston Howard single of pitching a no-hitter in his major league debut at Yankee Stadium. Rohr's hopes for a no-hitter were kept alive in the ninth inning when Yaz made a sensational catch of a Tom Tresh line drive.

"One of the big differences in 1967," Yaz recalled, "is that I was able to work out the preceding winter. In earlier years, I was finishing up my college work. But I had completed my degree at Merrimack College so I had time to focus on my conditioning. I reported to spring training in great shape."

By the time the 1967 All-Star game rolled around, Yaz was among the top five in the American League in batting average, home runs, and runs batted in. The Red Sox were only six games out of first place at the All-Star break, and it was clear that the team had as good a shot at the American League pennant as anyone.

When he looks back at the 1967 All-Star Game held in Anaheim, California, one fact stands out for Yaz. "I remember we had four guys on the team. I was on it, along with Rico [Petrocelli], Tony [Conigliaro], and Lonnie [pitcher Jim Lonborg]. To me, it was an acknowledgement that we were a team to be reckoned with. We had arrived."

Fellow All-Star Rico Petrocelli has fond memories of Yastrzemski's 1967 All-Star Game performance. "The game started in the twilight [4:15 PDT] and the hitters were having trouble seeing the pitches. That is, all the hitters except Yaz. He had a remarkable ability to tune out any distractions. Every time I looked up that day, it seemed he was on base. He was like that all year."

The 1967 American League All-Stars managed only nine hits over 15 innings as they fell to their National League counterparts 2-1. But Yaz rapped out two singles and a double hitting in the shadows on a sultry, 92-degree day. His two walks for the day meant he had accounted for five of the eleven American League base runners.

The 1967 Red Sox held New England fans spellbound all summer and into the fall, as they battled for first place in the most exciting pennant race in American League history. Their thrilling win over the Minnesota Twins on the last day of the season touched off one of the great celebrations in Boston history. While a different Red Sox hero seemed to emerge daily, the one constant was Yaz.

Former teammate George Scott remembers it this way, "Yaz hit 44 homers that year, and 43 of them meant something big for the team. It seemed like every time we needed a big play, the man stepped up and got it done."

The storybook season came to an end when the St. Louis Cardinals won the World Series four games to three, but Carl Yastrzemski's place was indelibly etched in baseball folklore. Yaz came within one vote of a unanimous selection as the Most Valuable Player of the American League. He was selected by *Sports Illustrated* as the "1967 Sportsman of the Year" at year-end. And he achieved baseball's "Triple Crown", leading the American League in batting, runs batted in, and home runs. In all the baseball seasons that have followed, no other player has been able to match his Triple Crown feat.

ALL-STAR MVP

Between 1965 and 1979, Yaz was named to 15 consecutive All-Star teams. The game he remembers best is the 1970 All-Star Game held in Riverfront Stadium in Cincinnati. That game was one of the most hotly contested match-ups in All-Star history.

"I remember that I started out in left field, then I was shifted to center, and I finished the game at first base. What I remember most is Pete Rose crashing into Ray Fosse [Cleveland catcher] to score the winning run for the National League in the twelfth inning." Almost as an afterthought, he mentions, "I won the MVP trophy that night. I gave the trophy to [then] President Nixon, and now it is in his library in California."

Yaz had four hits, to go along with a run scored and a RBI to earn his MVP honors that year. He and Ted Williams [1946] are the only two American Leaguers with four hits in an All-Star Game. Never one to focus on personal statistics, when asked about this record, Yaz responds, "I never knew that before. To tell you the truth, I was so sick of losing to the National League that I didn't pay much attention to that stuff."

It is sometimes written that Yaz had a "career year" in 1967, but never again approached that standard. It should be noted that in 1970 he led the American League in runs scored, on-base percentage, total bases, slugging average, and he came within .0001 of winning the batting title. When coupled with his all-time high of 23 stolen bases, you have a year that would have been a career year for almost any other player.

Those 23 stolen bases made him only the second player in Red Sox history to steal more than 20 bases *and* hit more than 20 home runs in a single season. Former All-Star outfielder Jackie Jensen was the first Red Sox player to achieve this combination in 1954, and Jensen duplicated this feat during the 1959 season.

THE LATER YEARS

In February 1971, Carl Yastrzemski signed a three-year contract that was reported to pay him $500,000 over the three seasons. At that time his contract was the largest in baseball history.

Yaz returned to the All-Star team each year from 1971 to 1974. In 1971 he earned his sixth Gold Glove for fielding excellence, and in 1974 he led the

American League in runs scored. But the next All-Star Game that stands out in his memory is the 1975 game played in Milwaukee.

"What I remember best is being a teammate of Hank Aaron. He was finishing out his career as a designated hitter with the Brewers, and it was just great sitting with him on the bench after seeing him across the diamond all those years.

"I got into the game as a pinch-hitter and homered off Tom Seaver. My home run tied the game 3-3 so it felt pretty good. The thing that still kills me is that he [American League Manager Alvin Dark] didn't put me in to play left field. The guy he put in there [Claudell Washington of the Oakland A's] made a couple of errors that cost us the game. I think I could have made a difference in the outcome. I was really sick of losing to the National League at that point."

Yaz's play throughout the post-season in 1975 reminded fans that he had always been at his best in clutch situations throughout his career. After playing first base during the regular season to make way for emerging superstar Jim Rice, Yaz returned to left field after Rice was injured in late September. Carl Yastrzemski played his old position in virtuoso style as he helped lead his team to a three-game sweep over the defending champion Oakland A's in the Championship Series. His stellar play in the field and at bat continued into the World Series against the Cincinnati Reds. Although the Red Sox lost to the Reds in seven games in one of the greatest World Series ever played, Yaz had scored 11 runs, and batted .350 during the 10 post-season games.

From 1976 to 1983, Carl Yastrzemski made the American League All-Star team six times. On July 14, 1977, he notched his 2,655th hit, moving past Ted Williams as the all-time Red Sox base hit leader. In 1979, he became the first American Leaguer to accumulate more than 3,000 lifetime hits *and* over 400 career home runs.

His final All-Star game in Chicago in 1983 really stands out in his mind. That game marked the 50th anniversary of the first All-Star game, and

Always close to the Yawkeys, Carl posed with Mrs. Yawkey during the 1989 Yaz Day ceremonies at Fenway when the Red Sox officially retired #8.

the National League brought a streak of 11 straight victories into the game.

"I had made up my mind to retire at the end of the season, so I knew it was my last All-Star game. What I remember about the game is that Fred Lynn [his former Red Sox teammate] hit a grand slam homer to break the game open for us. I knew then that I was going out an All-Star game winner. It was a great feeling."

HALL OF FAMER

On October 1, 1983, the next-to-the-last game of the season, 33,491 of the Fenway Faithful gathered to pay tribute to Carl Yastrzemski. The pre-game ceremony lasted for about an hour, and then came Yaz's turn to speak. After 23 years of never flinching in a pressure situation, Yaz broke down and cried when he stepped to the microphone.

A final farewell to the fans as Carl closed out his brilliant 23-year career with the Red Sox in 1983.

Once he regained his composure, he asked for a moment of silence for his mother and for former Red Sox owner Tom Yawkey. After thanking his family and everyone connected with the Red Sox, he finished with the words, "New England, I love you."

Yaz then broke into a victory lap along the perimeter of the entire ballpark. He reached out and touched as many hands as he could along the way. "I wanted to show my emotions," he said in the clubhouse after the game. "For 23 years, I always blocked everything out. I wanted to show these people that deep down, I was emotional for all that time."

In January of 1989, in his first year of eligibility, Carl Yastrzemski was elected to Baseball's Hall of Fame. His vote total that year was among the highest recorded in the history of the Hall of Fame.

If anyone worried that Red Sox fans would forget Yaz

after his retirement, those fears were assuaged at the time of his Hall of Fame induction ceremony. On a picture-perfect Sunday afternoon in July, an estimated 25,000 fans crowded the lawn around the Hall of Fame to pay tribute to Yaz. Before the ceremony, recordings of Jess Cain (former Boston radio personality) singing *"Caaarl Yastrzemski . . . Caaaaarl Yastrzemski"* echoed from one edge of the crowd to the other.

Fellow inductees Johnny Bench [Cincinnati Reds catcher] and Red Schoendienst [St. Louis Cardinal second baseman] were greeted warmly by the crowd. But the greatest crowd response was for Carl. He acknowledged Ted Williams, who was seated on the stage with his fellow Hall of Famers, with the following story:

"I remember in 1961 when I was a scared rookie, hitting .220 after the first three months of my baseball season, doubting my ability. A man was fishing up in New Brunswick. I said, 'Can we get a hold of him? I need help. I don't think I can play in the big leagues.' He flew into Boston, worked with me for three days, helped me mentally, and gave me confidence that I could play in the big leagues. I hit .300 for the rest of the season. I'd like to thank Ted Williams."

EPILOGUE

Carl Yastrzemski retired after 23 seasons with some of the greatest offensive statistics ever compiled [see box next page]. But many fans remember him for his standout defensive play, especially for his earlier years in left field, as well. When asked about his career highlights, the seven-time Gold Glover recalls two fielding plays.

"I remember the throw I made to get Bob Allison [Twins] at second base in the last game of the 1967 season. And I remember cutting off Reggie Jackson's line drive in the 1975 playoffs in Oakland. Those are the plays that stand out to me."

The baseball careers of Ted Williams and Carl Yastrzemski are inexorably linked. Their paths crossed directly for the last time when they were introduced before the 1999 All-Star Game at Fenway Park as two of the 100 greatest baseball players of the 20th century. The crowd reaction when Yaz was introduced shook the ballpark to its ancient foundations. The response of the crowd when Ted was driven from the far reaches of centerfield to a spot near the pitchers' mound nearly equaled the decibel count of the jet fly-by following the National Anthem.

Carl Yastrzemski was selected to replace Ted Williams in left field for the Boston Red Sox in 1961. Today, more than 40 years later, it is abundantly clear that no one will ever replace Ted Williams in the hearts of Red Sox fans. But it is equally clear that Carl Yastrzemski has rightfully earned a place alongside Ted as one of the greatest all-around ballplayers to ever grace the game of baseball.

Carl Michael Yastrzemski: the man we affectionately call Yaz.

Carl Yastrzemski's Ranks in
Major League Baseball History

CATEGORY	CAREER TOTALS	ALL-TIME MLB RANK
Games Played	3,308	2nd
At-Bats	11,988	3rd
Base on Balls	1,845	6th
Base Hits	3,419	6th
Doubles	646	7th
Extra Base Hits	1,157	8th
Total Bases	5,539	8th
RBI	1,844	11th
Runs	1,816	15th
Home Runs	452	27th

Source: MLB.com 2004

15.
Dick Radatz Interview
February 1999

I interviewed Dick Radatz over lunch at J.C. Hillary's in Dedham, Massachusetts. We all know that Dick Radatz is a big man, he comes by the nickname "The Monster" honestly, but you don't realize how big he is until you stand next to him. Once you adjust to his size, the next surprise is how smart he is.

Most of us have heard Dick Radatz on sports talk radio speaking, in his words, on behalf of "the old bastards." But that is his media persona. Speaking with him one-on-one, his views are much more thoughtful and sophisticated.

Dick is justifiably proud of the fact that he stuck around and earned his degree from Michigan State. He played in an era when there were very few college graduates playing major league baseball. And he put his degree to good use in business when his playing days were over.

Radatz is adamant that he didn't blow out his arm pitching so often in the 1962 to 1964 seasons. His profile describes the reasons for his rapid decline after three glorious seasons.

Two facts will probably surprise you about Dick Radatz. First, he is as graceful as any man I have ever seen on the dance floor. Second, we split a couple of appetizers over lunch and never did get around to ordering entrees. So much for stereotypes about big men.

DICK RADATZ
"THE MONSTER"

What stands out in Dick Radatz's memory as he reflects on the 1963 All-Star Game is the fact that he was the first pure relief pitcher to earn All-Star status. "I was the first pitcher ever named to an All-Star team who had never started a game in the big leagues. I was proud of that distinction then, and I'm still proud of it today."

Radatz recalls walking into the American League locker room in Cleveland's Municipal Stadium and being in awe of the talent assembled. "My locker was next to Mickey Mantle's, and I looked around the room and saw future Hall of Famers like Al Kaline of the Tigers, and Brooks Robinson of the Orioles. I remember saying to myself, 'What am I doing here?' Then I got into the game for the last two innings and struck out five National League All-Stars. That was really the first time I realized how important pitching in relief had become."

The fact that Dick Radatz struck out five National League All-Stars is impressive by itself. When you add the fact that three of those five strikeout victims are now enshrined in baseball's Hall of Fame it is even more impressive. Radatz struck out the San Francisco Giants' Willie Mays and Willie McCovey, and Duke Snider of the Los Angeles Dodgers. All three of these former greats can now be reached care of Cooperstown, New York.

"THE MONSTER"

At 6'6" and 240 pounds, his fans knew Dick Radatz affectionately as "The Monster." From 1962 to 1964, the sight of Dick Radatz lumbering in from the bullpen to the pitcher's mound struck fear in the hearts and minds of American League batters.

It might be an exaggeration to say that this former Red Sox star invented the role of "stopper" or "closer." But it is no exaggeration to say that while pitching for the Red Sox between 1962 and 1964, Radatz established a standard for relievers that has seldom, if ever, been equaled.

During this three-year period Radatz led the American League in saves twice while pitching for teams that never reached the .500 levels. His total of 118 wins or saves accounted for more than 50 percent (see next page) of the Red Sox victories. Adding to this feat is the fact that Radatz was pitching under the "old" saves rule. In his era, a reliever had to face the winning or tying run, or pitch two perfect innings, to earn a save. Playing under the liberalized save rules of today, his total would have been even higher.

Year	Wins	Saves	Total Wins and Saves	Red Sox Wins	Radatz Wins and Saves as % of Red Sox Wins
1962	9	24	33	76	43%
1963	15	25	40	76	53%
1964	16	29	45	72	63%
TOTAL	40	78	118	224	53%

But raw statistics tell only a small part of the story. To truly understand how dominant Radatz was in his prime, you need to hear from his contemporaries.

Johnny Pesky first joined the Boston Red Sox in 1942 and he managed Radatz during the 1963 and 1964 seasons. Dick Radatz contributed to the majority of his team's wins during Pesky's two-year tenure.

"I have seen all of the great relievers over the years, and I'm here to tell you that Dick Radatz was as good as any of them. When he was in his prime, he was virtually unhittable. I'll never forget the feeling of standing on the mound at Fenway and watching that guy coming in from the bullpen to save another game. When he took the mound, you felt there was no way you could lose. I don't know where we would have been without him."

Former Red Sox pitcher Gene Conley was a 15-game winner in 1962. "It gave me a great feeling to see that big guy coming in to relieve me. He was as good as any reliever I have ever seen. My only regret is that he didn't come up a year earlier. I might have won more than 11 games in 1961."

But the superlatives aren't limited to his former manager and teammate. Ralph Houk, who managed the New York Yankees during Radatz's prime, called him "the greatest relief pitcher I have ever seen."

MICHIGAN STATE SPARTAN

Dick Radatz grew up in Berkley, Michigan, a small town just outside of Detroit where he excelled in basketball and baseball during high school. "I was a pretty good pitcher, but, to be honest, my first love was basketball. At 6'6", I was a big man for the times, and I could jump pretty good."

Radatz went to Michigan State on a combination basketball-baseball scholarship, and he was the starting center role on the freshman team. He really thought that his future was in basketball rather than baseball.

"I was doing just fine, but in the middle of the season, a player by the name of Johnny Green came out of the service and joined the team. The first time we both went up for a rebound, his hands were so far above mine that I knew my dreams of basketball stardom at Michigan State were over. I didn't feel too badly because he [Green] went on to make All-American, and he had a great career in the NBA with the New York Knicks."

Radatz decided to concentrate on his pitching career, and putting together a

great career with the Spartans. He made All-American in his senior year, and earned his degree in 1959.

The Red Sox signed him upon graduation and assigned him to their Raleigh, North Carolina, farm club. Former Red Sox catcher Russ Gibson remembers catching Radatz in Dick's first professional game.

"Dick had an unbelievable fastball. He had great control of it, and it just exploded in on the hitters. The hitters couldn't touch him for a few innings. Finally they got a few hits off of him, and I figured we would mix it up a little bit. I put down two fingers for the curve ball, and Dick shook me off. I gave him the sign again, and he still shook me off.

"Finally I went out to the mound and I said, 'I know you went to college, so you must know that two stands for a curve ball.' Dick said, 'I don't have a curve ball. Just keep putting down one finger for the fastball, and I'll take care of the rest.' That's what I did, and he just blew them away!"

Radatz did well as a starter in Raleigh, and he continued to excel in 1960 with the Red Sox farm team in Minneapolis. When he reported to spring training in 1961, he was hoping to be a starter for manager Johnny Pesky in Seattle, the Red Sox' top minor league entry.

"My arm was a little sore that spring," Radatz recalls, "and I was holding back, but Pesky finally used me for four innings and I struck out 11 batters. He came to me after the game and told me they were going to bring me to Seattle, but as a reliever. I said 'Don't do that to me, Johnny. I'm a starter.' "

John Pesky has the same memory. In 1961, every pitcher wanted to be a starter. "He was all upset that he was going to the bullpen. Of course, this was before the importance of a closer had really caught on. There had been some great relievers like Johnny Murphy with the Yankees, and Jim Konstanty of the Phils, but going to the bullpen was still viewed as a demotion. You know, he really found a home in the bullpen, and he did a lot to define the role of the closer in baseball."

THE ULTIMATE STOPPER

Radatz dominated the Pacific Coast League with Seattle in 1961, and he earned a spot with the major league team the following season. The 1962 Boston Red Sox finished in eighth place in the American League, but their rookie pitcher led the league in relief wins (9), pitching appearances (62), and saves (24). Manager Mike "Pinky" Higgins often brought him in for the seventh inning of a tight game and left him in to finish the game. In his first season, he averaged two innings per appearance in his league-leading 62 games.

In 1962, Higgins took his strategy of letting Radatz finish his games to a whole new level. Radatz came in to start the seventh inning in New York at Yankee Stadium, and nine innings later he was still on the mound. He left for a pinch-hitter in the sixteenth inning and ended up with the win as the Red Sox scored six runs for a 9-3 victory.

When Johnny Pesky took over as the Red Sox manager in 1963, he knew how important Radatz was to the ball club. "There was one time I had used him six or seven games in a row. I told him to stay home so I wouldn't be tempted to use him. Darned if he doesn't show up in the middle of the game. We end up going into extra innings, and I can hear him popping fastballs in the bullpen. I finally brought him in for the thirteenth inning, and of course we won the game. I don't even want to think about where we would have finished without him."

Dick Radatz recalls the 34th All-Star Game in 1963 with fondness. "The National League had beaten us in 11 of the previous 17 games, and with hitters like Willie Mays, Hank Aaron, and Roberto Clemente, they were pretty tough. But we hung in there. Frank Malzone singled to drive in a run, and then scored the tying run in the third inning."

"I felt terrific when manager Ralph Houk brought me in for the top of the eighth. We were only down 4-3, and they had their best hitters coming up, so he showed a lot of confidence in me. As it turned out, I gave up a single to Bill White [St. Louis Cardinals first baseman and future National League President], and Ron Santo eventually brought him around with a bloop single. But with five strikeouts in two innings I felt pretty good about my performance. I finally realized that relief pitchers were an important part of the game."

One of Dick Radatz's great moments came against the New York Yankees. He came on in ninth inning relief against the Yankees with the bases loaded, no one out, and the Red Sox clinging to the lead.

"I struck out Roger Maris, Mickey Mantle, and Elston Howard on ten pitches. I was so excited, I threw my arms up over my head, and that became my trademark for the rest of my career."

The Red Sox improved one notch in the standings to seventh place in 1963, and Radatz posted 15 relief wins to lead the league, finishing second to Baltimore Orioles relief ace Stu Miller with 25 saves. His 162 strikeouts in 132 innings equaled 1.23 strikeouts for each inning pitched. Confirming the increased recognition of the importance of relief pitching, Radatz finished fifth in the balloting for the Most Valuable Player in the American League.

It is hard to believe, but Radatz actually improved upon his 1963 statistics the following season. In 1964, he appeared in 79 games, led the major leagues with 29 saves, and won 16 games for an eighth-place Red Sox team. His selection to the 1964 All-Star team was a forgone conclusion.

1964 ALL-STAR GAME

The 35th edition of the "midsummer classic" was held at Shea Stadium in New York right next door to the World's Fair. "The game was a big deal that year", Radatz remembers. "We really wanted to take the game back from the National League. Their domination had gone on long enough." But the game would turn out to be Dick Radatz's worst baseball memory.

A crowd of over 50,000 fans was on hand for the festivities, and they cheered every move of former hometown favorite Willie Mays. The American League managed to take the lead 4-3 in the top of the seventh, and American League manager Ralph Houk brought in Dick Radatz to hold the National League at bay. Radatz proceeded to retire the National Leaguers 1-2-3 in the seventh inning and to duplicate this feat in the eighth inning.

"I felt great that day. I walked Willie Mays to open the inning, but I had two strikes on him, and he fouled off five pitches before I lost him. I remember when

With teammate Don Schwall.

he was trotting to first the crowd cheered so hard that I could feel the ground shaking. I thought 'Boy, this is really exciting!' I was really into it.

"Then Willie stole second, and Orlando Cepeda singled him in to tie the game. But I was still in control out there. We got a couple of more outs and then I walked Johnny Edwards [Cincinnati catcher] intentionally. Up steps Johnny Callison of the Phils," Radatz remembers.

"In those days, they gave a brand new Corvette to the MVP of the All-Star Game. When the inning began, I was all but in the driver's seat of that 'Vette. Well, Johnny Callison turned on my fastball and drove it into the stands for the game-winning home run. The National League had its victory, and Johnny Callison had himself a new Corvette. Years later when I saw Johnny at an old-timers game, he said, 'Man, I never saw a car back out of one garage and into somebody else's so fast in all my life.' "

Despite his All-Star Game disappointment, Radatz picked up where he had left off and finished the 1964 season with his fastball blazing. He ended the year with 181 strikeouts in 157 innings and a sparkling 2.29 earned run average. He led the American League in games finished with a remarkable total of 67.

THE LATER YEARS

The following season was a major disappointment for Dick Radatz and for the Red Sox. He did manage nine wins in 1965 to go with a respectable 22 saves, but his earned run average nearly doubled, and the once dominant closer became merely mortal.

After more than 200 appearances and 400 innings during a three-year period, the sense was that Radatz had been burned out. "That wasn't it at all," Radatz counters. "The fact is that in spring training I worked hard to develop a sinker to go with my fastball and slider. I wanted a pitch to get the left-handed contact hitters out, and I was sure the sinker was the answer. What happened was I changed the angle of my delivery and my whole motion was out of whack. The season was almost over before I realized what had happened.

"In today's game I would have looked at videotape of my delivery and spotted it right away. But we didn't have any of that technology in those days."

When he got off to a slow start in 1966, the Red Sox traded him in June to the Cleveland Indians for pitchers Lee Stange and Don McMahon. Radatz pitched reasonably well for the Indians but, in the spring of 1967, Cleveland traded him to the Chicago Cubs where he struggled with his control. "Ultimately, I went to a psychiatrist who hypnotized me. After that I threw everything over the plate, which created a different problem," laughs Radatz.

Dick Radatz finished out his major league career with the Montreal Expos in 1969. "My son Dick, Jr., who was 10 at the time, said 'Dad, do you think we could go fishing?' All of a sudden it dawned on me that I was missing seeing my family grow up. I knew it was time to quit."

LIFE AFTER BASEBALL

After a successful sales career in the Detroit area, he returned to the Greater Boston area in 1984. "Gerry Moses [former Red Sox catcher] had me come back for a fundraiser. I remember going to a Celtics game at the Boston Garden and the fans gave me a standing ovation. I told him that more people recognized me in Boston in one hour than had recognized me in Detroit in 10 years. I always had an affinity for Boston and the fans, and they have reciprocated over the years."

Radatz is a regular on local TV and radio outlets, and he is a partner in National Pastime Legends, which conducts training programs for youth baseball coaches in the area. His son Dick Jr. owns and operates a summer collegiate baseball league in the Midwest, his daughter, Leigh, runs a coronary care unit at Massachusetts General Hospital, and his daughter, Chris, lives back in Michigan and is the mother of his two grandchildren.

Asked if he reflects on the Johnny Callison 1964 home run when he watches the All-Star Game each year, he responds, "I used to wake up in the middle of the night screaming when I would dream about it. Now I can laugh about it. I just try to enjoy the game."

Dick Radatz was inducted into the Boston Red Sox Hall of Fame in 1997. His save total of 104 games ranks second to Bob Stanley on the Red Sox all-time pitching records, and his 49 victories in relief is second to Stanley as well.

Dick Radatz has served as the pitching coach for the North Shore Spirit during 2003 and 2004. He serves under manager John Kennedy, former Red Sox super sub, working with the pitching staff of this Lynn-based Northeast League team.

In his prime, Dick Radatz was one of the premier relief pitchers in the history of baseball.

Radatz at the 1984 Old-Timers' Game at Fenway Park.

16.
Dick Williams Interview
April 2002

I sent Dick Williams a letter telling him that I would call him on April 27, 2002, and outlined the topics I would like to cover. Unfortunately the letter went astray and when Williams answered the telephone for all he knew I could have been a telemarketer. But he never missed a beat and filled two hours with some wonderful memories and outspoken comments.

Throughout the interview, his wife of 50 years, Norma Williams, was at his side perfecting his observations and letting him know if he went too far. Dick is quick to acknowledge that Norma is entitled to sainthood for putting up with him all these years.

Dick Williams spent his last two years in the major leagues as a utility player for the 1963-64 Boston Red Sox. When he took over as the rookie manager of the Boston Red Sox in 1967, he knew that he had to get rid of the country club atmosphere. He had his players working on fundamentals throughout spring training camp in Winter Haven, Florida. The most famous Williams in club history, Ted, left camp early muttering about pitchers playing volleyball.

While I talked with Dick, the television in my adjacent room was following Derek Lowe's no-hitter against Tampa Bay. Dick got a big kick out of that development and it brought back to him memories of Billy Rohr's one-hitter in Yankee Stadium on Opening Day in 1967.

Dick Williams tends to be very outspoken, so we let Norma Williams decide what was on- and off-the-record. His on-the-record quotes tell a very colorful story.

DICK WILLIAMS
MEMORIES OF THE IMPOSSIBLE
DREAM TEAM

When Dick Williams took over as the new manager of the Boston Red Sox at the beginning of spring training in 1967 he was determined to change the direction of the ballclub. The team had placed ninth in the American League during the two previous seasons, and the club had not finished within 20 games of first place since 1959.

"I wanted to get the team working together as a unit. And I wanted to emphasize the fundamentals I had been taught as a young player in the Brooklyn Dodgers organization. I knew I had to make some very dramatic changes."

No one in baseball considered the Red Sox to be serious contenders for the 1967 pennant. Asked what he remembers of the team's chances at the time, Williams recalls, "I knew we had a lot of good young talent. Reggie Smith, Mike Andrews, and Gibby [Russ Gibson] had all played for me in Toronto and we had won the International League Championship the previous two years. And I had played with Carl Yastrzemski, Tony Conigliaro, and Rico Petrocelli when I was with the Red Sox in 1963 and 1964, so I knew that we had a decent nucleus."

Dick Williams took that nucleus, along with a number of timely additions by General Manager Dick O'Connell during the season, and shaped it, cajoled it, and browbeat it into a pennant contender. By the end of the season the team had captured the hearts of New England *and* the American League pennant.

ROOKIE MANAGER

"Before we even got to spring training, I eliminated the position of team captain. It was important that the players knew there was only one boss: me. Early on, two of our pitchers showed up late for the workouts. They tried to blame it on the hotel telephone operator. Claimed they never got their wakeup call. I fixed that pretty quickly. I told the hotel to wake up every player at 7 A.M.

"I knew that to get ready for the season, we had to use every minute of spring training. The players were used to going their own way. There was no commitment to fundamentals. On the day of the first full squad workout, I gathered the players around the on-deck circle and told them they were going to re-learn the game inch-by-inch, and base-by-base."

The team wrapped up spring training with a 14-13 record in the Grapefruit

League. Asked for a prediction for the upcoming season, Williams responded: "We'll win more than we'll lose."

The Red Sox opened the 1967 season at Fenway Park, splitting a two-game series with the Chicago White Sox. The team then journeyed to New York for the Yankees' home opener. That game provided the first sign that this would be a special year for the Boston Red Sox.

Dick Williams started rookie left-hander Billy Rohr against the Yankees. Catching him was another rookie, Russ Gibson. Both players were making their major league debut. Rohr's sinker had the Yankee hitters beating the ball into the ground and he held the Yankees hitless through eight innings.

"I still think about that game. Rohr retired their first two batters in the ninth inning easily, and veteran Elston Howard was coming up. I went out to the mound to settle him [Rohr] down and give him some advice on pitching to Howard.

"Howard lined a 3-2 pitch into right field, and the kid ended up with a one-hitter. I still wonder if I had left him alone, whether he would have gotten the no-hitter. He only won two more games in the big leagues, and my move might have cost him the memory of a no-hitter."

THE IMPROBABLE DREAM

The team went 8-6 in April, and right fielder Tony Conigliaro and shortstop Rico Petrocelli both ended the month with batting averages of .333. During May, the Red Sox played .500 ball (14-14) and all 10 American League teams were within ten games of one another. The Detroit Tigers had a one-half game lead over the White Sox, while the Red Sox held third place, four and one-half games off the pace.

Yankee Stadium produced another indication that this would be a different Red Sox year on June 21, 1967. In the second inning of that memorable game, Yankee pitcher Thad Tillotson hit Red Sox third baseman Joe Foy on the batting helmet with a fastball. Since Foy's grand slam home run the previous evening had led the Red Sox to a 7-1 win, there was little doubt that Tillotson's pitch had a purpose.

In the bottom of the second inning, Red Sox pitcher Jim Lonborg nailed Tillotson on the shoulder with a pitch. At that point, both benches emptied. And both bullpens emptied. It was very obvious that this Red Sox team would not go down without a fight.

"Jim Lonborg had a tremendous year for us," Williams offers. "He learned to pitch inside and he made himself into one of the best pitchers in the American League. All year long, whenever we had to have a win, he was the guy who got it for us."

As the 1967 All-Star Game approached, the Red Sox were very much in the hunt for the American League pennant. But when Jim Lonborg took the mound for the last game before the annual three-day break, the team had lost five straight.

"I think Lonborg's performance in that last game before the break was a turning point. He shut the Tigers out for seven innings and we went on to win 3-0. It meant we finished out the first half of the season on a winning note. When we came back from the break, we went on our long winning streak. Lonborg's win was the start of our drive for the pennant."

At the halfway point in the 1967 season, Williams was right on track with his spring training prophecy: the Red Sox had won 41 and lost 39. To many, he seemed like an overnight sensation, but his path to becoming the youngest manager in the American League had taken quite a few twists and turns.

ST. LOUIS NATIVE

Dick Williams was born in St. Louis, Missouri, on May 7, 1929. As a youngster he played all sports, but baseball was always his first love.

"We lived close to old Sportsman's Park where the Cardinals and the Browns [now the Baltimore Orioles] played. They both had Knothole Gang clubs that let kids in for free. You were supposed to be at least 10 years old, but every year from the time I was seven I would grab my older brother Ellery's pass and act like I was 10. I used to leave school at 3:15, and get to the ballpark about the second inning."

The country was in the midst of the Depression when Williams was a young fan, so buying a baseball bat was out of the question. One of Williams' favorite baseball memories is the day that former St. Louis Cardinals star outfielder Pepper Martin gave him a broken bat. "I ran all the way home, and then I started worrying how my parents would feel about it. But my dad found some tape and helped me reconstruct my bat. Years later, I met Pepper Martin and thanked him for the bat."

The Williams family moved to Southern California when Dick was a teenager. After starring in baseball and football at Pasadena Junior College, he signed a minor league contract with the Brooklyn Dodgers in 1947.

MAJOR LEAGUER

A highly-regarded prospect, Williams made it to the big leagues in 1951. The Dodgers of that era were a powerhouse, winning six pennants between 1947 and 1956. Williams remembers that only Jackie Robinson made an effort to make the young rookie feel comfortable.

"That team had been very successful and they were very close. No one made an effort to make me feel welcome as a rookie—no one except Jackie Robinson, that is. Maybe he realized how tough it is to fit in. Whatever it was, he went out of his way to make me feel welcome and I will always remember that."

The following season, shortly after Williams had won the starting leftfielder's job, disaster struck. Diving for a routine fly ball, Williams wound up with a three-way shoulder separation. Following that injury, he went from being a highly-prized prospect to a well-traveled big league jack-of-all-trades.

"In the next 11 years, I was traded six times, spent time with five different organizations, and played four different positions. And I had to become a smarter player. I spent a lot of time studying strategy and human nature. That injury put me on track to become a manager."

Williams spent his last two major league seasons as a part-time player with the Boston Red Sox. "The place was a country club. Players showed up when they felt like it and took extra work when it didn't interfere with a card game," Williams told his biographer Bill Plaschke.

At the end of the 1964 season, then Red Sox Farm Director Neil Mahoney offered Williams a spot as a player/coach for the Red Sox Triple A farm team in Seattle. When the Seattle franchise was moved to Toronto prior to the 1965 season, Williams was named to manage the club. Dick Williams' return to Fenway Park was only two years in the future.

THE IMPOSSIBLE DREAM

When play resumed after the All-Star break, the 1967 Red Sox were in fifth place, six games out of first place in the American League. The team got off on the right foot by taking three out of four from the defending American League champion Baltimore Orioles. The Red Sox closed out an abbreviated homestand by sweeping the pennant-contending Tigers in a two-game series. The team was starting to jell.

"We went down to Baltimore and Jim Lonborg beat them in the series opener with a great effort," Williams recalls. "Then we beat them again the next night. We would have swept them three straight, but the final game was rained out before it became official.

"When we got to Cleveland we had won six in a row, and then we beat them on Friday night and Saturday afternoon. After we swept the Indians in a double-header, we headed back to Boston with a 10-game winning streak.

"We couldn't believe it when we landed at Logan Airport and saw the crowd of fans waiting for us. All I could think was that there were more fans there than the team averaged at Fenway the year before. There were more fans there [estimated by the Massachusetts State Police at between 10,000 and 15,000 fans], than we drew on opening day."

In 1967, the hit Broadway musical of the day was *Man of La Mancha*, featuring the hit tune "Impossible Dream." *The Boston Globe* had first used the term "Impossible Dream" to describe the team in a headline following a particular thrilling June victory. Once the team returned home with their 10-game win streak, seemingly every future reference was to the "Impossible Dream Team."

The California Angels snapped the team's win streak on July 25, but the club remained in second place through the end of the month. On July 31, Carl Yastrzemski's batting average of .322 led the team and ranked third in the American League. Yaz was clearly setting the pace for the team.

"Carl Yastrzemski had the best season in 1967 that I have ever seen. And I have watched a lot of baseball. He reported to training camp in wonderful shape. He had worked out all winter.

"I think that inwardly he was relieved not to have the role as team captain. He played great all season long that year. Time and again he came through when we had to have a hit."

At the beginning of August, Red Sox General Manager Dick O'Connell acquired veteran Yankee catcher Elston Howard to provide stability for the

Williams referred to Dick O'Connell (left) as "the best general manager I ever played under."

upcoming pennant drive. This followed an earlier O'Connell trade for starting pitcher Gary Bell, and the acquisition of super-sub Jerry Adair.

"I can't say enough about the job Dick O'Connell did for us that year," Dick Williams states emphatically. "Every time we needed a player, Dick went out and got him for us. He was instrumental in our success that year. And he was the best general manager I ever played under."

MANAGER OF THE YEAR

The Red Sox remained within four games of the American League lead throughout August, and by the end of the month they had climbed to first place. Dick Williams was pulling out all the stops by then. He was one of the first baseball managers to use videotape.

"Dick O'Connell arranged with one of the TV stations to borrow their equipment. We used it to tape George Scott batting. We wanted to show him that he was going after bad pitches and to show him that he was putting on weight. When we showed it to George all he said was, 'That's not me.'"

September produced the greatest pennant race in the history of the American League. The Red Sox remained in first place or within one game of first place, throughout the month. With one week remaining in the season the Red Sox, White Sox, Tigers and Twins all remained in the hunt.

"I remember with just a couple of games left, the White Sox were playing Kansas City in a doubleheader. The only way I could follow the games was to sit in my car and listen. I went out to my car with a six-pack of beer. When the second game ended, my six-pack was gone and so were the White Sox. Kansas City took both games."

Asked what he remembers about the last weekend of the season when the Red Sox swept the Twins to win the American League pennant, Williams replies, "I remember Yaz getting a base hit just about every time he came to the plate. I remember Jim Lonborg coming through for us one more time. And I remember Dalton Jones coming through with a big hit. That's the way it was all year. A different player coming through for us every day.

"And I remember listening to the second game of the Tigers' doubleheader, first in Tom Yawkey's office and then in our clubhouse. When the Tigers lost and we had the pennant outright, we really celebrated. We left the clubhouse around midnight, and the fans were still dancing in Kenmore Square."

The Red Sox took the heavily-favored St. Louis Cardinals to a seventh game in the World Series, but the Cardinals won Game Seven behind Bob Gibson's third great pitching performance of the series. "I pitched Jim Lonborg in the seventh game on two days rest because he was the one who got us there and he deserved a chance to see if he could win it. I just wish he had three days of rest. He and Gibson would probably still be pitching."

MANAGERIAL CAREER

The 1968 Red Sox never really did get on track. Star right fielder Tony Conigliaro missed the entire season following his tragic beaning in August, 1967, Jim Lonborg broke his leg skiing during the offseason, and pitcher Jose Santiago blew out his arm in mid-season.

The team improved slightly in 1969, but Dick Williams was replaced as manager with nine games left in the season. "It's tough to go from 'Manager of the Year' to out of a job in that short period of time," Williams reflects. "But you move on."

In 1971 Dick Williams took over as manager of the Oakland Athletics, managing for three years under the A's colorful owner Charlie Finley. "We had orange baseballs, multicolored uniforms, and a lot of fun," Williams recalls. "And we won a World Series which is the greatest thing that you can do in baseball."

Williams's next stop was with the California Angels where he managed for three seasons. In 1977, Dick headed north of the border where he managed the Montreal Expos for five seasons.

He moved to San Diego in 1982, managing the Padres to their first World Series appearance in 1984. His final managing position was in Seattle where he managed the Mariners in 1986 and 1987.

During his 21 years as a major league manager, Dick Williams won 1,571 regular season games. In the history of major league baseball, only 15 managers have won more regular season games than Dick Williams.

Dick Williams' last managerial role was for the West Palm Beach Tropicals in the short-lived Senior League. The co-owner of the Tropicals was current Red Sox Principal Owner, John Henry. "John Henry was a terrific owner and a great fan," Williams remembers. "He's a good man," he adds.

For a number of years Dick Williams was an advisor to the New York Yankees. In 2002, he was doing color for UNLV and the Pacific Coast League Las Vegas 51s.

A KINDLER, GENTLER DICK WILLIAMS?

One of Dick Williams' former players is quoted as saying, "Dick Williams was the best manager I ever played for. But as soon as I'm out of baseball, I'm going to get in my car and run him over!" Reminded of the quote, Williams chuckles. "I know who that was, and we're friends today. A lot of my players didn't like me. Some of them even hated me. But every single one of them cashed his World Series check."

Asked if he has mellowed, Williams repeats the question aloud. Norma, his wife of 50 years, shouts an emphatic "No!"

Today Dick and Norma Williams live in a suburb of Las Vegas, Nevada. He is still plain spoken but clearly he is a family man. "When I started out managing in Toronto, money was so tight that we couldn't afford to move the whole family there. Norma sent our oldest child Rick, who was 10 at the time, to live with me so I wouldn't be so lonesome.

"Rick made friends with all of the neighbor kids and there would be a whole bunch of them over for lunch everyday. The problem was I didn't have enough money to feed them and myself. I spent the whole season making a meal out of the clubhouse food.

"Rick [who will be forever known to longtime Red Sox fans as

the team's batboy "Ricky"] is a scout for the Montreal Expos. He has been a major league pitching coach, and he lives in St. Petersburg, Florida. He has a son Willie and a daughter Marissa. Our daughter Kathi lives in California with her three children Erika, Matt, and Leo, Jr. She graduated from Duke and she is a research scientist. Our son Marc graduated from Seattle University. He lives in the area so we get to see a lot of him."

Dick Williams has warm memories of Red Sox fans. "I always loved the Red Sox fans. They are great fans. Wherever I go, I tell people that Boston sports fans are the best anywhere. And not just baseball, that includes basketball, hockey and football, too. I'll always remember the great Red Sox fans."

And it is certain that Boston Red Sox fans will always remember Dick Williams, rookie manager of the 1967 American League pennant-winning Impossible Dream Team.

17.
Rico Petrocelli Interview
July 1997

I was scheduled to interview Rico Petrocelli at McCoy Stadium in Pawtucket, Rhode Island. At the time he was the hitting instructor for the Red Sox Triple A affiliate, working with players who hoped to make the one-hour trip to Fenway Park.

When I caught up with Rico, he was standing behind the batting cage watching the PawSox hitters take batting practice. He apologized for being tied up and I told him not to worry about it. It may have only been the minor leagues, but I was happy to follow him around for a couple of hours.

As we headed for the PawSox dugout it was obvious that he was the most recognizable person on the field. Cries of "Rico . . . Rico" echoed throughout the stands of the half-filled ballpark.

While Rico reflected on his 13 seasons with the Boston Red Sox, he patiently signed autographs for the many fans who dangled their requests from the roof of the PawSox dugout. He also took time to introduce me to Red Sox pitching prospect Carl Pavano. I thought then, and I still think today, that Pavano would look awfully good in a Red Sox uniform.

Boston Red Sox fans have a great deal of affection for Rico Petrocelli. Not only do we associate him with the memorable teams of 1967 and 1975, but also he came to Boston as a young man and he elected to make his home among us.

RICO PETROCELLI
MEMORIES OF THE IMPOSSIBLE
DREAM TEAM

As Rico Petrocelli, hitting coach for the Pawtucket Red Sox, steps into the home dugout, a middle-aged fan, with two youngsters in tow, leans over the railing and shouts, "Rico, I just want to say thank you for that catch on the last play of the '67 season!"

"Thank you for remembering, I appreciate it," Rico smiles in response. "That happens all the time," Rico marvels. "It was over 30 years ago, but lots of fans talk about it as if it was just yesterday."

Moments earlier, Rico's familiar number "6" had been perched beside the batting cage where he offered the young PawSox batting tips and encouragement. He spent the most time with 21-year-old Michael Coleman, who had just been brought up a level from the Trenton farm club. "The kid has the same compact swing that I had. He reminds me a lot of myself at his age."

BROOKLYN BORN

Americo Peter "Rico" Petrocelli was born in Brooklyn, New York, on June 27, 1943. He grew up in the Sheepshead Bay section of the city, the youngest of five brothers.

"All of my brothers were good athletes, but when they were younger they all had part-time jobs to help out with the family. As the youngest, I was able to concentrate on sports, and baseball in particular. My brothers would come to my games and cheer me on. I owe them a lot."

Rico's association with the Red Sox goes back over 40 years but, growing up, he was a New York Yankees' fan. His allegiance to the Yankees went with the territory.

"When I was younger, the Dodgers were still in Brooklyn, and the Giants were still in New York, so we followed them as well, but after they both moved to the West Coast, it was all Yankees in our house. My brothers would take me to Yankee Stadium when the Red Sox came to town because we wanted to see Ted Williams hit, but we always rooted for the Yankees."

By age 15, Rico had already attracted the attention of the baseball scouts. After an outstanding schoolboy career, legendary Red Sox scout Bots Nekola signed him one week shy of his eighteenth birthday. His choice of the Red Sox may not have been popular in his Sheepshead Bay neighborhood, but Rico had begun an affiliation with the Red Sox that would last a lifetime.

LIFE IN THE MINORS

Rico began his Red Sox career in the low minors at Winston-Salem, North Carolina. It was quite an adjustment for a city boy.

"I was used to the pace of New York City, and I couldn't believe how slowly things happened down there. It was a big adjustment. I even saw my first cow!"

But he handled the cultural and baseball adjustments well, and the following season he was advanced a notch to the Reading farm club. At the end of the Reading schedule, the Red Sox brought him to Boston for the last two weeks of the 1963 major league season.

"Being called up to the big leagues at age 20 was a big thrill for me. I got to travel with the club and to see the difference between life in the majors and life in the minor leagues. I even got my first big league base hit."

The following year, Rico was installed as the starting shortstop for the Red Sox farm team in Seattle. Clearly he was on the fast track to Fenway Park. Despite an injury-plagued 1964 season with Seattle, Rico went to the 1965 Red Sox spring training camp in Scottsdale, Arizona, with a "can't miss" label firmly attached to his brief minor league resume.

WELCOME TO THE SHOW

If you talk to a Red Sox fan who remembers that Rico began his big league career in Boston as a switch-hitter, you have located a real student of the home team.

That famous catch! 1967

When an injury hampered his swing in 1964, he moved over to the left side of the plate. He did well enough that he continued the practice at the beginning of his rookie season. But Rico was blessed with a swing from the right side that was tailor-made for Fenway Park.

The switch-hitting experiment was quickly abandoned, and the result was 210 lifetime major league home runs.

"We didn't have a very good team in 1965. In fact, we lost 100 games. But I was getting to play regularly, and I was learning quickly. In retrospect, I could have used another year or two in the minors, but I was learning the game at the highest level of baseball. One thing I learned was that I hated to lose!"

The 1966 Red Sox posted a 72-90 record, and finished in ninth place in the American League standings. That season stands as one of the low points in Boston Red Sox history. Interest in the team had fallen dramatically, and attendance had dropped off to about 10,000 fans per game.

"Our record in 1966 was terrible, but we had guys like Yaz, Lonborg, and Tony Conigliaro who were ready to become stars, and young guys like George Scott, Joe Foy, and myself, who were really starting to develop. We knew we had a brighter future than our record showed."

THE IMPOSSIBLE DREAM TEAM

When rookie Red Sox manager Dick Williams arrived at spring training in 1967, he was committed to building a winning team, and to changing the team's image as a losing franchise. One of his first acts was to appoint Rico Petrocelli as the unofficial captain of the infield. He told Rico, "Take charge out there. You're the veteran of this crew, and I want you to move people around."

"Dick showed a lot of confidence in me, and gave me a lot of responsibility. It really meant a lot to me. For the first time I really felt like a big leaguer, like I really belonged up there."

Still only age 23 when the 1967 season began, Rico anchored the young infield defensively, and stepped up his production at the plate. By the end of June, he was batting .296 with 8 home runs, and 32 RBI. His performance earned him a spot on the 1967 American League All-Star team.

When the Fourth of July rolled around, the Red Sox were within four games of first place, close on the heels of the Tigers, Twins and White Sox. Best of all, the Red Sox chances were a prime topic of conversation around New England, and twice as many fans were showing up at Fenway Park compared to 1966.

"We surprised a lot of people," Rico recalls, "but *we* weren't surprised as a team that we were in the thick of it. Nobody really noticed, but we had played well as a team in the second half of 1966. We were a little surprised that neither the Tigers nor the Twins opened up a big lead, but we expected to be competitive from the very beginning."

Asked when he knew they were serious contenders, Rico responds, "After we won 10 games in a row on the road in late July, we knew we were in it to stay. I'll never forget the crowd that met us at Logan Airport when we got back from

Cleveland after winning our tenth straight. They announced on the plane that there was a big crowd waiting for us, but we thought maybe that meant about 500 people. When we got there and looked out at 10,000 fans waiting for us, we were in shock."

All the world loves an underdog, and at 100-1 to win the pennant, the Red Sox were the longest of long-shots. And the team kept coming back just when they were counted out. In late August they were down 8-0 against the California Angels but rallied to win 9-8. One week later, Jose Tartabull and Elston Howard collaborated to nip the White Sox' Ken Berry at the plate for the final out in a crucial victory.

"We all couldn't wait to get to the park every day. It was just a great place to be that year. The fans were so excited and so supportive. If you made a mistake, you could hear them say 'that's all right . . . you'll get them the next time.' You ask if the fans make a differ-ence? They made a *tremen-dous* difference that year."

OCTOBER 1, 1967

It seemed only right that the Red Sox storybook season would come down to the final day. The team had lost two games to the lowly Cleveland Indians earlier in the week, but the White Sox faltered, the Tigers lacked a knockout punch, and the Red Sox turned back the Minnesota Twins on Saturday to set up Sunday's showdown.

Rico remembers the mood in the clubhouse before that game as upbeat. "We were deadly serious about beating the Twins, but we were also very loose. We felt like we had already exceeded everybody's expectations, so we had nothing to lose. We took the field expecting to win, but we were not tight."

The game provided all of the drama that anyone could have hoped for, and the ending that all Red Sox fans longed for. Trailing 2-0 in the bottom of the sixth, pitcher Jim Lonborg dropped down a perfect bunt that ignited a five-run Boston rally. The Red Sox brought a 5-3 lead into the ninth inning, and all of New England collectively held its breath to see if the Impossible Dream could really come true.

The inning got off to an inauspicious start as a Ted Uhlaender's ground ball took a bad hop, and nailed Rico Petrocelli directly under his right eye. After get-ting the okay from trainer (and subsequent team owner, Buddy LeRoux) Rico insisted on staying in the game. The next hitter, the ever-dangerous Rod Carew, grounded sharply to second baseman Mike Andrews. Andrews tagged Uhlaender and threw to George Scott at first to complete the double play.

Only pinch-hitter Rich Rollins stood between the Red Sox and their first share of the pennant in 21 years. Rico remembers, "Lonnie threw him a pitch that rode in on Rollins' hands. He tried to turn on it, but he was jammed, and all he could do was lift a weak popup in my direction. It may have been my easiest chance of the year, but it seemed to stay up there forever. What I remember most is the silence . . . there were 36,000 people there, and no one made a sound. When it landed in my glove, I squeezed it as hard as I could."

Within seconds of his catch, at least 5,000 fans had vaulted the railings to begin the wildest celebration ever held at Fenway Park. The fans lifted winning pitcher Lonborg on their shoulders and paraded him triumphantly towards right field.

"I started towards Lonborg, but the crowd had taken him almost immediately. I ran for the safety of the dugout, still holding the ball. We never anticipated that mob scene on the field. I gave it [the ball] to Jim when he finally made it to the clubhouse."

1967 WORLD SERIES AND BEYOND

Rico and his mates fought the good fight in the World Series against the St. Louis Cardinals, which immediately followed the season finale. In Game Six, his fourth inning home run preceded round-trippers by Reggie Smith and Carl Yastrzemski. The three home runs in one inning set a World Series record. His two home runs in that game helped to force a seventh game showdown. But the heavily-favored Cards ultimately prevailed as the journey of the Impossible Dream team came to an end.

Over the next eight seasons, Rico established himself as one of the premier infielders in major league baseball. In 1968, his production dropped off, along with that of most of his teammates. But 1969 was probably his best season in the major leagues.

"I turned 26 that season and I had matured in a lot of ways. I had been learning on the job and things came together for me. I finally got my swing where I wanted it to be."

In 1969 he was named to the American League All-Star team for the second time. That season he hammered out 40 home runs to establish the American League standard for shortstops that lasted until Alex Rodriguez powered 42 homers in 1998. He finished in the top 10 in the American League in 10 major offensive categories.

His fielding prowess kept pace with his improvement in offensive production. His 14 errors in 154 games tied the American League record for the fewest errors by a regular shortstop. This remarkable combination of hitting and fielding earned Rico seventh place in the American League MVP balloting, even though the Red Sox finished a distant 22 games behind Eastern Division winner

Baltimore.

Rico followed up his breakthrough 1969 season with 29 home runs in 1970. That season he led the American League with 10 sacrifice flies, he ranked fourth in extra base hits, and he went over the century mark in RBI for the first time with 103.

THE HOT CORNER

In 1971, Rico faced a major defensive adjustment. After 10 seasons in professional baseball, playing almost exclusively at shortstop, the Red Sox asked him to move over to third base.

"It was an adjustment, to be sure. But the Red Sox had brought in Luis Aparicio, who was one of the greatest defensive shortstops in the history of the game. I knew he had to be the everyday shortstop.

"And at least I was playing on the same side of the infield. I was used to seeing the ball come off the bat at that angle. The tough part is that at short you have time to adjust, but at third base you only have time to react. But I think I did okay there."

To Red Sox fans, Rico's shift to third seemed better than okay. Playing in a career-high 156 games, he committed only 11 errors for the season. And his offensive didn't suffer at all. His 28 home runs ranked fourth in the American League, his 56 extra base hits placed him third, and his 91 walks was fourth best.

By the time the 1972 season rolled around, Rico was a fixture at third base. He continued to field his new position well and his offensive production con-

tinued at a high level. A succession of injuries curtailed his playing time over the few seasons, but Rico Petrocelli and the Red Sox seemed synonymous to Red Sox fans.

When the Red Sox magic season of 1975 got underway, Rico and his long-time friend Carl Yastrzemski were the only players remaining from the 1967 season. "That 1975 season was so great," Rico recalls. "It was different than 1967 because we knew we would be in the running coming out of spring training. But we had two great young players in Jim Rice and Fred Lynn. And when you are winning, the enthusiasm rubs off on you."

Rico shook off a beaning that season and played a steady third base for 115 games that season. In that year's exciting World Series against the Cincinnati Reds, he was a defensive stalwart, and batted a sparkling .308. "That was such an exciting series. I really thought we were going to finally get that World Championship."

Petrocelli was bothered by inner-ear problems in 1976, and his playing time and offensive production suffered as a result. He was hopeful of earning a spot as a utility player in 1977, but the Red Sox gave him his outright release on March 26 that year.

LIFE AFTER BASEBALL

Following his release from the Boston Red Sox during spring training in 1977, Rico has applied his talents to a number of activities. In addition to coaching at the minor league level, he has enjoyed a successful career in radio and television. He has become a fixture on the local scene, providing insight on past and present Red Sox teams.

From 1986 to 1988 he coached and managed in the Chicago White Sox minor league system, leading their Birmingham entry to their league championship in 1987. In 1992 he managed the PawSox, he continued to work in the Red Sox minor league system from 1993 to 1995, and in 1996 he took over as the PawSox hitting coach. Under his tutelage, the 1996 Pawtucket club established an International League record for home runs, and produced the highest batting average and slugging average in franchise history.

Rico and his wife Elsie have been married for over 40 years, and they lived in Lynnfield, Massachusetts, for most of their married life. The Petrocellis currently live in southern New Hampshire, and Rico maintains an office in Nashua. The common thread in all of his business ventures is some connection with baseball. They have four grown sons, and Rico finds the experiences with his boys to be helpful in understanding the issues of the minor league players he worked with over the years.

When asked at what point he and his family first thought of Boston as home, Rico replies, "Without a doubt it was during the 1967 season. People made us so much a part of their lives that we felt as if we belonged here. We would be out to dinner and people would come over and say, 'we don't want to bother you, but we want to thank you for a great season,' or 'good luck tomorrow.' They made us feel so much at home that we knew we would never leave."

RED SOX HALL OF FAMER

Rico Petrocelli was inducted into the Red Sox Hall of Fame on September 8, 1997, along with eight other distinguished past Red Sox players and former General Manager Dick O'Connell. Rico's fellow inductees included former teammates Dick Radatz, Luis Tiant, and Carlton Fisk.

"It was a great honor to be included within that distinguished group. That was easily the most important distinction in my baseball career. It was almost overwhelming."

Asked if he could speak to Red Sox fans personally what would he say, Rico answers, "I would thank them for me and for my family for their constant support over the years. It has meant an awful lot to all of us. Every one of us connected with the Red Sox organization wants very much to bring a World Championship to Boston. The Red Sox fans of New England deserve it."

18.
Conigliaro Family Interview
July 2002

I interviewed Billy and Richie Conigliaro about their big brother Tony at the Tides Restaurant & Pub on Nahant Beach. Driving through the North Shore to get there, I couldn't help but think of how closely Tony C. was associated with the area. Tony spent his earliest years in Revere, learned to play baseball in East Boston, and eventually the family moved to Swampscott.

It was moving to hear how much the memory of Tony means to his two brothers. They shift from one story to the next, sometimes finishing the other's sentences. There is a mix of love, sadness, and quite often humor, in their stories.

One point that Billy and Richie emphasized over and over was how hard Tony worked at his career. "You always read about Tony dating some attractive young lady, or hanging around the clubs, but we saw him at home working out. He was always coming up with some contraption to strengthen his wrists or his forearms."

The other point that Billy and Richie hammered home was how important family was to Tony C. "For all of us, family has always been the most important thing in our lives and it always will be."

Tony C. was a proxy for every youngster who grew up in New England dreaming of stardom with the Boston Red Sox. He was the best player on your sandlot team; the one you always thought that would make the grade. Lots of younger brothers worship their big brother. But nobody does it better than Billy and Richie Conigliaro.

TONY CONIGLIARO
"TONY C"

In June of 1962, Tony Conigliaro of Swampscott, Massachusetts, was a star out-fielder for St. Mary's High School of Lynn. By April of 1964, the 19-year-old Conigliaro was a starting outfielder for the Boston Red Sox.

In his first at-bat at Fenway Park, Tony Conigliaro hit the first pitch thrown to him for a home run. In his rookie year he belted 24 roundtrippers to set a major league record for home runs by a teenager. In 1965 he hit 32 homers to lead the American League, making him the youngest player to ever lead the league in home runs. In June of 1967 he hit his 100th major league home run. At age 22 years, 6 months and 16 days, he was the youngest player in the history of the American League to reach that level.

But Tony Conigliaro was more than a home run hitter and more than raw statistics. Tony C. was a local hero.

JOHNNY PESKY REMEMBERS

Red Sox favorite Johnny Pesky, who joined the big league ball club in 1942, was the team's manager when Tony C. reported for spring training in 1964. Pesky will always remember the first time he saw Tony hit.

"I thought he was the best young hitter I had seen in a long time. He reminded me a bit of Ted Williams when Ted was a teenager. They were both tall and lean. And you could see right away that Tony worked as hard on his hitting as Ted used to.

"He had played only a short season in the minors but you knew right away that he was going to be a good one. Of course his parents, Sal and Teresa, lived around the corner from us in Swampscott, so I knew I was getting a good kid."

When Ted Williams was a teenager playing in the Pacific Coast League, Hall of Famer Lefty O'Doul watched the young phenom taking batting practice. O'Doul told Williams, "Whatever you do kid, don't let anyone change that swing." After Williams watched Conigliaro hit in spring training Ted's only advice to Tony was, "Don't change a thing."

Although the 19-year-old Conigliaro was a long shot to make the big league club, Pesky gave him plenty of playing time. Tony made the most of his opportunity, playing well in the outfield and hitting big league pitching with power.

"I remember one home run he hit," Pesky reminisces. "It cleared a fence in center field that was probably 450 feet from home plate. One of the writers went out to measure it and figured it had traveled about 530 feet.

"But I had to fight to bring him to Boston with the big league club. They wanted to send him to the minors for more seasoning, but I wanted him in my outfield."

When the writers asked Pesky if Tony had made the team he responded, "Do you want me to be shot by the fans back home? Yes, Tony will be in there."

HOME TOWN BOY MAKES GOOD

To get to Fenway Park from Tony Conigliaro's original hometown of Revere you take the Blue Line to Government Center and then change for the Green Line. Tony's journey to Fenway involved thousands of hours on the baseball fields of Boston's North Shore.

In his autobiography, *Seeing It Through*, with Jack Zanger, Tony recalled his early days on the baseball diamond. "I'd get up every day, put on my sneakers, ask my mother to tie the laces for me and run out the door to the ballfield across the street from my house. That's all I wanted to do. I was there so much that the other mothers in the neighborhood began saying my mother wasn't a very good one because she let me stay out there all that time."

Tony's younger brother Billy spent three seasons with the Boston Red Sox, two of them playing in the same outfield with his big brother. "I don't know if people realize how hard Tony worked to get to the big leagues and how hard he worked to stay there. He would spend hours swinging a lead bat or squeezing a ball."

Richie Conigliaro is the youngest of the three brothers. "I remember pitching to Tony in the parking lot of Suffolk Downs. We had moved to East Boston from Revere and our house was right above the track. Tony hit a line drive back at me and it caught me right in the forehead. I went down for the count!"

The local legend of Tony C. began in the East Boston Little League where he excelled. In his autobiography, Tony lauds his coach Ben Campbell. "Every kid in the world should have a little league coach like Mr. Campbell. I think that the course that I followed all through baseball was started right there under Mr. Campbell."

Tony's excellence on the baseball diamond continued as he moved from Little League to Pony League ball. "Tony stood out at every level," brother Billy remembers.

THREE-SPORT STAR

Tony was a three-sport star at St. Mary's High School in Lynn. Tony and his father Sal drove from their East Boston home to school every day. Sal would finish work at the nearby Triangle Tool and Dye Company and pick Tony up from practice for whatever sport was in season.

Baseball scouts first took notice of Tony in his sophomore year. They had turned out in droves to scout pitcher Danny Murphy of St. John's Prep in Danvers, who eventually signed with the Chicago Cubs for a six-figure bonus. Murphy only gave up four hits that day and three of them were to Tony Conigliaro.

In addition to his baseball prowess, Tony excelled at basketball and football. On the basketball court he set the St. Mary's school's scoring record with 417 points in his senior year. And on Thanksgiving he led the football team to victory over their larger Lynn public high school rivals.

In his junior and senior years at St. Mary's Tony hit over .600 and pitched his team to 16 victories. After his American Legion baseball season ended in September 1962, Tony signed with the Red Sox for a bonus of $20,000.

His first stop was Bradenton, Florida, for winter ball. At Bradenton, Tony learned how hard he was going to have to work to make it to the major leagues. He also established a lasting friendship with catcher Mike Ryan of Haverhill, Massachusetts. Conigliaro and Ryan both made it to the Red Sox in 1964 and continued as teammates through the Impossible Dream season of 1967.

Tony spent the 1963 season in Wellsville, New York, playing for the Red Sox farm club in the New York-Penn League. His .363 batting average and 24 home runs earned him an invitation to the Red Sox spring training camp in Scottsdale, Arizona, in 1964.

NEXT STOP KENMORE SQUARE

The hometown boy was an overnight sensation. By midseason he was averaging 100 letters per day, most of them from teen-age girls. He finished the season with a .290 batting average and 24 home runs. If he hadn't had his arm broken by an errant pitch late in the season his offensive totals would have been even more impressive.

If Tony was concerned about a "sophomore slump" in his second season, his numbers didn't show it. His 32 home runs led the American League and he drove in 82 runs.

Tony made an impromptu appearance at brother Billy's high school graduation from Swampscott High School that year. Tony took the microphone after a brief introduction from the principal and informed the crowd; "My brother Billy has just been selected first by the Boston Red Sox in the major league draft."

By the 1966 season, Tony C. was an established major leaguer. The Red Sox finished a distant ninth in the standings that year, but Tony rapped out 28 home runs and upped his RBI total to 93.

Long-time Red Sox broadcaster Ken Coleman had an interesting perspective on Tony C.'s status as a hometown hero. "In addition to broadcasting in Boston, I worked in Cleveland and Cincinnati over the years. Most of the hometown players I saw had some trouble with that role. It seemed to make it tougher for them. But not Tony. He actually seemed to relish his role as the hometown hero."

THE IMPOSSIBLE DREAM SEASON

Tony C. and his brother reported together to spring training in 1967. They made it a point to report early.

"Tony ran me into exhaustion during our three weeks together. He had more to do with my eventually making it to the big leagues than any other person."

The 1967 season started slowly for Tony. First he was injured by a John Wyatt fastball in batting practice during spring training. Then a bad back bothered him. At the end of May he was batting .304 but he had only contributed two home runs.

His home run drought didn't worry his teammates. Teammate Russ Gibson recalls, "Tony had a beautiful home run swing. You would see him lift one over the left-field wall at Fenway and you'd think, 'What a great Fenway swing this guy has.' Then we would go to someplace like Kansas City with a deep outfield and he would drive one 420 feet just over the fence. He had a knack for hitting them just far enough for a home run."

By mid-June the Red Sox had established themselves as pennant contenders and Tony C. was on a tear at the plate. Like many fans, Richie Conigliaro recalls the Red Sox game on June 15th as one of the season's turning points.

"I was 14 that year and I got to a lot of games. I used to ride in with Tony all the time. Of course I was scared to death when we got there because he drove like a madman. I remember that game against the White Sox because it was almost like a playoff game.

"It was 0-0 after ten innings and then the White Sox scored a run in the top of the eleventh. Joe Foy got on and then Tony hit a home run to win it 2-1. I remember the crowd went crazy and his teammates mobbed him at home plate."

Tony's dramatic home run had helped to coin a memorable phase. The following day a *Boston Globe* headline writer used the phrase "Impossible Dream" to describe the 1967 team's exploits to date.

As June came to an end, Tony's home run total for that month stood at nine. To cap it off, he was named to the American League All-Star team.

On July 23rd Tony hit his 100th career home run in the ninth game of a ten-game Red Sox winning streak. At the time he was believed to be the youngest player in major league history to reach this milestone. Later it was discovered that New York Giants Hall of Famer Mel Ott had topped Tony's record by a matter of days. When you consider that Ott had already played 117 major league games before he turned age 19, Tony's age in his rookie year, Conigliaro's achievement is even more remarkable.

As the temperatures of July and August rose, Tony's bat got even hotter. He totaled 8 home runs and 18 RBI for July. By mid-August he was up to 20 home runs and 67 RBI.

On August 18, 1967, Tony spoke with his business manager Ed Penney who told him, "I saw Ted Williams recently and he told me to tell you to stop crowding the plate. He said you should get back before one of those guys hits you."

That evening, pitcher Jack Hamilton of the California Angels hit Tony C. on the left side of his head with a fastball that sent Tony writhing on the ground with pain. Tony's teammates rushed to his side. His family joined a bedside vigil at Sancta Maria Hospital that evening. Tony C.'s 1967 season was over.

The Red Sox received permission from the Commissioner's Office to allow Tony to sit on the Red Sox bench for the season's final game. Tony did his best to celebrate with his teammates as the team clinched its first American League pennant in 21 years. Finally, overcome by depression, Tony put his head in his hands and cried in front of his locker.

Red Sox owner Tom Yawkey spoke for all Red Sox fans when he took Tony in his arms and said, "Tony, you helped. Those games you won for us in the early part of the season, well, they're just as important as today's game."

It is important for Red Sox fans of all ages to remember that without Tony C., the Impossible Dream season would never have been possible.

COMEBACK PLAYER OF THE YEAR

Tony Conigliaro attempted a comeback at spring training in 1968 but he simply could not see well enough to hit at the major league level. While trying his hand at pitching in the fall Instructional League that year, a few solid hits encouraged him to try again in 1969.

On opening day in Baltimore in 1969, Tony hit a tenth inning home run and scored the winning run in a 12-inning victory over the Orioles. On Opening Day at Fenway Park one week later, the fans gave Tony C. a series of ovations that rocked the ballpark to its foundations.

In one of the great comebacks in sports history, Tony drove in 82 runs in 1969 and hit 20 home runs. He was voted the Comeback Player of the Year, and he received the Hutch Award for being the player, "who best exemplified the fighting spirit and burning desire of the late pitcher and manager Fred Hutchinson."

It is often written that Tony Conigliaro was never the same player after his tragic beaning. That is simply not true. His eyesight was never the same again, but 1970 was his finest offensive season.

"When we would throw the ball to one another," Billy Conigliaro remembers, "if he closed his right eye he wouldn't be able to catch my return throw. He used his peripheral vision to hit the ball."

In 1970 Tony C. set career highs in home runs, runs scored, and RBI. His 116 RBI placed him second in the American League, and his 36 home runs ranked him fourth. The brothers Conigliaro combined for 54 home runs, establishing a major league record for brothers playing on the same team.

That fall the unimaginable happened: the Red Sox traded Tony C. to the California Angels. For Red Sox fans it was as if Mayor Menino were to trade the USS *Constitution* to Baltimore for the USS *Constellation*.

Tony C. never adjusted to life as a California Angel. He retired in mid-season with a batting average of .222. "I think being traded 3,000 miles away broke his spirit," Richie Conigliaro speculates.

Tony had been out of baseball for three- and one-half seasons when he phoned Red Sox General Manager Dick O'Connell to ask if he could try another comeback at the 1975 spring training camp. O'Connell told him that he was welcome if he would pay his own way.

Defying all odds, Tony hit the cover off the ball in spring training. When the Red Sox opened at Fenway Park that season, Tony was the designated hitter. He singled in his first at-bat and the crowd gave him a three-minute standing ovation. But hamstring and groin injuries hampered his comeback, and he retired from baseball for the last time in August 1975.

After baseball, Tony enjoyed a successful career as a television broadcaster in San Francisco. In January 1982 he interviewed for the color job on Red Sox telecasts. Tony suffered a heart attack while Billy Conigliaro was driving him to the airport for a return trip to the West Coast.

Tony never really recovered from this episode, and he died on February 24, 1990, a little over a month following his forty-fifth birthday. Nearly 1,000 people gathered at St. Anthony's Church in Revere to mourn his passing.

WE ARE FAMILY

"When people think about his career, I hope that people will remember that family was always first for Tony. Baseball was very, very important to him, but family was always most important. He came home to visit and to eat our mother's cooking every chance he got," Richie Conigliaro remembers.

"That's true of all of us," Billy adds. "If something great happened to one of us, Tony included, the first thing we would do is call home to tell the family about it. We have always been a very close-knit family."

The Conigliaros have learned over time that fame has its price. But they deal with it with humor rather than rancor. Billy recalls what it was like as a schoolboy when your big brother plays for the Boston Red Sox. "When I would strike out some fan was sure to yell, 'Hey Conigliaro, you're a bum, just like your brother Tony!' "

"You think you had it tough?" Richie laughs. "There I am trying to play high school baseball, and I've got one brother starting in right field for the Red Sox and the other brother starting in center field. When I would strike out they would yell, "Hey Conigliaro, you're a bum, just like your brother Tony *and* your brother Billy!' "

The Conigliaro brothers treasure their brother's memory, and enjoy reminiscing about his human qualities. Asked if either of them have their brother's fine singing ability, they both roll their eyes. "He was a ham," Richie adds.

Tony's appeal to the ladies is also fair game. "Remember Mamie Van Doren?" Richie asks. "How could I forget," Billy responds in reference to Tony's well-publicized romance with the Hollywood starlet.

"I remember one time," Billy continues, "when I spotted a very attractive young lady sitting behind the Red Sox dugout. I asked the batboy to have someone bring her a note to meet me after the game. A little while later he comes back with a baseball. I figure this is great, she wants me to autograph the ball. Then I notice some writing on the ball. I read it and it says, 'Meet me after the game: Tony Conigliaro.' My brother had spotted her before me!"

WHAT MIGHT HAVE BEEN

When his former teammate Dalton Jones is asked what Tony might have accomplished if he remained healthy for a full career, Dalton answers with a straight face, "He would have hit over 800 home runs before he retired, he would have gone to Hollywood and become a movie star, and then he would have come back to Massachusetts and been elected Governor. And I'm only half-kidding," he adds with a smile.

Baseball researchers have built a computer model that allows you to match players' performances with the statistics of every player who has ever played the game. When you enter Tony's batting statistics, his closest match at ages 20 and 21 is former Yankee great, Hall of Famer Mickey Mantle. For his abbreviated 1967 season at age 22, his match is Hall of Famer, and current Washington Nationals manager, Frank Robinson.

There is near unanimous agreement that if Tony had been able to play a full career in good health then he would have been a shoo-in for baseball's Hall of Fame. Johnny Pesky says, "I would bet my house on it!" His uniform number "25" would now be displayed on the façade in Fenway's right field along with the numbers of the five other Hall of Famers who played ten or more seasons with the Red Sox and finished their career with the club. But in fact, Tony's number "25" was retired in the hearts and minds of Red Sox fans a long, long time ago.

It is hard to believe that Tony C. has been gone for over 15 years now. But for as long as New England kids play baseball with snow shoveled to the sidelines, and dream of someday starring for the Boston Red Sox, the spirit of Tony C. will always be among us.

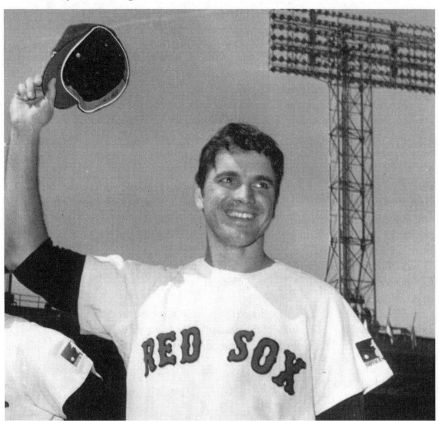

19.
Jim Lonborg Interview
July 1997

I interviewed Jim Lonborg in his office at his dental facility in Hanover, Massachusetts. As a long-time patient of the good doctor, it was a relief to focus on baseball rather than dental hygiene.

The first thing that strikes you about Jim Lonborg is the balance in his life. Family comes first for Jim, but he has managed to establish a thriving dental practice. And he finds time to make appearances for the Jimmy Fund and other charitable causes.

Since I had known him for over five years, Jim Lonborg was the first former player I approached for an in-depth interview when I decided to write Lightning In A Bottle, *the story of the 1967 Boston Red Sox. The first thing he said was, "I never wanted to be like the former high school star athlete, still wearing his letter sweater 20 years later. My baseball days were many years ago, and my focus is on my life today."*

At that point, I though my nascent baseball writing career was over before it had even begun. And then he added, "But, because it's you, I'll do it." Now that was a close call!

Asked what the 1967 Boston Red Sox season means to him today, Jim Lonborg offers, "It is an important part of who I am. It helps to define me as a person today. It will always be a wonderful memory for me."

JIM LONBORG
"GENTLEMAN JIM"

"When I think about the 1967 season, the first thing that comes to mind is that last game against the Minnesota Twins, when we had to win to at least clinch a tie for the pennant," Jim Lonborg recalled.

"I have a great picture hanging in my den that shows me leaping on the mound with my arms raised, Rico Petrocelli reaching to squeeze Rich Rollins' pop fly for the last out, and Carl Yastrzemski in left field raising his arms in celebration. The picture tells it all."

That October 1, 1967, game against Minnesota was the most important Red Sox game since their 1948 American League playoff game against the Cleveland Indians. The Twins game represented the culmination of a storybook season which began with the Red Sox as 100-1 underdogs to win the pennant, and featured enough come-from-behind wins to earn the team the nickname "the cardiac kids." A 10-game winning streak in July established them as legitimate contenders, and they stayed in the thick of the pennant race until the final, fateful game of the season.

There was never any question that Jim Lonborg would be the choice to pitch the most important game of the season. He led the pitching corps with 21 victories to date, and time and again that season he had come through with a victory to keep the Red Sox in the hunt. He was the undisputed ace of the staff, and he was on his way to winning the Cy Young Award as the outstanding pitcher in the American League in 1967.

GO EAST YOUNG MAN

While Jim Lonborg was the obvious choice to pitch the decisive final game of the 1967 season, he certainly couldn't have predicted it five years earlier. "Baseball was kind of a detour from medicine for me. I had enrolled at Stanford as a premed student in 1960, and I played whatever sport was in season during my teenage years. It wasn't until 1963, after my junior year at Stanford, that I started to focus on baseball as a career. That summer I pitched in the Basin League in South Dakota, the Cape Cod League of the west, and I really started to put it all together."

Jim Lonborg grew up in San Luis Obispo, California, over 3,000 miles from Fenway Park. His father was a professor at California Polytechnic Institute, and Jim treasures his memories of growing up in a loving and caring environment.

"The Dodgers and Giants didn't move to the west coast until 1958, so we didn't have the major league influence that kids in New England have from the Red Sox. I was well into my teens before my father drove us down to Los Angeles to see my first big league game. The emphasis in our home was on the whole person. It was a wonderful way to grow up."

Following his 1963 season in the Basin League, the Red Sox offered Lonborg an $18,000 bonus to sign with the club. "The Baltimore Orioles had expressed some interest, but they had just given Jim Palmer [fellow Basin Leaguer and future Hall of Famer] $100,000 so they probably didn't have enough money left to top the Red Sox offer. I'm glad it turned out that way."

THE RED SOX YEARS

After finishing his fall semester at Stanford, Lonborg reported to the Red Sox spring training camp where he was assigned to their Winston-Salem, North Carolina, team in the low minors. The Red Sox quickly recognized his potential and he was rushed through their minor league system.

The pitching-poor Red Sox put him on the fast track, and he arrived at Fenway in 1965. He was handicapped by his lack of experience and a poor-hit-

ting Red Sox club, and he went a disappointing 8-17 in his rookie year. In 1966 he split his time between starting and relieving, and his record improved to 10-10.

The following winter he went to Venezuela to pitch winter ball. "I worked on throwing my curve ball for a strike on 2-1 and 3-2 counts. At the major league level you need to be able to use every pitch you have effectively. After I finished up down there, I went skiing for a couple of weeks, and reported to training camp in the best shape of my life."

The irony of Lonborg using a ski trip to tune up for the 1967 season will not be lost on long-time Red Sox fans. It was an ill-fated skiing excursion in December 1967 that resulted in his broken leg and three subsequent seasons of frustration for Jim and his fans.

The 1967 Red Sox spring training camp was very different than any other that Lonborg had attended. It was run by rookie manager Dick Williams who was intent on changing the teams image as a country club. "Dick was very purposeful," Lonborg remembers. "If we weren't throwing or running windsprints, he had the pitchers playing volleyball. He kept us focused all season long."

To spend 10 minutes with Jim Lonborg is to understand how he earned his nickname "Gentleman Jim." He is thoughtful and well-spoken. But Lonborg was determined to change his image with the hitters in 1967. "As a pitcher, you have to establish that the whole plate belongs to you. If you let the hitters lean over the plate at will, you're giving up the outside of the plate to them. I was determined to pitch inside and to make the outside of the plate a longer reach for them."

Under the tutelage of pitching coach Sal "The Barber" Maglie, who was the master of the brushback pitch throughout his career, Lonborg set about to reclaim the whole plate. In the process, he managed to lead the American League with 19 hit batsmen.

"I never really felt that I really hit them—they just failed to get out the way," Lonborg recalls, emphasizing the subtle distinction. "My fastball sailed in on right hand hitters, and my curve broke in on lefties. If they were standing too close to the plate, they simply couldn't get out of the way.

"Baseball is a contest between the pitcher and hitter. And whoever 'owns' the inside of the plate wins that contest. I always felt that the inside of the plate belonged to me."

The combination of experience, conditioning, and determination turned Lonborg into one of the better pitchers in baseball. When the beginning of July rolled around, Lonborg led the American League with 10 wins and 120 strikeouts. He was an easy choice for the All-Star team for Orioles manager Hank Bauer.

As the pennant race tightened, Lonborg became even more tenacious. He flew to Boston on August 1 from Atlanta, where he was on two weeks duty with the National Guard, and stuck around long enough to notch his fifteenth victory. On September 12 he tripled off the fence in right-center to lead his club to his twentieth victory.

OCTOBER 1, 1967

After a disappointing two-inning outing against the Cleveland Indians on September 27, Jim was ready for the ball in the crucial final game against the Twins. "It took me a little while to find my rhythm, and the Twins jumped out to a 2-0 lead, but after I settled into my groove, I knew I could hold them."

Hold them he did, but the Twins were hanging tough, and when Lonborg led off the home half of the sixth inning, the Red Sox still trailed 2-0. Ever the thinking man, he noticed that third baseman Cesar Tovar was playing back. Lonborg dropped down a surprise bunt and legged out a base hit that keyed a five-run Red Sox uprising.

"I had made up my mind standing in the on-deck circle that I was going to drop a bunt down. I knew Tovar was back and I thought the element of surprise might work for me. And I could run pretty well at that time." The Twins countered with a run in the eighth, to make it 5-3, but there was no way that Lonborg was going to relinquish the lead. With two down in the ninth, and close to 35,000 Fenway Faithful on their feet in anticipation, he jammed Rich Rollins with a fastball, and Rico waited anxiously for the harmless popup to settle in his glove.

"When I look at that picture of the last out, I think about how fortunate I was. That could never happen today. First of all, there would be a relief pitcher standing on the mound. And with the playoff format coming into play in 1969, it has been almost 30 years since you could win the pennant outright on the last day of the season. And finally, you couldn't let 10,000 people out on the field to celebrate the way they did that day. That crowd was purely spontaneous, filled with good will, and delirious with joy. I will *never* forget that moment.

"At one point I looked around and realized I was the only player left on the field. And the crowd was carrying me out towards right field away from our dugout. But a couple of Boston's 'finest' came to my aid and spirited me back to the clubhouse. What a memory that is."

1967 WORLD SERIES AND BEYOND

It seems hard to believe, but Jim Lonborg pitched an even better game against the St. Louis Cardinals only four days later in the World Series. He took a no-hitter into the eighth inning against the slugging Cardinals, and settled for a 5-0, one-hit victory. In Game Five, with the Red Sox trailing in the series 3-1, Lonborg limited the Cards to three hits as the Red Sox squeezed out a 3-1 victory.

When Red Sox fans look back on the 1967 World Series they remember the heroics of the Cardinals' Bob Gibson, who won three games to lead St. Louis to a World Championship. But after Game Five, Jim Lonborg had actually outpitched Gibson. Lonborg had held the potent Cardinals lineup to four hits and one run while pitching two complete games.

Lonborg came back on just two days' rest to pitch in Game Seven at Fenway Park and gave his team five strong innings. But he ran out of gas in the sixth inning, and the Cardinals prevailed 7-2 to clinch the series. It should be noted, however, that in a stretch of just eight days, Jim Lonborg achieved three clutch victories while limiting the opposition to a total of 11 hits. To date, no Red Sox pitcher has ever again equaled this standard of excellence over this period of time.

His unfortunate off-season skiing accident limited Lonborg's effectiveness for the Red Sox in 1968-70. During that period he won only 17 games for Boston. At one point he was sent back to Triple A Louisville in effort to regain his major league form.

"I tried to come back too soon," Lonborg remembers. "I was favoring my injured leg and I ended up hurting my arm. It was a really frustrating time for me."

In 1971 he bounced back with 10 wins, but the Red Sox traded him to the Milwaukee Brewers during the off-season. The blockbuster trade included George Scott and Billy Conigliaro along with Lonborg, while the Brewers shipped Marty Pattin, Lew Krause and Tommy Harper to Boston.

"That trade was hard for me. Rosemary and I had just gotten married and I really thought of Boston as home. But I was fortunate that the Brewers were a classy operation. I played winter ball in Puerto Rico before the 1972 season and I knew I would have a good year."

He won 14 games in his one season with the Brewers, but was traded to the Philadelphia Phillies on October 31, 1972. After eight seasons in the American League he was headed to the senior circuit.

PHILADELPHIA STORY

Jim Lonborg enjoyed a great deal of success with the Phillies over the next seven years. In 1974 he won 17 games, and his 16 complete games ranked third in the National League. His high point was the 1976 season when he went 18-10, helping the Phillies to reach the playoffs. The Phillies made it into the postseason in 1977 as well, and Lonborg started games in the NLCS both years.

Red Sox fans consider Jim Lonborg to be "one of their own." But he actually won more games in a Philadelphia uniform (75 wins) than the 68 wins he posted with the Red Sox.

When the Phillies released him in June of 1979, Lonborg decided he wasn't quite ready to give up pitching entirely: he pitched five games for the Scituate, Massachusetts, town team. "I had gotten in shape to play a whole season, and it

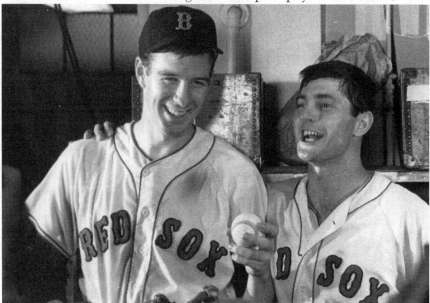

Jim and Yaz, 1967.

seemed like it might be a good thing to do with the community. A sense of community is very important to our family.

"The only problem was that I had learned to set up the hitters over the years, to waste one on the inside to set up my curveball. But these kids climbed out of their cars and started swinging. There was no setting up the hitters in that league."

DR. JAMES R. LONBORG

The end of Jim Lonborg's baseball career meant that he could return to his original love: medicine. He enrolled in the Tufts Dental School in Boston, and spent the next four years in friendly competition with fellow students freshly out of school.

"I missed baseball, and the friendships you make in the game, but it was time to move on to another career. And it was also time to spend as much time as possible with my family. You miss out on an awful lot at home when you are constantly traveling with the ballclub."

Today Dr. Lonborg maintains a thriving dental practice in Hanover, where he has been located for 20 years. He and his wife of nearly 35 years, Rosemary, have raised six children in their lovely 200-year-old Scituate home.

Asked what his current ties are to baseball, Lonborg responds, "I get to a Red Sox game when I can, and I follow nearly every game by radio. And I love

to coach and watch my two sons pitch." Son John had recently graduated from Scituate High School and hoped to pitch at UMass Amherst next year. Son Jordie was entering his junior year at Scituate High the next fall, and is the stylish southpaw pitcher of the family.

"I also provide some baseball background for Rosemary to use in her baseball books." Rosemary Lonborg has written three children's books and is the recipient of a prestigious Ben Franklin Book Award. Ironically, the impetus for Rosemary's first book, *The Quiet Hero: A Baseball Story*, was Roger Clemens' infamous temper tantrum that got him thrown out of a crucial playoff game against the Oakland Athletics in 1990.

Old Timer's Game

Rosemary adds, "I've never

wanted to make too much out of that aspect, but I felt very strongly that young people needed a positive role model to emphasize the importance of good sportsmanship. My book tells the story of Jim's relationship with our two younger boys, and focuses on team play and abiding by the rules."

Rosemary's latest book (at the time), *The Bird Of Baseball: The Story of Mark Fidrych*, received a glowing endorsement from *Sports Illustrated* that spring. Her book focuses on the Cinderella Story of Northboro's Mark Fidrych and his rookie season in 1976 with the Detroit Tigers.

"Mark is a fascinating individual, and someone that kids can really relate to. People tell me they have had trouble finding the book, but they can always drop a note to Fidco Distributors, PO Box 1072, Northboro, MA 01532, and get a copy that way. It was a fun book to work on."

The popular press continually harps on the lack of role models in professional sports. All you have to do is read a few excerpts from son John Lonborg's 1997 graduation address to his classmates at Scituate High to know that this is not always the case:

"Although in 1967 I was not even a twinkle in my father's eye, I know that he and his "Impossible Dream" proved something to our parents' generation, waaaay back then. And it is a lesson even now, 30 years later, that our generation can benefit from.

"Believe in yourself! Never let anyone tell you that your dream is impossible. And most importantly, never stop dreaming!"

The apple doesn't fall very far from the tree.

GENTLEMAN JIM

Jim Lonborg was inducted into the Red Sox Hall of Fame in 2000. His 10 games of 10 or more strikeouts places him sixth on the Red Sox all-time list, and his 784 strikeouts ranks eleventh.

One final anecdote about the day the Red Sox won the American League pennant for the first time in 21 years tells a lot about Jim Lonborg the person. Jim was perhaps the last player to leave the Red Sox clubhouse that day. About the only sounds in the old ballpark came from the crew dealing with the post-celebration cleanup. Only one other man remained at Fenway.

Lonborg made the long trek to the top of the ballpark. He found his way to the office of the man who *was* the Boston Red Sox: Thomas Austin Yawkey. He found Mr. Yawkey sitting in solitary reflection in his office. Jim had lost his cap, his belt, and his undershirt to the crowd in the post-game celebration, but he had ended up with the game ball. He walked over to Yawkey, handed him the ball, and said, "If anyone deserves this, you do."

Dreams do come true.

20.
Eddie Kasko Interview
July 2004

I caught up with Eddie Kasko by telephone in his Richmond, Virginia, home. Two hours later I had discovered what a great storyteller he is and what a terrific sense of humor he has.

I didn't know a lot about Eddie Kasko before I started his profile. I remembered that he had a nice career in the National League and that he finished up as a utility player with the Red Sox in 1966. Naturally, I remembered him as the Red Sox manager from 1970 to 1973, especially the team's near miss in 1972. And I was aware that he was a front office fixture with the Red Sox for many years.

When our interview was over I had a newfound respect for Eddie Kasko. I learned that he had put together a distinguished 40-year career in professional baseball despite facing major obstacles at every critical point. He was a guy who kept drawing lemons and making them into lemonade.

I learned that Kasko played for the Houston Astros before they were the Astros. He was a member of Houston's first expansion team, then known as the Colt 45's, and they played outdoors throughout the intolerable Houston summer. He remembers killing mosquitoes in the Colt 45's dugout that were "as big as small birds."

When the interview was over, I remember thinking that Eddie was a guy you would like to have a beer with sitting around talking baseball. There is a lot more to Eddie Kasko than I ever realized.

EDDIE KASKO
ADOPTED SON OF
NEW ENGLAND'S TEAM

Former Boston Red Sox manager Eddie Kasko spent over 40 years in professional baseball, but his career was almost over before it had barely begun. "The New York Giants signed me from a tryout camp when I was a kid right out of high school. I went to their minor league spring training camp and found I was one of eight shortstops there. I was the last one cut, but I headed home to Linden, New Jersey, figuring I had better get a job.

"But there were no good jobs and all I wanted to do was play ball. I had been to a total of five tryout camps before Baltimore, an independent minor league team in the International League at the time, signed me. It never occurred to me that I would spend my whole career in baseball. I was just happy to have a job with a ballclub."

Eddie Kasko ultimately spent 10 seasons in the major leagues, achieving All-Star recognition and batting .318 in the 1961 World Series. He managed the Boston Red Sox for four seasons between 1970 and 1973, averaging 86 wins per season. He then spent 21 years in a variety of management positions with the team, including Vice President of Baseball Development, retiring at the end of 1994.

NEW JERSEY BORN

Eddie Kasko was born and raised in Linden, New Jersey, just outside of New York City. "My parents were hard-working immigrants from the old country. They ran a small, neighborhood grocery store and they worked long hours. My father didn't know anything about baseball and he couldn't understand my passion for the game. He used to say, 'Why are you always running off to play ball in the park? Your future is here with the store.'"

Asked if he grew up a Yankee fan, Eddie provides the right answer. "No, I was a fan of the National League. I would play hooky from school and go into the city to watch the Dodgers in Ebbets Field and the Giants at the Polo Grounds. I guess the Dodgers were my favorite team.

"I played only baseball as a kid growing up. I wasn't a great athlete and I was pretty slender, so baseball was my best sport. Baseball was the big sport when I was growing up and we had some pretty good teams. I wasn't even the best player on my high school team. We had a catcher who went on to play in the minors. There were no baseball scouts beating down our door.

"When I would go to a tryout there would be hundreds of kids there with the same idea. At the end of a Giants tryout with about 350 kids there, I remember the guy called six of us aside and said, 'How would you guys like to play for the New York Giants?' Of course we all had visions of playing at the Polo Grounds. When I got to their minor league spring training there were over 100 players in camp.

"I would show up every day and there would be fewer guys there. I finally asked where they had all gone and somebody told me to check the bulletin board. I saw there were only two of us left at shortstop and the other guy was in his mid-twenties. I figured I was next and I was right."

Kasko returned to Linwood and looked for work, but he wasn't ready to give up on his dream of playing baseball. He didn't catch the eye of another major league team, but a 1949 tryout camp for the minor league team in Baltimore resulted in the next best thing.

THE LONG TREK TO THE MAJORS

"Baltimore offered me a contract at $250 a month, and of course I jumped at it. My father couldn't believe that I was going to make my living playing ball. 'They are going to pay you to play baseball? Why would they do that? Look at all the guys down at the park who play for free.' "

Baltimore was an independent team in the top-flight International League, and it had its own minor league system. "By the time I was signed they had already stocked their minor league system so they kept me with the top team. This was at the Triple A level so there were a lot of former major leaguers on their way down, hoping for another chance. I watched the veterans and learned how to play the game at a high level, and I learned how to act like a professional ballplayer. I wasn't playing to speak of, but I learned how to handle myself and that was very valuable."

Baltimore assigned Kasko to their Class D team in Suffolk, Virginia, for the 1950 season. "That was really the low minors," he recalls. "And if you don't believe me, let me tell you that we were called the 'Goobers,' and our uniform had a big peanut on it as our logo. But I was playing regularly and that was all that mattered."

Eddie Kasko's baseball career was interrupted by service in the U.S. Army. "It was at the time of the Korean War, and the draft was in place. I remember when I reported for induction that they had us count off. Every fifth man became a Marine and was sent off to fight in Korea. Fortunately, I was a three.

"I spent two years in the Army, nearly all of it at Fort Leonard Wood in Missouri. I was a combat engineer and I spent most of my time as an instructor. I also had the opportunity to play a lot of baseball, which was good."

After his honorable discharge from the Army, Kasko headed to Richmond, Virginia, for the 1954 season. Forty years later, he still calls Richmond home. Asked how a guy from New Jersey would end up spending his entire adult life south of the Mason-Dixon line, Eddie responds, "Well, as is often the case, there was a woman involved. In my case it is my lovely wife, Catherine, and she has lived in this area all of her life.

"I was living with a family here while I was playing for Richmond, and their daughter told me she had the perfect girl for me. She introduced me to my future wife and I realized the daughter was right. Catherine and I celebrated our forty-sixth wedding anniversary last February." Asked if it was the best decision he ever made, Eddie quickly agrees and adds, "And it has certainly helped that she was already a baseball fan."

MAJOR LEAGUER

Eight years after he signed his first professional baseball contract Eddie Kasko finally made it to the big leagues. His first stop was with the St. Louis Cardinals and he is quick to admit that he was somewhat in awe of his new teammates.

"I remember the first day of spring training we were due in the clubhouse at 10 A.M. I made it a point to get there at 8 A.M. and I wandered around just look-ing at the names over the lockers. It was knee-knocking time. I'm looking at Stan Musial's locker, Alvin Dark's locker, guys who were headed to the Hall of Fame.

"But I was fine once the workouts started. You're so focused on playing well that you don't have time to worry about who is across the diamond from you. I was just busy trying to stick with the team."

Stick with the team is exactly what Eddie Kasko did, and he managed to get into 134 games with the 1957 Cardinals. He played mostly at third base beside Alvin Dark at shortstop.

"I had always been a shortstop but one time in the minors our third baseman got hurt and they asked me if I could play there. I said, 'Oh sure.' Of course I really hadn't played there but you grab every chance you get to play. And being able to play third got me a regular job as a rookie in the big leagues. Alvin Dark was very generous giving me tips on how to play the infield. And I picked his brain every chance I got.

"I remember one time we were having trouble hitting a pitcher but Alvin had good success. He told me, 'You watch him closely. He's tipping his pitches.' I watched and watched but I couldn't see anything. Finally Alvin told me, "When he brings his glove over his head and his fingers flare out, he's going to throw a curve.' I think that's when I realized how much there was to learn in this game."

THE CINCINNATI KID

Kasko played a second season with the Cardinals in 1958, but in October he was traded to the Cincinnati Redlegs as part of a six-player swap. When Fred Hutchinson was named Cincinnati's manager during the 1959 season, Eddie was reunited with his first big league manager.

"I used to kid him that he was following me around, but Hutch had a tremendous influence on me. He was a terrific manager. Whenever I see the term 'player's manager' I think of Hutch. There was never any doubt that he was in charge, believe me he set the rules, but he let the players play the game. He understood the role of the manager and the role of the players."

Kasko came into his own in the 1960 season with Cincinnati, batting a career high .292. He was voted the team's most valuable player over better-known team-mates such as Frank Robinson and Vada Pinson.

In 1961 Kasko's skills were recognized beyond Cincinnati as he was named to the National League All-Star team. "They played two games that year. I didn't get to play in the first one but I did get to play in the second one in Boston. It was the first time I had seen Fenway Park and I liked it right away. It reminded me of Crosley Field in Cincinnati. Small and unique."

The 1961 Cincinnati Reds won the National League pennant and met the powerful New York Yankees in the World Series. "I remember kneeling in the on-deck circle in Yankee Stadium and looking around. That was another knee-knocking time. But we beat them in the second game at the stadium and we actually thought we had a chance to take them. Three straight losses back in Cincinnati took care of that. The Yankees had a powerhouse team that season."

After two more seasons in Cincinnati, Kasko was traded to Houston for the 1964 season. That year his fielding average was tops among all National League shortstops. He was named the Astros' first captain in 1965.

"In Houston we had a mix of veterans and youngsters. Getting a chance to compare notes with guys like Nellie Fox and Robin Roberts really contributed to my baseball knowledge. And I can remember young Joe Morgan [Hall of Famer and current ESPN analyst] asking us questions the way I used to pepper Alvin Dark with questions."

NEXT STOP KENMORE SQUARE

In April 1966, Kasko was traded to the Boston Red Sox for Felix Mantilla. After nine seasons in the National League changing leagues was a bit of an adjustment for him. "It took some getting used to. I grew up a National League fan and I had played my whole career over there. And my back was starting to bother me so I didn't play that much.

"But I liked the organization and I liked the city. And Tom Yawkey was one of the finest men I have ever met. He was such a gentleman."

Bothered by injuries all year, he appeared in only 58 games with the 1966 Boston Red Sox. "In October I got a telegram from General Manager Dick O'Connell that simply said, 'Released: will call in a few days.' Dick called to say that I was invited to camp with the team the following spring, and I had a shot at making the team. But what they really wanted me to do was to manage the Red Sox Triple A team in Toronto. Dick Williams had been named the Boston manager so his old job was open.

"I was flattered that he offered me their top minor league job and I was a little surprised. The team had asked me to work with Rico Petrocelli during 1966 and I think I was helpful to him. I guess that made an impression on the team.

"I told my wife about the offer, and she said, 'Why are you even thinking about playing again? The job as manager is a great opportunity. You like the organization and you like their people. Why don't you just pick up the telephone and accept?' As usual she was right and that's exactly what I did."

Before he left for spring training with his new team, Kasko recognized that he had a problem. "I was very excited about the upcoming season and then I realized I had no idea what the pitchers did in training camp. I had been going to spring training all those years, but always two weeks after the pitchers reported. I started trying to contact old pitching friends like Bob Purkey. I shouldn't have worried, though. The Red Sox had arranged for Charlie Wagner [long-time Red Sox scout and advisor] to go to spring training and organize the pitchers."

Kasko managed in Toronto in 1967 and continued as the Red Sox Triple A manager when the franchise was shifted to Louisville, Kentucky. "In those days you didn't have a full-time coach to help you out, even in the high minors. You would be coaching third base, trying to run the game, and worrying about who would pitch the next inning all at the same time. I found I really enjoyed managing."

BACK IN THE MAJORS

At the end of the 1969 season Eddie Kasko received a surprising telephone call from Red Sox General Manager Dick O'Connell. "He was calling to say that they were letting Dick Williams go and that they wanted me to take over as manager for the 1970 season. I told him, 'If you think I can do a good job, that's all I need to hear. Working with good people is all that really matters.' "

The Boston Red Sox introduced Eddie Kasko as the new manager of the team on October 2, 1969. It was announced that he had received a two-year contract.

The starting lineup for the 1970 Boston Red Sox mirrored the 1967 team except that Carl Yastrzemski played primarily at first base, and Billy Conigliaro joined brother Tony as a starting outfielder. The pitching staff had turned over almost completely however. New faces, Gary Peters, Ray Culp, and Sonny Siebert, were expected to lead the team back into contention.

The 1970 Red Sox got off to a good start. On May 5 they were in second place in the American League East, 1.5 games off the pace. But the team lost 16 of their next 23 games, falling 12 games behind the Baltimore Orioles. At the All-Star break they were in fourth place.

Jim Lonborg had reeled off four straight wins to start the season, but his arm gave out and he was sent to Louisville to rehab. There was not enough pitching depth behind the "Big Three" and the team could never put together a sustained winning streak. At the end of the season the team had matched their 1969 record of 87-75, finishing in third place a full 20 games behind the eventual World Series winner, the Baltimore Orioles.

"My good friend Charlie Wagner, who I still talk to every week, gave me some good advice when I started out as a manager. He told me that being a manager wasn't anything like being a player. He said, 'You have to prove to the players every day that you are smarter than they are. And they will test you every single day.' He was right."

The team had made a number of moves in the off-season, trading Tony Conigliaro to the Angels and Mike Andrews to the White Sox, and the reconfigured 1971 Red Sox got off to another good start. On June 4 the team was leading the Eastern Division, but the team lost 11 of the next 17 games and quickly they were eight games out of first.

Under the heading, "The more things change, the more they stay the same," Boston sportswriters were calling for Kasko's dismissal. In late June, veteran sportswriter Larry Claflin wrote in *The Sporting News*, "Is another Red Sox manager in trouble? Already, yet with a team that just spent a month in first place, every newspaper in Boston is openly speculating that Eddie Kasko will be replaced at the end of the year unless the team plays well enough that his contract will have to be renewed."

In mid-August the 1971 Red Sox were in second place, still within striking distance of the division-leading Orioles. But the team played .500 baseball the rest of the way and finished third with a record of 85-77. Eddie Kasko may not have had the vote of the writers, but he did have the support of the front office. The Red Sox extended his contract to cover the 1972 season.

"At the major league level you have a lot of resources at your disposal, much more than in the minor leagues. And it took me a while to figure out how to make full use of those resources. But I got much better at it as time went on."

CLOSE CALL

The start of the 1972 season was delayed for 10 days by a player strike. The Red Sox had their season shortened by seven games. Their eventual rival for the division championship, the Detroit Tigers, had their schedule cut by six games. That one-game difference would turn out to be very important in the final days of the season.

The Red Sox started slowly in 1972. At the end of June they were in third place, but they were seven games under .500 and eight games out of first. They put together a seven-game winning streak to start July, and climbed above .500 as the month closed. Led by rookie catcher Carlton Fisk and the rejuvenated Luis Tiant, the team climbed to within two games of the division lead at the end of August, and claimed first place with a 10-4 win over the New Yankees on September 7.

The team flew into Detroit for the final three games of the season, leading the Tigers by one-half game. Trailing 1-0 in the series opener, the Red Sox had runners on first and third when Carl Yastrzemski laced a Mickey Lolich fastball off the top of the fence in center field. Tommy Harper easily scored the tying run from third, the speedy Luis Aparicio was heading towards home, and Yaz had triple on his mind from the moment he left the batter's box.

As he rounded third base, the usually sure-footed Aparicio stumbled and fell to the ground beyond third. Third base coach Eddie Popowski screamed at him to get back to third and then Aparicio fell again. Yaz was the most surprised person in Tiger Stadium when he arrived at third to find Aparicio waiting there. Yaz was tagged out, the rally was over, and the Tigers prevailed 4-1 to move into first place.

Eddie Kasko can still picture that scene as if it was in slow motion. "I was tracking both Luis and Yaz, but as Aparicio approached third I shifted my focus to Yaz. I was sure that Luis would score but I thought it might be close for Yaz at third. All of a sudden I couldn't see Luis. I actually started looking around the dugout thinking maybe he had already come in. When I saw them both at third I was stunned. I can actually laugh about it now, but it sure wasn't funny at the time."

The Tigers won 3-1 the following night to clinch the Eastern Division title. Red Sox owner Tom Yawkey, who had made a rare road trip to watch his team, announced at the end of the series that Eddie Kasko would be signed to a two-year contract extension.

The 1973 Red Sox won 89 games, their high-water mark since the 1967 Impossible Dream Team. The pitching staff featured five starters with 13 or more wins led by Luis Tiant's 20 victories.

At mid-season the team was in second place, trailing Baltimore by only three games. In late August they put together an eight-game winning streak but the Orioles matched them win for win and could not be caught that season.

As the 1973 season was coming to a close, Eddie Kasko took the call from General Manager Dick O'Connell that all managers eventually receive. "He told me he was sorry but they were going to make a change. They

With members of his 1970 coaching staff: (standing) Charlie Wagner, Eddie Popowski; (kneeling) Don Lenhardt, Kasko, and Doug Camilli.

were going to bring Darrell Johnson in from Louisville to manage the club in 1974. I told him that I understood completely and that I appreciated the opportunity they had given me. I offered to attend the press conference they were holding the next day to announce the change. I think he really appreciated that."

KEY CONTRIBUTOR IN THE FRONT OFFICE

"Now that the decision was made to go with Darrell Johnson as the manager, Dick O'Connell asked me what I was going to do. I told him I was going to look for another job. He said, "No, no, we want you to stay with the team. We want you to be our Executive Scout.' I asked him if that meant I would be scouting for executives, and he laughed."

"My job for the next four years was to scout the major league teams and I loved it. I was evaluating major leaguers for potential trades and doing advance scouting. I was able to use our home in Richmond as my base and go up to Boston when it was necessary. Then in 1978 they asked me to take over as scouting director. I told them I would accept the job provided I could continue to work out of Richmond and they agreed.

"We came up with a schedule of when I would be in Boston and it really worked out very well. I inherited a great scouting staff. We had 17 scouts located all over the country. I spent my time checking in with them so it really didn't matter that I wasn't in Boston. But I'll tell you, I never could have done it without the help of my assistant, Debbie McIntyre. She was the one in Boston holding everything together.

"I figured out early on that I couldn't give the scouts a lot of help in projecting whether an 18-year-old kid was going to be a big leaguer in five years. Most of them had been doing it so long it was like second nature to them. But I realized that I could help them by providing the resources they needed. That was the biggest contribution I could make for them."

After 14 years as scouting director, Kasko was promoted to Vice President of Baseball Development. He was responsible for the operation of the team's minor league system and the scouting department in that role. Looking back at his career in the front office, he is particularly proud of the players who were signed and later became outstanding major league players.

"Roger Clemens and Wade Boggs are two of the signings that come immediately to mind. Mike

Expressing a difference of opinion.

Greenwell was another great signing and so was Bruce Hurst. Right there in New England, Mo Vaughn was a terrific signing, and even though he didn't end up playing for us, signing Jeff Bagwell out of Connecticut for $35,000 was a great move.

ADOPTED SON OF RICHMOND

Today Eddie Kasko and his wife Catherine live in their long-time home of Richmond, Virginia. They have two grown sons, Michael and James, and plenty of time to dote on their granddaughters Casey, Abbey, Stephanie, and Kate. "We had boys ourselves and now we have all girls for grandchildren. They are just great."

He still follows baseball closely and watches as much as he can. "We get the Braves down here on TV all the time and I catch the Red Sox on national television whenever I can." Commenting on Red Sox fans, Eddie offers, "The Boston fans are great. They are really knowledgeable fans. They remind me of the St. Louis fans in that way. Red Sox fans are demanding and they can be a little tough, but that's only because they want a winner so badly."

Given the opportunity to offer some advice to Red Sox manager Terry Francona, Eddie strikes a positive note. "He has to remember that it is a long season. And he shouldn't take any criticism personally. He shouldn't take it to heart, it goes with the job."

Asked how much he loves baseball, Kasko responds with feeling, "Boy, an awful lot. It has given me a wonderful life with so many great experiences. You know, I grew up in a fairly rough area. There wasn't a lot of opportunity there and I'm not exaggerating when I say that a lot of the guys I grew up with ended up in jail. I know how fortunate I am to have spent my life in baseball."

From 1967, the year Eddie Kasko took over as manager of the Red Sox top farm team in Toronto, through the 2004 season, the Red Sox have had more winning seasons (32) than any other team in major league baseball. He would be the first one to tell you that an achievement of that magnitude is the result of the collective efforts of the organization. But it should be noted that Eddie Kasko was among the key contributors to that accomplishment.

His name doesn't appear among the major league leaders based on his ten-year career in the big leagues. But Eddie Kasko may have led the majors in overcoming adversity during his more than 40 years in baseball.

He went to five tryout camps as a teenager before he managed to secure a toehold in professional baseball. It took him another eight years before he finally made it to the majors. He lost his job as manager of the Boston Red Sox, but he remained with the organization and continued to contribute to the team's success.

It is sometimes written that the key to success in life is converting adversity to advantage. Eddie Kasko was a master at doing exactly that.

21.
George Scott Interview
July 1999

I interviewed George Scott at Fraser Field in Lynn, Massachusetts, several hours before he was scheduled to manage the Massachusetts Mad Dogs in that evening's game. Our session began in his office, and then we moved on to the stadium.

George "Boomer" Scott is one of the most beloved players in Red Sox history. He makes the top 10 list of every Red Sox fan who is age 40 or older. Fans loved his colorful quotes, they loved his fielding grace at first base, and they loved his long "Taters" best of all.

I had always wondered why The Boomer called his home runs "Taters," and it was one of the first questions I asked him. George gave me a rather long, involved explanation, and I have done my best to capture his explanation.

In addition to managing the Mad Dogs, Scott ran a "Boomer's Mississippi Barbecue-Southern Style" concession at Fraser Field. Our interview continued as George fired up the barbecue pit. When he poured lighter fluid on the smoldering flames, I pictured a headline, "Former Red Sox Star and Obscure Writer Injured in Barbeque Blaze." But George assured me that it always worked for him.

I also questioned him about the shell necklace that he wore later in his career with the Red Sox. "Those were the teeth of second basemen," he informed me with a straight face. I didn't believe him, but George "Boomer" Scott has always been good for a colorful quote.

GEORGE SCOTT
"THE BOOMER"

When Red Sox rookie George Scott was selected to the American League All-Star team in 1966, the 22-year-old first baseman had played fewer than 100 major league games. Scott, who was managing the Massachusetts Mad Dogs of Lynn, Massachusetts, when the 1999 All-Star game was played at Fenway Park, remembers being in awe of the baseball talent assembled in St. Louis for that year's midsummer classic.

"My legs were like spaghetti, I was shaking so much. I'm sitting in the dugout, everybody else is running around having fun, but I can't take my eyes off the field. I'm watching Willie Mays, Clemente, Stargell, Koufax, and I'm saying to myself, 'Are you in the right place?'

"When they called my name for the introductions, I thought I was going to pass out, I was so nervous. But once I got in the game, I felt like I belonged there. I didn't get a hit, but I put the ball in play against Sandy Koufax and Juan Marichal. That was pretty amazing in itself, 'cause I struck out about 150 times in my rookie year!"

George Scott burst upon the baseball scene in 1966 like a meteor across the evening sky. He had accumulated 20 home runs by the All-Star break. His fielding at first base was nearly flawless, and he had impressed one and all with his enthusiasm for the game. The question of the day was: who is George Scott, and where in the world did he come from?

GREENVILLE, MISSISIPPI: MY HOMETOWN

George Scott was born and raised in Greenville, Mississippi, in the heart of the Mississippi Delta. Located on the Mississippi River in the southwestern corner of the state, Greenville is referred to by the local chamber of commerce as "Mississippi's Queen City."

"I grew up on a farm," George recalls. "I woke up every morning looking forward to working. Farming is hard work, but I loved it. I never lifted weights. I never worked out. I was naturally strong from working so hard on the farm. It's just part of the life"

Scott was a three-sport star in high school in Greenville. "I was a better football player than a baseball player. I played quarterback in my senior year. But to be honest with you, my first love was basketball. I remember John Wooden [legendary UCLA basketball coach] talking to me about going to UCLA and helping them win some more national championships."

Boston Red Sox scout Milt Bolling worked hard to convince Scott that his best potential was on the baseball diamond. "The Red Sox offered me $10,000 to sign with them right after high school graduation. That was a lot of money for an 18-year-old kid in the Mississippi Delta. It was just my momma and me, so I took it. I never regretted it."

Scott's first professional baseball stop was at the Red Sox' lowest farm team in Olean, New York. His fine play at bat and in the field at Olean earned him a promotion to Wellsville, New York, the following year. "The first player I met in Wellsville was Tony Conigliaro. I was a pretty confident athlete, but Tony was even more confident than me. He was my friend. I still miss him very much."

Despite his limited baseball experience, Scott rose rapidly through the Red Sox minor league system. By 1965 he had advanced to the Red Sox Double A farm team in Pittsfield, Massachusetts, where he came under the tutelage of long-time Red Sox instructor Eddie "Pop" Popowski.

"Pop was terrific with me. He was a wonderful influence. I really learned how to play baseball under him," Scott remembers. The Scott-Popowski combination worked well enough that George won the Triple Crown in the strong Eastern League that season. His outstanding year earned him an invitation to spring training with the major league club in 1966.

"The Red Sox were very honest with me when I went down to Winter Haven that year. They told me they weren't going to rush me. They just wanted me to get a taste of the big leagues in spring training. They planned to send me to the top farm club in Toronto for the regular season. But the way I hit in pre-season, they had to keep me with the big club. I went to Boston to open the season, and I ended up in 162 games. That was as many games as any rookie ever played in the big leagues."

"THE BOOMER"

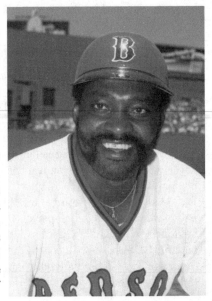

Baseball has some wonderful nicknames, and the Red Sox have had their share over the years. Mention "The Monster" and almost every fan will identify Dick Radatz. Most fans will link Ken Harrelson with "The Hawk." But the player most closely tied to his nickname is George Scott as "The Boomer."

"Joe Foy [the late Red Sox third baseman of 1966-68] put that name on me. One night when we were both rookies in 1966, we came into the clubhouse after a win, and he looked at me and said, 'Man, you really put a boom on that ball.' He was talking about a home run I had hit earlier. The other players started calling me 'Boom.' Over time it became 'Boomer,' and eventually I just became 'The Boomer.' Hardly anybody calls me George."

The Boomer's offense tailed off during the second half of the 1966 season, but his fielding prowess at first base continued to earn rave reviews. The irony is that Scott had played everywhere in the infield except first base during his minor league career.

"Joe Foy had won the Triple Crown in the International League in 1965, and he was a third baseman. Billy Herman [Red Sox manager 1965-66] took me aside in spring training and told me I had a better shot at making the big leagues as a first baseman. So I moved over to first and it felt natural from the start. I didn't have any trouble over there."

THE IMPOSSIBLE DREAM TEAM

George Scott spent 14 seasons in the major leagues, nine of them in a Red Sox uniform. His favorite Red Sox season is unquestionably the 1967 Impossible Dream year.

"I knew things were going to be different right from the start in spring training with Dick Williams. All of a sudden, doing even the little things right became important. I had my problems with the man [Williams], but he taught me how to win. I still use some of the things he taught me in my managing."

Manager Dick Williams demanded excellence from Scott and his teammates from Opening Day to the last pitch of that year's seven game World Series. It was a MVP year for Carl Yastrzemski, a Cy Young Year for pitcher Jim Lonborg, and an unexpected hero emerged almost daily. Throughout this season of high drama, George Scott was a paragon of consistency.

Dick Williams remembers George Scott fondly. "I loved Boomer. He was a great kid. Sometimes I had trouble getting through to him. I tried every way I could to get him to listen to me."

At one point an exasperated Williams told the Boston writers, "Talking to George Scott is like trying to talk to cement." Dick is a little more philosophical today. "That was a little harsh," he offers in understatement.

"But I saw this talented ballplayer who could become a star if he took some instruction. I got frustrated because I couldn't get him to listen to ways that he could improve. Everything I said or did was intended to make him a better player."

Scott must have been listening to some of Williams' words of wisdom. He reduced his strikeouts from the previous year and still raised his slugging average. George was a much more disciplined hitter in 1967 than he was in his rookie year.

DOWN TO THE WIRE

The 1967 season featured Yaz at the plate and Jim Lonborg on the mound, but George Scott contributed key hits and fielding gems at first base throughout the season. The crucial, next-to-last game of the year against the Minnesota Twins typified Scott's contribution that year.

With the scored tied 2-2 in the sixth inning, Scott stepped in as the first batter to face Twins reliever Ron Kline. The Boomer lined Kline's first pitch into the center-field bleachers to give the Red Sox their first lead of the day. The headlines trumpeted Yastrzemski's three hits and four RBI, but it was George Scott who had put his team ahead to stay.

He finished the season batting .303, which placed him fourth in the American League. And his fielding at first base was even better than his hitting. Younger Red Sox fans that enjoy Doug Mientkiewicz's play around first base would have loved The Boomer. His fielding prowess earned him the first of eight Golden Gloves for fielding excellence at first base.

Scott continued his fine play during the World Series against the St. Louis Cardinals. He contributed two of the Red Sox' six hits against the Cards' Bob Gibson in the opening game. He finished his outstanding season with six hits during the seven-game World Series loss to the Cardinals.

Scott enjoys looking back at the Impossible Dream season. "That was such a great year. Every time we needed a big hit, Yaz delivered. And Lonnie [Jim Lonborg] had so many big wins for us. Reggie [Smith] had a great year. And of course Tony [Conigliaro] came through so many times before he got hurt."

If everything seemed to go right for Scott and his Red Sox teammates in 1967, almost nothing went right in 1968. Winning his second straight Gold Glove was little consolation as Scott's batting average fell to an embarrassing .171. Dropping from the fourth-best batting average in the American League to below "the Mendoza Line," may have been the result of some bad off-field advice to swing for the fences.

In 1969, Scott filled in at third base for over 100 games, and in 1970, splitting his time between third and first base, he brought his batting average back up to .296. The 1971 season saw his full-time return to first base, where he earned his third Golden Glove as the best-fielding first baseman in the American League.

MILWAUKEE-BOUND

In October of 1971, George Scott and five other Red Sox players were traded to Milwaukee for four Brewers including Tommy Harper. "I hated to leave Boston. But Milwaukee turned out to be great for me. It's a good baseball town and good people."

Scott spent five productive years with the Brewers. In his first season away from Boston, he stole 16 bases in 20 attempts, demonstrating remarkable agility for a big man. He also continued his stranglehold on the American League Gold Glove award, topping all first basemen in each of his five years with Milwaukee.

His best season with the Brewers came in 1975 when he led the American League in home runs and RBI. His 36 home runs, or "Taters" as George called them, marked a career high. Pressed for the origin of the term Taters, Scott responds, "It comes from my background down on the farm. When you're playing ball with guys like Reggie Jackson, you have to come up with your own thing."

That's how I happened to call my home runs Taters." Asked if Taters relates to potatoes, Scott replies, "Of course."

The Boomer's outstanding 1975 season earned him his second spot on the American League All-Star team. Appropriately, the game was played in Milwaukee's County Stadium that year.

"The thing I remember best about that game was the way the crowd reacted to Hank Aaron. I got a nice hand from the home crowd, but they went wild when Henry was introduced. I'll never forget that All-Star game for that reason.

"In fact, the best part of being in Milwaukee was being Hank Aaron's teammate in '75 and '76. I had the locker next to him, and we used to talk every day. I think I learned more from Hank Aaron than anyone."

RETURN OF THE PRODIGAL SON

In December of 1976, George Scott and Bernie Carbo were traded by the Brewers to the Red Sox, in exchange for Boston first baseman Cecil Cooper. "I asked to be traded to the Red Sox. I liked Milwaukee enough, but I really missed Boston," is Scott's recollection.

It was a triumphant return for The Boomer who responded to the trade with 33 home runs and 103 runs scored. His production resulted in a third trip to the All-Star game.

"I was one of eight Red Sox who made the team in 1977. We played in Yankee Stadium that year. I came up against Goose Gossage in the last of the ninth with a man on. Goose threw me nothing but heat. I crushed a ball into the left-field stands." George Scott had produced a Tater on what was to be his last at-bat as an All-Star.

The 1978 season ended in disappointment for the Boston Red Sox when they lost a one-game playoff for the American League pennant. It was a disappointing year for The Boomer as well. Scott batted .233 and produced only 12 home runs in 120 games.

Scott began the 1979 season with the Red Sox, but he was traded to the Kansas City Royals in mid-June. He ended the season with the New York Yankees, batting .318 in 45 at-bats.

Unable to land a major league job in 1980, The Boomer continued his playing career in Mexico. Eventually he became a player-manager in the Mexican League, continuing until 1984.

LOOKING BACK

George Scott is justifiably proud of his outstanding major league career. "When you look at my numbers you have to remember that the pitchers were better during my career. I hit against guys who were winning 30 games [Denny McLain for the 1968 Tigers], and guys with an ERA of one-something [Bob Gibson's 1.12 ERA, also in 1968.] I hit 271 home runs against some very good pitchers.

"Sometimes I think I should have stayed in Milwaukee [with the Brewers]. There wasn't as much pressure there and I was very popular with the fans. Maybe I would have become a designated hitter for them eventually. They might have kept me in the organization. But I don't regret coming back to Boston. I love the fans here."

The Boomer is philosophical when he remembers his running battle with Red Sox manager Dick Williams. "I loved Dick Williams. And I still love him today. He was just trying to drive me to the maximum. He was tough on me but I know now he was just trying to make me better.

"He gave me a hard time, but he gave everybody a hard time. Heck, he gave Yaz a hard time. He made me realize that baseball is a dog-eat-dog game. He taught me that you have to be a dog in this business. That helped me through my whole career. He (Williams) made me a better person."

Dick Williams is happy to join the love-fest. "I loved Scotty. We had an old-timers' game in Boston and they brought me back to manage. I told The Boomer I wanted him to manage the team. I put him in charge and he got a big kick out of it."

MASSACHUSETTS MAD DOGS

On a warm summer evening, the Massachusetts Mad Dogs' home park, Fraser Field in Lynn, is heavily populated with youngsters and their parents. A father is overheard pointing out the Mad Dogs' manager and telling his young son that George Scott was one of the best first basemen to ever play for the Boston Red Sox.

Like many baseball fans, that father knows the game. In a 1982 poll of fans, Scott was voted as the second-team first baseman on the All-Time Boston Red Sox team. The Boomer played more games at first base (988) for the Boston Red Sox than any player in the team's history. And his 154 Taters in a Red Sox uniform place him thirteenth on the Red Sox all-time home run list.

George Scott became the Mad Dogs' manager when the team was founded in 1996. At the time of our interview, the Mad Dogs were part of the 16-team Northern League, which is an independent league. The team had a loyal fan base, drawn primarily from the North Shore of Boston.

"I love what I'm doing," George Scott stated with a passion. "I learned a lot from my time in the big leagues and I do my best to pass it on to these kids."

Mike Kardamis, the Mad Dogs' General Manager, may be The Boomer's biggest fan. "I've worked in professional baseball since I graduated from UMass, and I've learned an awful lot from The Boomer. Our players really respect him, and he is great with the fans. He understands baseball, both how it is played and how it is run.

"We work very hard on our ties to the community. Any time I ask Boomer to make an appearance, he always comes through. You should see the reaction he gets when he speaks to a group. Everybody loves The Boomer."

Not only was George Scott the manager of the Mad Dogs, but he had the barbecue concession at Fraser Field as well. Many athletes lend their name to a product, but George Scott prepared "Boomer's Mississippi Barbecue-Southern Style" personally before each home game. "This sauce is from a secret recipe my momma gave me," he remarks as he prepares an evening's fare alongside the left-field line. "My momma has been the biggest influence in my life."

At the time of our interview, George and his wife Edith had lived in Randolph, Massachusetts, for a number of years. At that time, his 13-year-old son Brian had shown an early aptitude for baseball. "We'll have to see," said George speaking philosophically about his son's prospects in the game. A highlight of each year is a return trip to Greenville, Mississippi, to visit his mother and the community he grew up in.

When asked how much he loves the game of baseball, Scott replies, "I love baseball more than I can ever put in words. You're a pretty good writer, but even you don't have words to say how much I love this game. Baseball is my life."

The Boomer was back: back in the game of baseball that he loves so very much.

George hoping to connect for one of his famous "taters."

22.
Mike Andrews Interview
March 1997

I met with Mike Andrews in his office at the Jimmy Fund. During the hour and one-half we spent talking, I almost felt guilty taking him away from the good work he does helping to raise money for the Dana-Farber Cancer Institute's important work.

Over the years, almost every player I have interviewed has referred to the ties the Red Sox have to the Jimmy Fund. And it is never mentioned in the context of all the time the player has spent visiting patients or going to fundraisers. Instead they speak of how much pride they take in the Red Sox connection to the Jimmy Fund.

I have been amazed at the level of detail that so many players remember about the games they have played. Jim Lonborg can tell you what the count was when he got Rich Rollins to pop up for the last out of the 1967 season, and what kind of pitch he threw him. Mike Andrews is quick to acknowledge that he is not in that category.

Whenever I ask Mike about a game or a play, he always responds, "I can't even remember what I had for breakfast this morning. I played in well over 1,000 professional games, and most of the details run together."

But Mike does remember the role the Impossible Dream Team played in bringing baseball back to the forefront in New England. And he does remember how so many of the players on that team made a commitment to the Jimmy Fund that has lasted for over 35 years.

MIKE ANDREWS
MEMORIES OF THE IMPOSSIBLE
DREAM TEAM

Mike Andrews, former Red Sox second baseman and current Chairman and Executive Director of the Jimmy Fund, is clearly a man who loves his job.

"Winning the pennant with the Red Sox in 1967 was a great thrill. Playing in the All-Star Game, and two World Series, are memories that I will always treasure. But nothing that I ever achieved in baseball could possibly compare with the tremendous satisfaction I get from my job here at the Jimmy Fund."

Andrews, who spent eight years in the major leagues, celebrated his twenty-fifth anniversary with the Jimmy Fund in February. "I see some real similarities between baseball players and my colleagues here at the Jimmy Fund and the Dana-Farber Cancer Institute. Ballplayers are totally consumed by their sport; they tell you not to take the game home with you, but that's easier said than done," Andrews laughs.

"The physicians, researchers and staff here are the same way. They are all completely committed to our mission, and to our vision. This is their life's work."

ROOKIE SECOND BASEMAN

At six feet, three inches, Mike Andrews became the tallest regular second baseman in baseball history, when he took over the starting duties for the Red Sox in mid-April in 1967. Andrews was on the bench on Opening Day, nursing a bad back that had cropped up during spring training. Mike's absence from the starting lineup gives rise to one of the most popular Red Sox trivia questions: who played second base on Opening Day in

Back in uniform again for an Old-Timers' Game at Fenway in the 1980s.

1967? Serious Red Sox fans know that the answer is nominal center fielder Reggie Smith.

Mike Andrews chuckles at the memory. "Reggie was such a great natural athlete that when I couldn't play, they knew he could get the job done at second. He did fine, but one game he was taken out hard by the runner on a force play at second base. He was okay, but he looked like he had been injured.

"Reggie was just too valuable to the team to take a chance on his getting banged up at second. I was expendable," Mike laughs. "Bad back or not, Dick Williams told me to get back in the lineup. Dick didn't have much patience for injuries."

The "experts" almost universally picked the 1967 Red Sox team for the second division. But Andrews, and many of his teammates, didn't feel that way.

"I never liked to lose. Reggie Smith, Russ Gibson, and I were all rookies in 1967, and we had won the International League championship the year before in Toronto, so we didn't think about losing. We had played under new Red Sox manager Dick Williams at Toronto, and we knew he didn't want to hear about losing. We never thought of ourselves as a second-division team."

Rookie manager Williams had promised at the end of spring training: "We'll win more than we'll lose." On Memorial Day that year, a Fenway crowd of over 32,000, watched as the Red Sox swept a twin bill over the California Angels, improving their record to 22-21. Williams had been writing Andrews' name into the lineup on a daily basis, and Mike had become the most consistent Red Sox second-sacker since Hall of Famer Bobby Doerr had retired in 1951. The team would stay above .500, and Andrews would remain entrenched at second base for the balance of the season.

Andrews is described by former teammate Russ Gibson as the "ultimate team guy." Gibson recalls, "He did the important things that don't show up in the box score. When he came up with a man on second, he made sure he moved him

A young Andrews takes his swings in spring training.

along to third . . . He always made the double play at second, even when the runner came in hard.

"When you think of '67, you think of Yaz, and Lonnie [Cy Young Award-winner Jim Lonborg]," Gibson continues. But you have to realize that first, and foremost, we were a real team. And Mike Andrews personified that team. He was the ideal teammate"

On July 22, 1967, the Red Sox won their tenth straight game in Cleveland, and a crowd of about 15,000 fans descended upon Logan Airport to welcome their conquering heroes. Andrews remembers that crowd and the day distinctly.

"That was probably the point when we realized that we had a good shot at the pennant. We had played good, consistent ball, and no one team was pulling way out front. We had believed in ourselves all along, but from then on we really started to focus on making a run for it."

UNSUNG HERO

Andrews left the headlines to Yastrzemski, Lonborg, and the late Tony Conigliaro, but opposing teams recognized how important he was to the Red Sox. While the Red Sox prepared for their triumphant return from Cleveland, the Indians' General Manager Al Rosen told Boston writers, "Without Mike Andrews, you Red Sox would be nothing."

Asked when he first became aware of the Jimmy Fund, and its bond with Red Sox, Andrews responds, "I was aware of it from day one . . . we all were. Right away you were struck by Mr. Yawkey's devotion to the cause, and we all revered that man. Ted Williams had only been retired for seven years, and his commitment to the Jimmy Fund was legendary. We all looked up to Yaz. And he is one of the biggest supporters the Jimmy Fund has ever had. And we had a bunch of local guys like Gibby [Fall River native Russ Gibson], and Mike Ryan [Haverhill], who had grown up with the Jimmy Fund and they made sure we knew all about it."

By the end of August 1967, the Red Sox were acknowledged as legitimate contenders. The Minnesota Twins, Detroit Tigers, and Chicago White Sox all took their shot at opening up a lead atop the standings in the American League, but Boston stayed with them every step of the way. Mike Andrews has a special memory of that time.

"I remember it as a lot of fun, but the tension really started to build up. I will always remember Bill Koster, who was the original Executive Director of the Jimmy Fund, asking me to speak to a 12-year-old patient just before one late-season game. I was happy to do it, we all were, but I have to admit I was a little distracted. We had a nice chat . . . he told me how he was looking forward to playing ball the next season, and I wished him well."

"Later, Bill Koster took me aside and said, 'I really appreciate you helping out at the last minute. We have to send that young man home. There's nothing more we can do for him. I know your visit meant a lot to him.' All of a sudden, whether I batted .250 or .260 didn't seem to matter that much. It put a lot of things in perspective for me.

"Over the years, a lot of the players have told me they have had the same experience. You might go 0-4, or you might get knocked out of the game, but when you come over to visit with these kids, you realize you can't feel sorry for yourself. You really have nothing to complain about."

THE STUFF THAT DREAMS ARE MADE OF

The New England weather grew colder as September dawned, but the American League pennant race grew even hotter. The Red Sox, led by Carl Yastrzemski, responded to the pressure by turning up their intensity another notch. Over the last 12 pressure-packed games, Yaz had 23 hits, and batted an unbelievable .523.

"Yaz came through over and over for us in '67," Andrews recalls. "Of course, I would be remiss if I didn't point out that he has performed at that same level for the Jimmy Fund for over 40 years. He is one of our MVPs."

The Red Sox swept the Twins in two crucial games in the last weekend of the season to bring the pennant to Boston for the first time in 21 years. Andrews contributed two key hits in the Saturday game, and started a crucial double play in the last inning of the final game.

"I'll always remember beating Minnesota on the final day of the season and the crowd coming on the field. That was a once in a lifetime experience. We really shared the experience with the fans that day."

In his view, the loss of the World Series to the St. Louis Cardinals, four games to three, didn't detract from the achievements of the Impossible Dream team at all. "Our exciting season brought baseball back to the forefront in New England. To this day, when someone says 'that's impossible,' the response is often 'don't forget the '67 Sox!' It really is part of the New England folklore. We use it here [at the Jimmy Fund], all the time."

THE RED SOX AND THE JIMMY FUND

If the odds against the Red Sox winning the pennant in 1967 were 100-1, the odds against Dr. Sidney Farber achieving his goal of eradicating cancer in children when he began his work in 1947 were even greater. Yet today, better than two out of three children walk away disease-free from Dana-Farber's Jimmy Fund Clinic, and from many other cancer treatment centers around the world.

New England's favorite charity, the Jimmy Fund, and New England's favorite sports team, the Boston Red Sox, are inexorably linked. "The Red Sox are tied in with almost everything we do," says Andrews. "Whether it is raising money, or visiting sick kids, or volunteering, the Red Sox are always there."

It is actually something of a long shot that Mike Andrews is in his present position, and that the Red Sox are the baseball team so closely tied to the Jimmy Fund. Sixty years ago, Andrews was a toddler growing up 3,000, miles away in

Torrance, California. An outstanding high school athlete, he was best known for his football exploits before the Red Sox signed him to a minor league contract.

When the Jimmy Fund received its first national exposure through the famous Ralph Edwards 1948 radio broadcast, the Braves were the Boston baseball club identified with the charity. The 1948 Boston Braves won the National League pennant by six and one-half games, while the Boston Red Sox lost a one-game playoff to the Cleveland Indians, depriving the city of its one opportunity for a "Streetcar Series." Nearly 120,000 Boston fans trekked to old Braves Field to watch the three home World Series games against the Indians, giving the Braves a total season attendance that surpassed the Red Sox for the first time in 15 years.

By 1952, the Braves had fallen to seventh place in the National League, and home attendance had fallen below the 300,000 fan level. In the spring of 1953, owner Lou Perini received permission from his fellow owners to move his franchise to Milwaukee. Boston was about to become a one-team baseball town for the first time in over 50 years.

One of Perini's last official acts on behalf of the Boston Braves was to meet with Mr. and Mrs. Thomas A. Yawkey to pass the mantle of Jimmy Fund support to the Red Sox. The Yawkey's enthusiastically agreed, and announced on April 10, 1953, that they would join with the Variety Club as a Jimmy Fund sponsor. Thus was born one of the great philanthropic partnerships of all-time.

GO EAST YOUNG MAN

When the 1967 World Series came to an end, Mike Andrews piled his young family into their car and drove 3,000 miles to their California home. In the sixties, a young ballplayer with a family had to hustle to make ends meet. An off-season job at the local Sears & Roebuck awaited Andrews. "We all had to work during the winter in those days," Andrews recalls with a chuckle.

A series of phone calls from teammates convinced Andrews that he should return to the Boston area. "Guys like Gibby were telling me, 'You have to come back. These fans can't get enough of us. You'll be out every night speaking at a function of some kind.' The Andrews family repeated their cross-country trip just months after returning to California. Peabody, Massachusetts, became their adopted home.

Mike settled in as the regular Red Sox second baseman for the next several seasons. In 1968 he was one of the few players who improved on his 1967 season, advancing to fifth in the American League in on-base percentage (.368) and times on base with 229.

The 1969 season was probably Andrews' best in the big leagues. He reached double-figures in home runs (15) and his .293 batting average ranked the tenth highest in the league. His offensive production and fine play earned him a spot on the American League All-Star team.

Mike Andrews had another fine season in 1970. He increased his home run output to 17, and he was tenth in the American League in walks. And the Red

Sox finished a respectable third in the Eastern Division under new manager
Eddie Kasko.

TRADED

Being traded is part of baseball, and that is exactly what happened to Andrews
just before Christmas in 1970. Andrews was traded to the Chicago White Sox for
future Hall of Fame shortstop Luis Aparicio.

"I remember I was devastated when I found out I had been traded. We had
really settled in with Boston as our new home. We knew we were going to stay
here permanently no matter where I ended up playing.

"It was never quite the same for me after that," Andrews recalls. "I had some
good years with the White Sox. I really enjoyed playing for Chuck Tanner in
Chicago. But I lost a little bit of my spark when I left the Red Sox."

Andrews had two decent seasons with the White Sox. He hit a solid .282 in
1971, and in 1972 he was in the top 10 in walks in the American League, while
his 18 sacrifice hits ranked second best in the league. But in 1972, his batting
average declined to .201, and the White Sox gave him his outright release in July.

At that point fate, in the person of Dick Williams, intervened. Dick Williams
was en route to guiding the Oakland Athletics to their third-straight American
League pennant, and had his sights set on a second straight World Series win.

Dick Williams knew that Mike Andrews would make a great backup second baseman for his A's.

"I always got along with Dick Williams. I had played for him in the minors
and I played three years in Boston for him. You know the old cliché, 'tough but
fair?' That was Dick Williams. He always treated me fairly."

Andrews appeared in 18 games with Oakland over the last two months of the
1973 season, mostly as a late-inning defensive replacement. And he celebrated
winning his second American League pennant as the A's defeated the Baltimore
Orioles three games to two.

WORLD SERIES CELEBRITY

Andrews was eagerly anticipating his second World Series, hoping for his first
World Championship, but he expected to be far from the spotlight. But the spotlight found Mike Andrews and he became a national figure in a very unusual cir-
cumstance.

In Game Two of the World Series, following the A's 2-1 opening game win,
Mike Andrews was charged with two key errors in the twelfth inning. The A's lost
10-7 and A's owner Charlie Finley insisted that Williams put Andrews on the disabled list and replace him with Manny Trillo.

This happened over 30 years ago, but Dick Williams is still steaming mad
over the incident. "First of all, Mike took an error on a ball that took a bad hop.
And the second error really should have been charged to first baseman Gene
Tenace. I decided right then and there that I was getting the hell away from
Charlie Finley whether we won the Series or not. I had had enough of that man."

Dick Williams was outraged and Andrews' teammates were equally upset.
They wore armbands at their practice before Game Three. Finally,
Commissioner Bowie Kuhn moved to void Finley's decision and ordered Mike
reinstated to the A's. Dick Williams used Mike Andrews as a pinch-hitter in Game
Four, and 55,000 fans at Shea Stadium gave him a standing ovation.

The Oakland A's went on to win the World Series and, true to his word, Dick
Williams resigned as their manager. Mike Andrews wanted to get as far from
Charlie Finley as he possibly could, and that is exactly what he did. Mike played
the following season in Japan.

After playing the 1974 season in Japan, he concluded that it was time to
retire from the game and get on with his life. "Actually, I was ready to go back to
Japan for another season," Andrews recalls. "But my wife, Marilyn, put her foot
down. And she was right. Our kids were getting older and it is a major adjustment
to pick up your family and move them to Japan for the season."

JIMMY FUND ALL-STAR

Andrews did a little broadcasting and sold life insurance, but in early 1979, long-
time Jimmy Fund supporter Ken Coleman asked him if he would like to do some
work for the Jimmy Fund.

"I told Ken I would try it part-time, but very quickly I realized that this was what I really wanted to do with my life. I've been here ever since."

In his role as Chairman and Executive Director, Andrews is accountable for raising the money needed to continue this critically important effort. "Our fundraising activities involve thousands of individuals, and range from small neighborhood activities to major corporate efforts. Every single dollar is important to our continued success."

Over 100 Jimmy Fund golf tournaments are held to generate donations each year. Each August, John Hancock sponsors a day at Fenway Park which gives fans a chance to hit one over the "Green Monster" in return for a generous donation to the Jimmy Fund. And in September, the Boston Marathon Jimmy Fund Walk brings out thousands of walkers to retrace this famous course, and to raise substantial sums for this great cause.

The "406 Club" was formed in 1995, to honor longtime Jimmy Fund supporter Ted Williams by raising over $2 million to fight childhood cancer. Members pledge to contribute $1,000 to the Jimmy Fund every year for five years. "Being able to plan on pledges at this level means an awful lot to our program," Andrews emphasizes.

All of these activities keep Mike Andrews and his staff quite busy. But getting Mike Andrews to use the word "I" in a sentence is a real effort. Mike's former Red Sox teammates describe him as the "ideal teammate." He certainly is the ideal person for his job with the Jimmy Fund. Mike Andrews is now an all-star at his position seven days a week.

23.
Ken Harrelson Interview
June 2002

I sat with Ken Harrelson in a quiet corner of the Fenway Park press box several hours before the Red Sox were scheduled to play the Chicago White Sox. The Hawk has been a color analyst on White Sox telecasts for many years, but the quiet of the ballpark seemed to rekindle his emotional ties to Boston.

He was clearly nostalgic when he reminisced about how much being a part of the Impossible Dream team meant to him. And he was obviously sincere when he said his only regret was that it was Tony Conigliaro's injury which brought him to Boston.

Ken Harrelson joined the 1967 Red Sox in late August, and he contributed to their memorable season. But it was in 1968, when most of the heroes from '67 slumped, that the Hawk emerged as a folk hero. He was flamboyant in a town that prefers its heroes to be understated, but he was so likeable that he pulled it off.

Some of Ken Harrelson's strongest memories revolve around the time he spent for the Jimmy Fund and spending time with young cancer patients. He pointed to a seat near to the Red Sox dugout and recalled speaking with a young patient seated there before a game. Ken Harrelson was overcome with emotion as he recounted the phone call he received the next morning from the parents, telling him that the youngster had passed away.

Unable to go on, Ken Harrelson patted me on the shoulder, and left the area. Then you remember the reason why everybody loved the Hawk. It was because he cared passionately about everything he did.

KEN HARRELSON
"THE HAWK"

On August 20, 1967, Ken "Hawk" Harrelson was a first baseman for the tenth place Kansas City Athletics earning the princely sum of $12,000 per year. On August 21 he was a 25-year-old unemployed first baseman. On August 28 he signed a contract with the pennant contending Boston Red Sox for $150,000, reportedly the highest salary in major league baseball at the time.

The Hawk went on to play a key role in the Red Sox pennant-winning season and to play in the World Series. The following season he led the American League in RBI and became one of Boston's best-known public figures. In April of 1969 he was traded to the Cleveland Indians and in 1971 he retired from baseball.

THE HAWK LANDS IN BOSTON

"Kansas City was down at the bottom of the standings, but we knew we were the team of the future," Harrelson remembers. "I had teammates like Reggie Jackson, Joe Rudi, and Catfish Hunter. And our manager, Alvin Dark, was just the right guy for us. He was teaching us and grooming us for the future.

"There was an incident with pitcher Lew Krausse, and Charlie Finley [Kansas City Athletics' owner] didn't like the way Alvin handled it, so he fired him. I told the writers after the game that Mr. Finley's actions were a detriment to the club and to baseball. The headline the next day was 'Harrelson Calls Finley Menace to Baseball.'

"I got a call from Charlie the next morning and we went at it pretty good. Finally he

told me that he had scheduled a press conference for noon and I was to retract everything. I told him I would clarify the term 'menace' because I had never said that, but that I would stand by everything else.

"He called me later that morning and all he said was 'you'll never play for the green and gold again.' All I could think at the time was 'I'm out of a job.' So I called the Commissioner's office to clarify my status. By the time I hung up I realized I was a free agent, and the only guy swinging a bat better than me at the time was Yaz.

"Then the telephone started ringing. First the White Sox called and made me a nice offer. Then I heard from Haywood Sullivan who made me a better offer. Next I heard from Paul Richards of the Braves. He made me the best offer to date. I called Haywood back to tell him that I was going to Atlanta, and the next thing I knew Dick O'Connell called back from the Red Sox.

"Dick asked me what it would take to bring me to Boston. This was before players had agents and I didn't know quite what to say. So I threw out the figure of $150,000, and Mr. O'Connell said 'done.'"

MEET YOUR NEW BOSS

Ken Harrelson was signed in an effort to fill the power void created when star right fielder Tony Conigliaro was struck in the head by a Jack Hamilton fastball on August 18 in a game against the California Angels. He had to adjust to a new set of teammates and the Red Sox had to adjust to the flamboyant Hawk.

"I had just played a series in Boston. In one game I hit a three run homer off of Lonborg [Jim] to win the game, and I doubled off the center-field wall to win another. At one point Dick Williams [Red Sox manager] was standing on the top step of the dugout screaming 'stick it in his ear' and I walked halfway from the batter's box to the Red Sox dugout and asked him if he wanted to come out and say that. Nobody moved.

"When I joined the Red Sox in New York at the end of August, Dick had me up to his hotel room. We talked generally and finally he said, 'I hope that incident isn't going to get in our way.' I told him that was behind us and we were fine from there."

Ken Harrelson's Red Sox career began with a bang. In his first at-bat in Yankee Stadium he hit a home run and the Red Sox moved into a tie for first place. Three days later he had a double, triple, and a home run as the Red Sox defeated one of their leading competitors, the Chicago White Sox.

Although his production fell off during the rest of September, he had won the hearts of the fans. He would flash the peace sign as he ran to his position in right field and he kept up a running conversation with the fans in the grandstand.

"I'm really two different people," Hawk insists. "There's Ken Harrelson who is actually a shy guy and pretty much of a loner. Then there's The Hawk who is outgoing and loves the spotlight. The fans in Boston really brought out The Hawk in me."

GEORGIA ON HIS MIND

The Hawk was the toast of the town in Boston, but 10 years earlier basketball was his first love. He was a high school basketball All-American at Benedictine Military Academy in Savannah, Georgia, and he had his choice of college scholarships.

The greatest single influence in Ken Harrelson's life was his mother, Jessie Harrelson. "My mother had always wanted me to be a baseball player. And let me tell you, no one has ever loved their mother more than I loved mine. There may be others who loved their mothers as much, but nobody has ever loved their mother more.

"She was divorced from my father when I was eight years old and she raised me all by herself. She was making $56 a week as a secretary but I never lacked for anything.

"I remember playing in a high school tournament in Atlanta and she would drive from Savannah to Atlanta to watch me play. That was a long trip in those days. Then she would turn around, drive home and go to work the next day," Harrelson recalls, emotion choking his voice. "She was always there for me.

"The president of the local gas company paid my tuition and costs at Benedictine and some of their supporters would chip in some cash when I had a good game. And I was making pretty good money playing semi-pro baseball. It really helped out at home."

Basketball may have been young Harrelson's game of choice, but he followed big league baseball closely. "I loved Ted Williams as a youngster. But I have to admit that my absolute favorite was Mickey Mantle. I think I liked Mantle better because he was younger, closer to my age.

"I remember that the Yankees played an exhibition game in Savannah on their way north from spring training when I was a kid. I went up to Mick after the game and said, 'Mickey, can I please have your autograph?' His reply was, 'Get lost, kid. I'm in a hurry,' says Harrelson, chuckling at the memory. "We became good friends years later and I used to kid him about that all the time.

"I had my heart set on playing basketball for Adolph Rupp at Kentucky. They sent an assistant coach down to watch me play and I had a great game. But they decided I wasn't tall enough to meet their needs. I ended up signing a baseball contract with the Kansas City Athletics for a $30,000 bonus. That really made my momma happy."

HENRIETTA HAWK

Ken Harrelson progressed rapidly through the Kansas City farm system. He was called up to the major leagues in June 1963. He appeared in 79 games that year, splitting his time between first base and the outfield. Kansas City Athletics teammate Dick Howser, who later managed in Kansas City, gave Harrelson his trademark nickname.

"We were playing winter ball down in Florida and my hitting was terrible. Dick Howser started calling me 'Henrietta Hawk' after a well-known comic strip character of the time. I didn't like that at all, so I asked him what it was going to take to get him to stop calling me Henrietta. He replied, 'Go out tomorrow and get a couple of base hits.' That's exactly what I did, and it has been Hawk ever since."

The Hawk has been known to stand for hours signing autographs. It is a lesson that he learned from former Cleveland Indians outfield great Rocky Colavito, who was a teammate in Kansas City. After a particularly good game he was rushing past the fans gathered outside the Kansas City clubhouse when he felt a hand on his shirt collar.

"It was Rocky and he dragged me bodily back into the clubhouse. He said, 'Listen. Those people out there pay your salary. If somebody wants your autograph, you sign. If I ever see you ignore the fans again, I'll beat the stuffing out of you.' He made a tremendous impression on me. To this day I sign every autograph, if I possibly can."

Hawk hit 23 home runs in 1965 and established himself as the team's regular first baseman. The following season he was traded to the Washington Senators, but Kansas City reacquired him in June 1967. Until he made the headlines on August 20 that year, he expected to be a part of a future Athletics powerhouse.

REMEMBERING 1967

"When I think back to 1967 I always wish that I wasn't there because Tony Conigliaro got hurt. That was a tragedy. Tony was a great player. I wish I had ended up in Boston for another reason.

"My first big surprise when I arrived in Boston was the media coverage. In Kansas City we had one beat writer and when I got here we had about 40 guys covering us at home. I couldn't get over it.

Carl Yastrzemski's clutch hitting in September of 1967 made a lasting impression on Hawk. "Yaz was the greatest clutch performer I ever saw. George Brett is my all-time favorite player, but if the game was on the line, Carl is the guy I would want up there. I have been watching baseball for a long time, and his performance during the last two weeks of the season [1967] was the best I have ever seen. Every time we needed a big hit, Yaz came through."

Hawk was a central performer in one of the biggest plays of the 1967 season. The Red Sox and the Twins squared off at Fenway Park on October 1, 1967, with identical records of 91 wins and 70 losses. The Twins took a 2-0 lead into the sixth inning, but Carl Yastrzemski's single tied the game at two runs apiece.

Ken Harrelson stepped in with Dalton Jones at third and Yaz on first, with starting pitcher Dean Chance still on the mound. He worked the count to 3-2 and then Chance came in with a wicked pitch ("a spitter," Harrelson recalls emphatically). Hawk got good wood on the ball, but it went directly to Twins shortstop Zoilo Versalles on one hop.

"It looked like a tailor-made double play ball, but for some reason Zoilo went home with it. His throw was high, and Dalton slid home easily. I thought it was a really stupid play but, boy, it sure helped us."

The Hawk's RBI turned out to be a crucial one, as the Red Sox went on to beat the Twins 5-3. When the Tigers lost the second game of a doubleheader, the Red Sox were headed to the World Series for the first time since 1946.

"Playing in the World Series was a great thrill. The game I remember best is Game Six at Fenway Park. We had been down three games to one, but in Game Five Jim Lonborg pitched his third straight great game to bring us back to Boston.

"Yaz had three hits in the sixth game, including a home run, and he made a great catch in the late innings. He had gotten us that far, and it was almost as if he was going to personally assure that we would get a chance in Game Seven.

"Hitting behind Yaz that year really inspired me. I vowed to have a better offensive year in 1968 than Yaz. He became my benchmark."

CAREER YEAR

The Hawk returned to Savannah after the Red Sox lost Game Seven of the World Series, and he began a conditioning program. "I worked harder in that off-season than I had ever worked before. When I reported to Winter Haven in February 1968 I was in the best shape I had ever been in."

Harrelson greeted teammate Carl Yastrzemski at home plate during the 1967 World Series.

Hawk's dedication won him a trip to the 1968 All-Star Game in Houston's Astrodome. He pounded American League pitching all year, leading the Red Sox in home runs and RBI. And he was as popular off the field as he was in Fenway Park. At one point he had an interest in a nightclub and a submarine shop, and he was the host of his own television show. He did more to popularize the Nehru jacket in Boston than the first Prime Minister of independent India did.

"I was disappointed that we couldn't repeat in 1968. Lonnie got hurt in the off-season and Tony C. missed the whole year. We hung in there as long as we could, but then Jose Santiago, who was having a great season, blew his arm out. I had played with Jose in Kansas City and he was one of the two nicest men I ever met in baseball. Frank Howard of the Washington Senators was the other guy.

"I finished ahead of Yaz in home runs and RBI, but he had a sore wrist for most of the season and he never told the writers. But he still won the American League batting title."

The Hawk ended up with 35 home runs, which placed him third in the American League, and his 109 RBI topped the league. His achievements earned him recognition as Player of the Year in the American League as selected by *The Sporting News*.

On April 19, 1969, the unthinkable happened: The Hawk was traded to the Cleveland Indians. "It literally broke my heart. I loved the city of Boston and I dearly loved the Red Sox fans. But I told Dick O'Connell that I understood. They were picking up a good starter in Sonny Siebert, a top reliever in Vicente Romo, and Joe Azcue was a good catcher. The Red Sox had to make the deal."

After toying with the idea of retiring, The Hawk finally reported to the Indians. But there were few fans on hand in Cleveland's Municipal Stadium to bring out the Hawk in Ken Harrelson. In 1969 the Indians attracted only 620,000 fans to a stadium that could seat 80,000 per game. Playing in relative obscurity, the Hawk's average fell to .222.

The Hawk was injured in both the 1970 and 1971 seasons. During those two seasons combined he played in only 69 games for the Indians. Following the 1971 season he announced that he was retiring from baseball to pursue a career as a professional golfer.

FORE!

Anyone who had ever watched Ken Harrelson hit a golf ball recognized that he had the natural talent to succeed as a professional golfer. "I could hit off the tee as well as anyone and my overall game matched up. But it turned out that I didn't have the temperament to make it as a pro. I would be going along having a great round and something would happen to set me off. You simply can't succeed as a professional on that basis.

"But I consider myself the luckiest guy to ever set two feet on this earth. I got to pursue my dream and to compete professionally in two sports. The Red Sox contacted me in 1974 to ask if I was interested in broadcasting. I thanked them, but I told them I wanted to give golf one more year. In 1975 I had decided to walk away from golf, and on the day I was going to play my last round, the Red Sox called and offered me the chance to audition for a TV job.

"I started out with Dick Stockton, and then with Ned Martin, who I loved working with. I did the Red Sox games for seven seasons, and then I got an offer to telecast the White Sox that was too good to pass up."

Hawk's only departure from telecasting came in 1986 when he agreed to serve as the general manager of the White Sox. "That's the toughest job in baseball. I was okay until I had to start letting people go. Even when it is absolutely the only decision, it's terrible. I didn't want any part of messing peoples' lives up."

Family is obviously a very important part of Ken Harrelson's life. "We are an extremely close family. My wife Aris and I have two wonderful children. Our daughter Christa Hawthorne married a terrific guy a year and a half ago. And our son Casey is a great guy who I think has a future as a professional golfer."

LOOKING BACK

Asked where the 1967 season fits on his list of favorite memories, Harrelson answers, "I have had some great thrills in sports. I played in an All-Star game, I was the American League Player of the Year in 1968, and I got to play in the British Open. But the 1967 season is far and away my favorite memory.

"I have only held on to three mementos over the years. I have a collage that Mickey Mantle gave me and I have my award for Player of the Year. And I have this," he says, holding up his 1967 Red Sox World Series ring.

"And I remember the time we all spent getting to know the patients through the Jimmy Fund. Those kids helped us to realize that going 0-4 didn't mean a thing. For that matter they helped us to understand that going 4-4 wasn't very important either." Even 35 years later, Ken Harrelson is overcome with emotion as he recalls the personal relationships he had with some of the Jimmy Fund youngsters.

Harrelson shows the 1967 World Series ring that he proudly cherishes at a May 2002 BoSox Club luncheon.

"Tell the Red Sox fans to never change. Tell them to stay the great fans they have always been," Harrelson concludes.

Ken Harrelson played in only 183 games for the Boston Red Sox. While he appeared upon our stage for only a brief time, he remains one of the team's better-known former players. No other member of the Boston Red Sox has ever played so briefly for the team and achieved such a lasting love affair with the New England fans.

24.
Carlton Fisk Interview
June 2000

I caught up with Carlton "Pudge" Fisk about one month before his induction into baseball's Hall of Fame. Considering the demands on his time, I was pleased to get an hour with him on the telephone.

It seemed odd to be speaking with Pudge at his permanent residence in suburban Chicago. Like many long-time Red Sox fans, when I think of New Englanders who grew up to play for the team, Pudge Fisk is the first player who comes to mind. He made it clear that a large part of his heart still resides in New Hampshire.

"We spend the winters in Florida. When we are leaving, if we are heading to New Hampshire for a visit we say, 'we're heading home.' Otherwise, we say 'we're going back to Chicago.' "

I always enjoy it when I ask a good question and the response is, "No one has ever asked me that before." In this case I asked Pudge to identify his second most memorable home run.

That question stumped him for a minute. But I know you will find his answer to be of interest.

CARLTON "PUDGE" FISK
NATIVE SON OF NEW ENGLAND'S
TEAM

It is only about 150 miles as the crow flies between Charlestown, New Hampshire, and Cooperstown, New York. But Carlton Fisk's journey from the playing fields of Charlestown to the Baseball Hall of Fame in Cooperstown required 26 seasons as a professional baseball player, over one million air miles, and a determination to overcome injuries that threatened to end his career when it had barely begun.

"To tell the truth, getting elected to the Hall still hasn't sunk in entirely. I'm still getting used to it," Carlton Fisk acknowledged in an interview a few weeks before his induction into Baseball's Hall of Fame.

"It's hard for me to get used to the idea of being alongside great players like Ted Williams, Bobby Doerr and Yaz. It's quite an honor for a guy from a small town in New Hampshire."

It may be hard for Carlton "Pudge" Fisk to get used to, but his election to the Hall of Fame has been inevitable since he played his last major league game in 1993. When he retired, Pudge had played in all or part of 24 big league seasons, and he had caught more games (2,226) than any player had in major league history. His 376 home runs place him fifty-seventh on baseball's all-time list and his 351 home runs as a catcher represented the lifetime standard for that position at the time.

THE PRIDE OF CHARLESTOWN,
NEW HAMPSHIRE

Carlton Fisk was born in Bellows Falls, Vermont, on the day after Christmas in 1947. "The nearest hospital was in Bellows Falls, but my mother had me back home in New Hampshire the first chance she got," Pudge laughs. "Actually, I played Legion ball in Vermont so I feel an attachment to the state, but I am a New Hampshire guy through and through."

Asked about his nickname of "Pudge," he recalls, "According to family legend, I had an aunt who took one look at me in the crib, and remarked, 'He certainly is a pudgy little fellow.' No one remembers exactly who or when, but it has been my nickname all my life."

Charlestown, New Hampshire, is the quintessential small New England town. It is located in western New Hampshire, separated from Vermont by the

Connecticut River. Cecil and Lee Fisk raised Carlton, his three brothers, Calvin, Cedric and Conrad, and his two sisters, Janet and June, in this close-knit community.

Pudge's nickname continued to be appropriate through the eighth grade. At age 13 he was about 5' 5" tall, and chubby. His high school coach, Ralph Silva, has memories of Pudge tripping all over his feet and trying to play soccer as an eighth grader.

In a January 2002 interview with *The Boston Globe*, Silva described an amazing transformation before Fisk's freshman year. "Over the summer he went to work on the farm with his dad and his brothers and he came back for his freshman year 6 feet 3, 175 pounds, and solid as a rock. I guess it was throwing around the bales of hay and bringing in the corn," Silva speculates.

"What was even more incredible was not only did he grow in stature, he grew in coordination and all that stuff. How that happens, only the good Lord knows. I was appreciative, I know that!"

BASKETBALL STANDOUT

Pudge excelled at soccer, basketball and, of course, baseball, during his four years at Charlestown High School. However, his first love was basketball. "I was a big Red Sox fan," Fisk recalls, "but I was probably an even bigger Celtics fan. Bill Russell [Boston Celtics Hall of Fame center] was my hero."

Fisk's first appearance before Boston sports fans was in the Boston Garden during his sophomore year. The Charlestown "Forts" appeared in a preliminary game in the New England High School tournament, taking on the Vermont entry from Winooski.

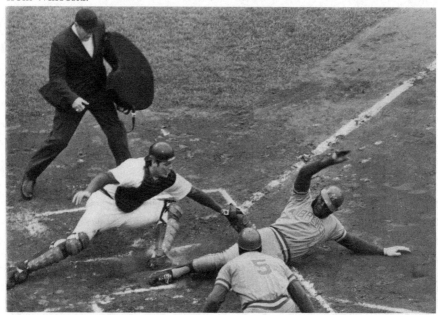

High school coach Silva still remembers Fisk's performance on the basket-ball court against Hopkinton (NH) for the state semi-finals when Pudge was a senior: 40 years later he still marvels at Fisk's determination.

"He scored like 42 points and had 30-some odd rebounds. Of course, in baseball he had many, many, many great games. But in this basketball game, you knew this was the kind of guy who rises to the occasions and would fight what-ever obstacles there were."

Pudge played shortstop and pitched for Charlestown High during the base-ball season. "I loved playing baseball, but we were hard-pressed with the New England spring to get in 12 games. There wasn't enough time to really identify your best position. It was more like, 'Well, you played short Tuesday, so why don't you pitch on Friday?'" Pudge remembers.

"I was a big kid, so eventually they put me behind the plate. At first I wasn't wild about catching. I still enjoyed playing all over. But I came to enjoy being in the middle of things. To be involved in every pitch." In classic New England understatement, Fisk adds, "I guess it was the right choice."

THE ROAD TO FENWAY

After graduation from Charlestown High School, Pudge matriculated at the University of New Hampshire on a basketball scholarship. In his heart, he could still picture himself in a Celtics uniform.

"I played freshman basketball and baseball at UNH, but when I enrolled, my primary focus was still on basketball." Asked when he first recognized that he had a better chance at a professional baseball career, Fisk laughs at the memory. "We were playing the University of Rhode Island freshman, and when I looked across the court I realized that every single player on their team was taller than me. Right then and there, I decided to concentrate on baseball."

After the freshman baseball season at UNH, Pudge played briefly for the Orleans entry in the Cape Cod Summer League. In January of 1967 the Boston Red Sox made Fisk their first draft choice, and the fourth overall selection of the winter baseball draft. "That's not as big a deal as it might sound," Fisk demurs. "It was a very small draft!"

Fisk signed with the Red Sox, but his first tour of duty was with Uncle Sam. "It was the Vietnam era, and I joined an Army Reserve Unit in Chester, Vermont, to satisfy my military obligation. I completed my active duty requirement during the 1967 season, and drilled on weekends and for two weeks in the summer after that. Many of my teammates over the years had the same requirement."

His professional baseball season finally began in 1968 with the Red Sox farm team in Waterloo, Iowa. He batted .338 in 62 games and showed signs of power with 12 home runs. His fine play earned him a promotion to the Red Sox minor league team in Pittsfield, Massachusetts, for the 1969 season.

Fisk found the pitching in the Eastern League a little tougher, batting .243, but his outstanding defensive work impressed the Red Sox front office. He was called up to the Red Sox in September to get a taste of life in the big leagues. He went hitless in two games, but his brief stay makes him one of a select group of players whose major league career spanned four decades.

Pudge graduated to Pawtucket, which was the Red Sox Double A farm team at the time, for the 1970 season. He batted only .229 for the season, but his handling of pitchers continued to draw raves. At the time, the Red Sox projected him as a potential major leaguer based on his superb defense behind the plate.

In 1971, he moved up to the Red Sox top farm club, then located in Louisville, Kentucky. His strong play in the fast Triple A International League earned him another September call-up to Fenway Park. Pudge made the most of this opportunity, batting .313 and contributing two home runs in 14 games at the big league level.

ROOKIE OF THE YEAR

When Carlton Fisk reported to spring training in Winter Haven, Florida, for the 1972 season, no one questioned his abilities behind the plate. However, some observers doubted his ability to hit major league pitching on a consistent basis. All Pudge did to silence his critics was to hit .293, and rap out 22 home runs in 131 games. In recognition of his outstanding season he became the first player selected unanimously as the American League Rookie of the Year.

"I wasn't that surprised to hit so well. I was behind most players at my age (24) because I had fewer at-bats and I was still learning how to hit. The players from California and Florida get a big head start on the New England kids. While we're shoveling the snow off the field, they've already played 30 or 40 games. I was pleased that I hit so well, but I always thought I could do it."

Pudge followed his outstanding rookie season with his first All-Star year in 1973. He missed the first few weeks of the 1974 season with a serious injury, but he was at an All-Star pace when near-disaster struck on June 28 in Cleveland. The Indians' Leron Lee crashed into Fisk on a play at the plate and Pudge's knee was torn apart as a result of the collision.

"I couldn't find one doctor who would give me any encouragement that I would ever play again. Worse

The ever-imposing presence behind the plate.

than that, they all felt I could face serious impairment later in life. No one gave me any chance to come back. It was a pretty lonely, discouraging time. I even had to put together my own program to rehabilitate myself," Fisk recalls.

THE 1975 BOSTON RED SOX
Defying all medical odds, Fisk reported to spring training in 1975 ready to reclaim his starting catcher's job. Unfortunately, a broken arm sidelined him for the first 63 games of the season. After returning to the lineup in June he was a major contributor to the Red Sox American League Championship. During the September pennant drive he had 17 RBI and 10 extra base hits. His season average of .331 was a career high, and he batted .417 in the three-game sweep of the Oakland A's for the American League Pennant.

When fans think of the 1975 World Series they think of the mound magic of Luis Tiant, Dewey Evans' catch of a Joe Morgan line drive, and the clutch play of veteran Carl Yastrezemski. But mostly they think of Carlton Fisk's dramatic game-winning twelfth inning home run in Game Six. The video shot of Pudge using body English to keep his drive fair ranks as one of the great sports clips of all time.

"Fred Lynn was on deck at the time, and I told him, 'I'm going to get on and I want you to drive me in.' I wasn't thinking home run, I just wanted to put the ball in play safely." Asked if he ever got tired of talking about his home run, Pudge reflects, "There was a time when I was in the midst of my career when I used to think, 'That was a long time ago. I've done a lot more than that in my career. Why don't they ask me about our chances for the playoffs?' Now? Never."

Questioned about his second most memorable homer, Pudge hesitates for a moment before answering, "I've never really thought about that. No one has ever asked me that question before. I did hit three consecutive home runs off Roger Clemens over several games.

"I was playing for the White Sox and he was still with the Red Sox at the time. And I don't bring this up to take anything away from Roger. Just the opposite. I remember it so well because he was so great. Of course, he knocked me down on the fourth at-bat. That was okay. I knew it was coming."

Fisk earned All-Star honors for the fourth time during the 1976 season. In 1977, he became the fifth catcher in major league history to both score and drive in over 100 runs. In 1978 he caught a career-high 154 games, and he was widely acknowledged to be the premier catcher in the American League.

Injuries struck again in 1979 and he was limited to 91 games that season. Fisk rebounded in 1980, catching in 115 games, and earned American League All-Star honors for the seventh time.

THE LATER YEARS
Carlton Fisk hit the game-tying home run on Opening Day at Fenway Park on April 10, 1981. Unfortunately, when he put on his Sox before the game they were

White, and he was in the visitors' dressing room. Pudge had signed with the Chicago White Sox as a free agent in January of 1981.

"That was a very strange experience," Pudge exclaims with emotion in his voice. "The strangest part was arriving at Fenway Park and heading into the visitors clubhouse. After all those years of going in the other door, it really seemed odd.

"But the fans at Fenway were always great to me. Even in a visitors' uniform. I think the Boston fans are the best in all of baseball."

Pudge Fisk went on to play in all, or parts of, 13 seasons for the Pale Hose. He helped to lead the White Sox into the postseason in 1983. In 1985, he had 37 home runs to set the American League record for players performing primarily as catchers. In 1991, he caught over 100 games, and he was named to the American League All-Star team at the age of 43. When his career ended in 1993, he had established himself as one of the premier players in the history of the Chicago White Sox.

Although he played less than half of his career in Boston, he still ranks twelfth in home runs and seventeenth in total bases and RBI on the Red Sox all-time list. He was inducted into the Boston Red Sox Hall of Fame in 1997.

"IN THIS LEAGUE WE RUN THOSE OUT"

Carlton Fisk was an 11-time American League All-Star, he caught more games than any player in major league history, and his home run total as a catcher was the record for that position when he retired. His credentials for the Hall of Fame are impeccable. Yet, there was more to the player and the man than mere statistics. His professionalism, his work ethic, and his commitment to the game were legendary.

For many, Fisk's defining moment as a professional baseball player occurred in a May 1990 game between the White Sox and the Yankees. Pudge was behind the plate, and sometime baseball player, and long-time NFL defensive back "Neon Deion" Sanders was at the bat. Sanders lofted a high pop-up to the infield, but never left the batter's box. Fisk flipped back his mask, got right in Deion's face, and informed him in his best New Hampshire accent, "In this league, we run those out!" The 42-year-old Fisk participated enthusiastically in the melee that followed.

Fisk sputtered to reporters, "Yankee pinstripes. Yankee Pride," after the game. "I'm playing for the other team, and it offended me." The famous New Hampshire statesman, Daniel Webster, "The Great Orator," would have been proud.

If you had asked Normal Rockwell to sketch a picture of a big league catcher, he would have painted Fisk upon the pitcher's mound, mask atop his head, instructing his pitcher on the finer points of pitch selection. Moreover, if you commissioned central casting in Hollywood to scour the lengths of our region to find the consummate native to represent New England and baseball, they would have sent you Carlton Fisk.

HALL OF FAME INDUCTION

Carlton Fisk made his first tour of the Baseball Hall of Fame in May 2000. All of the scheduled inductees visit Cooperstown in advance of the July ceremonies to acclimate themselves and enjoy a leisurely visit of the facilities.

"I had been to Cooperstown three times to play in the Monday exhibition game, but I had never had the time to tour the Hall." During his May visit, he headed for the plaques honoring fellow Red Sox greats.

"I went to Tom Yawkey's plaque first. It kind of jumped out at me. I made sure I looked at Yaz, Ted Williams and Bobby Doerr. They were right up there with my contemporaries, Tom Seaver, Steve Carlton and Johnny Bench. It made me wish that I had spent time there before."

Other members of the Hall of Fame Class of 2000 included Sparky Anderson, who managed the Cincinnati Reds in the 1975 World Series, and Tony

Perez, the slugging first baseman for The Big Red Machine. "The tie-in with the '75 Reds is kind of nice. It makes the ceremony even more special."

Pudge reflected on his choice of his hat for the occasion: "There really was never any doubt in my mind that I would go to the Hall with a Red Sox cap on. I was born in New England and I grew up a Red Sox fan. I played for the Red Sox.

"Not many New Hampshire boys have had that privilege. To be honest with you, there were many times when I would look in a mirror, see myself in a White Sox uniform and ask myself, 'What am I doing here?' It never really felt right."

The 1975 World Series Game Six hero was on hand to toss out the ceremonial first pitch before Game Four of the Red Sox-Yankees ALCS at Fenway Park, October 1999.

THE HOMECOMING

In March of 1999, Carlton Fisk rejoined the Boston Red Sox as Special Assistant to then General Manager Dan Duquette. "I'm looking forward to working with the young catchers in our system. I think I have a lot to offer them. I am happy to help out wherever I can," Fisk emphasized at the time.

The Boston Red Sox retired Pudge Fisk's number on September 4, 2000. His Red Sox "27" stands proudly alongside the numbers of Bobby Doerr, Joe Cronin, Yaz, and Ted Williams on the right field façade of Fenway Park. His number is flanked by "42" which was retired by major league baseball in 1997 in honor of the great Jackie Robinson.

Pudge was clearly pleased to be back with the team. Commenting on his return to the Red Sox, he asks, "Who was it, Thomas Wolfe, who wrote, 'You can't go home again?' Well, it turns out he was wrong. You *can* go home again."

Welcome home, Pudge. Welcome back home where you really belong.

Carlton "Pudge" Fisk's Rank in Major League Baseball History

CATEGORY	CAREER TOTALS	ALL-TIME MLB RANK
Seasons	24	8th
Games	2,499	45th
Home Runs	376	57th
At Bats	8,756	73rd
RBI	1,330	76th

Source: 2004 MLB.com

25.
Bob Montgomery
Interview
April 2000

I managed to track Bob Montgomery down on the telephone at his Saugus, Massachusetts, home on a rainy Sunday morning. Known as one of the better golfers in Red Sox history, it was raining too hard for even Monty to be out on the fairways.

It is always interesting to talk one-on-one with someone you have spent hours listening to on the radio or television. You feel as if the voice is off a beat, like there should be a three-second delay.

Monty's conversational style is identical to his broadcasting delivery. He provides insightful comments and communicates them with conviction. There is nothing contrived about his broadcasting style.

Bob Montgomery spent his entire career with the Boston Red Sox and for most of that time he was a backup catcher. Backup catchers like Joe Garagiola and Bob Uecker poked fun at their role and parlayed their humor into a cottage industry. But Bob Montgomery offers a more serious view of the role and makes some interesting observations.

Monty is one of only a handful of former players who took the time to call me to tell me he enjoyed his article. His daughter was born after his playing days were over and she hadn't realized how much he had achieved as a major leaguer. The surest route to a man's gratitude is through his daughter's heart.

BOB MONTGOMERY
"MONTY"

Bob Montgomery made his major league debut with the Boston Red Sox on September 6, 1970. He remained with the Red Sox, primarily as a backup catcher, through the 1979 season. During his decade with the club, the team finished in second place or better five times, played in the most exciting American League playoff game in baseball history, and participated in what is widely considered the best World Series of all time.

"I feel like I was very fortunate to have played in the big leagues throughout the seventies," Monty states emphatically. "I had Hall of Fame teammates like Yaz and Carlton Fisk, and a couple of guys, Jim Rice and Luis Tiant, who I think belong there. And I played against Hall of Famers like George Brett, Catfish Hunter, and Jim Palmer. There were some wonderful players during that decade. I believe it was one of the great eras for baseball.

"When I look back on those Red Sox teams of the seventies, I feel that if we had one more pitcher we would have been a dominant team. Just one more starting pitcher and the Red Sox would have been the team of the seventies."

THE 1975 BOSTON RED SOX

The 1975 Red Sox are best remembered for the pitching heroics of Luis Tiant, the outstanding rookie years of the "Gold Dust Twins" of Fred Lynn and Jim Rice, and the leadership of Carl Yastrzemski. Yaz and Lynn were American League All-Stars, and the Red Sox led the league in slugging, on-base average, and hitting with a team batting average of .275. The club won 95 games, 47 of them at Friendly Fenway and 48 on the road.

When Red Sox fans think back on the highlights of the 1975 season, their first thought is of Pudge Fisk's dramatic twelfth-inning home run to win Game Six of the World Series. Few fans recall that when the 1975 season began, the regular Red Sox catcher was Bob Montgomery. Carlton Fisk had missed large portions of the 1974 season due to an injury. Bob Montgomery played in 88 games behind the plate that season for the Sox. Then in spring training before the 1975 season, Fisk suffered a broken arm, and Bob Montgomery filled the void once more. Monty was the regular catcher through the first two months of that year. More importantly, he was the Red Sox best clutch hitter during that period.

When Fisk returned to regular duty in June, Monty resumed his accustomed role as the number-two catcher. He appeared in 62 games that season and made a number of important contributions to the team's first place Eastern Division finish.

"When it came time to face the Oakland A's in the American League Championship Series a lot of people thought we would have a tough time. After all they were the three-time World Series champs. Well, we didn't feel that way at all. We had played well against the A's all season, and we expected to beat them. Our three straight wins surprised a lot of people, but it didn't surprise us.

"It was the same way when it came time to face the Cincinnati Reds in the World Series. Everybody was talking about the Big Red Machine and how they were going to roll all over us. But we didn't feel that way in the least. We knew we had a very strong club and we knew we were going to give them a battle. And we darn near pulled it off!" Monty recalls reflecting on the Reds' one-run win in Game Seven.

NASHVILLE NATIVE

Bob Montgomery was born and raised in Nashville, Tennessee. If you listen very closely, you can still hear a hint of Nashville, but his strong voice resonates with the timbre of a professional announcer.

Monty was an all-state athlete in three sports at Nashville's Central High School. In baseball he was a pitcher, first baseman and an outfielder. "I did pret-

Making the tag on Boomer.

ty well in the other sports, but baseball was my first love. My dad was a pretty good sandlot player, and my brother Gerald played in the Red Sox minor league system. When I was a youngster, Nashville was the Cincinnati Reds farm club in the Southern League and I used to go to a lot of their games. I knew at an early age that baseball was the sport I wanted to pursue as a career."

Veteran Red Sox scout George Digby signed Monty in June of 1962 right after his high school graduation. The 18-year-old Montgomery reported to Olean, New York, where he played third base and batted a respectable .273. He didn't know at the time, but he had embarked on a journey to reach the major leagues that would last for almost 10 full seasons.

MINOR LEAGUE ODYSSEY

Monty was promoted to Waterloo, Iowa, for the 1963 season. That year he received some advice that eventually paid off in a 10-year big league career. "Len Okrie was our manager and he took me aside and said, 'If you want to make it to the majors, you're going to have to make yourself into a catcher. You don't have the power to make it at the corner positions in the majors, but you could make it as a catcher.'

"Len had played in the majors as a catcher, so I took his advice to heart. I played in a few games at catcher towards the end of the season, and I came back to Waterloo in 1964 as a full-time catcher. I made the All-Star team that season so I guess I made the right decision."

Asked if it was difficult to make the transition to catcher, Monty responds, "Not really. It even gave me one advantage: I hadn't developed any bad habits over the years. I could concentrate on learning to do the right things in a professional situation. I took to it very quickly."

Over the next six seasons, he progressed steadily through the Red Sox minor league system. But he had some formidable competition in the Boston depth chart at catcher. In addition to fellow Nashville native Bob Tillman, the Red Sox had two fine young catchers in future big leaguers Mike Ryan and Russ Gibson.

You spend a lot of time on buses when you play for nine years in the minor leagues, but Bob Montgomery never got discouraged. "I never thought about quitting. I had one goal in mind: to play baseball at the big league level. I stayed focused on that goal and just moved a little closer every year."

In 1969 he got in to over 100 games at catcher for the Red Sox top minor league team in Louisville, Kentucky. Batting a solid .292 against the tough International League pitching, he had moved within one rung of his goal. The Red Sox sent him back to Louisville for the 1970 season and Monty demonstrated that he was more than ready. During this final season in the minor leagues he appeared in 131 games, batted .324, and slugged 14 home runs. After earning recognition as an International League All-Star for two years running, Fenway Park was clearly in his sights.

His outstanding play earned him a September call-up to the Boston Red Sox. At age 26, with parts of nine minor league seasons behind him, Bob Montgomery had finally made it to the big leagues. And it was more than a courtesy call. He appeared in 22 games and rapped out 14 base hits. Bob Montgomery had begun a major league career that would last for the balance of the decade.

BOSTON TRANSPLANT

The 1971 season was his first full year in the big leagues and Monty made the most of it. Sharing the catching duties with Duane Josephson, he appeared in 67 games and established himself as a fine handler of pitchers. The Red Sox finished third that year under manager Eddie Kasko. Monty remembers Kasko warmly. "Eddie Kasko was a terrific baseball man and a really good guy to play for. I really respected Eddie's baseball knowledge."

In 1972 Carlton Fisk claimed the starting catching position and Monty's playing time fell to 24 games. Despite his diminished workload he continued to contribute to the team on and off the field. The BoSox Club recognized him as their Man of the Year in 1972 for his "contributions to the team and his outstanding co-operation in community endeavors."

In 1973 Monty continued his number-two catching role and contributed to the offense with a .320 batting average. The Baseball 2000 Preview Issue of *Sports Illustrated* included an article entitled "What is the Cushiest Job in Baseball?" spotlighting backup catchers. The theme of the article is that the backup works only occasionally, has a great seat for the ballgame, and is well-paid for his modest efforts. Bob Montgomery has a very different perspective.

"The backup catcher has to be ready to enter the game on a moment's notice, because the regular catcher is always vulnerable to injury. You have to be ready in case you're asked to pinch-hit, and you have to help out warming up the pitchers if necessary. When I was playing, I was focused on every single pitch, even if I hadn't played in a week."

His perspective was validated in 1974 when Fisk was injured in a collision in Cleveland and Monty took over as the regular catcher in June. With Montgomery behind the plate, the team was in first place as late as September 9. The Red Sox ended up in third place, but their late season victories over the Yankees allowed the Baltimore Orioles to squeak by the New Yorkers. Monty played in 88 games that season. He had found himself a home.

"It was around then that I started to think of Boston as home. I bought a place in Dedham and began to spend a good part of the year around the area. It felt like I belonged here."

1975 AND BEYOND

Monty performed yeoman duty as the regular Red Sox catcher during the first two months of the 1975 season. He delivered the winning RBI in four of the Red Sox' first 11 victories in the early going. "I knew my limitations and I stayed within myself. I did have a knack for putting the ball in play, and during those first few weeks I was fortunate to come up with some key hits," is his explanation for his clutch hitting.

He jumped back into the breach in August when Fisk was out with a split finger, and he also filled in at first base for six games that season. Monty remembers 1975 as a year with many highlights.

"Everyone talks about the Fisk home run in Game Six of the '75 Series, and with good reason. But the performance that stands out in my mind is Luis Tiant in Game Four in Cincinnati. We had lost two in a row and we had to win Game Four to stand a chance. Luis threw 163 pitches and simply refused to let the Reds beat us. To me that was as great an effort as I've ever seen on a baseball diamond."

Asked to name the best pitcher he ever handled, Monty quickly responds, "Luis Tiant." Asked to name the most difficult pitcher he ever caught, he is just as quick to respond, "Luis Tiant." Explaining this seeming contradiction, he adds, "Luis was such a great craftsman and a terrific competitor that he was clearly the best. But for the same reason that he was difficult for hitters, he was difficult to catch. He would hide the ball from the hitters until the very last second, and they had trouble picking up the pitch. Well, remember, it was just as difficult for the catcher to pick up Luis' pitch coming in!"

The 1976 season was a disappointing one for the Red Sox and for Bob Montgomery personally. The team fell out of contention early in the season and

Receiving a helping hand from teammate Tommy Harper.

third base coach Don Zimmer was tapped to replace Darrell Johnson as manager in mid-season. Monty's playing time was cut in half and the team finished in third place, 14 games off the Yankees' division leading pace.

"It was just one of those years," Monty remembers. "It seemed like everything that could go wrong did go wrong. There was nothing memorable about that season at all. It's best forgotten."

In 1977, Zimmer's first full season as manager, the Red Sox improved to 97 wins, just three games behind the Yankees. Bob Montgomery saw limited playing time but made the most of it with a .300 batting average.

The 1978 season was one that Monty remembers vividly. "Now *that* was a memorable season. Of course, we had that big lead over the Yankees and then they came in over the Labor Day weekend and swept us four straight. I didn't coin the phrase, but the best description was a first place team, the Red Sox, chasing a second place team, the Yankees.

"Those two teams were so evenly matched that you knew it would come down to the wire. We really felt we were going to beat them in that one game playoff, and we were pretty certain that whoever won that game would almost certainly go on to win the World Series."

Bob Montgomery enjoyed playing for Don Zimmer. "Zim was a guy who was willing to take a calculated risk. I remember one time I was batting in Chicago with one out and the bases loaded. I looked down for the sign, and the hit-and-run was on. I was so surprised, I had to step out of the box and take another look. I singled through the infield and brought two runners home. Zim said to me later, 'I always wanted to try that play.' Of course, I was a contact hitter so he was pretty confident I would find a hole in the infield."

Bob Montgomery's final year with the Red Sox came in 1979. "That was a frustrating year for me. We played a game in Cleveland in early April where the temperature dropped below freezing. The

At an Old-Timers' Game at Fenway in the late 1980s.

next morning I couldn't even raise my arm far enough to brush my hair. I had to go on the disabled list. That was the only injury I ever had as a player."

He recovered well enough to get into 32 games and bat a career-high .349, but he knew that his career was winding down. His last game was a forgettable 16-4 loss to the Baltimore Orioles on September 9. But with his last at-bat, Bob Montgomery became a footnote in baseball history. Grandfathered under the major league baseball rule that required all players to wear batting helmets, he became the last player to wear a "hard liner" in his cap.

He went to spring training with the Red Sox in 1980 and he played well in spurts. But approaching age 36, he knew his big league career was over.

RECENT YEARS

"After I retired from baseball, I went into broadcasting. I was on a sports talk radio show with Clif Keane and Larry Claflin for awhile. And I used to sit in the stands at Red Sox home games and practice doing the color on the games. I used to sit there with a tape recorder just as if I was on live."

In 1982 Monty was hired by Channel 38 to do the color for their Red Sox telecasts. It was an association that would last through 14 seasons. Red Sox fans remember his insightful observations and comments on the game within the game.

"I felt that as a former catcher I gave the fans a sense of what goes on between the pitcher and the catcher. I think I helped fans to anticipate certain situations and to understand a lot of the thinking that goes into making decisions." His television role came to a close when Channel 38 ended their Red Sox telecasts after the 1995 season.

In April 2000 Monty was in sales and marketing with Unison in Boston. The state-of-the-art signage in the Fleet Center is an example of the company's products. "It is a real change in focus for me. I learn something new every day. It reminds me of baseball in that way."

Monty now lives in Saugus with his wife Ann and teenage daughter Loren. His fatherly pride is evident as he described Loren's athletic prowess and the scholarship she had just been offered by Quinnipiac College in Connecticut. Bob Montgomery is considered to be one of the Red Sox better golfers over the years, and he is a serious model train buff.

He sums up his career this way: "I was what they call a 50/50 player. That is, I didn't help you an awful lot, but I didn't hurt you either." His self-assessment is too modest by far. He was probably the premier backup catcher in the major leagues throughout the seventies, and he made a significant contribution to the great Red Sox season of 1975. Red Sox fans remember him fondly for his steady play with the team and for his enjoyable commentary in the broadcast booth.

26.
Luis Tiant Interview
May 2000

I interviewed Luis Tiant at Northeastern's Kent Street baseball field in Brookline, Massachusetts. His Savannah (GA) College of Art and Design baseball team took batting practice while we talked. Luis gave me his full attention, but he watched everything that took place on the field throughout our conversation.

If you stand at just the right spot on Kent Street you can actually see the light towers of Fenway Park. It seemed incongruous to me that I was sitting with one of the great pitchers in Red Sox history, within sight of Fenway Park, and Luis was sitting on the bench beside me wearing a black and yellow cap with an enraged bumble bee on it.

But Luis made it very clear to me that he was just happy to be a part of baseball. And he was particularly pleased that his son, and namesake, was working with him as his assistant. The two things that are most important to Luis are family and baseball.

Luis' English is about 1000% percent better than my Spanish. But sometimes I have had trouble catching every word when he is interviewed on the radio or television. However, if you are sitting beside him and the subject is baseball or his family, you will never miss a word.

As I drove away, I couldn't help wishing he were back with the Boston Red Sox where he belonged. He gave me a great big Luis Tiant smile when we said goodbye. But the next time I saw him on Yawkey Way, he was back with the Red Sox as a Special Assignment Instructor, and his smile was twice as broad.

LUIS TIANT, JR.
"EL TIANTE"

He whirled, and he twirled. At the midpoint of his pitching motion, Luis Tiant would turn his back completely to the hitter, and he appeared to be counting the crowd in the center-field bleachers. When he corkscrewed around for his delivery, the hitter knew he could be facing any one of six different pitches thrown from three different arm slots. The result of this baseball ballet, more often than not, was a series of outs culminating in yet another Red Sox victory.

Between 1973 and 1977, Luis Tiant won 96 regular season games, and three post-season games for the Boston Red Sox. It could be argued that other Red Sox pitchers have been equally effective over a comparable period of time. But no other Red Sox pitcher has ever captivated the fans and captured their hearts the way Luis Tiant did for an extended period of time.

EL TIANTE

Luis Tiant was named to the American League All-Star team five times during his 19-year career. But he was not the first baseball All-Star with that name. His father, Luis Tiant Sr., was a perennial All-Star as a pitcher for the New York Cubans of the Negro Leagues. Luis Sr. was a stylish southpaw who pitched for the Cubans from 1930 through 1947. On one occasion, the senior Tiant defeated a barnstorming team made up of major league all-stars, striking out Babe Ruth in the process.

Luis remembers being compared to his father back in the late 1950s. "When I pitched winter ball in Cuba, the old-time fans would say 'you are a very good pitcher, but your father was better.' I remember watching my father pitch when I was a youngster, and trying to copy his motion."

Luis was born in Marianao, Cuba, the only child of Luis Sr. and Isabel Tiant. "When I was a youngster, my father tried to keep me from playing baseball. The players in the old Negro League really had a tough life, and he didn't want me to go through it. He used to say, 'Go to school. Study English. Forget about baseball.' I have spent more time in this country than in Cuba, so his advice to study English was good."

Luis followed his father's advice and studied English, but he also followed his heart and pitched every chance he got. "Finally my father's friends said, 'You have to let him play. He is terrific. Go watch him pitch.' The first time he came to see me, he hid behind a pole. Finally he did come up to me after the game to congratulate me.

"But it was my mother who had to talk him into letting me go with the Cuban team to the Latin American Games in 1957 when I was 16. She used to say 'Hey, leave him alone. If he wants to play, let him play.'"

THE LONG ROAD TO THE MAJORS

Luis Tiant began his professional baseball career in 1959, at the age of 19, with the Mexico City Tigers. His second season with the Tigers led to 17 victories and an introduction to his future wife, Senorita Maria del Refugio Navarro. In 1961, his outstanding pitching caught the eye of the Cleveland Indians and they signed him to a minor league contract for the 1962 season. Luis and Maria were married on August 18, 1961.

When the 1961 season ended Luis was anxious to return to Cuba to show off his new bride and to play for the Havana team in the Cuban Winter League. But conditions in his native country had deteriorated following Fidel Castro's rise to power on New Year's Day in 1959. The United States had severed diplomatic relations with the country, and nearly 500,000 Cubans had emigrated from their country.

"When I called my father to tell him I was coming home, he said, 'Don't do it. I don't think you will be able to get out again. Don't come home.'"

A distraught Tiant headed to Puerto Rico with Maria for a season of winter baseball. Stops in Charleston, South Carolina, and Burlington, North Carolina, preceded his assignment to the Indians' top farm club in Portland, Oregon. By

July of 1964, Luis was standing Pacific Coast League hitters on their heads with a 15-1 record.

Luis didn't skip a beat when the Indians called him up from Triple A to the majors in July of 1964. He went 10-4 for the Indians during the balance of the season, and he turned in a sparkling ERA of 2.74 over 127 innings. During the next three seasons he was a mainstay of the Tribe pitching staff, winning 35 games while splitting his time between starting and relieving.

1968 ALL STAR GAME

The 1968 season was Luis' breakout year. He won 21 games while compiling an eye-popping ERA of 1.60. In recognition of his outstanding performance, he was named as the starting pitcher for the American League in the All-Star Game in Houston, Texas.

"I remember that game very well. We played in the Astrodome and it was the first time I had pitched indoors. I remember looking into the National League dugout and seeing guys like Willie Mays, Henry Aaron, and Don Drysdale. All I could think was, 'Wow!' But mostly I remember that game because it was televised back to Cuba, and my mother and father got to watch me."

Tiant gave up only one unearned run and struck out two National Leaguers during his two-inning stint. Willie Mays scored the only run of the contest, crossing the plate after Luis had induced Willie McCovey to ground into a double play.

"I talked to my parents right after the game. My mother said she wanted to reach right into her TV and hug me. I think my father wanted to know why I had thrown a wild pitch."

Tiant's win total fell to nine in 1969, and the Indians traded him to the Minnesota Twins that winter. Luis reeled off six quick victories for the Twins in the early months of the 1970 season. His fast start earned him a spot on the American League All-Star roster once more. But he had developed arm trouble and he didn't pitch in that year's game at Riverfront Stadium in Cincinnati.

"It was the first time I had serious arm trouble and it scared me. I tried pitching later in the 1970 season, but my arm wasn't up to it."

The Twins released him from his contract that winter and Tiant signed a minor league contract with the Atlanta Braves. After a disappointing trial in Richmond, the Braves released him as well. At the age of 29, it seemed like his big league career might be over. But the Red Sox took a chance on Luis, and signed him for their Triple A club in Louisville, Kentucky.

Jose Santiago was a former Red Sox star hurler assigned to Louisville, trying to work his way back to the majors as well. He remembers Luis' time with the club. "It was obvious that his arm was almost back to normal. The Red Sox talked to me about coming back to Boston, and I said, 'Bring Luis back instead. He's ready. I'm not.'"

LOO-EEE! LOO-EEE!

Manager Eddie Kasko remembers Luis' pitching performance at the end of 1971, "He went 1-7, but you could see he was almost all the way back to his old form. We took a lot of heat for his record, but I was sure that he was about to turn his career around."

Kasko had seen enough of the old Luis Tiant at the tail end of the 1971 Red Sox season to include him on the pitching staff for 1972. Used mainly in relief during early stages of the year, he became a starter during the second half of the season. He finished the year with a 15-6 record and a league-best 1.91 ERA. His "second career" had officially begun.

Luis followed up with 20 victories in 1973, and he upped that total to 22 wins in 1974. During this period the Fenway Faithful started a ritual of chanting "LOO-eee, LOO-eee," as he would make his way from the bullpen to the pitchers mound to start the game. At tense moments during the game, fans would pick up the mantra again. Luis remembers those moments warmly. "They really gave me a lift. When you hear the fans pulling for you like that, you reach down a little deeper."

Luis' stellar performance in 1974 earned him his third selection as an American League All-Star. He pitched in the forty-fifth annual mid-summer classic held at Riverfront Stadium in Cincinnati.

"My wife Maria had just had a baby, and I flew home to Mexico City to be with her. I wanted to stay but she told me to go back for the All-Star Game. I pitched lousy. [Tiant gave up two earned runs in two innings, and took the loss for the American League.] I probably should have stayed with my family."

THE SEASON OF '75

The 1975 season is the year that Luis remembers best. "We won our division, and then we beat the Oakland Athletics for the American League Championship. Then we had the great World Series with the Reds. It was a great year."

Luis remembers the 1975 World Series for another special reason. The intercession of U.S. Senators Edward Brooke and George McGovern helped persuade the Cuban government to issue visas to Luis Sr. and Isabel Tiant to come to the United States to watch their son in the World Series. Long-time Red Sox fans still treasure the memories of watching Tiant's parents cheer him on at Fenway Park. But no one cherishes that memory more than Luis.

Asked if having his parents in the stands added to the playoff pressure, Luis demurs. "I was very aware they were there. And I wanted to win for them. But it is very important for a pitcher to stay within himself. If you try to do more than you are capable of, that's when you get in trouble. I just tried to pitch my regular game.

"I knew where my parents were sitting and I would look up there when I was walking off the mound when the inning was over. It was a nice feeling. But when

I was pitching to the hitters I had to forget about it. You have to stay focused."

Although almost 25 years had passed when we talked, Tiant was very emotional when he talked about his 1975 reunion with his parents. "I hadn't seen my parents in many years. My mother came to Mexico City in 1968 to visit us, but I hadn't seen my father since 1961. It meant everything to me to have them there."

The 1975 World Series is regarded as one of the best in history, and Luis played a major role in the drama. He shut out the Cincinnati "Big Red Machine" in Game Two at Fenway to even the Series at one game each. He reached back and fired 163 pitches in Game Four at Cincinnati, earning the victory that knotted the Series at two games apiece.

Game Six of the World Series was a contest for the ages. Luis took the mound once again and held the Reds scoreless through four innings. The Reds got to him for three runs in the fifth. "I had beat them in the other two games with breaking balls. I went more with fastballs in Game Six. They finally caught up to me in the fifth."

Luis left the mound to a thundering ovation from over 35,000 fans when he was relieved in the eighth inning. "When Bernie Carbo tied it with his home run in the bottom of the eighth, I was in the clubhouse half-dressed. I still ran into the dugout to give him a hug. Same thing when Fisk hit the winner in the twelfth. I couldn't go out in the field, but I was in the dugout in my skivvies. I thought we were going to win the next night [Game Seven] right up to the final out. What a great Series!"

FOUR TIME ALL-STAR

All-Star honors came his way for a fifth time in 1976. "We played in Philadelphia that year. I held the National League scoreless in the fifth and six innings. I think I was just getting used to pitching to them."

Following 12 victories for the Red Sox in 1977, and 13 wins in 1978, Luis signed as a free agent with the New York Yankees for the 1979 and 1980 seasons. The sight of Luis Tiant in Yankee pinstripes is one that Boston Red Sox fans would just as soon forget.

The Yankees declined to re-sign him for the 1981 season, and he spent part of the season pitching for the Pittsburgh

A touching moment for father and son. Luis Sr. threw out the ceremonial first pitch before one of the 1975 World Series games at Fenway Park.

Pirates. The following year, the California Angels picked him up in mid-season after a scout spotted him pitching well in Mexico. Luis finally retired from baseball in 1983.

Luis Tiant played professional baseball for 25 years. He played winter ball, mostly in Venezuela, during 21 of those years. Over 14 full, and five partial major league seasons, he won 229 games. Only 59 pitchers in the history of major league baseball have won more games. His 2,426 strikeouts place him thirty-second in major league history.

Although he spent only one-half of his career with the Red Sox, he ranks fourth in wins, third in innings pitched, and fourth in shutouts among the all-time Red Sox pitching leaders. Luis Tiant was inducted into the Red Sox Hall of Fame in 1997.

FOREVER YOUNG

A popular Red Sox trivia question is: "How old is Luis Tiant, *really*?" Tiant smiles at the question, but he is clearly tired of the doubts surrounding his age. "I pitched professionally for 25 years. When you are around that long, people start wondering how old you really are. When Tony Perez [former Cincinnati Red great] was traded to the Reds in 1980, he told people, 'My father used to take me to see Luis Tiant play when I was a kid.' Tony and I are about the same age and we grew up playing ball together in Cuba. But when he said that, people took him seriously.

"Every spring in the 1970s Peter Gammons [then of the *Boston Globe*, now of ESPN], used to write, 'Luis Tiant is a year older, and we're not sure how old he is anyway. This might just be the year he runs out of gas.' Finally I said, 'Peter, you write that stuff every year, and every year I go out and win 20 games. Stop writing that junk. I'll know when I can't pitch any more, and I'll tell you.' "

THE LATER YEARS

Luis has done a number of things after his retirement as an active player. For a period of time, he worked in Public Affairs for the Massachusetts Lottery Commission. He also worked as a roving pitching instructor in the Dodgers' minor league system.

In 1999 he was in his second year as head baseball coach at the Savannah (GA) College of Art and Design. The school has about 4,500 students, and enjoys a high academic rating. "I love it. My son [Luis Jr.] is my assistant coach and that's really nice. The tough part is remembering that these kids are students, not professional athletes. Their studies have to come first."

Luis took in a Celtics game in April 1999, while his team was in town for a game with MIT. He was introduced to the crowd at the Fleet Center, and scenes of his glory days with the Red Sox were shown on the message board. The crowd brought him to his feet twice with standing ovations. "A couple of my players told me later, 'Coach, we were crying. We couldn't help it. It was so moving.'" Luis smiles at the memory.

It is only one mile or so from Fenway Park to the Northeastern University baseball diamond. But the small crowd on hand to watch Luis' team play the Huskies is a reminder that Luis is a long way from the major leagues. During a break in the interview, two long-time Red Sox fans politely ask Luis to sign Red Sox programs from the 1970s. "Luis, you were the best pitcher we ever had," one fan offers. "If anyone belongs in the Hall of Fame, it's you, Luis," adds another.

Today, Luis Tiant is a Special Assignment Instructor for the Boston Red Sox, instructing young pitchers in their system during the season. He also assists the Red Sox with clinics and special appearances throughout the season.

Luis can also be heard on the Red Sox Spanish Radio Network, adding color to J.P. Villaman's play-by-play. The busy Tiant also finds time for his eatery El Tiante, which is a fan favorite on the Yawkey Way concourse. Luis manages to find time to visit with fans on the concourse and he always draws a crowd.

"Boston fans are the greatest. They have always been great to me and to my family. Boston is my home away from home," Tiant says with feeling.

If there ever truly was an adopted son of New England's team, Luis Tiant is that man.

Luis Tiant's Rank in Red Sox History

CATEGORY	CAREER TOTALS	ALL-TIME BOSTON RED SOX RANK
Games Started	238	3rd
Innings	1,774	3rd
Wins	122	4th
Shutouts	26	4th
Strikeouts	1,075	5th
Complete Games	113	7th
10-K Games	9	8th
Winning Percentage	.601	12th
Games	274	14th

Source: 2004 *Boston Red Sox Media Guide*

27.
Dwight Evans Interview
May 2000

When I talked to Dwight Evans in his North Shore home, he was convinced that his life in baseball was over. Like a lot New Englanders, he was hopeful that the dot.com world represented his future. It was unfortunate that the dot.com bubble burst, but it feels right that Dewey has reconnected with the Red Sox organization.

Dwight Evans is a very articulate guy. And in his interview he showed a good understanding of why Red Sox fans gravitate towards certain players and why some players draw the wrath of fans.

Dewey might be the most underrated player in the history of the Boston Red Sox. He is a member of the Red Sox Hall of Fame and the Boston Baseball Writers voted him the team's Most Valuable Player four times, so he certainly has received recognition.

But when you search for matches to his career numbers, the names that pop up are Al Kaline, Tony Perez, and Billy Williams. All three of these former players are in the Hall of Fame, but only Kaline made the defensive contributions that Evans did.

I was hoping for a fascinating story of how Dwight Evans got the odd nickname "Dewey." The origin turns out to be pretty ordinary. Dwight Evans acknowledges that he has learned to live with "Dewey."

DWIGHT EVANS
"DEWEY"

Dwight "Dewey" Evans was arguably the greatest right-fielder in the history of the Boston Red Sox. Evans spent all or parts of 19 distinguished seasons as the Red Sox regular right fielder, and in 1982 he was selected for the team's All-Time outfield, along with Ted Williams and Carl Yastrzemski, by vote of the fans. He was inducted into the Red Sox Hall of Fame in 2000.

"Dwight Evans was the best Red Sox right fielder I ever saw." These are the words of all-time Red Sox favorite Johnny Pesky, who has been associated with the team for over 60 years.

"We have had a lot of outstanding right fielders over the years, and I have seen almost all of them," Pesky continues. "Jackie Jensen was a terrific right fielder, a great ballplayer. And Tony Conigliaro was a wonderful ballplayer as well. But if you force me to pick one, I have to go with Dwight Evans. He could do it all."

THE 1975 BOSTON RED SOX

The 1975 Red Sox featured the heroics of Pudge Fisk, the great rookie years of Jim Rice and Fred Lynn, and the clutch pitching of Luis Tiant. But when writers asked their World Series opponents the Cincinnati Reds which Red Sox player impressed them, Dwight Evans was mentioned most frequently.

Pete Rose told reporters at the time, "We had heard all about Fisk and Lynn. And we knew all about Yaz and Tiant. But nobody told us much about Evans and he can really play the game. He's been a big surprise to us." Reds manager Sparky Anderson called him, "The surprise package of the Red Sox and a great future star."

Dwight Evans had given the Reds plenty of reason to notice him. He rapped out seven hits over the seven-game Series and he fielded flawlessly throughout the Series. His clutch two-run homer in the ninth inning had tied Game Three of the Series. Evans' spectacular catch off the bat of Joe Morgan in Game Six was called, "The greatest catch I have ever seen under the circumstances," by Sparky Anderson.

The 1975 season firmly established the 23-year-old Evans as a premier major league outfielder. Bothered by hamstring and shoulder injuries early in the year, he batted .327 after the All-Star break. His 15 outfield assists placed him among the league leaders, and his 8 double plays topped the American League. He was at the big league level to stay, but the route had not always been easy.

CALIFORNIA BORN

Dwight Michael Evans was born in Santa Monica, California, on November 3, 1951. His family moved to Hawaii soon after he was born.

"I spent my early years in Hawaii. Every day was a beach day there, so all the kids spent their time by the water. I never really played any baseball until we moved back to California when I was nine."

When the Evans family moved to Northbridge, California, a small community north of Los Angeles, Dwight got involved in Little League baseball right away. Playing mostly at third base and taking his turn on the mound, he took to the game immediately.

"When I was about 11-years-old, my father took me to see a Dodgers game. They were playing in the old Coliseum [the Los Angeles Dodgers' temporary home before Dodgers' Stadium was built], and I loved it. I think I had a passion for baseball from that point on. That was what hooked me on baseball."

Dwight was an All-Star selection at the Little League and Colt League levels. His first baseball setback came as a sophomore at Chatsworth High School. "I tried out for the junior varsity baseball team and I didn't even get a uniform. I was very disappointed, but I didn't give up. I kept playing every chance I got."

His perseverance paid off in his junior year. He made the varsity and he earned All-Valley recognition in the competitive San Fernando Valley League. The following season he was selected as the Most Valuable Player in the league and the major league scouts were on his trail.

"It was kind of funny. We would get these cards to fill out from the major league teams. I heard from most of the major league clubs, but I never heard from the Red Sox. I was surprised when they drafted me."

Long-time Red Sox Southern California scout Joe Stephenson had followed Dwight's development as a schoolboy. Based on his recommendation, the team selected Evans in the fifth round of the June 1969 draft. After signing the 17-year-old to his first professional baseball contract, the Red Sox sent him to their farm club in Jamestown, New York.

FAST-TRACK TO THE MAJORS

"Life in the minor leagues was a big adjustment. I was pretty much the best player in my high school league, but when you get there you find out everyone was the best player back home. And we had a number of guys who were coming back from the Vietnam War so they were a little older. We had more players than uniforms, so for the first week or so I was practicing in my Levi's and sweatshirt.

"And, of course, growing up in Hawaii and southern California, living and playing in the northeast was an adjustment. I was a kid really, and most of the guys had played more ball than I had. There were times when I wondered if I belonged there."

Evans eventually got a uniform and hit a solid .280 in 100 at-bats. The following year he advanced to the Greenville, South Carolina, farm club where he led the league in triples. In 1971, he compiled 36 extra base hits in 118 games in Winston-Salem, North Carolina, earning him a promotion the following season to the Red Sox top farm club in Louisville, Kentucky.

At age 20, Evans struggled in the early going against the Triple A pitching. Louisville manager Darrell Johnson told Evans early in the season, "You are my everyday right fielder whether you hit .100 or .300." Manager Johnson proved to be both an astute judge of talent and a prophet when Evans finished the season with a batting average of exactly .300. His league leading 95 RBI and recognition as the Most Valuable Player of the International League earned him a September call-up to the major leagues.

WELCOME TO THE SHOW

When Evans joined the team in mid-September, the 1972 Red Sox were neck-and-neck with the Detroit Tigers for first place in the Eastern Division of the American League. Manager Eddie Kasko made immediate use of his talents, and he fielded sensationally in 18 crucial games.

"The first major league field I was on was Yankee Stadium. It was before they renovated the park, and the monuments were still on the playing field in deep center field. I couldn't help looking around like a little kid. It was quite a thrill."

Evans may have been a bit awestruck by Yankee Stadium but it didn't prevent him from playing like a seasoned veteran. He contributed 15 hits in the midst of a pennant race, including a key home run against Baltimore's Eddie Watt.

Dwight remembers his first look at the left field wall in Fenway Park. "I had heard a lot about it, and I had seen it on TV, but until I stood at home plate I didn't realize how beautiful it was, or how close it was. I was thinking something like, 'So near and yet so far.' It can be a real distraction for a hitter."

The 1972 Red Sox finished second, a heart-breaking one-half game behind the Tigers. But Dwight Evans had established a toehold on a major league career. And his major league career would encompass another 19 outstanding seasons.

Evans struggled a bit at the plate in 1973, his first full season in the majors.

However, his career-low .223 average was more than offset by his stellar play in right field. In 1974 he raised his average to .280 and he continued to impress observers with his outstanding defense.

"I felt comfortable in the outfield from day-one in the majors. I really worked on my fielding and I took a lot of pride in it. Hitting at the major league level proved to be a real challenge. I knew the pitching would be better, but the superior defense at the major league level makes a big difference. I would nail a line drive only to find that they had positioned me perfectly. Or I would hit one into the gap, and someone would make a great catch."

THE GREATEST WORLD SERIES

The 1975 season was a memorable one for the Boston Red Sox and for Dwight Evans. The team clinched the Eastern Division title on September 27 and went on to sweep the Oakland A's in three games for the American League Championship. Asked if he recalls a particular turning point, Evans responds, "When you are going good the way that team was, everything seems to fall into place. We felt good about our chances all year, right through the World Series. We were confident from Opening Day right through the last game of the World Series."

The 1975 World Series provided Evans with national recognition. His spectacular catch of Joe Morgan's line drive in Game Six ranks with the top defensive

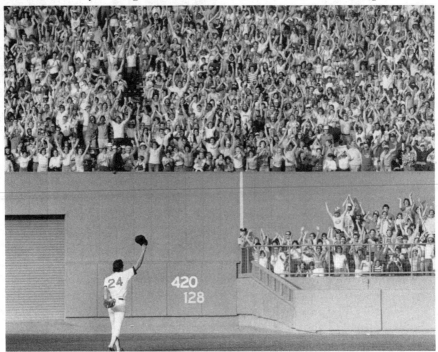

Evans in 1976.

plays in World Series history. "It wasn't my best catch, but it was my most important one. When I watch the replay, it looks a little awkward to me. I anticipated
that the ball would drift towards the right field line, but it stayed straight as an
arrow. It was a great thrill to catch that ball."

In 1976, Evans was honored with his first Rawlings Gold Glove for fielding
excellence. That season, Dwight showed the first promise of the offensive power
that would blossom in the 1980s. He was second in the American League with 34
doubles and his 56 extra base hits ranked fourth.

His 1977 season was marred by injuries, but 1978 brought him his second
Gold Glove and his first selection to the American League All-Star team. Dwight
Evans' all-around excellence had established him as an elite major league player
as the decade of the 1980s rolled around.

POWER SURGE

A surprising thing happened for Dwight Evans in 1981: he led the American
League in total bases, and tied for the lead in home runs. It was a strike-shortened season to be sure, but he still outdistanced sluggers like Dave Winfield of
the Yankees and Eddie Murray of the Orioles.

His 1982 season was almost as strong offensively and he won his fifth Gold
Glove for defensive excellence. That year he led the American League in games
played, appearing in all 162 contests, and his 291 times on base topped the Junior
Circuit as well.

In 1983 his offensive production tailed off slightly but he won his sixth Gold
Glove. The following season he led the league in games played with 162, and in
extra base hits with 77.

Most premier offensive players increase their production through their late
twenties, maintain that level for a few years, and then their production gradually
decreases as they advance through their thirties. Dwight Evans had a totally different pattern: he was a much better hitter in the second half of his career than
during his first half.

In his first eight full seasons with the Red Sox, he averaged about 15 home
runs per year. For his last 10 years with the Red Sox, he averaged 25 home runs.
In fact, during the period 1981 through 1990, Dwight Evans hit more home runs
than any other American League player. And during that same period he had
more extra base hits than any other major leaguer.

"There were a number of reasons why I was a better hitter in the second half
of my career. For a number of years, I was trying to pull the ball. Eventually I
realized I was a better gap hitter, and I started to use the whole field. Also, during my early years with the Red Sox, our young son had some serious medical
issues. I'm not using that as an excuse, but unless you have had a child in that situation, you have no idea how totally consuming it is.

"I also have to give a lot of credit to Walt Hriniak, who was our batting coach
when my hitting came around. He worked with me continually. Walter was the
hardest-working man I ever saw in baseball."

ONE PITCH AWAY

"When we lost to the Reds in the 1975 World Series it was a real disappointment. But I was only 23 years old at the time, and we all thought we would be back in the Series for years to come. It never occurred to me that it would be another 11 years before we had another shot at a world championship."

Eleven years may have gone by, but Evans picked up right where he had left off with his clutch hitting and outstanding defense. He knocked in 11 runs during the seven-game 1986 World Series against the Mets and he contributed eight hits, including two home runs. His overall batting average for the 1975 and 1986 World Series was exactly .300.

"I always liked to hit in the clutch. I wanted to be at the plate when the game was on the line. I have to admit that I lost a little concentration when we were up by eight runs or down by 10 during the regular season, but in the World Series, every at-bat is crucial."

THREE TIME ALL-STAR

When the 1987 season began, Evans was 34 years old, but his offensive production was still on the upswing. That year he made his third American League All-Star team and he reached career highs in home runs and RBI. He finished fourth in the balloting for the American League MVP Award, and he led the American League in walks for the third time in his career. The Boston Baseball Writers Association voted him the Most Valuable Player of the Boston Red Sox for the fourth time, an achievement that is only surpassed by Carl Yastrzemski's six-time selection.

Dewey maintained a high level of production over the next two seasons. But in 1990, his offensive output declined and the Boston Red Sox granted him his release at the end of the season.

Dwight Evans finished out his major league career in 1991 with the Baltimore Orioles. For Red Sox fans, the sight of Evans in a Baltimore uniform was akin to watching the *Constitution* sail off to join her sister ship the *Constellation* in Baltimore Harbor.

DEWEY

"I wish I could tell you a really interesting story about how I got my nickname," laughs Evans, "but there isn't one. When I was playing in the minors we had a pitcher named Don Newhauser, who later pitched for the Red Sox, and he was 'Newey.' Somehow I became 'Dewey' and it stuck. I wasn't wild about it at first, but it became my name. I like it."

RED SOX AND MAJOR LEAGUE LEADER

Dwight Evans ranks fifth or better in 10 of the all-time batting categories of the Boston Red Sox. Only Carl Yastrzemski appeared in more games or had more at-bats in a Red Sox uniform. Only Yaz and Ted Williams had more walks, doubles, extra base hits and runs scored than Evans did.

Fielding records are not tracked in the same volume as batting records, but his eight Gold Gloves for defensive excellence establish Dwight Evans as the all-time Red Sox leader. In fact, only Willie Mays, Roberto Clemente, Al Kaline, and Ken Griffey, Jr. have won more Gold Gloves than Evans.

Dwight Evans was such an outstanding fielder, that many Red Sox fans are unaware that his lifetime batting statistics place him among the elite players in baseball history. Evans ranks among the top 100 players in baseball history in eight offensive categories.

Johnny Pesky feels that Dwight Evans' career was comparable to the achievements of Detroit Tigers Hall of Fame right fielder Al Kaline. "I consider Evans and Kaline to be parallel ballplayers. Kaline was a shade faster than Dewey, but they had comparable power and they were both exceptional fielders."

LIFE AFTER BASEBALL

"After my major league career was over, I worked in the White Sox minor league system as an instructor for a couple of years. Then, in 1994, I was the batting coach for the Colorado Rockies. I enjoyed that season, but I was away from my family too much, and I'm a very family-oriented person. At the end of that season I walked my daughter down the aisle and walked away from baseball," Dewey laughs.

At the time of our interview, Evans was the Vice President of Athlete Relations for AthleteNow.com. "I'm really excited about this opportunity," Evans emphasized then. "This is a terrific firm with a lot of potential. I haven't been this energized since I was playing in the big leagues!"

But like so many former players, baseball was still in Dewey's blood. He rejoined the Red Sox as a roving instructor in 2001, and he was the hitting instructor for the big league

Dwight was inducted into the Red Sox Hall of Fame on May 18, 2000. Executive VP and GM Dan Duquette made the presentation.

team in 2002. Currently he is a player development consultant for the club.

Evans reflected on the Red Sox fans. "They cheered you when you made a good play, and they booed you when you deserved it. I discovered early on that what they really wanted was maximum effort at all times. I thought that was very fair. The fans always treated me very well. More than anything else, I played for the Red Sox fans."

Dwight "Dewey" Evans: the greatest right fielder in the history of the Boston Red Sox.

Dwight Evans' Rank in Major League Baseball History

CATEGORY	CAREER TOTALS	ALL-TIME MLB RANK
Walks	1,391	24
Games	2,606	33
Home Runs	385	46
Doubles	483	57
RBI	1,384	63
At Bats	8,996	60
Runs	1,470	65
Years	20	82

Source: 2004 MLB.com

28.
Don Zimmer Interview
March 2003

To the best of my knowledge I was the first representative of Red Sox Nation to enter the Yankees clubhouse after the New Yorkers had been dubbed "The Evil Empire" during the winter of 2003. I must confess that my media credentials "Affiliation: Boston Red Sox" felt like a bull's-eye hanging from my neck. Worse than that, I had trouble finding their clubhouse at Legends Field, their spring training home in Tampa, Florida.

A cordial gentleman glanced at my credentials and told me to follow him. I had been chatting with him for a couple of minutes before I realized that Hall of Famer Reggie Jackson was my guide. I knew I was supposed to hate these guys, but he couldn't have been nicer.

The first thing that catches your eye when you walk into the New York Yankees locker room is the message over the passage way to their dugout. Written in large script is this quote from Joe DiMaggio: "I want to thank the good Lord for making me a Yankee." I don't know if the players pay much attention to it, but it is certainly a reminder that there is some history with this team.

Zim greeted me cordially and walked me to the Yankees dugout where we talked for about 45 minutes. At one point, out of the corner of my eye I could see a Yankee player playfully whack Zimmer on the shoulder. When I looked up I saw Derek Jeter giving me his 1,000 watt smile and his best, "How ya doin'?" At that point I wished somebody would be rude to me.

Don Zimmer was close to the ideal interview subject. He is a great storyteller, he has over 50 years of baseball memories, and he is very honest. Never for a moment did I imagine that seven months later I would be sitting in Fenway Park watching him charge across the field at Pedro Martinez.

DON ZIMMER
THE 1978 BOSTON RED SOX
REMEMBERED

The 2003 baseball season marked Don Zimmer's fifty-fifth year in professional baseball. At that point, he had played for, coached or managed with 11 major league teams in 13 big league cities. His seven seasons with the Boston Red Sox as coach and manager from 1974 to 1980 is his longest consecutive tenure with one team.

Don Zimmer led the 1978 Red Sox to 99 wins and a share of the regular season Eastern Division crown with the New York Yankees. The team's 99 victories remains the highest win total since the 1946 Red Sox won 104 games. Zimmer's 411 wins as Red Sox manager between the middle of 1976 and the end of the 1980 season ranks sixth among all Red Sox managers. His winning percentage of .575 is second only to the legendary Joe McCarthy (.606) among Red Sox managers who have guided the team in 350 or more games.

THE REAL ZIM

A popular misconception about Don Zimmer is that he has a steel plate in his head as a result of a "beaning" in 1953. "Zim" was seriously injured that year when he was hit in the head by a pitch while playing for St. Paul in the Brooklyn Dodgers minor league system. His life hung in the balance while he lay unconscious in the hospital for six days.

Instead of a steel plate, Zim has four tantalum buttons inserted in holes that were drilled in his skull to relieve the pressure. "Those players who said I sometimes managed like I had a hole in my head were wrong. I actually have four holes in my head," Zim is fond of saying.

Another source of confusion is selecting a likeness for Don Zimmer. Up close and personal in the Yankees dugout he looks most like a caricature of your favorite uncle. Think of him as your gruff, favorite uncle with kind blue eyes, the one who everyone looks forward to seeing at their family reunions.

And finally, Don Zimmer does not have negative feelings about his time in Boston with the Red Sox. "I always enjoyed the fans in Boston," Zimmer states emphatically. "And I'm not saying that because you are writing for a Red Sox magazine. I tell everyone the same thing.

"I'm always running into fans from Boston and they'll tell me, 'Oh Zim, we loved you in Boston. We wish you never left.' I have a lot of fun with them. I ask them, 'Did you ever boo me?' and of course, they say, 'Oh, no. Never.' Then I tell them, 'Gee, there were 30,000 fans booing me at every game, and I can't find a single one of them.' It's all in good fun."

THE 1978 BOSTON RED SOX

The 1978 Boston Red Sox were expected to give the 1977 World Champion New York Yankees a run for their money. Their 97 victories the previous year fell short of the Yankees' 100-win mark, but the Red Sox had made a number of off-season moves to improve the team.

To shore up their pitching staff, General Manager Haywood Sullivan entered the free agent market to acquire relief pitchers Dick Drago and Tom Burgmeier. In a major coup, Sullivan lured free-agent Mike Torrez, who had won 14 games for the Yankees the previous year, to Boston.

Sullivan was busy in the trade market as well. He traded outfielder Rick Miller to the California Angels for second baseman Jerry Remy, a native of Somerset, Massachusetts, and current Red Sox telecaster. And at the end of spring training Sullivan pulled off a blockbuster trade. The Red Sox traded pitcher Rick Wise and three promising youngsters to the Cleveland Indians for future 20-game winner Dennis Eckersley.

Don Zimmer had a good feeling about his team when they left Winter Haven, Florida, to start the regular season. "After you spend six weeks with your club in the spring, you have a pretty good feel for how you're going to do. You

Zim would sometimes have an occasional word for the umps.

really know whether you are going to contend or just be in the middle of the pack. And I knew our 1978 team was going to be in it to the end.

"We had a terrific offensive team. Jim Rice at that time was as good as anybody in the game. And we knew what Yaz, Fred Lynn, and Fisk could do. Picking up Eckersley really helped the pitching staff. You can never have enough pitching because even the best offense will go into a slump. And you need pitching to win those 2-1 and 3-2 games."

The 1978 Red Sox opened on the road with a record of 2-3, but reeled off eight straight wins when they returned to the friendly confines of Fenway Park. The team lost four in a row on the road at the end of April, finishing the month at 11-9, two games out of first place.

On May 13 they improved their record to 21-11, and moved into sole possession of first place. By mid-June the Red Sox were 26-4 at home and boasted an overall record of 45-19 for a winning percentage of .703. "Our offense was really rolling," Zimmer recalls. "When you've got a hitter having the kind of year that Jim Rice had, and your ninth hitter [third baseman Butch Hobson] ends up with 17 home runs, you've got quite a lineup. And we were getting outstanding pitching at the time."

The team took four out of six games from the Yankees during the last two weeks of June, and opened up a nine and one-half game lead on the Bronx Bombers. At the All-Star break the team had won 57 games and was playing .850 ball at Fenway Park.

"I knew we weren't 13 or 14 games better than the Yankees, regardless of the standings," Zim remembers. "Everything was breaking our way, and we earned it. But the Yankees just couldn't seem to get going. I never thought we would just run away with it that year."

In late July the Yankees fired Billy Martin and the team began to jell. Bob Lemon was a popular choice with Yankee players as Martin's replacement, and they quickly narrowed the Boston lead to six games. A two game sweep at Yankee Stadium by the Red Sox in early August, opened some daylight, but the race was clearly on.

THE SECOND BOSTON MASSACRE

The two teams matched victories throughout August, and when the Yankees arrived at Fenway Park on September 7, the Red Sox lead had been cut to four games. The Yankees took the opener by a score of 15-3, and followed it with a 13-2 drubbing the next day. In the third game on Saturday, Yank Ron Guidry ran his record to 21-2 as he shut out the Red Sox 7-0.

On Sunday, the Red Sox started rookie Bobby Sprowl and the Yankees swept the series with a 7-4 win. The two teams were in a dead-heat for first place. "I took a lot of heat for starting Bobby Sprowl, but we thought he was ready. I never even considered starting Bill Lee. He had lost seven straight starts when I pulled him from the rotation in mid-August. He had given up 54 hits and walked 16 in his last 42 innings. He couldn't get anybody out."

The Yankees decisive four-game sweep temporarily derailed the Red Sox Pennant Express. They lost five of the next six games, including the first two games of a crucial three game series in Yankee Stadium. Trailing the Yankees by three and one-half games with only two weeks left in the season, the Red Sox defeated the Yankees 7-3 in the series finale with Dennis Eckersley picking up his seventeenth win.

"About that time most people had given up on us. But that team never quit. When you're only a couple of games back, you know you still have a chance. And we kept battling and winning. Of course, the Yankees kept winning too. But we won our last eight ballgames and forced them to a playoff."

THE SECOND AMERICAN LEAGUE PLAYOFF GAME

"I remember that Monday was a beautiful day. Usually at that time of year you'll get a cold day and the wind blowing in. I remember talking to Joe Mooney [head groundskeeper] that morning and he said the wind would be blowing out lightly all day. Of course, that eventually cost us the game."

Fenway Park was overflowing on Monday afternoon, October 2, 1978, as the Red Sox squared off with the Yankees in the winner-take-all playoff game. This was only the second playoff game in American League history and ironically both games took place in Fenway Park. Almost exactly 30 years earlier, on October 4, 1948, the Red Sox had lost a one-game playoff to the Cleveland Indians by a score of 8-3.

The Yankees started their ace pitcher Ron Guidry and Boston countered with 16-game-winner Mike Torrez. The Red Sox jumped out to an early 1-0 lead on captain Carl Yastrzemski's second inning solo home run. The lead was increased to 2-0 when Jim Rice, who would win American League MVP honors for his outstanding season, singled in shortstop Rick Burleson.

Torrez had pitched well for the Red Sox through six innings, and there was only minor concern when Yankee shortstop Bucky Dent stepped to the plate with two men on in the top of the seventh inning.

"When you have watched as many games in Fenway Park as I have," Zimmer recalls, "you know when the ball leaves the bat whether it is an out or whether it will reach the wall. When Bucky's ball left the bat I said to myself, 'Good, that's an out.' Then when Yaz turned around I said, 'That's not so bad, it's going to hit the wall.' Not to take anything away from Bucky Dent, but when that ball ended up in the net, I was as surprised as anyone in the ballpark."

The Red Sox battled back and came within one run of tying the game in the bottom of the ninth inning. But when Yankee third baseman Graig Nettles squeezed Carl Yastrzemski's popup for the final out of the game, it was the New York Yankees who would advance to the post-season.

"I was kind of numb after the final out. When I got to the clubhouse I closed the door to the media and gathered the team together. They were crying, and for the first time in my baseball life I was crying right along with them. What else could you do?

"I told them, 'There's not a guy in the clubhouse who should hang his head. I couldn't be more proud of the way you played those last 20 games. Everybody gave up on you, but you wouldn't quit. This is just something you have to live with. It's baseball.' "

WESTERN HILLS HIGH SCHOOL

Don Zimmer was born in Cincinnati, Ohio, on January 17, 1931. He starred in football and baseball at Western Hills High School, but baseball was his first love. He signed with the Brooklyn Dodgers for a $2,500 bonus and reported to their Class D farm club in Cambridge, Maryland, in 1949.

"I went back to a reunion at Western Hills a while back and we counted up that the school had sent 14 players to the major leagues. Red Sox fans will remember Clyde Vollmer who was the first to make it to the big leagues. Everybody remembers Pete Rose, of course. And four of us went on to manage in the majors. Myself and Rose, plus Jim Frey who was my close friend and classmate, and Russ Nixon was the fourth."

Zimmer was a highly regarded prospect in the Dodgers system. A sure-handed shortstop with a strong arm, he had speed and surprising power at 5'9". At the time of his first beaning in July 1953, he was leading the American Association with 23 home runs and 67 RBI.

BROOKLYN-BOUND

Don Zimmer shook off his near-fatal beaning and earned a promotion to the big leagues in July 1954 when regular Dodgers shortstop Pee Wee Reese was side-

lined with an injury. He tripled in his first major league at-bat at old Shibe Park in Philadelphia and played well until Reese returned to the lineup one week later.

Early in the 1955 season Zim hit two long home runs into the upper deck at Ebbets Field in Brooklyn. When he returned to the dugout after the second blast, Dodger catcher and future Hall of Famer Roy Campanella grabbed him by the biceps and announced, "No wonder this little guy can hit balls like that. He's got arms like Popeye." Popeye has been Zimmer's baseball nickname for almost 50 years.

Zim had 15 home runs in only 280 at-bats in 1955, and played in four games during the Dodgers' World Series victory over the Yankees. His future with the Dodgers was bright. But in July 1956 he was hit on the left cheekbone by a fastball thrown by Hal Jeffcoat of the Cincinnati Reds.

For the two weeks following his beaning he had to wear a blindfold to keep his eyes stationary. He was out of uniform for the balance of the season. This second injury affected his vision and probably kept him from achieving elite status as a player.

The Dodgers moved to Los Angeles in 1958 and Zimmer enjoyed his best year with the club, hitting 17 home runs and stealing 14 bases. When Pee Wee Reese retired before the 1959 season it looked like Zim would finally take over as the Dodgers' starting shortstop.

But Zimmer never found his hitting stroke in 1959, and Maury Wills established himself as the Dodgers shortstop of the future. Zim had the consolation of earning another World Series ring as the Dodgers defeated the Chicago White Sox in five World Series games, but the Dodgers traded him to the Chicago Cubs during spring training in 1960.

CHICAGO CUBS CAPTAIN

The 29-year-old Zimmer started his Cubs career by homering against former teammate Don Drysdale on opening day at the Memorial Coliseum. He split his time that season between third base and second base, playing in a career-high 132 games. The Cubs named him their captain in 1961, and he was selected to the National League All-Star team.

"That was one of the years they played two All-Star Games and I played in both of them. Today I tell my grandkids I was good enough to play in two All-Star games. Why does anyone have to know they were both in the same year?"

The newly formed New York Mets made Don Zimmer one of their early selections in the draft held to stock the new expansion clubs. Zimmer's off-season home was near the Mets' St. Petersburg spring training headquarters and he posed for photographers as the first player to wear a Mets uniform.

Zimmer's days as a regular were behind him, but he was highly valued as a utility player. The 1962 Mets traded him to the Cincinnati Reds in midseason, and Zimmer thought he was headed back to his hometown. But the homecoming was short-lived when the Reds traded him to the Los Angeles Dodgers before the 1963 season.

The well-traveled Mr. Zimmer was sold to the Washington Senators in June 1963.

Zim finished out his major league playing career under his former Dodgers teammate, manager Gil Hodges. In 1966 Zim played for the Tokyo Toei Flyers, earning $30,000 for the season, which was $9,000 more than his highest big league salary of $21,000.

BACK ON THE BUS

After 18 years in uniform, 12 of them at the major league level, Zim was back in the bushes, starting over as a minor league manager. His first job was in the Reds' farm system in Knoxville, Tennessee, where he earned about one-third of what he made in Japan. In mid-season he was promoted to manage the Reds' Triple A club in Buffalo.

After a second season in Triple A for the Reds in 1968, Zim joined the minor league system of the newly formed San Diego Padres. After two seasons of managing in the minors for San Diego, he accepted an offer to return to the majors as a coach with the Montreal Expos under manager Gene Mauch.

In 1972 he signed on as the third base coach for the San Diego Padres under manager Preston Gomez. Less than one month into the season Gomez was fired and Zimmer was named to replace him. After an apprenticeship of only five years, he was a big league manager.

The San Diego Padres had lost over 300 games during their first three years as an expansion franchise and they didn't fare much better under Zimmer. The team went 54-88 over the balance of the 1972 season and they lost 102 ballgames in 1973. He was not rehired for the 1974 season.

BOSTON: 1974 TO 1980

Manager Darrell Johnson hired Zim as his third base coach for the 1974 season. He remained in that role until the Red Sox fired Johnson in July 1976, and Zimmer took over as manager. Zim led the 1977 Red Sox to a tie for second place in the American League East, two and one-half games behind the Yankees. "One of the great things about the Red Sox was knowing every season that you would be in contention right to the end," Zimmer emphasizes. "You knew that in September you would be playing for something."

Zimmer chuckles when he remembers Opening Day at Fenway Park in 1979. "I went to home plate to exchange lineup cards before the game and 30,000 fans booed me. Jeff Torborg was the Indians' manager and he said, 'Wow. This is one tough audience. You win 99 games, go to a playoff, and they boo you like that?' We had a good laugh over it."

In 1979 the Red Sox won 91 games and finished third, 11 games behind the Baltimore Orioles. In 1980 the team fell to fourth place, and Ralph Houk replaced Zimmer as the Red Sox manager for the 1981 season.

Shortly after his release by the Red Sox, Zimmer was hired to manage the Texas Rangers. He managed the Rangers to a strong first half in 1981, but the team faded in the second-half of the strike-shortened season. Rangers' owner Eddie Chiles fired Zim in the middle of the 1982 season. Darrell Johnson, who had preceded Zim as manager of the 1976 Red Sox, replaced him as the Rangers' manager.

Zim coached under manager Billy Martin for the New York Yankees in 1983. He then coached with the Chicago Cubs under old friend Jim Frey from 1984 until Frey was fired in 1986. He finished out the 1986 season as a coach under the Yankees' Lou Piniella.

In 1987 he moved to the San Francisco Giants as a coach under his old Dodgers teammate Roger Craig.

When Frey was hired as the General Manager of the Chicago Cubs he brought back Zimmer to manage the club from 1988 to 1991. He led the Cubs to the post-season in 1989 earning Zim National League "Manager of the Year" honors. His 1989 Eastern Division Champion Cubs were known as "The Boys of Zimmer."

Zim returned to Boston as a coach for Butch Hobson in 1992. During the three following seasons he served as a coach for the Colorado Rockies. In total, he has served as a coach for seven major league teams over 22 seasons.

BACK IN THE BRONX

Don Zimmer joined the Yankees as Joe Torre's bench coach in 1996. Zimmer and Torre enjoyed an extremely close relationship. When Torre left the team in 1999 to be treated for prostate cancer, Zimmer managed the team to a 36-21 record until Joe's return as manager. During his first eight years with the Yankees Zim added four World Series rings to go with the two rings he had earned as a player with the Dodgers.

But Zim still holds fond memories of his time in Boston. "I had seven wonderful years in Boston. And that is not b.s. I really enjoyed my time there. I played for a great owner in Tom Yawkey, and I had two excellent general managers in Dick O'Connell and Haywood Sullivan. Sure, I got booed a lot, but it goes with the territory. Overall the fans were great there. Red Sox fans are second to none.

"I tell these guys," waving his arm in the direction of the 2003 New York Yankees working out at Legends Field in Tampa, Florida, "that my two favorite ballparks are Fenway Park and Wrigley Field. They say, 'ah, that's just because you are an old-timer.' And I am," Zim adds.

Don Zimmer and his wife Jean live in Treasure Island, close

Don returned to Boston in 1993 to accept the Judge Emil Fuchs Memorial Award for Long and Meritorious Service to Baseball as voted by the Boston writers at the annual dinner in January. Television personality and emcee Dick Flavin made the presentation.

to the Yankees' Tampa spring training headquarters, and not far from Tropicana Field. Zim and his wife, who is universally known as "Soot," were married at home plate in Elmira, New York, in 1951. "Our honeymoon was the ballgame after the wedding ceremony. I played and Soot watched."

The Zimmers have two grown children. Son Tommy has three sons of his own, and their daughter Donna, who lives in Windham, New Hampshire, has one daughter.

Asked if he has any message for Red Sox fans, Zim laughs. "Yeah. Tell them I hope you finish second. I hope you have a heck of a year. No, I can put it better than that. I hope you finish second to the Yankees, and your team has a great year for your fans."

Don Zimmer is the consummate professional baseball man. He is perhaps the ideal symbol of the Red Sox-Yankee competition, the best rivalry in baseball. Don Zimmer: we hope *you* finish second, back at you.

29.
Rick Burleson Interview
July 2000

I tracked Rick Burleson down by phone in San Antonio, Texas, just before he was leaving for the ballpark to manage his San Antonio Missions. At the time he was in his second year of managing in the Dodgers' minor league system. Currently he is managing the Louisville Riverbats, the Cincinnati Reds' Triple A team.

Burleson is known as one of the most intense players in Red Sox history. I'm not sure if you can feel intensity through a telephone line, but Burleson seemed to attack every question I asked. Attack in a good sense, as if every answer was important.

At the time of the Iranian hostage crisis, the ever-quotable Bill Lee offered, "I don't know what the big holdup is. All they have to do is send in Rick Burleson and Rico Petrocelli. They'll have the whole thing resolved in 24 hours."

Ironically, Don Zimmer christened Burleson "Rooster" because of the way Rick's hair stood straight up after infield practice. But the nickname stuck because of his combative playing style and aggressive strut.

When Derek Jeter crashed into the stands to catch a foul ball in July 2004, a New York Times *columnist wrote that no player in Red Sox history would have done the same thing. I sent the columnist an e-mail suggesting that he send a copy of his article to Rick Burleson. I still haven't heard back from the columnist.*

RICK "ROOSTER" BURLESON
THE 1975 BOSTON RED SOX
REMEMBERED

When you mention the name Rick Burleson to a long-time Red Sox fan, the immediate response is: "The Rooster." Burleson, a four-time American League All-Star and a Gold Glove winner, is generally regarded as one of the most intense players in the team's history. He was the Red Sox starting shortstop from early in the 1974 season through 1980, and every step he took on the playing field exuded a determination to win.

"Don Zimmer [former Red Sox coach and manager, and current Yankees coach] gave me that nickname," Burleson recalls. "Zim used to hit grounders to me during infield practice, and one day when we got back to the dugout my hair was sticking straight up. He took one look at me and said, 'The Rooster.' That was probably 25 years ago, but it stuck."

Burleson's intensity as a ballplayer had a lot more to do with the staying power of the nickname than his hairstyle. Generously listed in the program at 5-feet-10 inches and 165 pounds, the adjective used most often to describe his play was "feisty."

Former Red Sox pitcher Bill Lee remembers Burleson in spring training before the 1974 season. "Some guys don't like to lose, but Rick got angry if the score was even tied. He was very intense and had the greatest arm of any infielder I had ever seen. The moment he reported to camp, he brought a fire to the club that we had been lacking."

THE 1975 BOSTON RED SOX

When the 1975 Boston Red Sox reported to spring training in Winter Haven, Florida, an air of cautious optimism surrounded their camp. It was clear early on that second-year manager Darrell Johnson would have to find a spot in the line-up for two rookie outfielders by the names of Jim Rice and Fred Lynn. But there was never any doubt that Rick Burleson would be the starting shortstop day-in and day-out.

Johnny Pesky, who has been associated with the team for over 60 years, remembers Burleson's years with the Red Sox fondly. "He was like a breath of fresh air. He was a real scrapper. He played hard every day, and he did everything well. And boy, did he have a gun for an arm! He could fire it over to first from the hole at shortstop as well as anybody."

The 1974 Boston Red Sox led the American League's Eastern Division by seven games in late August, but an eight-game losing streak in September placed them out of contention. Rick Burleson had been called up from Pawtucket in early May that season. He appeared in 114 games and batted a solid .284.

"I remember Darrell Johnson saying to me at the end of the 1974 season, 'Next year we're going to win it all.' I had a real good feeling when I reported to camp in 1975."

The 1975 Red Sox got off to a strong start and continued to play well throughout the season. When All-Star catcher Carlton Fisk's spring training injury forced him to the sidelines for over two months, backup catcher Bob Montgomery filled the void. Monty did an outstanding job of handling the pitching staff and he chipped in with four game-winning RBI in the early going. The team took three out of four games from the visiting New York Yankees in late June, and the Red Sox moved into first place to stay.

Rick Burleson remembers a doubleheader against the Yankees in late July as a crucial point in the 1975 season. "We played a Sunday doubleheader against the Yankees. I remember it was played in Shea Stadium because Yankee Stadium was being totally renovated. Bill Lee shut them down in the first game and Fred Lynn made a sensational catch in the ninth inning of a 1-0 win. Then we beat them 6-0 in the second game. There was still a lot of baseball left to be played that season, but we knew we were the team to beat."

The Baltimore Orioles made a run at the Red Sox in September of 1975. A Baltimore disc jockey flew to Nairobi, Kenya, and hired a witch doctor to place a curse on the Red Sox, but Luis Tiant put an end to that nonsense with a 2-0 September shutout of the Birds. When the Yankees beat the Orioles on September 27th the Red Sox clinched their first American League East title.

"I remember I had a speaking engagement that night. The Yankees win came late that Saturday, and when I arrived at the function, the guests were all excited about clinching the title. That's how I found out we had won the division. My wife and I spent the evening celebrating the good news with all those nice people!"

UNSUNG HERO

The Eastern Division Champions won 95 games and led the American League in batting, slugging and on-base percentage. Fred Lynn led the American League in runs scored, and he joined fellow rookie Jim Rice with over 100 RBI. Rick Wise led the team's pitchers with 19 wins. Luis Tiant and Bill Lee were close behind with 18 and 17 victories respectively.

Dwight Evans' spectacular defense in right field has been well chronicled, and veterans Carl Yastrzemski and Rico Petrocelli have been deservedly credited with anchoring the young team. Catcher Carlton Fisk's heroic home run in Game Six is easily the best-remembered event of the entire 1975 season.

In retrospect, Rick Burleson's contributions to the team were overshadowed by the spectacular achievements of his teammates. Rick Burleson would never make that statement, but the Boston Baseball Writers agreed when they voted him as the team's Unsung Hero.

CALIFORNIA KID

Rick Burleson was born in Lynwood, California, and grew up in southern California as a Dodgers' fan. "I remember watching the Dodgers in the Coliseum before Dodger Stadium was built. Sandy Koufax and Maury Wills were their big stars then."

Rick played baseball, basketball and football as a youngster but gravitated to baseball because of his size. He was a shortstop and pitcher until a broken arm at age 14 cut short his pitching career. Burleson played for strong teams at Warren High of Downey, California, and his Connie Mack team won the National Championship in 1969.

In addition to his relatively small stature, a medical condition caused

Receiving congrats from teammate Jerry Remy following a home run.

Burleson to focus on baseball. "I have spondylosis, a back problem where a couple of vertebrae are set out in my lower back. When I played football, I couldn't stand up right after a game, and I would end up at the chiropractor. For some reason, baseball never bothered my back even when I'd dive or swing hard."

The Red Sox made Burleson their number one secondary selection in the Winter Draft of 1970, and he began his career with Winter Haven in the Florida State League. He progressed through the Red Sox system to Greenville, South Carolina, and on to Winston-Salem, North Carolina, for the 1971 season. In 1972, he was promoted to the Pawtucket club, then a Red Sox Double A farm team.

"I had kind of a rough start," Burleson recalls. "My one God-given talent was a strong throwing arm. Everything else I had to work hard at. Nothing came easy for me."

Burleson played in 136 games in 1972 and his strong defense earned him the Triple A shortstop job in 1973. Pawtucket became the Red Sox top farm team that year, and he played another year at McCoy Stadium under future Red Sox manager Darrell Johnson. His 146-game season topped the International League.

Rick played winter ball in Venezuela in the off-season, and after one month in Pawtucket to start the 1974 season, he was ready for prime time. Called up to the Red Sox in early May, Burleson vividly remembers his first game.

"I made three errors in my first game with the team. That tied an American League record. That was a tough start! But I hit a home run in my second game, and I was fine after that."

THE 1975 POSTSEASON

The Red Sox drew the three-time World Series Champion Oakland A's as their 1975 American League Championship Series opponents. But Luis Tiant shut down the mighty A's in the Series opener, and the Red Sox were on their way. Boston swept the vaunted A's in three straight, and Rick Burleson contributed a .444 batting average.

The 1975 Cincinnati Reds were strong favorites to handle the Red Sox easily in the World Series. The "Big Red Machine" had won 108 regular season games and they were determined to add a World Championship to their list of accomplishments.

The 1975 World Series is considered by many observers to be the best World Series ever played. The Big Red Machine had stalled in Game One as Luis Tiant mystified the Reds in a 6-0 Red Sox victory at Fenway Park. A ninth inning double by Ken Griffey, Sr., gave the Reds a come-from-behind 3-2 win in Game Two.

The Reds took the Series lead with another come-from-behind win in Game Three, but Luis Tiant knotted the Series with a gritty 5-4 victory in Game Four. The Reds regained the edge with a Game Five win, and future Hall of Famer Carlton Fisk thrilled the nation with his game-winning twelfth-inning home run in Game Six.

The Red Sox held a 3-0 lead in the sixth inning of Game Seven, but two other future Hall of Famers, the Reds' Tony Perez and Joe Morgan, saved the day for Cincinnati. Perez's sixth-inning home run, and Morgan's ninth-inning single gave the Reds a 4-3 win and a World Championship.

Burleson looks back on the 1975 World Series with a sense of irony. "The Reds were a great team and we almost beat them. We knew we had a great team. I had only been in the majors two seasons, one full season actually. I thought we would be back in the playoffs every year. We all did, really."

How important was Rick Burleson to the Red Sox team that came so close to a World Championship? Statistics do not tell the whole story for a "gamer" like The Rooster, but he only missed 36 innings over the course of the entire season and nine of those were in the final meaningless regular season game. On a team of acknowledged power hitters, he finished second in game-winning hits and third in RBI.

Bill Lee recalls Rick Burleson as the glue that held the 1975 Red Sox together. "Burleson might have been our least expendable player. Shortstop was the one position our depth couldn't cover. Luckily, he only missed four games that year. He was a scrapper. I would load the bases and he would trot over and say, 'Keep the ball down and make them hit it to me. I'll turn two.'"

ALL-STAR SHORTSTOP

The 1976 season was a disappointing one for the Boston Red Sox, but Burleson raised his batting average to .291 and continued his stalwart defense. In 1977,

Burleson coaching third base for the Red Sox in 1993.

baseball fans voted him as the starting shortstop for the American League All-Star team. "That was a great honor," Burleson offers, recalling the game played at Yankee Stadium. "I remember what a thrill it was playing in front of all of those fans. I flew my father in to attend the game. It's a wonderful memory."

Burleson earned All-Star honors for a second time in 1978, but a torn ligament prevented him from playing in the game. He was a major participant in the 1978 playoff game against the Yankees, and he still remembers virtually every detail.

"I remember that Goose Gossage walked me on four pitches in the ninth inning. Jerry

Remy hit a line drive to right and Lou Piniella speared it so I had to stop at second. I tagged up to move to third on Jim Rice's long fly ball. I was still there, hoping to score the tying run, when Yaz popped out to Nettles to end the game.

"What I remember the most is the clubhouse after the game. Not only how quiet it was, but looking at the bags we had packed to go on to Kansas City to start the playoffs. It was a sad sight to look over there at the luggage."

Burleson was named an American League All-Star for the third straight year in 1979 and he led American League shortstops with a .980 fielding percentage. The 1980 season was another fine year for the seven-year veteran, and the Boston Baseball Writers Association voted him the team's Most Valuable Player for the second year in a row.

But 1980 would be Rick Burleson's last year with the Boston Red Sox. The following December he was traded, along with Butch Hobson, to the California Angels for Carney Lansford, Mark Clear and Rick Miller.

"It was tough to be traded. I had spent eleven years with the Boston Red Sox organization. It was the only team I had ever been with. It was kind of nice to be traded to my home in southern California, but I hated to leave Boston."

LATER YEARS

Burleson's career with the Angels got off to a great start. He was named an American League All-Star for the fourth time, and he matched a career-high with a .293 batting average. But in early 1982 he suffered a serious shoulder injury and he spent the balance of his career with the Angels hoping to regain his All-Star form. In 1986 he appeared in 93 games with the Angels and he played in four games against the Red Sox in the American League Championship Series.

"I enjoyed my time with the Angels. And we had a terrific team in 1986. That was the third time in my career that I came close to a championship.

"But it always felt kind of strange to come back to Fenway with a visiting team. I remember it really felt funny to be back in Boston for the post-season and be in the visitors dugout."

Rick Burleson signed with the Baltimore Orioles for the 1987 season. After appearing in 62 games as a designated hitter and occasional second baseman, he was released by the club. His 13-year big league career was over.

"I hope when people think of me they will remember that I played every day. I wanted to play every inning of every game, and I wanted to play hard all the time. That was always my objective."

MANAGING IN THE MINORS

At the time of our interview Rick Burleson was the manager of the San Antonio Missions in the Los Angeles Dodgers farm system. The Missions are a Double A franchise playing in the Texas League. Burleson guided them to a second-place finish in the first half of the 2000 season.

"I really enjoy managing. It is a real challenge working with a 23-man roster. I coached at the big league level for a number of clubs, but Don Zimmer once told me that he wanted big league coaches who had experience managing in the minors. Naturally I would love to get back to the big leagues."

Burleson's big league coaching portfolio includes a stint with the Oakland A's in 1970 and 1971 as their hitting instructor. He returned to Boston, coaching under Butch Hobson, in 1992. After one season as hitting coach, he took over as the Red Sox third base coach for the 1993 season.

"I realized it takes a unique set of skills to be an effective hitting coach. That is one of the toughest jobs in baseball." Asked for his memories of Red Sox fans, Burleson responds, "The fans in Boston are very knowledgeable. They were always great to me. Of course, when I was coaching third and a runner got thrown out at the plate, I heard about it!"

After his time in Boston, Burleson was a member of the California Angels big league coaching staff from 1994 to 1996. In 1997, he joined the Seattle Mariners organization, managing the Lancaster Jethawks of the California League for two seasons. His affiliation with the Dodgers began in 1999, when he accepted the manager's job for their California League entry, the San Bernardino Stampede.

Johnny Pesky played a lot of shortstop and he has seen a lot of shortstops in his time. Asked if Rick Burleson reminded him of a young Pesky, Johnny chuckles, "He was a throw-back to an earlier era, that's for sure. What a fiery guy! I'll tell you what: I would want him on my team. I would find a place for him, that's for sure."

MARATHON MAN

Rick Burleson has an interesting observation on the 1978 season and that Boston Red Sox team. "That team won 99 ball games. That was a very good team. Under today's rules we would have been the Wild Card team. We knew whoever won the playoff game against the Yankees would beat Kansas City and go on to the World Series. Who knows what would have happened in a longer series?" Burleson muses.

Former Red Sox manager Jimy Williams was fond of comparing the baseball season to a marathon. The regular season is 26 weeks of executing the fundamentals and playing with intensity in every inning of 162 games. A video of Rick Burleson's career highlights would be short on dramatic game-winning home runs, but packed with examples of the little things that win baseball games.

The video would show The Rooster advancing the runner from second to third base when the at-bat called for him to give himself up, taking a hard slide from the runner while turning a crucial double play, and fouling off pitch after pitch until he got one he could handle. That is baseball. That is Rick Burleson.

30.
Bernie Carbo Interview
March 2004

I had a tough time reaching Bernie Carbo at his home in Theodore, Alabama. I have known Bernie for over 15 years and I have always had a difficult time tracking him down.

For the first six years I knew him, I couldn't get ahold of Bernie because he was out raising the devil. These days Bernie is hard to find because he is busy with his grandchildren and he is out spreading his vision of the Lord to groups all over the country.

Bernie is one of the more articulate former players that I have ever met. Current Red Sox fans probably think that Kevin Millar runs on with the media. If they spent an hour with Bernie, they would realize what the word loquacious really means.

Bernie spent only three and a half years with the team, but he is a legend among long-time Red Sox fans. It was nice to see him honored for his dramatic sixth game World Series home run at the Red Sox Hall of Fame dinner in November 2004.

Some players seem to peak during their big league careers. Many former players go on to even greater heights when their big league careers are over. Bernie Carbo is one former player who has totally turned his life around and become a positive force in people's lives.

BERNIE CARBO
THE 1975 BOSTON RED SOX
REMEMBERED

Ask a *casual* fan of the Boston Red Sox what they remember about the sixth game of the 1975 World Series against the Cincinnati Reds and the answer is certain to be, "Pudge Fisk's game-winning, twelfth-inning home run." Ask a *dedicated, long-term* Red Sox fan the same question and the answer is likely to be, "Bernie Carbo's eighth-inning home run that tied the game, and set up Fisk's home run."

Bernie Carbo immediately perks up at the mention of one of the most dramatic home runs in Red Sox history. "When I got to home plate after that home run, my teammates mobbed me and the fans were going crazy. It wasn't until I got to the dugout that I found out I had tied the game. I was so focused on keeping the inning alive that I hadn't paid any attention to the score. The fans were screaming my name. I think I could have been elected the Mayor of Boston."

BORN TO PLAY

Bernie Carbo was born in Detroit, Michigan, and grew up in suburban Detroit. "When I was 11 years old we moved to Nankan Township. My dad found a house right across from Edward Hines Park so I could play ball all the time. I was over there from morning to night."

Bernie developed the beautiful "inside-out swing" that he used to great affect at Fenway Park on the diamond of Edward Hines. "We usually only had eight or nine kids, so anything hit to right field was an out. I was the only left-handed hitter and the kids refused to switch around when I came up. It forced me to learn how to hit the ball to left field."

Bernie's Little League career began with a home run. "Our coach was a woman. She was a good coach and a nice woman. First time up I hit a ball that went between the outfielders. I slid into second base, I slid into third base, and then I slid into home plate for a home run."

Bernie was a good all-around athlete in high school, but baseball was his passion. "I think I always wanted to be a baseball player growing up. Whenever we had to do a book report, I would make up a baseball story. It was always about the Detroit Tigers and they always went to the World Series. I imagined myself as the star of the team. I never actually read the books, I just made them up."

The first baseball amateur free agent draft was held in 1965 when Bernie Carbo was 17 years old. A favorite baseball trivia question in Cincinnati is: "The second player selected by the Reds in the first free agent draft was Johnny

Bench. Who was the first player ever drafted by the Reds?" The answer is: Bernie Carbo.

"When I reported to Tampa after signing with the Reds, I was being interviewed by a sportswriter, and another player came over and asked me if I was the first draft choice. I told him I was. Then he asked me how much I signed for. When I told him, '$30,000,' he shook his head and walked away. I asked the writer who the player was, and he said, 'Johnny Bench. And he's upset that he only got $5,000.' "

SPARKY ANDERSON

Bernie Carbo had a tough time during his first few seasons in the minor leagues. "I was just a kid and I felt a lot of pressure, being the number one draft choice. I responded to the pressure by clowning around, making my teammates laugh."

Hall of Fame manager Sparky Anderson was making his own way through the minors and he took Bernie Carbo under his wing in 1968 at Asheville, North Carolina. In his autobiography, *Sparky* (Fireside: 1990), Anderson recalls working with Bernie Carbo. "I may have spent as much time working with Bernie Carbo as any player I ever managed. When I first met him his teammates called him 'The Village Idiot' and he liked it. I had Bernie out to the park every morning, hitting him fly balls and working on his hitting."

Bernie is quick to credit Sparky Anderson with salvaging his career. "He had me out there at 9 A.M. every morning. He moved me from third base to the outfield where I was more comfortable. He taught me to take the game seriously."

The following season Bernie hit .359 at Indianapolis, the Reds' top farm team. His outstanding season earned him recognition as the Minor League Player of the Year. A strong showing in the Puerto Rican Winter League and a good spring training propelled him to the Cincinnati Reds for the 1970 season.

THE CINCINNATI KID

"My first hit in the big leagues was a home run on Opening Day in Cincinnati. It was the longest home run in baseball history. I hit it out of the park onto Route I-75. It landed in a truck and they found it in Florida, 1,300 miles away. It was a great way to start my big league career."

Carbo stayed hot all through his rookie season, finishing with a .310 average and 21 home runs. *The Sporting News* named him the National League Rookie of the Year. But controversy found him when the Reds faced the Baltimore Orioles in the World Series.

"I was on third base with one out. Ty Cline tops a ball in front of the plate, and I break for home. I had to push the umpire [Ken Burkhart] out of the way to get to home plate. Elrod Hendricks [Baltimore catcher] never tagged me. I missed home plate, but I stepped on it when I went back to argue.

"*Sports Illustrated* got a great picture of the play that they ran for years. It shows Hendricks tagging me with his glove but the ball is in his right hand. Every time I see Earl Weaver [former Orioles manager] he says, 'You're still out, Bernie.' "

Controversy followed Bernie into the 1971 season when he deemed the Reds' contract offer inadequate and declined to report to spring training. His lack of pre-season training and his disillusionment with the Reds resulted in a drop in his batting average of almost 100 points, to .219 for the 1971 season. Bernie sat out spring training once again in 1972, and in May the Reds traded him to the St. Louis Cardinals.

Bernie played parts of two seasons with the Cardinals. Following a productive 1973 season in St. Louis, he was traded to the Boston Red Sox along with pitcher Rick Wise in exchange for Reggie Smith and Ken Tatum.

A GOOD ITALIAN BOY

"Boston was a big adjustment for me," Bernie Carbo recalls. "In Cincinnati we might have had two or three writers in the clubhouse. When I got to Boston for Opening Day, it seemed like there were 100 writers covering us. One writer says to me, 'Bernardo Carbo, you must be Italian.' 'No,' I told him, 'I'm Spanish.' I pick up the paper the next day and I read, 'Bernardo Carbo, a good Italian boy, joined the Red Sox yesterday.' "

It also took Bernie Carbo a while to sort out all of the faces in the Red Sox clubhouse. "Right after I joined the team I walked into the clubhouse and there

was an older gentleman straightening things up. I gave him $20 and asked him to get me a cheeseburger and some french fries. When the clubhouse kid delivered the food, he asked me if I knew who I gave the $20 to. I told him I didn't, and he said, 'You just asked Tom Yawkey to get your lunch.' I thought I was in big trouble, but Mr. Yawkey got a big kick out of it."

Bernie played well in 1974 and quickly became a fan favorite. A former Cardinal teammate sent him a stuffed gorilla, which Carbo named "Mighty Joe Young," and took with him on road trips. Eminently quotable, *The Boston Globe's* Clif Keene once wrote, "Bernie Carbo could talk for twenty minutes about a spool of thread."

Bernie Carbo's versatility was a key component in the Red Sox drive to the American League Championship in 1975. He played 85 games in the outfield, served as the designated hitter, and pinch-hit. In just over 400 plate appearances he finished tenth in the American League with 83 walks.

"Playing for Tom Yawkey made all the difference. I loved Mr. Yawkey like a second papa. When I got to Boston I was a disillusioned ballplayer. But then I wanted to play for the uniform, for the team. And for Mr. Yawkey.

"I went to him that season and told him I wanted to buy a house for my family. I asked him to advance me $10,000, and to take it out of my pay. I went to my locker a few days later and he had left a check for $10,000 in there. He never took a dime out of my pay."

1975 WORLD SERIES

The Red Sox swept the defending World Champion Oakland A's in three games in the 1975 American League Championship Series. But Bernie Carbo spent the ALCS on the Red Sox bench. After spending the first two games of the World Series against the Cincinnati Reds in the same spot, he was getting a little restless.

"I went into the Reds' clubhouse when we got to Cincinnati to visit with some of my old teammates. My former roommate Clay Carroll gave me a nice picture inscribed, 'Good luck in the World Series.' I told some of the guys that I was tired of sitting on the bench and it was time to get me into the Series. It wasn't very smart, but I was frustrated.

"Sure enough, in Game Three Darrell Johnson sends me up to pinch hit for Reggie Cleveland in the seventh inning. And who is on the mound to pitch to me? My old roomy Clay Carroll. And don't I hit a home run into the left-field stands? When I went back to the clubhouse after the game, my locker had been trashed. I asked the clubhouse guy what had happened and he told me that Clay Carroll had stormed in, torn his picture into a thousand pieces and thrown all my things on the floor."

The Reds won Game Three despite Carbo's pinch-hitting heroics, but Red Sox ace Luis Tiant came back with a gutsy 163-pitch effort in Game Four. Tiant's 5-4 victory tied the Series, but a 6-2 Reds' win the following evening sent the team back to Boston, one game from elimination.

GAME SIX

Rain forced postponement of Game Six for three straight days. The extended break in the Series gave Luis Tiant enough rest to start this crucial game. Fred Lynn raised Boston fan's hopes with a first-inning, three-run home run to give the Red Sox an early lead. Tiant dominated in the early going, but the Reds tied the game in the fifth inning and moved ahead in the seventh.

Trailing by three runs in the bottom of the eighth, the Red Sox stirred fans' hopes when Fred Lynn and Rico Petrocelli reached base to start the inning. But when Dwight Evans and Rick Burleson were retired, the Reds were only four outs from a World Championship.

"Darrell Johnson told me to grab a bat to pinch hit, but I never expected to bat. The Reds had a left-hander warming up in the bullpen [Will McEnaney] and I was sure they would bring him in. At that point Darrell would have sent Juan Beniquez up to bat in my place. I couldn't believe it when Sparky Anderson left Rawly Eastwick in to pitch to me."

To add to the drama, Bernie's old friend Johnny Bench was behind the plate catching for the Reds. With the count even at 2-2, Eastwick came after Carbo with a wicked pitch on the inside corner. "That was a tough pitch for me to handle," Carbo remembers. "The ball was almost in Bench's glove and I just managed to get my bat on it, to foul it off at the last second. Pete Rose [Reds' third baseman] called it a Little League swing. It was a terrible swing."

Roger Angell, was more eloquent than Rose in describing Carbo's swing in his World Series article for *The New Yorker*. Angell wrote, "Bernie Carbo, pinch-hitting, looked totally overmatched against Eastwick, flailing at one inside pitch like someone fighting off a wasp with a croquet mallet."

Late Red Sox announcer Ken Coleman had a totally different assessment of Carbo's performance. "Bernie got a totally un-hittable pitch to deal with, and he managed to get his bat on the ball to stay alive. I thought it was a great piece of hitting. And look at what he did next."

There is no disagreement about what Bernie did next. Rawly Eastwick did Bernie an enormous favor by coming back with a fastball in his wheelhouse. And Bernie did what he did so well. He turned on it and he drove it straightaway to center with power.

"When I hit that ball, I wasn't sure if it was going out. I ran as hard and as fast as I could, and I didn't really slow down even after I knew it was a home run. When I was approaching third base, I yelled to Pete Rose, 'Don't you wish you were that strong?' As I was passing him he said, 'Ain't this great, Bernie? Isn't this what playing in the World Series is all about?'

"I just barely got a piece of the pitch before. I turned around after that pitch, and Johnny Bench was jawing with the umpire about whether the pitch would have been a strike. I said to them, 'Wow. I almost struck out.' And then I hit the next pitch into the center-field bleachers."

The Red Sox and Reds sparred on into the twelfth inning, when Carlton Fisk hit his dramatic, game-winning home run. The Reds managed a 4-3 win in Game Seven to earn their World Championship, but Bernie Carbo had become a permanent part of Red Sox folklore.

BOSTON TO MILWAUKEE AND BACK

In 1975 most things went right for the Boston Red Sox. They won the American League Championship and they came within one victory of a World Series win. In 1976 hardly anything went right for the Red Sox. Distracted by contract negotiations and the failing health of owner Tom Yawkey, the team got off to a terrible start. On June 3 the team announced that Bernie Carbo had been traded to the Milwaukee Brewers for pitchers Tom Murphy and Bobby Darwin.

"I was devastated," Bernie Carbo responds, looking back on his trade. "The Boston fans loved me and I loved them back. I couldn't imagine going from Boston to Milwaukee. My wife at the time was eight months pregnant, and we had two little girls. I was crushed.

"I refused to report to the Brewers. They kept calling, but I told them I couldn't do it. I could see the light towers at Fenway Park from our place in Cambridge and I just kept staring at them. After about three weeks my wife told me, 'You have to report. You're driving me crazy.' Bud Selig [then the owner of the Brewers and currently Commissioner of Baseball] flew us all out and I played the balance of the season with the Brewers."

Bernie's exile to Milwaukee was relatively brief. On December 6, 1976, Bernie and George Scott were traded back to the Red Sox for first baseman Cecil Cooper. The prodigal son was returning home.

"It was great to go back to Boston. But Tom Yawkey had passed away while I was gone and it wasn't the same for me. When I heard on the radio that he had died I just cried and cried. I couldn't stop crying. In some ways I think my career died with Tom Yawkey."

Bernie Carbo made a significant contribution to the 1977 Boston Red Sox. His on-base average of .409 was the highest on the team, and his 15 home runs in only 228 official at-bats helped the team to set a franchise record 213 round-trippers.

The 1978 Boston Red Sox got off to a great start. By mid-June the Red Sox were 26-4 at home and boasted an overall record of 45-19 for a winning percentage of .703.

But manager Don Zimmer was using Bernie Carbo sparingly, and on June 15 the Red Sox announced that they had sold his contract to the Cleveland Indians.

"When I walked into the clubhouse after the game that night, I saw a crowd of reporters around my locker. No one had to tell me what was going on, I knew I was gone. I headed right to my car, still in my uniform, and drove right through the crowd leaving the ballpark. I just had to get out of there."

WINDING DOWN

Bernie finished out the 1978 season with the Indians, batting .287. In 1979 he rejoined the St. Louis Cardinals, where he was used primarily as a pinch-hitter, and batted .281 for the season. He started the 1980 season with the Cardinals but they released him in May, and he finished the season with the Pittsburgh Pirates. His big league career came to an end when the Pirates released him on October 8, 1980.

"People ask me what I would do if I had my big league career to do over. I tell them the same thing I tell young players today. I tell young players to stay focused and to be the best player they can be. I tell them to stay away from things that can distract you, and don't make bad choices. I made some bad choices.

"But when I look back on the positive things, I did get to play for 12 years in the big leagues. And I played with some great players, like Yaz and Jim Rice in Boston, I lockered next to Hank Aaron in Milwaukee, and I got to play with Willie Stargell in Pittsburgh. I have some great memories."

LETTING GO

When Bernie's baseball career was over he started a second career as a cosmetologist. For a number of years he operated a series of beauty salons in the Detroit area.

In 1989 Bernie moved his family to Winter Haven, Florida, where he played for the Winter Haven Super Sox in the newly formed Senior League. The league, which was limited to players over the age of 35, was formed to play in the period between the World Series and the beginning of spring training. His teammates included his long-time friend, former Red Sox pitcher Bill Lee.

The Senior League was not a commercial success and shortly after the league folded Bernie Carbo hit rock bottom. "My mother had committed suicide, my father had died, and my first marriage was coming to an end. Bill Lee called and I told him I wasn't even sure about the next day. Bill was so concerned that he had Ferguson Jenkins [former Red Sox pitcher] call me and talk to me. Fergie had experienced some personal losses so he knew what I was going through. Then Fergie called Sam McDowell at the Baseball Assistance Team."

BASEBALL ASSISTANCE TEAM

The Baseball Assistance Team (B.A.T.) was formed in 1986, primarily by a group of former major leaguers, to help members of the baseball "family" who have come on hard times and who are in need of assistance. Joe Garagiola has been their most visible public spokesman, and former Red Sox pitcher Earl Wilson is the President & CEO. Most of B.A.T.'s work is done anonymously, but Bernie Carbo is quick to acknowledge the assistance he received.

"The Baseball Assistance Team probably saved my life. Sam McDowell got me into rehab to get me treatment for my alcohol and drug addiction. And they worked with me for the next three or four years to be sure that I had my life in order and to help me with my finances. I don't know where I would have been without them.

"While I was in rehab, I had an anxiety attack and they moved me to a regular hospital. I was in a room with an older gentleman and he could tell from the conversations that I was battling addictions. He asked me if I knew God, and I told him I didn't. He told me that I had to get to know God, and he gave me my first Bible. He really changed my life. When he was leaving I asked him what his name was and he said, 'The only name you need to know is God's name.'

"I spent about three months in rehab and when I got out I established the Diamond Club Ministry. I speak primarily to young people about baseball, about Jesus, and about the dangers of addiction to drugs and alcohol. My ministry is non-denominational and I have spoken in Christian churches throughout the United States and all over the world. I have preached in Saudi Arabia and to Cuban refuges at Guantanamo Bay."

BERNIE CARBO TODAY

"After I had been preaching for a few months I was giving witness at a home for boys and I met this wonderful woman," Carbo recalls. "I told her, 'God told me that you need to be with me.' She told me that God hadn't told her that. But I persisted, and four months later we were married. She is a very special lady."

Today Bernie and his wife Tammy live in Theodore, Alabama, just south of Mobile. Tammy, who has a Masters Degree in psychology, is a counselor at the local middle school, and Bernie does some substitute teaching. He has three grown daughters from his first marriage, and his son, Bernie, Jr., who recently received his undergraduate degree, will be pursuing a Masters program. Two of Bernie's grandchildren live with Bernie and Tammy, and a third grandchild lives in Hawaii.

In 2003 Bernie managed the Pensacola Pelicans to a championship in the independent Southeastern League. He was named Manager of the Year for the league and in 2004 the Pelicans moved up to the more established Central League.

Bernie Carbo's Fantasy Camp takes place on the second weekend of November each year. "It's a fantasy camp for fathers and

Carbo returned to Fenway to participate in a 1980s Old-Timers' game. The fans obviously hadn't forgotten him!

sons. Last year we had a grandfather, son and grandson participate. We do it as a long weekend, Friday through Sunday, and we keep the numbers down so it will be a meaningful experience for everyone. I have another former major leaguer work with me, and we break the players into three teams. This year we will be doing it at Spring Hill College in Mobile, Alabama.

"We have a busy and full life, but the Diamond Club Ministry is our main focus," Bernie emphasizes. "I live my life for God, and he has blessed me."

Bernie Carbo has successfully turned his life around. It's hard to know if he would have done a good job as the Mayor of Boston. But it is certainly clear that Bernie Carbo has found his true calling in life.

31.

Jim Rice Interview

August 2000

I interviewed Jim Rice in the family room adjacent to the Red Sox clubhouse at Fenway Park. At the time he was in his sixth season as the team's hitting instructor. It was about four hours before game time, but Rice was already in his uniform and anxious to get out to the batting cage.

The best single word to describe Jim Rice up close and personal is imposing. You have an idea of how big he is from watching him on the field for all these years. But it isn't until you sit three feet away from him that you realize how big he really is.

And imposing is a good one-word description of his passion for the game. The man has studied the game from every angle and no detail seems to escape him. You get a sense of this from his role as an analyst on NESN, but it is even stronger in a one-on-one conversation.

Sometimes I like to throw in a little "free association" into my interviews. I'll ask a player to name the first thing that comes to mind when I mention the left-field wall. Pudge Fisk answered, "beautiful." Dwight Evans responded, "close."

When I asked Jim the same question, his answer was, "37 feet high." Jim Rice is obviously a man who has taken measure of the left-field wall. And he came out way ahead.

JIM RICE
ADOPTED SON OF
NEW ENGLAND'S TEAM

Jim Rice, present Boston Red Sox Special Organizational Instructor, and former All-Star left fielder, has been a part of professional baseball for 32 years. And for all 32 of those years he has been associated with the Boston Red Sox. Named to the Red Sox Hall of Fame in November 1, 1995, he was part of the original group of 10 former Red Sox players to be so honored.

Red Sox favorite Johnny Pesky, who has been a part of the team for over 60 years, and is one of Rice's biggest fans, recalls, "Not only was he one of the best ballplayers this team has ever had, but he may have been the hardest-working ballplayer I was ever associated with. He and I would go out to the park before anyone was even in the stands and I would hit ball after ball to him in left field. He probably had the best work habits I have ever seen, and I've seen a lot of hard-working ballplayers."

THE 1975 BOSTON RED SOX

The 1975 Red Sox are often remembered for the heroics of Pudge Fisk, and the pitching majesty of Luis Tiant, but the monster rookie season of Jim Rice was as big a factor as any in the team's success during the regular season. Rice began the season as the team's primary designated hitter but took over as the regular left fielder on June 2. From that game forward, his season really took off. During the next two months he batted .330, drove in 45 runs, and put together five, four-hit games.

Rice became an instant legend during a game in June of 1975. He tried to hold up on his swing in a game in Detroit and he snapped his bat in half. Long-time baseball observers said they had never heard of such a thing.

Rice ended the 1975 season with a batting average of .309 and 102 RBI in 144 games. Less remembered is the fact that he played 90 games in left field and did not make one single error. "Hitting always came naturally to me," Rice recalled recently, "but I had to work hard at my fielding. I take a lot of pride in the fact that I made myself into a good defensive outfielder."

His outstanding rookie year came to an untimely end when a Vernon Ruhle pitch broke his left hand in late September. He missed the last few games of the season and all of the post-season.

Rice is philosophical when asked if it was difficult looking on while his club swept the Oakland A's and came within an inning of upsetting the Cincinnati

Reds in the World Series. "It was hard not being able to play, but they were my teammates so you want to be with them." Would the result have been different if he had been able to play? "Maybe, but we will never know. You just have to accept things the way they are, and deal with them. I've always felt that things like that were in the hands of the Lord. If He had wanted me to play in the World Series, I would have been there."

ANDERSON, SOUTH CAROLINA NATIVE

Jim Rice was born in Anderson, South Carolina, on March 8, 1953. Anderson is a community of almost 30,000 citizens in the western part of South Carolina, set in the Blue Ridge Mountains. He was the fourth-oldest in a family of nine. By all accounts, Jim Rice is clearly the finest athlete that Anderson has ever produced.

Jim Rice won a total of 10 letters during his high school career for baseball, football, basketball and track. His varsity baseball career began when he was in the seventh grade. A local recreation center was named the "Jim Rice Community Center" in 1981.

His former baseball coach at Westside High remembered Jim Rice fondly in a 1986 *Boston Globe* interview. "I'll tell you what. If I had a son, I'd want him to be just like Jim. He wouldn't have to be a ballplayer, either. He's tremendous, because he likes people."

Jim Rice was the Red Sox' number one selection in the 1971 draft, and the fifteenth pick overall. Long-time Red Sox scout Mace Brown signed him shortly after his high school graduation.

THE ROAD TO FENWAY

Rice began his professional baseball career with the Red Sox farm club in Williamsport, Pennsylvania. The 18-year-old Rice scored 34 runs in 60 games and compiled 27 RBI. But adjusting to professional baseball was easier than getting used to life off the field.

"Playing professional baseball for the first time wasn't the hard part. Being away from home and having to take care of yourself for the first time was the hard part," Rice recalls. "You had to learn to adjust to people from all sorts of backgrounds, and you had to learn how to be self-sufficient."

Jim Rice spent the 1972 season playing for Winter Haven in the Florida State League. In his second year of professional baseball Rice led the league in hits and runs and rapped out 17 home runs. His exploits earned him an All-Star selection.

He earned All-Star honors again in 1973 for Bristol in the Eastern League. His league-leading batting average of .317 helped propel him to Pawtucket at the Triple A level at the end of the 1973 season. Moving up a level from Double A didn't slow him down at all as he batted .378 for the PawSox.

In 1974 Rice drove International League pitchers to distraction as he led the league in RBI, batting average and home runs with 25 in only 430 at-bats. His outstanding performance earned him recognition as the "Minor League Player of the Year," identifying him at the top among all prospective major leaguers.

SIXTEEN SEASONS AT FENWAY PARK

Jim Rice played in his first game with the Boston Red Sox on August 19, 1974. The 21-year-old Rice would go on to play 2,089 games with the team, placing him fourth on the all-time Red Sox list. While he appeared in only 24 games over the balance of the 1974 season, American League pitchers immediately recognized that he would be a force to deal with for years to come.

Rice took the American League by storm in 1975. He led the team with 22 home runs and he finished fourth in the American League batting race with a .309 average. He showed surprising speed for a man of his size, tying with fellow-rookie Fred Lynn for the team lead with 10 stolen bases.

Although his season-ending injury happened on September 21, he still finished fourth in the American League in runs scored. If he had been able to play out the season he might have won the American League RBI crown, and his 102 RBI still placed him fifth in the league.

In July of 1975 he hit a home run off Steve Busby of the Kansas City Royals that cleared everything in left-center field in Fenway Park. Beloved Red Sox owner, the late Tom Yawkey, thought it was the longest home run that he had ever seen.

Rice responds modestly when reminded of Mr. Yawkey's statement. "It may have looked that way from where he was sitting. He had a better view than I did. I couldn't really tell from the field."

As the 1976 season began there was some concern about the lingering effects of his broken wrist and the mythical "Sophomore Jinx." Rice quickly allayed those fears by increasing his home run output from 22 to 25, and producing a slugging percentage of .482.

With teammate, Rick Burleson, in 1978 after one of his major league-leading 46 home runs.

The 1977 season was Jim Rice's "breakout season." He made the American League All-Star team for the first time and he led the American League with 39 home runs. His 206 hits and 114 RBI placed him third in the league standings and his slugging percentage of .593 topped all American League batters by a comfortable margin.

Along the way Jim Rice made himself into a very credible left fielder. Long-time Red Sox Special Instructor Sam Mele remembers how hard Jim Rice worked on his fielding.

"At spring training, he would come to our door to ask if I could come out to work on his fielding. My wife Connie and I used to laugh, because it was like a little kid asking if I could come out to play catch. But the point is he wanted to improve so badly that he was willing to look a little silly. He and Dwight Evans would do the same thing. They both worked as hard as any two ballplayers I have ever seen."

A SEASON FOR THE AGES: 1978

In 1978, Jim Rice had a season that ranks among the greatest offensive achievements in baseball history. In doing so, he helped lead the Red Sox to a tie for first place for the regular season in the American League's Eastern Division and he was voted the Most Valuable Player in the American League. Rice led the major leagues in hits (213), triples (15), homers (46), RBI (139), and slugging (.600).

His most remarkable accomplishment in 1978 was compiling 406 total bases. He became the first major leaguer to exceed 400 total bases since Hall of Famer Joe DiMaggio reached this pinnacle with the New York Yankees in 1937. Twenty-two seasons later, no American League hitter has reached 400 total bases in a single season.

Asked to recall his 1978 records, Jim Rice talks first about his league-leading 15 triples. And his perspective is very enlightening.

"To hit a triple, you have to be thinking triple from the moment you leave the batter's box. You see a lot of guys stop at second and you wonder if they had a shot at a triple. Often they don't make it because they weren't thinking triple every step of the way."

Asked if Fenway is a particularly tough park to hit a triple in, Rice answers, "Not really. If you hit a ball in the triangle you have a great shot. If you put it right down the right-field line you can do it. You can hit some triples in this ballpark, if you want third base badly enough."

When most players and fans recall the Red Sox heart-breaking loss to the New York Yankees in the 1978 playoff game they immediately point to Bucky Dent's three-run homer. As a serious student of the game, Jim Rice has a different perspective.

"The Yankees won that game when Billy Martin [New York manager] replaced Reggie Jackson with Lou Piniella in right field. Piniella speared Jerry Remy's line drive in the ninth inning and Rick Burleson had to hold up on second base.

"I was the next batter, and my long drive to right field would have scored Burleson with the tying run if Piniella hadn't held Rooster at second base. It wasn't Bucky Dent that beat us, it was having Lou Piniella in right field making that play."

Rice continued his remarkable slugging in 1979. He led the majors again with 369 total bases, and he finished in the top four in the American League in hits, RBI, home runs, runs scored, batting average and slugging average. That season he was selected to his third straight American League All-Star team and along with Yaz and Dwight Evans, he was part of an all-Boston Red Sox starting outfield.

When the 1979 season came to a close he had become the first player in major league history to put together three consecutive seasons with over 200 hits and 35 home runs. No other major league player has ever matched this achievement.

THE 1980s

Over the next six seasons, Rice maintained his standard as one of the top hitters in major league baseball. He was an American League All-Star in four of those seasons. In 1983 he led the American League with 126 RBI and 39 home runs, and the Boston Baseball Writers Association selected him as the team's Most Valuable Player. His composite batting average during those six seasons exceeded .300. He was clearly at the elite level among major league players.

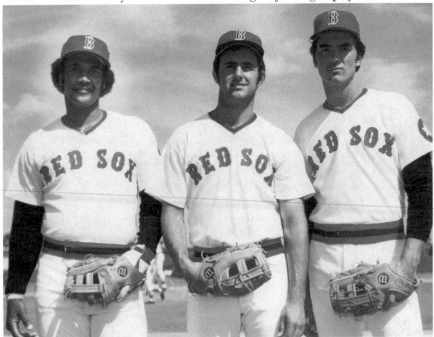

For several seasons, the Red Sox outfield was securely anchored by Rice, Fred Lynn and Dwight Evans.

Long-time major league manager Ralph Houk piloted the Boston Red Sox from 1981 to 1984, and he still raves about Rice's offensive skills. "Jim Rice may have been the strongest player I ever managed. And I managed some of the great ones. He powered our offense the whole time I was there. He was one of the hardest working players you will ever see."

At the height of his offensive prowess, Kansas City manager Whitey Herzog once deployed four fielders in the outfield in effort to thwart Rice. Asked about his unorthodox strategy, Herzog replied, "What I would really like to do is put two guys on top of the CITGO sign and two guys in the net."

In 1986, Rice put together yet another extraordinary season. He batted .324 and amassed exactly 200 hits. Rice was fourth in batting and RBI (110) in the American League, and his 39 doubles placed him third in the league. He finished third in the balloting for the Most Valuable Player in the American League, the sixth time he had finished in the top five in that category. And most importantly, he was a major factor in the Red Sox first place finish in the Eastern Division.

The Red Sox' dramatic American League Championship Series win over the California Angels was his first trip to the postseason. Rice contributed two home runs and scored eight runs as the team overcame a three-games-to-one deficit to earn their first trip to the World Series in 11 years.

Jim Rice batted .333 against the New York Mets in the 1986 World Series. He was on base 15 times in 7 games, but it wasn't enough. "We came awfully close to the World Championship, but we couldn't get it done. It wasn't meant to be. Things happen."

From 1987 to 1989 Jim Rice's offensive production dipped from major league leader to merely above average. When he retired after the 1989 season he had accumulated 382 lifetime home runs. At the end of the 2004 season this total placed him 48th in the history of major league baseball. Most of the players above him on the home run list played more seasons and had more at-bats to reach their totals.

PROFESSOR JIM ED

Jim Rice rejoined the Red Sox as their roving minor league hitting instructor in 1992. He traveled throughout the team's farm system for three seasons working with players at all levels.

In 1995, he joined the big league team as hitting coach under then manager Kevin Kennedy. Throughout his six years with the club, Red Sox hitters fared very well. In his first year with the team, Red Sox hitters led the major leagues with 286 doubles, and placed second in the American League with a slugging average of .455. In 1999 the team was second in the American League in doubles and triples and had the fewest strikeouts in the league.

Jim Rice is passionate on the subject of hitting. "A hitter needs to adjust after every pitch," Rice offers with intensity. "You'll hear some guys talking about adjusting from one at-bat to the next, but if you don't get around on a fastball on one pitch you have to make an adjustment before the very next pitch."

When he is told that former teammate Rick Burleson is quoted as saying, "If the hitter is going good he gets the credit, but if the hitter is bad the hitting coach gets the blame," Rice just laughs. "It goes with the territory."

In 1999, the Boston Red Sox, along with Major League Baseball, constructed a replica of Fenway Park at the corner of Washington and Ball Street in Roxbury. The facility is for the use by the community, and it was funded from ticket sales to the 1999 All-Star Workout Day. The park is named "Jim Rice Field" in honor of the former Red Sox slugger.

In July 2000, Jim Rice, Red Sox manager Jimy Williams and a number of other Red Sox personnel took part in a tribute to the former Negro League players in a ceremony at Jim Rice Field. The event celebrated the arrival of the Negro League Baseball exhibit that was on display at the Reggie Lewis Track & Athletic Center from July 22-28, 2000.

A PLAYER FOR THE AGES

In addition to his standing on the all-time home run list, Jim Rice ranks in the major league top-100 in four other important offensive categories at the end of the 2004 season. Among Red Sox players, Rice ranks in the top five in nine lifetime offensive categories. He also ranks fifth in putouts and eighth in lifetime

assists among Red Sox outfielders. But statistics tell only a part of the Jim Rice story.

Asked where he would place Jim Rice among the Red Sox all-time great hitters, Johnny Pesky responds, "Of course Ted Williams is in a class by himself. He is above every major league hitter I have ever seen. But Jim Rice is near the top of the next tier. He is right up there with Yaz and Bobby Doerr. He used the whole field," Pesky remembers. "Obviously he had tremendous power to left, but he used the power alleys in left center and right center as well. If the pitch was outside he would drive it to right. He used the whole field as well as any power hitter I have ever seen.

"And you talk about strong hitters. I saw him check his swing in Detroit and snap the bat in half and then I saw him do it again in Boston later in his career. I have been in baseball for over 60 years and I've never seen another hitter do that, and I saw Jim Rice do it twice," Pesky marvels. "He compares with any other outstanding hitter who has ever played the game. He belongs in the Hall of Fame."

Jim Rice has received strong support for baseball's Hall of Fame over the years, but he has always fallen short. Certainly his offensive production compares favorably with the achievements of Tony Perez who entered the Hall of Fame in 2000.

Former Red Sox pitcher Bob Stanley echoes Johnny Pesky's support for Rice's Hall of Fame candidacy. "He always played hurt. He never complained," says Stanley who played with Jim from 1976 to 1989. "He should already be in the Hall of Fame. He was amazing."

And former Red Sox southpaw Bruce Hurst feels strongly that Jim Rice belongs in Cooperstown. Hurst, who was a teammate from 1980-88, points out, "He didn't hit those magic numbers they look at like 500 home runs, or 3,000 hits. But in my mind he was definitely a Hall of Famer."

The number 406 has a nice symmetry when applied to former Red Sox players Jim Rice and Ted Williams. In 1941 Ted hit .406 to become the last .400 hitter in baseball. In 1978 Jim Rice accumulated 406 total bases to become the last American Leaguer to exceed 400 total bases. Jim Rice: a baseball player for the ages.

Jim Rice's Rank in Major League Baseball History

CATEGORY	CAREER TOTALS	ALL-TIME MLB RANK
Home Runs	382	48
Total Bases	4,129	59
Slugging Percentage	.502	64
Hits	2,452	91
At-Bats	8,225	98

Source: 2004 MLB.com

32.
Fred Lynn Interview
May 1999

Sometimes you get lucky when you schedule your interview. In Fred Lynn's case I was very fortunate in my timing. The night before our conversation, Nomar Garciaparra had homered three times and driven in ten runs in a game against the Seattle Mariners.

It was 7:30 A.M. when I contacted Fred by phone at his Carlsbad, California, home but he had already read a newspaper account of Nomar's performance and he had caught the highlights on ESPN. He acknowledged that it was a great spark to rekindle his memories of his terrific rookie season.

Fred Lynn had homered three times and driven in 10 runs for the Red Sox in Tigers' Stadium 24 years earlier. "Boy do I envy him, doing it at home," Lynn mused. "He must have been the toast of the town. I'm sure he didn't have to pay for his dinner."

Many of us felt that Fred Lynn made a terrible mistake leaving Boston. We hated to see him go, but more importantly, Fenway Park was tailor-made for his skills. He had a beautiful inside-out swing that allowed him to take advantage of the left-field wall, and the smaller dimensions of center field allowed him to roam at will on defense.

I couldn't get Fred to acknowledge that it was an error in judgment to leave. But if you read between the lines, I think you will agree that he regrets his decision. We will never know, but Fred Lynn just might have made it to the Hall of Fame if he had remained with the Boston Red Sox.

FRED LYNN
ALL-STAR MEMORIES

When former Red Sox All-Star center fielder Fred Lynn learned that Nomar Garciaparra had connected for three home runs and driven in 10 runs against the Seattle Mariners on May 10, 1999, his first reaction was, "Good for him!" Lynn's second reaction was, "I hope Nomar appreciates how fortunate he was to do it in front of the Boston fans."

Nomar's RBI total made him the first Red Sox player to drive in 10 runs since Lynn reached this level on June 18, 1975, in Detroit. Lynn and Garciaparra share the Red Sox' single game RBI record with Rudy York (1946) and Norm Zauchin (1955).

Fred Lynn was a 23-year-old rookie with fewer than 80 major league games under his belt when his 10-RBI game began. He still remembers almost every detail of his record-setting performance against the Tigers.

"I had gone hitless the night before and that broke my 20-game hitting streak. I took extra batting practice the next night, and I was 'in a zone' the whole game." Lynn drove in his 10 teammates that evening in Tiger Stadium with a single, a triple, and three home runs. His triple came within two feet of being his fourth home run of the game.

"It was quite a night to remember, but the park was less than half-full, and they were all Tigers fans. Nomar was really lucky to do it before the Boston fans in his hometown.

"After the game a bunch of us decided to go to the nicest restaurant in Detroit to celebrate. When we got there, they wouldn't seat us because I didn't have a sports coat on. I'm sure Nomar didn't have that same experience in Boston!"

ROOKIE OF THE YEAR AND MVP

When Fred Lynn reported to Winter Haven, Florida, for spring training camp in 1975, he was clearly the Red Sox center fielder of the future. But not even his biggest fan would have dared to predict the kind of rookie season that he would enjoy.

All Fred Lynn did in 1975 was to lead the American League in runs, doubles, and slugging average, to field his position spectacularly, and to contribute mightily to the first Red Sox pennant since 1967. His heroics earned him the distinction of becoming the first player in major league history to simultaneously earn his league's Rookie of the Year award and to be named the Most Valuable Player.

Lynn's blazing start at the plate in 1975 was matched by his acrobatic fielding in center field. Long-time Red Sox fans compared his circus catches to the defensive genius of Jimmy Piersall who patrolled center field with distinction for the Red Sox during the 1950s.

He made a tumbling catch on a line drive by the Yankees' Graig Nettles at a critical juncture in a June game which then Red Sox third base coach Don Zimmer called, "The greatest catch I have ever seen in baseball." His heroics earned him a slot on the American League All-Star team for the game held that year in Milwaukee's County Stadium.

"I remember being so nervous that I could barely hold the bat when I pinch-hit for Bobby Bonds [father of Barry Bonds] against Tom Seaver. The thing I remember best is Manny Sanguillen [Pittsburgh Pirates All-Star catcher] coming over to me before the game and rubbing my uniform saying 'You're so hot I want some to rub off on me.' I went 0-2 but it was a great thrill to be wearing the same uniform as guys like Hank Aaron and Rod Carew."

Fred Lynn maintained the same standard of excellence that earned him All-Star honors over the second half of the 1975 season. Fred Lynn's strongest memory of the second half happened in center field, not in the batter's box.

"It was a late-season game against the Yankees. We were hanging on to a 1-0 lead in the eighth inning when Graig Nettles hit a line drive into the gap. I dove and went tumbling, and came up with the ball in my glove. It preserved the lead and pretty much knocked the Yankees out of contention."

The contributions of Lynn and his fellow "Gold Dust Twin", Jim Rice, together with the accomplishments of the team's veterans placed the Red Sox in the American League Championship Series against the defending World Champion Oakland A's. Sparked by the all-around play of Carl Yastrzemski and the pitching of Luis Tiant, the Red Sox swept the A's in three straight, earning them a World Series slot against the Cincinnati Reds. Lynn contributed a key two-run double in the first game against Oakland, and batted .364 for the series.

The seven-game contest against Cincinnati's "Big Red Machine" is considered to be one of the most exciting World Series ever played. Joe Morgan and Pete Rose for the Reds, and Carlton Fisk for the Red Sox are the most remembered heroes, but Fred Lynn was a major factor as well. He fielded flawlessly and rapped out seven hits, including a three-run home run that gave the Red Sox an early lead in the epic Game Six at Fenway Park.

Fred Lynn sounds like it still hurts when he thinks back to the end of the heart breaking loss to the Reds in the Seventh Game. "I honestly didn't know how to act after losing Game Seven. We had always won when I was at USC, we had won the Little World Series when I was at Pawtucket. I had never been in a losing clubhouse before. I think it was the biggest disappointment of my life."

The Red Sox may have fallen to the Reds in the World Series, but the post-season awards flooded in for Fred Lynn's amazing rookie season. In addition to his American League Rookie of the Year and MVP trophies, he earned a Gold Glove for his fielding excellence and *Sport Magazine* named him their Pro Rookie of the Year. To top off the honors, the Associated Press named him the Male Athlete of the Year, and United Press International designated Lynn as their Athlete of the Year. The most asked question in the sports world at the time was: "Who is this guy, and where in the world did he come from?"

CALIFORNIA DREAMING

Fred Lynn was born in Chicago, Illinois, but grew up in sunny southern California. As a youngster in El Monte, California, a suburb of Los Angeles, he excelled in sports. "I played every game there was and I played them all pretty well. When I was at El Monte High School I played football, basketball and baseball. To be honest, baseball was number three on my list."

Fred Lynn fondly recalls his early exposure to major league baseball. "I remember going to a Dodgers game against the Giants when I was about 11 years old. Sandy Koufax pitched for the Dodgers and I got to see Willie Mays play. I can remember going to games at the old Wrigley Field [the original Angels home field] and the Memorial Coliseum when the Dodgers first came to town.

"I would have to say that Willie [Mays] was my favorite player. But Roberto Clemente was a close second. They could both do it all on the field. There were no holes in their game."

Asked for his greatest influence as a youngster, Lynn is quick to respond, "That would have to be my dad. He encouraged me to play all sports. I played three sports in high school, and I think it gave me a lot of confidence. Playing a variety of sports teaches you about competition also."

He matriculated at USC in 1970 on a football scholarship. "As a freshman, I lost the starting wide receiver's job to Lynn Swann, who went on to have a great career with Pittsburgh in the NFL. After a year of watching Swann in action, I figured I had better concentrate on baseball!"

Fred clearly made the right choice as he earned All-American honors in his sophomore and junior seasons. Playing under legendary college coach Rod Dedeaux, Lynn played a key role as the USC Trojans won three straight NCAA national championships.

The Red Sox made him their second choice in the 1973 draft, and Lynn made his professional debut in New Britain, Connecticut. He played well in New Britain and was promoted to play in the "Little World Series" with the Red Sox Pawtucket team.

He spent most of the 1974 season at Triple A Pawtucket where he batted .282 and hit 21 home runs. His fine all-around play earned him a September call-up to Boston where he batted .419 in 15 games.

Fred Lynn still clearly remembers his first big league hit. "It was a home run off Jim Slaton in Milwaukee. What a thrill. I'll never forget it."

NINE TIME ALL-STAR

Fred Lynn's offensive production fell off in 1976 when he was hobbled by a series of injuries. But he was still voted the starting center fielder in the All-Star Game, held in Philadelphia that year to tie in with the Bicentennial celebration. He managed a home run off of the Mets' Tom Seaver and he was so excited, "I can't

even remember my feet touching the ground." He finished the 1976 season with a batting average of .314.

Injuries dogged Lynn again in 1977, as they would throughout his career, but he scored a run for the American Leaguers in the mid-season classic held in refurbished Yankee Stadium. In 1978 he earned All-Star honors for the fourth straight time and he managed a single in four at-bats in the game played at San Diego Stadium.

Ask Red Sox fans about Fred Lynn and most will reply, "He had the greatest rookie year in baseball history, but he never reached that level again." The fact is that Fred Lynn's offensive production in 1979 exceeded his tremendous rookie output. In 1979 he hit 39 home runs and he led the American League in batting (.333) and in slugging (.637).

"During the winter before the 1979 season I started lifting weights. It wasn't like today when the players have conditioning coaches; we were on our own. I put on about 10 pounds lifting, and it was all muscle. As a result, my doubles turned into home runs. The next winter I decided to take up running. I proceeded to run off the 10 pounds I had gained, and I never hit over 25 home runs again in my career. I hope that today's players realize how fortunate they are to have professionals directing their conditioning."

Lynn's extra muscle came in handy at the 1979 All-Star Game at the Kingdome in Seattle when he took future Hall of Famer Steve "Lefty" Carlton deep for a two-run home run. "As a left-handed batter I really had to concentrate facing a left-handed pitcher. Carlton gave me a pitch I could handle, and I drove it. I was really happy because it gave us a 3-2 lead."

The 1979 All-Star Game featured an all-Red Sox outfield for the American League, with Lynn in center, Jim Rice in left, and Dwight Evans in right field. Fred Lynn ranks that trio as among the best in baseball history.

"I've seen a lot of baseball in my time, and I've never seen another outfield that was as good as ours. I'll match our three guys with any that have ever played the game. Our outfield, Jimmy, Dwight and myself, could all hit, and we could all field. We were the complete deal. And Yaz had moved to first, but you could still run him out [to left] and he was a great swing guy. I would match that group with anybody."

In the 1980 All-Star Game in Dodger Stadium, Lynn connected for his third home run in six All-Star games. His two-run homer off Dodger reliever Bob Welch gave the American League a 2-0 lead, but the National League battled back to a 4-2 win, for their ninth-straight All-Star victory.

LIFE AFTER FENWAY PARK

Following the 1980 season the Red Sox, anticipating some difficulty re-signing him in his free agency year, traded Lynn to the California Angels. The trade sent him back to his native southern California, but it did little to advance Lynn's baseball career.

"I missed Fenway Park. It was an ideal place for me to hit. And I really missed the intensity of the crowds. They used to get me going. I don't think I appreciated what a great place Boston was for me to play until I left. The fans in Boston stick with the team through thick and thin. They give it to you pretty good when you are losing, but they are there for you. It's different on the west coast.

"I hated to leave Boston. I know I had a reputation of being a west coast guy. I grew up there, but I had learned to love Boston. And the Red Sox were the team that signed me and gave me the opportunity to play in the big leagues. I have a lot of great memories of the city and the team. I think you have a special attachment to the team you start out with. I'm always going to be a Red Sox."

His offensive numbers fell in 1981, but he retained his All-Star status. He pinch-hit in the 1981 All-Star Game at Cleveland's Memorial Stadium, and he was the starting center fielder in the 1982 game in Montreal, the first All-Star Game played outside of the United States.

The 1983 game was the 50th anniversary of the All-Star Game. It was played at old Comiskey Park in Chicago, the site of the first game in 1933. Coming into the game, the National League boasted 11 straight victories. But the boasting

American League batting champion honors went to Lynn in 1979 when he hit .333 in 147 games. American League Chairman and former A.L. president and Red Sox shortstop, manager and general manager Joe Cronin presented Fred with a commemorative bat on the occasion.

didn't last long as Fred Lynn broke the game wide open with a grand slam home run in the third inning. He thrust his right hand in the air as the ball landed in the distant bleachers.

"I put my hand in the air because I knew we were going to win that game. I hated to lose, and I had played in eight straight losses to those guys. I was sick and tired of losing to them." Lynn's home run was the first, and still the only, grand slam in All-Star history. The American League coasted to a 13-3 victory that evening.

During his nine All-Star Game appearances, Lynn had compiled a .300 batting average, hit 4 home runs, and driven in 10 runs. This offensive record placed him among the most distinguished players in the history of the All-Star Game.

"I really got up for the All-Star games because you knew you were facing the very best players. It took every bit of your concentration to face pitchers of that caliber. I really got pumped up for the games."

That 1983 game turned out to be Fred Lynn's last All-Star Game. Following his 1984 season with the Angels, he moved on to the Baltimore Orioles. He hit 23 home runs in each of his three full seasons with the Birds, but injuries limited his playing time. In 1988 he started the season in Baltimore and then he moved on to Detroit where he remained for the 1989 season. Lynn finished his major league career as a National Leaguer, appearing in 90 games for the San Diego Padres in 1990.

Fred Lynn ended his major league career with over 300 home runs, and nearly 2,000 (1,980) base hits. There is no way to calculate the number of acrobatic catches he made in center field, but he does have five Gold Gloves to show for his fielding prowess. His career may not have reached the pinnacles forecast for him following his amazing rookie year, but it was a very distinguished major league career by any measure.

THE LATER YEARS

Today Fred Lynn lives in suburban Carlsbad, California, just north of San Diego. He was an announcer for ESPN for four years, and currently he is busy with personal appearances and special broadcasting assignments. His wife, Natalie, is an advertising executive and a Boston native. A return to Boston for the 1999 All-Star Game was a summer highlight for the couple.

Fred Lynn looks back on his major league career with pride and some misgivings. "For me, it was always about winning. The personal achievements were nice, but my focus was always on the team. After we were in the World Series in 1975, I had played for a national championship for five straight years: the NCAA's for three years, the Little [Minor League] World Series with Pawtucket, and then Boston. I thought it would always be like that. It just didn't work out that way."

Lynn had only one more shot at post-season play after 1975. In 1982 he batted .611 in a losing cause as the Angels lost to the Milwaukee Brewers in a five-game series.

Fred Lynn was inducted into the Boston Red Sox Hall of Fame in November

2002. He made it clear that a bit of his heart still belonged to the Red Sox. "When you get traded the bonds get severed. You stay in touch a bit, but everything has changed. It's great to reconnect with the club and come back where my career began.

"One of the best parts of this honor is being reunited with Jim Rice and Dwight Evans who played on either side of me. Now we are all in the Red Sox Hall of Fame, so we have come full circle."

Boston Red Sox fans look back on Fred Lynn's six years with great fondness. Most of all, they remember his splendid rookie season in 1975. A review of baseball's record books suggest that the only ballplayer who may have had a better rookie season than Fred Lynn was the fictional character Joe Hardy from the Broadway musical "Damn Yankees." Asked about this comparison, Lynn laughs and responds, "But he got old as soon as that season ended. I'm glad that didn't happen to me!"

In 1997 Nomar Garciaparra became the first Red Sox player to be named the American League Rookie of the Year since Fred Lynn earned this distinction in 1975. Both players followed up with outstanding second seasons. Here's how their first two years stack up against the first two seasons of all-time Red Sox great Ted Williams.

Player	Year	Games	Hits	2B	HR	SB	Bat. Avg.	On Base Avg.
Williams	1939-40	293	378	87	54	6	.336	.439
Lynn	1975-76	277	334	79	31	24	.323	.390
Garciaparra	1997-98	296	404	81	65	34	.314	.352

Note: Ted Williams' *lifetime* on-base average of .483 is the highest in major league history.

33.
Butch Hobson Interview
June 2003

I interviewed Butch Hobson in his office at Holman Stadium in Nashua, New Hampshire. I couldn't help feeling, looking around at the cramped quarters of the manager of the Nashua Pride, that we were a long way from the manager's office at Fenway Park. But Butch made it clear that he was perfectly comfortable in his surroundings.

Butch Hobson is a very intense personality. He takes his role as a manager in the independent Atlantic League every bit as seriously as he took his role as manager of the Boston Red Sox. Maybe it was my own mindset, but I couldn't help jotting down "football intensity" while we spoke.

The media often portrayed Butch Hobson as too soft on his players during his three-year tenure as manager of the Red Sox. Maybe there was some truth to that description and maybe there wasn't. Sitting there under Hobson's gaze, I knew that I wouldn't want to miss his hit-and-run sign.

I left our interview believing that Hobson is very comfortable with his life. He can watch his sons play Little League baseball in the field adjacent to Holman Stadium, and then manage that evening's game. And it is clear that he has a missionary's zeal to give his players a second chance in professional baseball.

I thought of Butch Hobson when I watched the Red Sox play the Anaheim Angels in the 2004 American League Division Series. Former major leaguer Curtis Pride was playing for Hobson at the time of our interview, and there he was in the series as a reserve outfielder for the Angels. And I knew Butch Hobson was proud.

CLELL "BUTCH" HOBSON
THE 1978 BOSTON RED SOX
REMEMBERED

When Red Sox fans remember former third baseman Butch Hobson they picture his uniform "number four" hurtling into the visitors dugout in hot pursuit of a foul ball, or belly flopping headfirst to stretch a single into a double. Hobson, who played quarterback and strong safety under legendary Alabama coach Paul "Bear" Bryant, brought a football player's intensity to the baseball diamond. And the Fenway fans loved him for his hustle.

"The fans in Boston were great to me. They are the most knowledgeable fans in the major leagues. They study the game and they know it inside out. They want blue collar players, guys who go all out on every play." Hobson, who manages the Nashua Pride in the independent Atlantic League adds, "People have been great to me anywhere I have gone in New England. These fans right here in Nashua are terrific."

Butch Hobson played all or part of six seasons at third base for the Red Sox between 1975 and 1980. His 30 home runs and 112 RBI in 1977 remains the standard for Red Sox third basemen. Hobson also managed the Red Sox to 207 victories between 1992 and 1994.

THE 1978 BOSTON RED SOX

"We really thought that was going to be our year," Hobson recalls looking back to spring training in 1978. "We had a great offensive team in 1977, one of the best ever for the Red Sox. And we signed Mike Torrez [pitcher] away from the Yankees during the off-season. Then at the end of spring training we made the trade with the Indians for Dennis Eckersley. We thought that our pitching would be strong enough to overtake the Yankees that year."

The Red Sox home opener on April 14, 1978, featured a capacity crowd and a thrilling win over the Texas Rangers. Dennis Eckersley's first start at Fenway was a memorable one as he pitched into the tenth inning before giving way to Dick Drago with the score knotted at three. Butch Hobson scored the winning run on a 395-foot Jim Rice single in the bottom of the ninth.

"The home opener was always exciting. The stands were packed and everyone was excited to be back. And a win gave everyone a good feeling," Hobson recalls.

The win in the home opener was an omen of things to come as the 1978 Red Sox would go on to win over 70 percent of their games at Fenway.

A 9-6 win over the Baltimore Orioles on May 1 improved their home record to nine wins against only two losses. They were two and one-half games behind the first place Milwaukee Brewers, but the pitching staff was sharp and Butch Hobson had picked up where his hot hitting left off in 1977.

The Red Sox won 23 out of 30 games in May. They moved into first place on May 24 and they would remain there for almost four months. At the end of May they had a solid hold on first place in the American League East with a record of 34-16.

When the Red Sox played New York for the first time on June 19, the Yankees were in disarray. Slugger Reggie Jackson, who had earned his nickname "Mr. October" with his home run heroics in the Yankees 1977 World Series victory, was feuding with manager Billy Martin. And the fiery Martin seemed to be feuding with everyone he met. The Yankees were hard-pressed to catch the Brewers, let alone the Red Sox.

"We knew things were tense with the Yankees, but we didn't pay a whole lot of attention to that," Hobson recalls. "Our focus was on our team, not theirs. But I do remember how intense that rivalry was. Neither team liked the other very much."

The Red Sox took two out of three from the Yankees at Fenway and then split two games with the Yankees the following week at the Stadium. At the end of June the first place Red Sox were 52-23 overall, and 33-6 at home.

ALL-STAR BREAK

As the All-Star break approached Butch Hobson was on track to exceed his outstanding offensive numbers of 1977. "I had something like 15 homers at the end of June. Then I tore up my hamstring and I was out for a couple of weeks. It was really disappointing because the team was going so well and I wanted to be a part of it."

The Red Sox continued their winning ways as Jack Brohamer filled in capably for Butch at third base. A Red Sox win over Milwaukee on July 18 gave them a nine-game lead over the Brewers. The Baltimore Orioles were in third place, and the New

A young Butch in Red Sox spring training.

York Yankees were a distant fourth, 14 and one-half games off the pace.

The Red Sox 8-2 win over the Brewers that day marked Butch Hobson's return to the lineup and featured an example of his heads-up play. George Scott scored on a close play that began with Hobson on first base. The Brewers catcher, Charlie Moore, argued the call on Scott heatedly but didn't bother to call time. Hobson never stopped running and came around to score before Moore realized what was happening. "I tell my kids to run as hard as they can because I scored on a pop-up to first base."

One week later, Billy Martin resigned as Yankees' manager and his temperamental opposite, low-key Bob Lemon replaced him. Lemon quickly stabilized the situation in New York, and the Yankees began one of the great late-season drives in baseball history.

By the beginning of August the red-hot Yankees had vaulted into second place, narrowing the Red Sox lead to six and one-half games. But the Red Sox swept the Yankees in a two-game series at Yankee Stadium in early August opening up a little daylight.

A lingering memory of Butch Hobson in 1978 is watching him tugging on his elbow after making the long throw from third to first. He said little about his arm problems at the time, and never used his injury as an excuse. "I had bone chips floating around in my elbow. It was an old football injury from landing on the

Astroturf. I was just working the bone chips back in place when fans would see me grabbing my elbow. I kept playing because it was the only thing I knew how to do."

The tide officially turned in early September when the Yankees came to Fenway for a crucial four-game series. When the so-called "Boston Massacre" was over, the Yankees had won four straight by a cumulative margin of 42-9. On September 10 the two teams were tied for first place in the American League East.

The Red Sox lost the first two games of their rematch at Yankee Stadium, and on September 16 they trailed the Yankees by five games. Dennis Eckersley won his 17th game in the series finale on Sunday, but with only 13 games remaining and the Yankees playing the best ball in the major leagues, Red Sox fans prepared for the worst.

REFUSE TO LOSE

But instead of the worst, they got the best. The Sox took three out of four games from the Tigers in Detroit. After losing the opening game in Toronto to the Blue Jays, the Red Sox simply refused to lose. The Red Sox took the two final games in Toronto and returned to Fenway, sweeping three in a row from the Tigers. The streaking Red Sox took two in a row from the Blue Jays and went into the final game of the season trailing the Yankees by one game.

On Sunday October 1 Luis Tiant shut out the Blue Jays 5-0, while the Yankees lost to the Cleveland Indians 9-2. The Yankees sent their luggage on to Kansas City where the League Championship Series would begin on Tuesday, but the players took the shuttle to Boston to play in the second-ever American League playoff.

The media described the Yankees as disappointed by their loss to Cleveland but optimistic about the one-game playoff. They had gone 52-21 over the last two and one-half months of the season, and their last trip to Fenway had been the four-game sweep of the Red Sox in early September. Taking the mound for the Yankees was their ace Ron Guidry with a record of 24-3. His winning percentage of .889 was the highest of any 20-game winner in the history of baseball.

In the Red Sox favor was their home record of 59-22, and the momentum of an eight-game winning streak. Also, starter Mike Torrez had won 16 games during the regular season and wanted to prove to the Yankees that they had made a mistake by not re-signing him after the 1977 season. The final factor favoring the Red Sox: all three of Guidry's losses had been to pitchers named Mike.

The 1978 Red Sox-Yankees playoff game featured drama, tension, heroic efforts, last minute hope, and finally disappointment for Red Sox fans. Noted *Washington Post* baseball writer Tom Boswell was moved to write a book describing the game entitled, *The Greatest Baseball Game Ever Played.* The final score was New York 5, Boston 4.

Asked if he has ever seen a replay of the 1978 playoff game, Hobson answers, "I've sat and watched it with my boys a couple of times. It gives them a chance to see their daddy hit, or not hit as the case may be. You know, it's funny. Everyone is still talking about the Bucky Dent home run but it was Reggie Jackson's home run in the eighth that won it.

"I know when Red Sox fans look back on 1978 they think of it as a nightmare. But when I look back on it I'm very proud of our team. We won 99 games, the same as a very good Yankees team. And we won 12 out of our last 14 games and the last 8 in a row after everyone had written us off. That team showed a lot of heart."

SWEET HOME ALABAMA

Clell Lavern Hobson, Jr. was born in Tuscaloosa, Alabama, on August 17, 1951. He grew up playing all sports, but he excelled at football and baseball. "When I got into high school my momma kept a close eye on my grades. She wanted to be sure I would be able to get into college so I concentrated on football and baseball."

His dad, Clell, Sr., was a three-year letterman at quarterback for Alabama, and coached Butch in football at Bessemer High School. Butch was named to the All-Jefferson County team as a quarterback and he was a prized college recruit. He was also named as the MVP for his high school and American Legion baseball teams.

"Football is the sport in Alabama, but I enjoyed baseball every bit as much. I came pretty close to going to Auburn because coach [Pat] Sullivan promised me I would play quarterback. Coach Bryant really wanted me, but he signed something like 16 quarterbacks that year. He liked to take high school quarterbacks and turn them into wide receivers or safeties.

"I really seriously considered Auburn but I knew I wouldn't get fed in my house when I came home for school breaks if I went there. That was pretty motivational. And coach Bryant told me I could play football and baseball, something he usually didn't do. I think maybe he saw that I had more of a future in baseball."

As Butch expected, coach Bryant moved him to strong safety in his sophomore year. But he did have the thrill of carrying the ball 15 times in the Orange Bowl against Nebraska, rushing for 59 yards. And he managed to play three years of varsity baseball at Alabama, capping his career with a .317 average and setting the Southeastern Conference home run record.

The Red Sox made Butch Hobson their eighth choice in the 1973 draft. It didn't take him long to accept their offer and report to the Red Sox farm club in Winston-Salem, North Carolina. As a June draft choice he appeared in only 17 games for Winston-Salem in 1973, but his professional baseball career was underway.

BIG LEAGUE BOUND

In 1974 Butch was the regular third baseman for Winston-Salem and he rapped out 120 base hits in 119 games. His 14 home runs and 75 RBI served notice that he had the power to play at the hot corner. His strong showing in his first full professional season earned him a promotion to the Red Sox Double A team in Bristol, Connecticut, for the 1975 season.

At Bristol he increased his home run output to 15 and he was called up to Boston when the parent club expanded their roster in September. "That was the year the Red Sox made it to the World Series and it was great just to be around those guys. I only got into a couple of games but it was special to get a taste of the big leagues."

Butch was invited to spring training with the major leaguers for the first time in 1976. The opening line of his biography for the Red Sox Media Guide that season read, "Butch is knocking on the door of the major leagues and coaches and minor league managers believe he is ready if anything should happen to Rico Petrocelli at third base." That line proved to be prophetic when Rico went on the disabled list in June. After being recalled from Pawtucket, Butch made his Fenway Park debut with a splash on June 28.

"That was pretty exciting. I was sorry that Rico was out but it was great to have the opportunity. I remember I doubled off the center-field wall and I also hit an inside-the-park home run. We beat the Orioles that night.

"After Rico recovered I got sent back to Pawtucket. But when Don Zimmer replaced Darrell Johnson he called me back up. I stayed with the team the rest of the season and played pretty regularly."

Zimmer installed Hobson as his regular third baseman from the start in 1977 and he appeared in 159 games that season. Hitting mostly in the ninth spot in the batting order, he still knocked in 112 RBI to finish fourth in the American League. His 30 home runs placed him eighth in the league in that category, and his 68 extra base hits ranked him sixth.

Floating bone chips in his right elbow and a hamstring injury slowed Butch in the field and at bat in 1978. Hobson had the bone chips removed by Dr. Arthur Pappas after the 1978 season and returned to form in 1979. He increased his home run total to 28, which was tenth in the American League, and his RBI total in 1979 climbed to 93 for the season.

The injury jinx resurfaced in 1980. Troubled by shoulder woes throughout, his batting average fell to .228, and his home run total fell to 11. The Red Sox traded Butch Hobson to the California Angels following the 1980 season.

"I was very disappointed when I was traded to the Angels. I guess the only thing that helped was that I was traded along with Rooster [Rick Burleson was also traded with Hobson]. I had played beside him at third base for all those years so that was comfortable. It was easier for Fred [Lynn] and Rooster in California because they were coming home. I never really got comfortable with the California lifestyle.

"Coming back to Fenway felt weird. It was very strange going into the visitors clubhouse. And it was really strange to look across to the Red Sox dugout and see so many old friends. It just felt funny."

The Angels traded Hobson to the New York Yankees during spring training in 1982. He appeared in 30 games with the Yankees that season but spent most of the year at the Yankees' Triple A farm team in Columbus. Butch spent the balance of his active career in the minors trying to play his way back to the major leagues.

"I just loved playing baseball and I wasn't ready to give up on my career. I needed to do everything I could to get back to the big leagues. I think the experience made me a better manager."

BORN TO MANAGE

Butch Hobson sat out the 1986 season after being released by the Yankees in spring training. The following season the New York Mets signed him to manage their Single A Columbia farm team in the South Atlantic League. In his second year as manager he guided Columbia to a second place finish in the second half of the season.

The Red Sox signed Hobson to manage their New Britain farm team in the Eastern League in 1989. In 1990 he guided the BritSox to the final round of the

Eastern League playoffs. The following season the Red Sox promoted Butch to Pawtucket where he managed the team to first place in the International League. He was named minor league Manager of the Year in 1991 by *Baseball America*.

In October 1991 Hobson was named as the 38th manager of the Boston Red Sox. After managing in the minors for five years, 40-year-old Butch Hobson had made it back to the majors as a big league manager.

Butch Hobson's first year as manager of the Boston Red Sox was a disappointment for Red Sox fans and for the rookie manager. The team played reasonably well at home (44-37), but an abysmal road record (29-52) left the team in last place in the Eastern Division. Plagued by injuries throughout, in mid-June the team lost star outfielders Mike Greenwell and Ellis Burks to season-ending injuries.

The 1993 Red Sox spent most of the season battling for the Eastern Division lead. After leading the pack for most of April, the team weathered a tough spell to reclaim the lead on July 23. Their roller coaster season continued and the Red Sox were only four and one-half games out at the end of August. The team eventually faded to fifth place, but strong seasons by Mo Vaughn and John Valentin gave Sox fans hope for the 1994 season.

Unfortunately, the 1994 season came to a premature end. The Red Sox played their last game on August 10 as a work stoppage shut down major league baseball. Kevin Kennedy was named to replace Butch Hobson as the manager of the Boston Red Sox in October 1994.

"I wish we could have done more during my time as manager," Butch reflects. "But I think we accomplished a lot with some of the younger players. I was proud of my teams. I know this. We were respected as a team. We played the game right, and we conducted ourselves professionally all the time. And I'm proud of that."

THE PRIDE OF NASHUA, NEW HAMPSHIRE

Butch Hobson took over as the manager of the Nashua Pride before the 2000 season. In his first season Hobson led the Pride to their first playoff appearance and the Atlantic League title. The following season he had them back in the playoffs, and after a difficult 2002 season, Hobson is optimistic about his current team.

"We've put together a good bunch of players. My pitching coach Rick Wise [former Red Sox pitcher] and I look hard for talented players with good character. This is a community-based team and it's important that our players represent us well.

"This is a good league. I consider this the equivalent of Triple A ball. We have former major leaguers like Rickey Henderson, and we have a lot of guys who were originally high draft choices. We work hard with the guys on fundamentals. If they do get the call, we want them to be ready."

The Nashua Pride team is a charter member of the independent Atlantic League. They play their home games at historic Holman Stadium, which has been substantially renovated in a joint effort between the Pride and the City of Nashua. Holman Stadium was home to the first integrated baseball team in the United States in this century. In 1946 the Brooklyn Dodgers signed Jackie Robinson and sent him to their farm club in Montreal. Shortly after, they signed Negro League stars Roy Campanella and Don Newcombe and assigned them to their minor league club in Nashua. Campanella and Newcombe excelled for Nashua and eventually became stars for the Dodgers.

Hobson feels a strong commitment to his Nashua players. "Some of these guys are here because they couldn't get it together in their prior organizations. We work hard with them because this is almost certainly their last chance. I tell them that there isn't anything they can do that I haven't tried myself. I did some pretty stupid things years ago, and I tell them I'm lucky to be alive. I tell them they don't have to be that stupid."

HOBSON'S CHOICE

There are three obvious passions in Butch Hobson's life: family, baseball and teaching. If you want to see his famous blue eyes sparkle, just ask him about his family. "My wife Krystine is terrific. I'm lucky to have her. We have three wonderful little boys. Our oldest, Kristopher Clell, we call him K.C., is twelve. Hank

Having a word with the umpire as Sox manager in 1992.

is ten years old and he's playing little league ball with K.C. And then our little guy, Noah is six and he's playing rookie ball.

"I have three older daughters who are all grown up. Allene is my oldest. My next two, Libby and Polly, were both born at Framingham Union Hospital in Framingham. And I have two grandsons who were just here for a nice visit.

"The Little League park is right in front of the stadium here. So I can go over and watch K.C. and Hank play in a 5:05 P.M. game and be back here coaching third base at 7:05 P.M. It really is a great set-up.

"I do a lot of speaking to groups and I talk in schools and to youth groups whenever I can. I talk to them about making smart choices. I tell them to be smart in selecting their friends and whom they associate with. Picking the right friends is so important.

"I tell the kids that I managed Mo Vaughn and Roger Clemens, and that I played with Yaz. The professional speakers do a great job, but I think after I tell the kids who I managed and played with they really listen. I have tried to take any mistakes I made and use them to help others."

Butch is active in the off-season teaching hitting and baseball to youngsters. He hopes to expand that activity in the future. "Right now Krystine and I are working to get a business going where we can do clinics all over New England, not just here in New Hampshire. Krystine is from Connecticut and we moved back to New England in 1999 to get her closer to home.

"We really love it here. As a player I didn't live here in the off-season but the fans always made me feel like they adopted me. Having moved here to Nashua, the people in this area really make me feel like I belong. I love these people. Of course, no one will ever mistake me for a native with this accent."

Looking back on his big league career Hobson offers, "My talent was average at best. I got as far as I did through hard work. I was fortunate to play in the big leagues. I was fortunate to be there when Yaz got his 3000th hit and his 400th home run. And I was fortunate to play with my pitching coach, Rick Wise."

Asked what single person has had the greatest influence on him, Butch takes his time before answering. "No one has ever asked me that before, but I would have to say my mother. She was always there for me. My daddy would call and give me some good advice about my game, and I really appreciated that. But my momma would call and tell me I looked great out there. That always helped. She was a very special person. She passed away about five years ago and we miss her."

Red Sox fans adopted Butch as of their own many years ago and now he has returned the favor. He set a standard for hustle and intensity for all Red Sox players to be measured against. That is Butch Hobson's legacy in Red Sox history.

34.

Dennis Eckersley Interview

August 2003

My interview of Dennis Eckersley may be my all-time favorite interview. And that is saying quite a bit. I have interviewed nearly 100 former Red Sox players and I have enjoyed every single session.

I interviewed Dennis Eckersley in Theo Epstein's private box while the Red Sox took batting practice before a night game against the Cleveland Indians. The Eck's comments about the activities on the field below were almost as interesting as his memories of his 24-year major league career.

It was a great setting for an interview, and he was every bit as articulate and honest as he is on the NESN post-game show. At the time, Dennis Eckersley was unsure about his chances for election to the Hall of Fame the following January. He had no reason to be unsure: he was easily elected to the Hall on his first appearance on the ballot.

When I asked Dennis who had influenced him the most over the years he was quick to name his father. I couldn't help asking him if he had ever told his dad that. Dennis thought about it for a minute and answered, "No, I don't think I ever have."

Debbie Matson, who is the Editor of Red Sox Magazine, *made it a point to send a copy of the article to Dennis's parents. Within days, his mother sent back a very nice thank-you note. It seemed like a perfect ending to the story.*

DENNIS ECKERSLEY
THE 1978 BOSTON RED SOX
REMEMBERED

When former pitching ace Dennis Eckersley looks back on the 1978 Red Sox, he focuses on the team's 99 victories and their late-season winning streak to force a one-game playoff with the Yankees. "The 1978 team was a very good club, but almost everyone had written us off with two weeks to go. Then we won eight in a row at the end to give ourselves a shot. We never gave up," the Eck remembers with feeling. "The playoff loss was devastating but that doesn't change the fact that it was a very good team."

Eckersley, who provides insightful analysis on NESN's pre-and post-game shows, was uniquely qualified to compare the 2003 Red Sox team with his 1978 team. "This year's team has a great offense and so did we with hitters like Jim Rice, Freddie Lynn and Carlton Fisk. The starting pitching is about equal, and I would give the '78 team the edge on defense. But this year's bullpen has a chance to be better than ours was. They are both strong teams."

Dennis Eckersley finished his 24-year major league career in 1998 with the Boston Red Sox. His 1,071 pitching appearances ranks third in major league history and his 390 career saves places him forth on the all-time list. He moved to Boston when he was traded to the Red Sox in 1978, and he has lived in the area for the past 25 years.

THE 1978 BOSTON RED SOX

Dennis Eckersley started spring training in 1978 with the Cleveland Indians in Arizona and finished it with the Red Sox in Winter Haven, Florida. On March 30 the Red Sox traded four players to Cleveland to obtain Eckersley along with catcher Fred Kendall.

"I was crushed when I found out I had been traded," Dennis recalls. "I had signed with the Indians as a 17 year old, and I had been with the organization my whole career. I had put together three good big league seasons with the team, and I had good friends there.

"The first time you are traded as a big leaguer it's a shock. It takes a while before you realize that no one is indispensable. As it turns out, getting traded to Boston was one of the best things that ever happened to me, but I didn't realize it at the time."

Opening Day at Fenway Park in 1978 still stands out in his mind. "I was the starting pitcher and the fans gave me a standing ovation. I'll never forget it. It was kind of like the ovation the fans gave Jeff Suppan the other night [August 5, 2003]. They couldn't have been nicer. I pitched into the tenth inning and we beat Texas in the last of the tenth. It was a great day.

"I didn't get my first win until my fifth start that year. I was pitching all right but it just didn't happen. And there were very big expectations for me. I was well aware of that. It felt good to finally get that first win over the Twins in early May."

Dennis Eckersley soon found his groove and he had accumulated nine wins when he took the mound in Cleveland against his former teammates on the last weekend before the All-Star Game. "That win in Cleveland was sweet," Eckersley says of his 12-5 victory. "It brought my record to 10-2. And I beat one of the guys [Mike Paxton] who I was traded for.

"We got off to such a great start that year. I really thought we were going to run away with it. Then we ran into some trouble as everyone remembers."

On August 30, Dennis beat the Toronto Blue Jays 2-1 at Fenway Park to run his record to 16-5. It was the Red Sox fourth straight victory and it improved the team's home record to an outstanding 51-14. The first-place Red Sox lead over the Yankees seemed secure at the time.

STRETCH DRIVE

Over the next 2 and one-half weeks the Red Sox lost 14 out of 17 games. The 14 losses included a demoralizing four-game sweep by the Yankees at Fenway Park, and two straight losses to New York at Yankee Stadium. When Dennis Eckersley took the mound at the Stadium on Sunday afternoon, September 17, the Red Sox were in second place, three and one-half games behind the Yankees.

"Oh man, that game was intense," Eckersley remembers. "We knew we had to win that game or it was all over. That was my biggest game of the year. Everyone had written us off, and you couldn't blame them. We had played terrible. Everyone had given up except the players. We thought we could still do it."

In Houdini-like fashion, the Red Sox sprang back to life, defeating the Yankees 7-3 as Eckersley won his 17th game, aided by a Bob Stanley save. Over the next week the reborn Red Sox took five out of seven games to move within one game of the Yankees. When Dennis Eckersley won his 20th game 5-1 over Toronto in the next-to-last game of the season, the Red Sox were still hanging on, one game behind the Yankees. Luis Tiant's 5-0 win over the Blue Jays the following day, coupled with a New York loss, created the historic playoff game with the Yankees.

"That playoff game was serious business. I was so nervous I kept pacing between the dugout and the clubhouse. I saw Bucky Dent's home run on a TV monitor in the clubhouse. NBC had put up a set for the post-game interviews and after the home run they started taking it down. I started yelling at them, 'Hey, don't do that. It's not over.' And it wasn't, but we couldn't quite pull it out.

"That loss was heartbreaking. But I was proud that we wouldn't quit. And I had it in my mind that we were going to be a dominant team for years. That made it easier to take. When you're young, you think things will go on indefinitely."

BIG LEAGUE DREAMING

Dennis Eckersley grew up in the Oakland, California, area, hoping for a career in major league baseball. "As far back as I can remember my dream was to play major league baseball. I played all sports and living in Oakland I dreamed of growing up to be John Brodie, Rick Barry and Juan Marichal. But I picked the right sport. When I think how I have gotten to know all three of my boyhood heroes, I realize how lucky I have been.

"I would get to two or three games a year to watch the Giants play in Candlestick Park. I grew up watching stars like Marichal, Willie Mays, Orlando Cepeda, and the Alous. It was great."

Eckersley signed a minor league contract with the Cleveland Indians as a 17-year-old just out of high school. "It was a good decision. I only spent three years in the minors and I made it to the big leagues by age 20. If I had signed with someone like the Dodgers with a lot of depth, it might have taken me five or six years to get to the majors."

He began his rookie season in the bullpen for Frank Robinson's Indians. He still treasures the memory of his first big league start. "It was against the Oakland A's and I pitched a three-hit shutout. Having grown up in Oakland, to shut out the world champion A's was a huge thrill. I remember feeling like I belonged in the big leagues. I'll never forget it."

His 13 wins earned him Rookie Pitcher of the Year honors for the American League. He followed up with 13 more wins in 1976, including nine complete games. The next season he pitched a no-hitter, out-dueling Angels' ace Frank Tanana.

"Jerry Remy was on deck when I got the final out and he loves to tell the story of how I was screaming at the last hitter, Gil Flores, to get in the batter's box so I could get my no-hitter over with. It wasn't quite like that. I wasn't that cool.

"The photographers were all scrambling to get a picture of the last out and he [Flores] was looking around to figure out what the commotion was. I was just telling him to forget about that and get in to hit. Now that I think about it, though, I was pretty cocky."

NEXT STOP: KENMORE SQUARE

Dennis Eckersley followed his 20 wins in 1978 with 17 wins and 17 complete games in 1979. His ERA of 2.99 led the team and ranked seventh in the American League. He finished fourth in the Cy Young Award voting.

"My early years with the Red Sox were very good and the fans were great to me. I pitched here with the Indians and I remember thinking, 'these fans are something else. They are really intense.' But I didn't know just how intense they really are until I got here. It might have been just as well."

In 1980 his win total dropped to 12 but it was still good enough to lead the Red Sox staff. He also topped the staff in complete games and strikeouts. There was a work stoppage the following season and Dennis managed nine wins in just 23 starts.

Eckersley rebounded for 13 wins in 1982 and he was named to the American League All-Star team for the second time. "I got to start the All-Star Game for the American League that year. That is every starting pitcher's dream and I am very proud of it. But I had pitched a lot of innings over the years, especially 1977-79, and I was starting to wear down.

"In 1983 I was just awful. I stunk. My arm wasn't right and I hadn't taken care of myself the way I should have. The Boston fans booed me right out of the ballpark. And rightfully so. It hurt and it humbled me but I deserved every boo I got, the way I pitched."

Dennis Eckersley's ERA of 5.61 in 1983 looks like a misprint for a career that averages 3.50. And things only got worse in early 1984 with the Red Sox. On May 25, 1984, he was traded to the Chicago Cubs for first baseman Bill Buckner.

"Under the terms of my contract I could have vetoed that trade. But I knew I needed a change of scene, a fresh start. I think Buckner felt the same way about Chicago. It worked out well for me."

The friendly confines of Wrigley Field proved beneficial to Eckersley as he cut his ERA in half and contributed 10 wins to help the Cubs earn a rare post-season appearance. "I enjoyed my time in Chicago. The fans are similar to the Boston fans. Maybe not quite as intense but just as passionate about their team."

In 1985 he won 11 games for the Cubs and finished in the top 10 in the National League in five pitching categories. But in 1986 he won only six games in 32 starts and the Cubs traded him to the Oakland A's on April 3, 1987, for three minor league pitchers. At age 32 with 12 big league seasons behind him, Dennis Eckersley's baseball career appeared to be winding down.

SECOND CHANCE

"The Cubs didn't know what they were giving up. They couldn't have known really. During the off-season I had decided to change my life and I went through rehab and got sober. When I came through it successfully I knew I had a second chance and I was a man on a mission. I felt like I was 25 years old again. I knew that most people don't get a second chance and I was determined to make the most of it. I turned my life and career around.

"When I got to Oakland I still wanted to start. But Tony LaRussa [A's manager] put me in the bullpen. I figured I could work my way back to the starting rotation. They used me to close in the second half and I had something like 13 saves but I still thought I could start.

"Before the next season Tony had a talk with me. He told me the A's had just picked up Bob Welch [former Dodger star pitcher]. All I said was 'Well, I guess I'm not going to start.' "

Dennis Eckersley may have been a reluctant closer but over the next five seasons he would emerge as the dominant closer in the game. In 1988 he appeared in 60 games for the A's and recorded 45 saves, one short of the major league record. He had 70 strikeouts in just 73 innings and amazingly, he walked only 11 batters. When his four victories in relief are added to his save total, he

The Eck, 1998.

accounted for almost half of Oakland's 104 wins as the A's easily won the American League's Western division.

The 1988 American League Championship Series matched the A's against the Boston Red Sox. Eckersley was even more dominant in this playoff series, saving all four Oakland victories in the A's sweep of the Red Sox.

Told that his late-inning appearances caused many Red Sox fans to consider an early departure from Fenway Park, Dennis can only laugh. "It wasn't that way for me at all. I might have looked confident but remember, I still lived here. And it was only a few years earlier that the fans had booed me out of town. I knew how much the fans wanted to see their team win and see me humbled. I didn't think it was easy in any way. I knew how dangerous those Red Sox hitters were. It was awfully sweet to get those four saves, but it wasn't easy. Not for a minute."

Dennis Eckersley went directly from a career high to a career low. The victorious A's were heavily favored to defeat the Los Angeles Dodgers in the World Series that followed, and Oakland had their ace closer on the mound with a one run lead in the opening game. In one of the more dramatic moments in World Series history, injured Dodgers' star Kirk Gibson hobbled to the plate and drove an Eckersley pitch into the right-field bleachers for a game-winning, two-run homer. The Dodgers players and their fans went into a frenzied celebration, while Dennis and his Oakland teammates stood by in shock.

"I have had people ask me: 'How could you ever recover from that?' I tell them, 'Listen, I was just lucky to be in that spot.' After you have been through what I had, it was amazing that I had a chance to be standing there. And I'm very proud of the fact that I saved more than 300 games after that experience. But man, did he ever hit that ball. It got out of there in a hurry.

"I've been together with Kirk Gibson a lot of times since. We've done card shows and other things together. We laugh and kid about it now, but it really hurt at the time. It was very humbling."

Dennis acknowledges that he has finally gotten around to watching the replay of the game on ESPN Classic Sports. "I had seen the replay of the home run 1,000 times. It follows me around wherever I go, I think. But I hadn't watched the game again until fairly recently. Mostly I couldn't get over how young I looked."

PREMIER CLOSER

In 1989, Dennis had 33 saves, third best in the American League, to go along with four wins. His ERA for the season was a sparkling 1.56. His control continued to be extraordinary, walking only three batters while striking out 55 in 57 innings. He saved three games in the A's American League Championship Series win over Toronto. Then the Oakland A's headed to the World Series against their Bay Area rivals, the San Francisco Giants.

"That was the year of the earthquake and baseball didn't seem all that important any more. We had 10 days between games and our focus was on our friends

and the community. But when the Series resumed I had one my greatest baseball experiences. We ended up sweeping the Giants in four games and I made the
final putout of the Series covering first base.

"There I was standing on first base with the ball. We've just won the World
Championship and I'm looking around Candlestick Park thinking how I used to
go there as a kid to watch my heroes. My dream then was to become a big
league player and here I was out on the field. That was my absolute highlight
in baseball."

Dennis Eckersley was 35 years old when the 1990 season began but he was
just reaching his prime as the premier closer of his era. He appeared in 63 games
that season, saving 48 of them and winning four games. He was selected to the
American League All-Star team for the fourth time, his second selection as a
relief pitcher.

His earned run average of 0.61 in 1990 is not a misprint: he gave up only five
earned runs all season, or fewer than one per month. To go with his meager five
earned runs, he parceled out a miserly four walks while striking out one batter
for each inning pitched.

"I was in a zone for most of that time. I had a lot to prove and a lot of time
to make up for. I really was at a point where I felt I could put the baseball exactly where I wanted it. Right on the corner of the corner, set up the fastball, turn
the ball over to get a grounder. Everything was working for me. It was almost like
magic."

The Oakland A's swept the Eastern Division champion Boston Red Sox in
four straight games for the second time in three years in the 1990 American
League Championship Series, and Dennis Eckersley picked up two more post-
season saves. But the A's were on the other end of a sweep in the World Series,
when the Cincinnati Reds upset them.

In 1991, Eckersley had 43 saves to become the first American League pitcher with 40 or more saves in 3 seasons. He struck out more than one batter per
inning that year while walking only nine batters in 76 innings of work.

MVP AND CY YOUNG AWARD WINNER

The 1992 season was arguably Dennis Eckersley's best year. His 51 saves and
seven wins earned him the American League MVP Award, the Cy Young Award
as the American League's best pitcher, and the Rolaids American League Relief
Pitcher Award. The total of his saves plus wins accounted for 60 percent of the
A's victories that season. Although the A's lost the American League
Championship in six games to Toronto, Eckersley picked up a save and finished
his fifth straight postseason series without issuing a walk.

"As good as I was for those five years, I was always aware of the slim margin
of victory. Every appearance was precious to me because I realized how close
defeat was. I walked that fine line realizing that something could go wrong. I
cared very deeply about my performance. God gave me another chance and I
wasn't going to waste it."

In 1993 Eckersley's achievements went from the level of "otherworldly" to above the average for mere mortals. His 36 saves ranked fifth in the American League and while he managed to strike out 80 batters while walking only 13 in 67 innings, he was no longer invincible. He slipped to 19 saves in the strike-shortened 1994 season, but he rebounded for 29 saves in 1995 at age 40. On May 4, 1995, Eckersley made his first fielding error in over eight seasons. His string of 470 errorless games established a record for major league pitchers.

"When I pitched badly I couldn't sleep that night. Most players tell you that they leave their mistakes at the ballpark but I don't think that's true. At least it was never true for me. I wouldn't have wanted to live with me after a tough loss. You have to care."

In February 1996 Dennis Eckersley was traded by Oakland to the St. Louis Cardinals. The trade reunited him with manager Tony LaRussa and rejuvenated his career. He saved 30 games for the Cardinals in 1996, helping them to the post-season. The Cardinals swept the Padres three straight in the first round of the playoffs and Dennis saved all three games. The Cardinals lost the National League Championship Series to the Atlanta Braves in seven games but Eckersley did not allow an earned run in three appearances and he picked up his fifteenth post-season save.

In 1997, at age 42, Dennis Eckersley saved 36 games for the St. Louis Cardinals, the fourth-best save total in the National League. This brought his career saves to 389, the third highest total in major league history. A free agent at the end of the season, he signed with the Boston Red Sox in December.

"It was great to finish up in Boston. A lot had happened to me during the 14 seasons I had played for other teams. Most of it for the better. I came back to Boston a different person than when I left."

On the mound at Fenway during his second tour of duty.

He made 50 relief appearances for the Red Sox in 1998. On September 26, the crowd at Fenway Park gave him a standing ovation as he took the mound for appearance number 1,071. Dennis Eckersley had broken Hoyt Wilhelm's major league record for career pitching appearances. He announced his retirement from baseball in an emotional press conference on December 10, 1998.

Asked if he watched the 46-year-old Jessie Orosco, wondering if he could still pitch at the major league level, Eckersley responded, "I pitched for 24 years in the major leagues. I was lucky I had baseball to change my life. It was a good run. You miss some things because the game is all-consuming. There are things outside of baseball that I need to attend to. I miss the game and I'm still adjusting but it's time to work on being a good person. I'm more of a whole person now."

HALL OF FAME NUMBERS

When Dennis Eckersley was first eligible for baseball's Hall of Fame in January 2004, other strong candidates for election included first-timers Paul Molitor and Joe Carter. Holdovers Jim Rice, Andre Dawson, and Bruce Sutter, who had drawn strong support in previous elections, were also strong contenders.

Asked if he thought about induction in the Hall of Fame, Eckersley answers, "Only because people keep asking me about it. If no one asked I probably wouldn't think about it because it seems too much to hope for. The standards are so high, and they should be, that it is hard for me to imagine. I would be thrilled if I'm lucky enough to make it someday, because it would be an incredible honor."

When you combine his 197 career wins and 390 saves, Dennis Eckersley has contributed to more victories than any other pitcher in major league history. He ranks in the top 100 in major league history in eight significant career categories (see box). He was among the 100 players selected for the All-Century Team that was introduced at Fenway Park before the 1999 All-Star Game.

"It was an unbelievable thrill to be out there with all those great players," Eckersley said, pointing at the field during a recent interview at Fenway Park. "To be on the same field with Ted Williams and my boyhood heroes. I was standing right down there next to Roger Clemens. It was an incredible feeling."

Eckersley clearly relishes his role as an analyst appearing on the NESN pre- and post-game shows. He was previously a color analyst for the Oakland A's, and he has filled in on occasion for Red Sox broadcasts "I want to do a better job of showing the audience how passionate I am about this game. I love baseball and sometimes it is hard to communicate that on television. I think I can bring that across even better."

Asked what single person has influenced him the most over the years, he reflects briefly and responds emphatically, "That would have to be my father. My father continually reminded me that I was as good as anyone else. Not that I was better than anyone else, but that no one was better than me. That thought has stayed with me my whole life, in every kind of situation. Yes, it would have to be my father, Wallace Eckersley."

Predicting the actions of the Hall of Fame voters is about as tough as fore-casting the weather in New England. But one thing is certain: in the hearts and minds of Boston Red Sox fans, Dennis Eckersley is definitely a Hall of Famer.

Dennis Eckersley's Rank in Major League Baseball History

CATEGORY	CAREER TOTALS	ALL-TIME MLB RANK
Games Pitched	1,071	3
Saves	390	4
Strikeouts	2,401	33
Walks & Hits Per 9 Innings		
(Lowest)	10.45	71
Innings	3,286	87
Walks Per 9 Innings		
(Lowest)	2.02	90

Source: 2004 MLB.com

35.

Bob Stanley Interview

February 1998

I interviewed Bob Stanley at his long-time home in Wenham, Massachusetts. As I walked up his front steps I remembered reading that someone had stopped in front of his home after the 1986 World Series and trashed a tricycle belonging to one of his youngsters. That certainly ranks as one of the most despicable acts in recent memory.

But that unpleasant memory is quickly erased as Bob escorts me into their kitchen, which is clearly the focal point of the home. The first phrase that comes to mind when you sit and talk with Bob Stanley for any length of time is "regular guy." It sounds trite, but Bob could easily be the guy you take the train to work with every morning.

It is February, and Bob's wife Joan points out that Bob always gets restless around that time of year. When you've been heading south for spring training every year for 25 years, I imagine you get the urge to pack your bags around Valentine's Day.

Most long-time Red Sox fans are aware that Bob Stanley has always been active helping to raise money for the Jimmy Fund. And they are generally aware that Bob's son Kyle had fought his own battle with leukemia.

While we were sitting around the family's kitchen table, there was a constant thumping sound just outside the kitchen window. "That's Kyle shooting baskets," Bob Stanley explained. And a very pleasant sound it was indeed.

BOB STANLEY
ADOPTED SON OF
NEW ENGLAND'S TEAM

Bob Stanley could claim that he is a "birthright" Red Sox fan. The former Red Sox right-handed hurler was born in Portland, Maine.

"I could do that, but it would be stretching the truth a little bit," Bob Stanley acknowledges. "I moved to northern New Jersey when I was only two years old."

"I did spend every summer in Maine as a kid, though. I grew up rooting for the Red Sox in the American League, and the Mets in the National League." Stanley cringes as he mentions the Mets, knowing how Red Sox fans will react to that bit of trivia. He quickly adds, "Make sure that you mention that I hated the New York Yankees."

"YOU'LL WATCH ME IN YANKEE STADIUM"

Bob Stanley grew up in Kearney, New Jersey, splitting his sports time between baseball and basketball. Like most kids with a New England connection, he was a die-hard Boston Celtics fan.

"Basketball was actually my first love growing up. I was a pretty good basketball player. But every time I see that movie, *White Men Can't Jump*, I'm reminded that I wasn't that good. I didn't have much of a vertical leap.

"I never really pitched until my senior year in high school. All our pitchers had graduated the year before and the coach decided to give me a try. And I did pretty well all things considered."

Stanley went 10-1 that year, but he didn't attract any attention from the baseball scouts until year-end. "We went into our last game, and the stands were packed with major league scouts who had come to watch the other team's pitcher. I pitched a perfect game through six innings, and we went on to win 10-1."

"By the time I got on the team bus I had the business cards for scouts of just about every major league team. That was the first time anyone had even noticed me. But I had already told my mother, 'Someday you'll watch me play in Yankee Stadium.'"

FAST-TRACK TO FENWAY

The Los Angeles Dodgers selected Bob Stanley early in the 1973 major league baseball draft, but since he was only 18 years old, he decided to give college a try. In less than one semester he concluded that his future was on the pitcher's mound and not in the halls of academia.

When the Red Sox selected him in the January 1974 draft, he quickly signed a contract. He was the Red Sox' first pick and the seventh overall choice. "That wasn't such a big deal," Stanley emphasizes. "It was the secondary draft so there weren't all that many hot prospects available."

Stanley still vividly remembers his first spring training camp. "I was an 18-year-old kid, away from home for the first time. I remember what it was like to compete for a job. We had all been local stars and now we were fighting for a spot.

"I really wasn't prepared for it. Camp was terrifying at times. And I had only pitched that one year in high school. Everybody there had more experience than I did."

The Red Sox assigned him to their low minor league team in Elmira, New York, where he began a 17-year professional baseball career. Stanley's six wins at Elmira in 1974 earned him a promotion to Winter Haven in the Florida State League for 1975.

Despite his league-leading 26 starts and a sparkling 2.93 era, he ended the year just 5-17. "We just couldn't score any runs. That was the year I learned to cope with losing," Stanley recalls.

In 1976 the 21-year-old really blossomed with the Red Sox Bristol, Connecticut farm club. Stanley produced 15 wins in the Double A Eastern League, and earned a spot on the Red Sox 15-player protected list in that winter's expansion draft.

"When I arrived in Winter Haven for Spring Training in 1977, I knew I had a shot at making the major league roster, but I knew I had to be at the top of my game. It's funny what you remember looking back on it. The minor leaguers all stayed at the Howard Johnson's and the big leaguers stayed at the Holiday Inn next door. I remember how much I wanted to move over to the Holiday Inn.

"I pitched well all spring, but on the day they were making the final cuts I gave up six runs in one inning. When I saw manager Don Zimmer approaching me after the game I thought I had blown it!"

"Zim said: 'Congratulations, you've made the team. Just don't have any six-run innings when we get up north.' After we shook hands, I went to the outfield and just ran, and ran, and ran. I had never been so happy in my life."

GLORY DAYS

Despite having only three years of professional baseball experience behind him, Stanley was an immediate success in the big leagues. In his rookie year he split his time between starting and relieving. He appeared in 41 games, earning eight wins to go along with three saves. Clearly he belonged at the big league level.

In 1978 he made a major contribution to the Red Sox' first place tie with the New York Yankees, compiling a 15-2 record as a middle-reliever. His teammates nicknamed him "The Vulture" in honor of his knack for swooping in from the bullpen and holding the opposition at bay until the Red Sox could take the lead.

On September 29, 1978, with the Red Sox desperate for starting pitching, Bob Stanley made what was only his third start of the season. The Red Sox, who were barely holding on in their quest to catch the New York Yankees, trailed the Bronx Bombers by one game going into the Friday night game against the Toronto Blue Jays. Stanley pitched brilliantly over six innings holding the Blue Jays to only one hit in an 11-0 Red Sox victory.

Bob Stanley gave up an eighth-inning home run to Reggie Jackson in the one-game playoff against the Yankees. Stanley grimaces while he volunteers, "That was a big run for the Yankees. I'm just lucky that all the fans remember about that game is Bucky Dent's home run."

The following season the Red Sox used him primarily as a starter, and he was selected for the 1979 American League All-Star team on the strength of his 16 victories. By this time, his nasty sinking fastball and pinpoint control had established him as one of the big leagues' premier pitchers.

"The sinker is a funny pitch," Stanley emphasizes. "I remember the first year I was in spring training, a bunch of the instructors watched me throw. One of them said, 'That's the best sinker I have ever seen,' and they all nodded in agreement. I didn't know what they were talking about. I didn't know I threw a sinker.

"The way I held the ball, and the way I delivered it, made the ball sink naturally. It wasn't something I was taught and it wasn't anything I was aware of. I guess God gave me this crummy body," he laughs, "but he truly blessed me with a strong arm and a natural sinker."

Bob Stanley began the 1980 season in the starting rotation, and pitched in 17 games before the All-Star break. But the Red Sox had concluded that his durability made him a natural reliever. Even though the move to the bullpen occurred in midseason, Stanley still finished eighth in the American League with 14 saves.

For the next six seasons the Red Sox bullpen would be Bob Stanley's principal residence, and he would establish himself as one of the top relievers in team history. The 1981 season was interrupted by a midseason work stoppage, but Stanley still managed 10 wins while appearing in long relief. His 35 appearances topped the Red Sox staff.

"MAN OF THE YEAR"

In 1982 Stanley established an American League record with 168 relief innings. His ERA of 3.10 was the team's best and while he was used primarily in long-relief, his 14 saves ranked ninth in the American League.

During his six years with the Red Sox Bob Stanley had become a fan favorite. His ritual of smashing beach balls from the bleachers with a bullpen rake was a Fenway favorite. Each year the BoSox Club honors a player for his contributions and cooperation with community endeavors. They named Bob Stanley "Man of the Year" at the end of the 1982 season.

"My wife Joan and I have always felt comfortable in Boston. We didn't grow up here but we made it our home. And I've always been happy to do my part off the field. It just feels right to give something back to the community."

In 1983, Bob Stanley established a Red Sox record with 33 saves. His outstanding work out of the bullpen earned him his second selection to the American League All-Star team. His 64 appearances that season topped the Red Sox and placed him fifth in the American League.

In 1984 Stanley led the Red Sox in appearances for the third time in four seasons, pitching in 57 games. Ralph Houk, who managed Bob Stanley during those four seasons, remembers him fondly.

"Bob Stanley was a workhorse for me," Houk remembered during a conversation in his Winter Haven, Florida, home. "He did everything I ever asked him to do. And I asked him to do a lot. He pitched long-relief for me, and I used him as a closer. I even started him in one game," Houk recalls fondly.

In 1985 new manager John McNamara used Stanley mainly in long-relief. His 48 appearances topped the Red Sox staff once again.

HARD TIMES

The 1986 season was a season of ups and downs for Red Sox fans and for Bob Stanley. The Red Sox won 95 games to easily outdistance the New York Yankees in the American League East. An heroic comeback against the California Angels propelled them into the World Series for the first time in 11 years.

Bob Stanley started strong in 1986, and had racked up 14 saves by mid-season. When Calvin Schiraldi emerged as the team's closer in the second half, Stanley returned to his role as a middle-reliever, and did heavy duty in leading the team with 66 appearances over the course of the season.

All Red Sox fans recall that Bob Stanley was on the mound when the New York Mets scored the winning run in the tenth inning of Game Six of the 1986 World Series. In the post-game news conference, Stanley told listeners: "I was booed on Opening Day, and I told the writers 'That's all right, I'll be standing on the mound when we win the World Series.' I had my dream right there in front of me and it didn't work out. No excuses."

Stanley bristles when Bill Buckner's name is mentioned. "People always remember the last thing that happened. They don't remember the other parts of the game, that we left 14 men on base."

Things went from bad to worse for Stanley in 1987. Roger Clemens held out in spring training, and "Oil Can" Boyd, who had won 16 games in 1986, was injured. Stanley agreed to step into the breach as a starter.

"I thought I could do it, but I had spent the last seven years in the bullpen. I was slotted in the rotation against the other team's number-one starter. Time and again I would come up against the other team's stopper. I was overmatched." His 4-15 record was by far his worst in a stellar major league career.

In 1988, Stanley made 57 appearances and contributed six wins to a Red Sox first place finish in the American League East. But when the 1989 season rolled around, he knew it would be his last. "I had lost my competitive edge. I could still pitch, but it wasn't enough. It was time."

Bob Stanley pitched in 43 games in 1989, running his 13-year Red Sox total to a franchise record 637 lifetime pitching appearances. To put that standard in perspective, Roger Clemens was second to Stanley at the beginning of the 2004 season with just 383 games pitched.

THE JIMMY FUND

Throughout his career with the Red Sox, Bob Stanley was extremely active with the Jimmy Fund. The entire Red Sox organization has been committed to the Jimmy Fund for over 50 years, and Bob Stanley has been a tireless worker for this cause.

"I always figured that God gave me a wonderful pitching arm, and it was up to me to give something back. I used to grab some of our young players who had

With rake in hand, Bob reenacted his familiar "burst the beach ball" one more time to the thrill of the fans during Bob Stanley Night!

gone 0-5, or been knocked out of the box early, and bring them along with me to the Dana-Farber Clinic for a visit. When we would leave a couple of hours later they would realize that going 0-5 wasn't really a big deal."

In 1985 Stanley was particularly moved by the plight of a 10-year-old boy with an inoperable brain tumor. Deeply depressed, the youngster had stopped talking, even to his parents. At the urging of Jimmy Fund Executive Director, Mike Andrews, Stanley paid a visit to the young man. He brought along assorted Red Sox memorabilia, including the uniform jersey he had worn when he set the Red Sox save record.

The youngster's physician called Stanley later that evening to say, "I don't know what you did, but that little boy is running up and down the halls talking to anyone who will listen." The child died a few weeks later, and he was buried, as he requested, in Bob Stanley's uniform number 46.

Months following Stanley's retirement from baseball, the Stanley family learned that their seven-year-old son Kyle had been diagnosed with leukemia. Ironically the diagnosis was identical to the tumor of the youngster that Bob had befriended five years earlier.

Thanks to the dedicated efforts of the researchers and clinicians at Dana-Farber's Jimmy Fund Clinic, significant medical advances had been made in the treatment of Kyle's form of leukemia. His treatment was successful, his recovery was complete, and today he is a happy, active teenager.

As Bob Stanley looks out the window of his kitchen at Kyle shooting baskets in the driveway, he reflects on his experiences. "You know, when I was standing on the mound at Shea Stadium in Game Six, I prayed to God that we would win. That prayer wasn't answered. When I learned that Kyle had leukemia, I prayed that he would be cured, and that prayer *was* answered. When you've been through what we've been through, you understand that baseball is only a game, and that family is what really matters. It truly puts things into perspective."

BACK IN THE GAME

Bob Stanley tried his hand at a number of things after he retired from baseball, but none of them really held his interest. About a year before our interview, he got the itch to get back into baseball.

"I called the Red Sox to see if they might have a spot in their minor league system, but they had already filled all of their slots. The Sox told the New York Mets that I was interested in coaching at the minor league level, and the Mets contacted me a couple of weeks later. I ended up as the pitching coach for their Pittsfield [Massachusetts] club in 1997. Believe me, we didn't walk many guys!" laughs Stanley, who was a control artist throughout his pitching career.

The Mets thought so highly of his work in Pittsfield that they have elevated him to St. Lucie to take over as their pitching coach in the strong Florida State League in 1998. "I wish I had known as much about pitching when I was 25 as I know now," quips Stanley.

Stanley has many great memories of his Red Sox career. And some of his warmest memories revolve around spring training in Winter Haven, Florida.

"Over the years as our family grew it became a real family adventure. We always stayed in the same two adjoining rooms at the Holiday Inn, right beside the kiddies' pool. My wife could sit outside the rooms and enjoy the sun while our kids napped. As the kids got older, we arranged for a tutor so the kids could keep up with their class work and we could be together as a family.

"Jerry Remy used to stay at the Holiday Inn with his family, too. We used to have an Easter egg hunt out there every year. One year there was one egg that nobody could ever find. The next year we were playing by the pool and I went into the bushes to find the ball and there was the missing egg. We had some great times."

Asked when he first thought of the Boston area as home, Stanley replies, "We've been here for over 20 years, and we were comfortable right from the start. We've raised our two daughters and our son here. We've been in the same house for 15 years. This *is* home."

"I have a lot more good memories of my career with the Red Sox than bad memories. I remember a lot more cheers than boos. They were great years."

Bob Stanley's place among the Red Sox all-time pitching leaders is firmly established. He was inducted into the Red Sox Hall of Fame in November 2000. In addition to being the all-time Red Sox leader in games pitched, he holds the club saves record and he is first in relief wins.

But for many long-time Red Sox fans, a different memory remains. It is also a warm memory of the Red Sox former spring training headquarters in Winter Haven, Florida. Most March evenings Bob Stanley could be found by the pool, playing baseball with his kids and any other kids who happened along.

Bob Stanley: all-time Red Sox good-guy.

Bob Stanley's Rank in Red Sox History

CATEGORY	CAREER TOTALS	ALL-TIME BOSTON RED SOX RANK
Games	637	1st
Saves	132	1st
Relief Wins	85	1st
Innings	1707	5th
Wins	115	6th
Relief Win Percentage	.582	12th
Strikeouts	693	19th

Source: 2004 *Boston Red Sox Media Guide*

36.
Jerry Remy Interview
March 2001

I interviewed Jerry Remy in the broadcast booth at City of Palms Park in Fort Myers, Florida. It was several hours before that afternoon's game against the Cincinnati Reds and the players were going through their spring training rituals below us.

The broadcast booth at City of Palms Park is fairly accessible to fans, and a couple of early arrivals headed up to get the inside story from Jerry on the team's chances. "Look me up in September," Jerry offered in his understated style, "I can give you a better idea then."

I first met Jerry Remy at a Red Sox fantasy camp in 1992, long before he became a cult figure. I was struck by the fact that he was less outgoing than most of the former Red Sox players on hand. In retrospect, I think that is why he has worn so well with Red Sox fans over 17 seasons.

In my research, I had read several stories mentioning that Jerry was on the field, along with several thousand other Red Sox fans, celebrating the team's dramatic victory on the last day of the 1967 season. "I've seen that several times," Jerry offered, "And I have no idea where it comes from. My mother and father would have killed me if I ever ran out onto the field like that!"

I think that is probably true for most of us. And because he is like most of us, a lifelong Red Sox fan from the area, we are happy to welcome him into our homes day after day throughout the long baseball season.

JERRY REMY
NATIVE SON OF
NEW ENGLAND'S TEAM

Most young fans of the Boston Red Sox dream of a future career with their favorite team. Jerry Remy, a native of Somerset, Massachusetts, has been fortunate enough to have two different careers with the team he rooted for as a youngster. Remy was an outstanding second baseman for the team from 1978 to 1984, and he has just finished his 17th season of color commentary for the Red Sox telecasts.

"I think I have the greatest job in the world," Jerry Remy said in an interview at spring training in 2001. "I'm still in the game. But I don't have the headaches that the players and the managers have. I'm with the team I want to be with, the team I rooted for as a kid. And I get to spend a lot of time at home with my family. I couldn't ask for a better job."

LOCAL BOY MAKES GOOD

Jerry Remy was born in Fall River, Massachusetts, on November 8, 1952. He grew up in Somerset, a small community about 50 miles south of Boston. He played all sports as a youngster, but baseball was his first love.

"I liked to play all sports but baseball was always special to me," Jerry emphasizes. "When I got to high school, the only sport I played competitively was baseball. But my goal was to get good enough to be able to play baseball at the college level. When I was a teenager it never occurred to me that I might go on to have a career as a professional baseball player. Fenway Park was only 50 miles or so away from home, but it seemed a lot further away than that."

Like most New England kids, rooting for the Red Sox was a family affair, part of his heritage. "My father and grandfather took me to quite a few games at Fenway when I was a kid. I remember when we were coming up the Southeast Expressway and we went by the gas tank, I knew we were getting close. Then when we got on to Mass Avenue, I would start looking for the light towers. Once I saw them I knew we were almost there.

"Of course, in those days, not every game was televised so it was a big thrill to see a game," Jerry reflects. "And we still had a black and white TV so when you would come up the runway and see the field for the first time, you couldn't believe how green it was."

Asked if there was one season that he remembered more than others and if he had a favorite player as a youngster, Jerry responds, "Like a lot of Red Sox fans, the '67 team, the Impossible Dream team, was my favorite. And Yaz was the player I followed most closely."

Remy played well enough in high school to earn All-Scholastic honors from *The Boston Globe* in his senior year. He also attracted the interest of Joe Lewis who was a scout for the Washington Senators (now the Texas Rangers). The Senators thought enough of his potential to select him in the June 1970 draft.

"I wasn't sure whether to sign with the Senators or to go on to college. I decided not to sign and I put in one semester of college. But I realized that I really wanted to pursue a professional baseball career. When the California [now Anaheim] Angels picked me in the January secondary draft I signed with them.

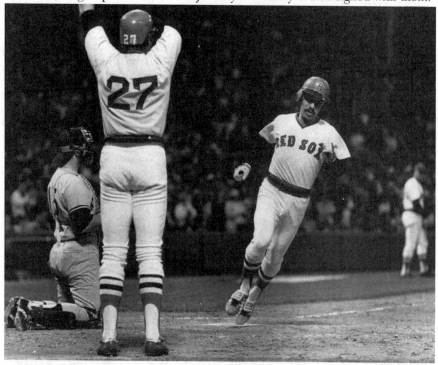

"I was an eighth-round draft pick, and that was in the secondary phase of the draft," Jerry points out. "Most of the top prospects had signed after the earlier round, so that gives you an idea of where I fit as a prospect."

THE ROAD TO THE MAJORS

When Remy reported to his first spring training camp he found that he had a lot of catching up to do. "We had a 16-game schedule in high school and I think two or three of them got cancelled every year. I get to the Angels' camp and there are all these kids from California and Texas who had been playing 50 to 60 games a year. Boy, was I behind their development."

His career was almost over before it began. "I almost got released my first spring. The Angels were ready to send me home, but one of their coaches, Kenny Meyers, stood up for me. He convinced them to have me come back for the Rookie League team in June so he could work with me. If he hadn't gone to bat for me, it would have been all over."

Remy worked diligently and moved steadily through the Angels' minor league system. "In my third year at Davenport, Iowa, I led the league in hitting because some of the things that Kenny Meyers had worked with me on started to kick in. All of a sudden people are starting to notice you. The following year at El Paso, Texas, I was leading the league in hitting when they promoted me to Triple A during the season."

Asked if he has any words of wisdom for New England youngsters who aspire to a career in the big leagues, Jerry suggests, "Kids should play every chance they get. Sure the weather is a factor, but our problem is simply that we don't play enough. If a youngster is serious about his game, he should look for every opportunity to play the game. There is no substitute for game experience."

Jerry Remy was named as the Angels' starting second baseman at the end of spring training in 1975. At age 22, after a slow start and four years of very hard work in the minors, he had reached the major leagues. And the manager of the Impossible Dream Red Sox team, Dick Williams, was his first big league manager.

"I still remember my first at-bat in the major leagues. My dad had flown cross-country to see me play. I singled to left field to drive in a run, and then on the very next pitch I proceeded to get picked off first base. When I got back to the dugout Dick Williams motioned for me to sit next to him. He said, 'Keep that stuff up and you'll be back in Triple A pretty fast.' That gave me a pretty good idea of how serious he was."

Jerry Remy put together an excellent rookie year in the big leagues. He played in 147 games and had 147 hits. He used his speed to great advantage, stealing 34 bases to finish fifth in the American League in that category.

"Speed was always my edge," Remy recalls. "I didn't have any power to speak of. I had to be quick fielding my position, and I had to be quick on the base paths."

His trips back to Fenway Park were not totally enjoyable for Remy. "I played very well at Fenway against the Red Sox, but it was very nerve-wracking. It was the only time my family and friends got to see me play, so I was nervous, almost sick. It certainly was a thrill to be playing in Fenway, and I did all right, but I was always happy when it was time to leave town."

In his second season with the Angels, Jerry raised his batting average five points to a respectable .263 and stole one more base for a total of 35. In his final year in California, the 1977 season, he played in 154 games and finished third in the American League for stolen bases, with a career high total of 41 steals. His 10 triples ranked eighth in the American League.

HEADING FOR HOME

On December 7, 1977, the California Angels traded Jerry Remy to the Boston Red Sox in exchange for pitcher Don Aase and cash considerations. Angels General Manager Harry Dalton told the Red Sox' Haywood Sullivan, "You have just traded for the best second baseman you've had since Bobby Doerr."

"I was very excited when I heard I had been traded to the Red Sox. All of a sudden I'm playing with Carl Yastrzemski, my boyhood hero, and guys like Fisk and the two guys who were rookies the year I broke in, Rice and Lynn. We had a very good team.

"It felt kind of funny being in the same locker room with Yaz, but he was great. And Carlton Fisk had called me in the off-season to tell me he was looking forward to playing with me. All the guys were terrific. And I knew I brought something the team needed: speed."

The 1978 Boston Red Sox got off to a great start. The team won 26 of their first 30 games at Fenway Park and on July 10 the Red Sox led the American League by nine games. Jerry Remy got off to a great start as well. His solid work at bat and in the field earned him a spot on the American League All-Star team.

"I was much more comfortable playing at Fenway on a regular basis. It meant my family and friends could see me play a lot and it took the pressure off. Billy Martin [New York Yankees manager at the time] named me to the All-Star team to replace Rick Burleson, who was injured. I didn't get to play in the game, but I didn't care. It was just a thrill to be there," the self-effacing Remy offers.

The New York Yankees were as hot in the second half of the 1978 season as the Red Sox had been during the first half. When the regular season ended on October 1 the two teams had identical records and the scene was set for the second playoff game in American League history.

Monday October 2, 1978, was a beautiful fall day and Fenway Park was the site of one of the most exciting, albeit disappointing games in Red Sox history. When Jerry Remy stepped to the plate in the last of the ninth inning, one man was out, the Red Sox were trailing 5-4, and Rick Burleson represented the tying run at first base.

"Gossage [Yankee reliever "Goose"] helped me out by throwing me a slider, something I could pull. When I came up I knew I didn't want to hit a ball on the ground, something that could end up as a double play to end the game. When I got my bat on the ball I knew from the time I hit it that Piniella [Yankee right-fielder Lou] wasn't going to be able to catch it. I could tell from the spin on the ball that it would fall in.

"I never realized that he [Piniella] lost sight of the ball, I was concentrating on running the bases. He stuck out his glove and there was the ball. If it gets by him, Burleson scores and I'm on third base. He made a great play, or a lucky play. But whatever, he made the play.

"I was disappointed when we lost, we all were. But you had the feeling that with the team we had we would make it to the World Series at some point. Looking back on the way it turned out I'm more disappointed now than I was then." Chuckling, Remy adds, "I watch that game all the time when it is on ESPN Sports Classics, and we always lose it. It always turns out the same way."

BEYOND THE PLAYOFF GAME

Jerry Remy and his Red Sox teammates reported to spring training in 1979 with high hopes for the coming season. These high hopes were never realized as the team finished in third place, 11 behind the Baltimore Orioles, and Remy suffered his first serious injury.

On July 1, 1979, at Yankee Stadium, he attempted to tag up and score from third base. "It was a shallow fly ball just into the outfield. Willie Randolph ended up catching the ball and throwing me out by 10 feet at home. I tried to slide around the tag but my spikes caught. It was really pretty painful," Jerry remembers, wincing as he recalls the trauma.

Remy played in only half of the Red Sox games in 1979 but he still managed to score 49 runs and to steal 14 bases. In 1980 he got off to an excellent start at the plate but he blew out his knee in mid-season. Despite his abbreviated season, he did manage to bat a career high .313.

The 1981 season was another fast start for Jerry Remy. On June 1 of that year he was leading the American League with a .366 average. Jerry laughs when he is reminded of his lofty batting average. "I should have saved the newspaper. Imagine me hitting .366, and leading the league in hitting."

Ongoing knee problems limited him to 88 games in 1981. But he still finished the year batting .307, which was tenth best in the American League. After a second surgery on his knee in December of 1981, and intensive offseason rehabilitation, he entered the 1982 season in great shape. He played in 155 games that season, scoring 89 runs and batting a solid .280.

The 1983 season was another excellent year for Remy. He appeared in 146 games rapping out 163 hits including 17 bunt base hits. Over the 1982 and 1983 seasons Jerry came to bat with a runner on third with less than two outs 48 times, and managed to drive 32 of those runners in.

"I used to try to put the ball in the air in those situations," Jerry states. "I wasn't a home run hitter so that was my chance to drive a runner in. I took a lot of pride in doing the little things in the game."

The 1984 season would turn out to be Remy's final year of professional baseball. He had undergone his third knee operation during the offseason. Thirty games into the season he dove for a Carlton Fisk ground ball and when he got to his feet his knee was worse than before the operation. Despite extensive efforts to rehabilitate his knee through the 1986 season, Jerry Remy's baseball career was over after ten big league seasons.

FROM THE DIAMOND TO THE BROADCAST BOOTH

"When my playing days were over I did some coaching for the Red Sox. I went down to New Britain [Connecticut] to work with the younger players in the minors. Then when the NESN job opened up I figured, what the heck, I'll throw my name in. I never anticipated getting it.

"After what I'm sure was long deliberation they hired me at NESN. So I said to myself, 'What do I do now? I have no clue.' I really didn't. It turned out to be the start of a whole new career that I had never anticipated.

"I wasn't comfortable at first. And I wasn't very good. I knew I wasn't very good, and I decided to really work at improving. It was probably halfway through my first year before I started to get comfortable. Then I started to like it. I was very fortunate that I had Ned Martin to work with. He helped me a lot."

Jerry Remy enjoys a reputation among his peers and fans as a hard worker, someone who really does his homework. Asked about his preparation before a game, he responds, "I sit in on the media's meeting with the manager, I review the notes that both teams provide us with, and you can get more information than you know what to do with on the Internet. When I first started in this job, I overprepared. Then I learned to talk baseball, to go with what I know.

"I make a real effort to anticipate what is likely to happen next, to help fans to understand the thinking that goes on. I feel good when I predict something and then it happens. I try to share with the fans what I learned from playing the game. I take a lot of pride in my work."

Baseball's long six-month season poses a particular challenge for announcers and Remy's low-key style wears well with fans. He also draws on his youthful experiences as a fan watching or listening at home.

"You are going into peoples' homes, in some cases every day of the season. And this is Boston. The fans are very knowledgeable," Jerry recognizes. "You want to be clear that you want the Red Sox to win, but if someone makes a mistake you have to point it out. These people want to hear the truth."

THE REM DAWG

During his first eight years Jerry did the color job exclusively for NESN. The 2004 season marked the ninth season that he has provided the color on all Red Sox telecasts.

"It seems hard to believe, but I have now been in this job for more years than I had seasons in the big leagues," Jerry marveled. "When I was playing it never even occurred to me that I would have this job."

Several Red Sox announcers over the years have had a national broadcasting role. In recent years announcers have moved from behind the microphone to the dugout as big league managers. Jerry Remy sounds like a guy who is very happy exactly where he is.

"I really love this job. I'm with the local team. I'm doing every Red Sox game. There's a different story every single day. I try to make it as comfortable as possible. I just want to be like the guy sitting in your house talking baseball. I've got a great job."

Remy and his family have lived in Weston, Massachusetts, for over 20 years. Jerry and his wife Phoebe have been married for 30 years. They have two sons,

Jerry finished his 17th season as a Red Sox broadcaster providing the color commentary for each game.

Jared and Jordan, who both graduated from Weston High School and a daughter Jenna who was a sophomore at the school at the time of our interview.

At this time Jerry Remy has become a cult hero to citizens of Red Sox Nation. He has his own website, theremyreport.com, and his book, *Watching Baseball: Discovering The Game Within The Game*, has achieved local bestseller status.

Jerry has been coming into our living rooms for 17 years now. He has almost become a member of our extended families. Jerry Remy is welcome at our house anytime.

37.
Bruce Hurst Interview
June 2001

While I was checking the time difference between Natick, Massachusetts, and Bruce Hurst's home in Utah, I realized just how far away he is. Bruce lived in Natick during his early years with the Red Sox, and moved to Wellesley during his later seasons with the club. The two towns are a world away from Gilbert, Utah.

Early in our telephone conversation I remembered how affable Bruce always seemed in his television interviews. He had left Boston 13 years earlier but memories of him as a really decent person returned quickly.

I mentioned watching him pitch at a game in 1985 when he was really struggling. The starter had been knocked out in the second inning, and Bruce Hurst was brought in to pitch in long relief. He was 1-9 at the time, and his reception from the fans was just brutal.

Bruce laughed at the memory. "If you weren't booing me, you should have been. I was just horrible during that stretch. The fans were just letting me know they thought I could do better."

Bruce Hurst pitched brilliantly that day in mid-1985. He went on to turn his year and his career around. He ranks among the better pitchers in Red Sox history. And he ranks among the nicest guys to ever wear a Boston Red Sox uniform.

BRUCE HURST
ADOPTED SON OF
NEW ENGLAND'S TEAM

Former Red Sox All-Star pitcher Bruce Hurst thinks that Boston fans are the best in baseball. "Boston fans really know the game and they are so intense. They always let me know when they thought I could do better and they were just as quick to cheer me when I was doing well.

"I didn't really appreciate them until I left Boston to join the San Diego Padres. Boston baseball fans are the best," Hurst said emphatically in a 2001 interview just prior to returning to Boston to take place in the Red Sox 100th anniversary celebration.

Bruce Hurst pitched for the Red Sox for all or parts of nine seasons beginning in 1980. He won more games during the 1980's than any other Red Sox left-hander. Bruce was the winning pitcher in two of the Red Sox three World Series victories in 1986 and he was named to the American League All-Star team in 1987. He ranks in the top 20 in five important Red Sox lifetime pitching categories.

ST. GEORGE, UTAH

Bruce Hurst was born 43 years ago in St. George, Utah. It is about 2,300 miles from Boston to St. George, but the difference is even greater in life style, climate, and culture. St. George was founded in 1861 when Mormon leader Brigham Young sent settlers there to grow cotton. Known as "Dixie" to the natives, the community of 20,000 is 350 miles from its spiritual focus in Salt Lake City. "You could call it isolated," Hurst agrees.

Professional sports seemed a long shot for Bruce Hurst as a youngster. At the age of one, his extreme bowed legs required corrective casts for a year. "Fortunately the casts and corrective shoes worked," Bruce recalls, "but I'm still pretty bow-legged," he adds, laughing.

Baseball and basketball were his passions as a youngster. "I would have to say that basketball was my first love. I was tall for my age, and nobody ever thought of Utah as a hotbed for baseball. But I did love baseball too."

Bruce was enough of a baseball fan that he slept with a Carl Yastrzemski poster over his bed. His first favorite team was the 1969 Amazing Mets. The irony of that choice would become apparent during the 1986 World Series.

Bruce Hurst was a serious baseball fan as a youngster growing up. He remembers collecting soft drink cans as a kid, and redeeming them so he could buy bubble gum to get the baseball cards that came with the gum. "I always watched the Game of the Week on Saturday, and I had enough cards that I could pull together the starting lineups for both teams and lay them out on the floor."

The youngest of five children, Bruce credits his two older brothers, Ross and Buck, for his early development as an athlete. "They were both a lot older than me, but they were good about letting their little brother hang around. Ross was a very good baseball player, close to professional potential.

"When I was around 12, a local man named Kent Garrett took an interest in me as a pitcher and really began working with me. He would talk to me about pitching fundamentals and breaking down my delivery points."

Years later, Hurst was honored with a parade in St. George following the 1986 World Series. During the speeches that followed at Dixie Junior College, he called Garrett up to the stage and presented him with the bat Hillerich & Bradsby had made for Bruce to use in the World Series.

By his senior year in high school Hurst had attracted the attention of the baseball scouts. Playing in the state tournament that June, Hurst had his left wrist broken by an errant fastball. Days later the Boston Red Sox made him their first round draft choice, and the twenty-second player selected overall in the draft. He may be the only Red Sox draftee who signed a contract with a cast on his writing and pitching arm.

THE ROAD TO FENWAY

Bruce Hurst's first stop in professional baseball was the Red Sox rookie team in Elmira, New York. "We had 30 guys, 25 lockers and three showers. It was quite an experience. I was 18 years old, and I had never been away from home for any length of time. It was a real adjustment. I was a long way from St. George, Utah.

"But our manager, Dick Berardino, was terrific. And I had some great teammates. Wade Boggs was on that team. Glenn Hoffman and Gary Allenson were there. We had a lot of talent."

He pitched well enough in Elmira to earn a promotion to Winter Haven in the Florida State League the following year. A good showing in the fall Florida Instructional League put Bruce on a fast track through the minor leagues. But then an injured elbow and lingering arm trouble slowed his progress. He was stalled in Winter Haven through 1979.

"Looking back on it, I hadn't pitched all that much during my high school years. I don't think my arm had developed enough to handle the amount of throwing you do on the professional level. I was pretty frustrated at the time."

WELCOME TO THE SHOW

An outstanding spring training performance in 2000, earned Hurst his first trip to the big leagues. Manager Don Zimmer and pitching coach Johnny Podres were impressed with the 22-year-old stylish southpaw and decided to bring him north with the big league club.

"I was as raw as any rookie who ever reported to the big leagues. I really wasn't ready, but they wanted to give me a shot. I remember my first game was against the Milwaukee Brewers. When they brought me in, we were down 13-1. The first thing I did was walk Robin Yount on four pitches, and that was the best thing I did. By the time they got me out of there, it was 18-1."

Bruce Hurst's first memories of Boston reflect his good nature. "I have always liked Boston, but in St. George all of the streets are laid out in a grid. I'm not sure how the streets are laid out in Boston, but I know it's not a grid. And I used to go in and order a chocolate milkshake and wonder why they didn't taste as good as they did back home. Finally I asked where the ice cream was, and the waitress said, 'Oh, you want a frappe!' "

Bruce was sent down to Pawtucket in mid-May for more seasoning. He pitched reasonably well during a September 1980 call-up. The biggest event in his life in 1981 was his marriage to his wife Holly in February of that year.

He split his time between Pawtucket and Boston in 1981, going 2-0 for the Red Sox. In 1982 he appeared in 28 games with the big club, and in 1983 he went 12-12 for the Red Sox. His 12 wins the following seasons showed that he had become an established major leaguer.

Bruce hit a rough patch in 1985. By midseason his 1-9 record earned him a demotion to the bullpen. "I went through a terrible spell where I couldn't get my changeup to work for me. And the fans really gave it to me. They would start booing as soon as I stuck my head out from under the bullpen roof. And I deserved it. I was awful. I understood it.

"I had experimented with the split-finger, and I remember my friend Danny Ainge [former Celtic great] saying 'just throw it.' I decided to go for it. I was tired of being a whipping boy, an underachiever. And that turned my whole career around." Hurst fought his way out of the bullpen, pitching impressively for a 9-4 record over the balance of the season.

AMERICAN LEAGUE CHAMPIONS

When the Boston Red Sox reported to Winter Haven, Florida, for spring training in 1986 there was a good feeling in the air. "We really felt good about our chances. We knew that Roger [Clemens] was going to be something special, we just didn't know how special. We had All-Star type players like Boggs, Jim Rice and Dwight Evans. And guys like Rich Gedman and Oil Can Boyd were really coming into their own," Hurst recalls.

The Red Sox and Bruce Hurst got off to a great start in 1986. On May 15, the Red Sox moved into first place and Hurst and Clemens were pitching as well as any combination in the American League. "I really felt good. My split-finger was doing just what I wanted it to. It made all the difference in the world."

Then in late-May disaster struck. Hurst, who was leading the American League in strikeouts at the time, collapsed on the Minneapolis Metrodome mound with a severe groin pull. The injury sidelined Hurst for almost two months. "It was tough," Hurst remembers. "We were playing well, and I had really found my groove."

Hurst returned to the mound in late July. By mid-August he had recaptured the form that he had displayed before his injury. On September 12 Hurst beat the Yankees 7-2 and the Red Sox increased their Eastern Division lead to 10 games. On September 27 Hurst's six-hit, 2-0 win over the Toronto Blue Jays clinched at least a tie for the division title.

"After pitching well in the game when we clinched a tie for the title, I knew I was all the way back. That was my first really big game test and I felt very good about my performance."

Bruce Hurst's stellar pitching in September earned him recognition as the American League pitcher of the month. And

A jubilant Bruce Hurst reacts to his 2-0 win vs. the Blue Jays on September 27, 1986, at Fenway Park to clinch a tie for first place in the A.L. East Division.

despite missing almost one-third of the season, his 11 complete games topped the Red Sox staff.

The California Angels surprised the Red Sox with an 8-1 trouncing in the Opening Game of the American League Championship Series at Fenway Park. But Hurst came back with a 9-2 complete game win the next day to knot the series at one game apiece. He pitched well for six innings in the crucial fifth game in Anaheim, and Dave Henderson's late game heroics kept the Red Sox hopes alive with a dramatic 7-6 win in 11 innings.

"When I was a youngster throwing the ball against a wall, I remember looking up at the sky and watching the jet planes flying over head. Like a lot of kids I would daydream that I was up there flying from city to city as a professional ballplayer. When we were flying back to Boston after Game Five at one point I looked down, and we were directly over St. George, Utah. It made me smile and brought back a lot of great memories."

OPENING GAME STARTER

The Red Sox beat the Angels easily in Games Six and Seven back at Fenway Park and the American League Champions prepared to meet the New York Mets in the World Series. Manager John McNamara named Bruce Hurst to start the first game of the Series on Saturday night.

"I remember being excited about starting the opening game of the World Series. It was an honor, and I was excited. I was nervous too, but it was a good kind of nervous. I had been pitching so well that I knew I could overcome the nerves."

Hurst and Ron Darling hooked up in a classic pitchers' duel in the Series opener. Hurst pitched eight innings of shutout ball, holding the Mets to four hits and allowing only one runner to get as far as third base. Hurst was lifted for a pinch-hitter in the ninth inning, but Calvin Schiraldi shut down the Mets in the last of the ninth for a 1-0 victory.

The Red Sox took Game Two at Shea Stadium, but the Mets turned the tables by sweeping the first two games at Fenway Park. Hurst took the mound for Game Five and held the Mets scoreless through the first seven innings. His teammates managed to score four runs against Dwight Gooden. Hurst held on for a complete game and a 4-2 Red Sox victory.

Following Hurst's second World Series victory in Game Five, Mets slugger Darryl Strawberry told the media, "Clemens is tough. But he's no Bruce Hurst."

After the Red Sox lost Game Six in heartbreaking fashion on Saturday night, the heavens opened on Sunday and the driving rain forced postponement of Game Seven. Manager McNamara named Bruce Hurst to start Game Seven on three days rest. He pitched brilliantly for five innings and the Red Sox led 3-0. The Mets finally got to him for three runs in the sixth and he left after six innings with the score tied at three. The Mets scored three in the seventh and two in the eighth inning, winning the World Series with an 8-5 victory.

"I just plain ran out of gas in the sixth inning. I tried to reach back for more, but it just wasn't there. I wish I could have hung on to get it done but my tank was empty. I honestly didn't have a thing left."

ALL-STAR PITCHER

The 1987 season was a great year for Bruce Hurst, but a disappointing one for his team. "We never really got on track. There might have been a little carryover from the disappointing end to the year before, but mostly we just never got it together. Things never jelled for us."

The Red Sox finished fifth in 1987 but Bruce Hurst managed a personal best of 15 wins. His outstanding effort earned him a spot on the American League All-Star team.

"The thing I remember best is sitting on the bus to the ballpark, and looking around at players like Dave Winfield and Reggie Jackson. It took a little getting used to thinking of them as my teammates. It was a little overwhelming."

But the record shows that Hurst is being his usual modest self. He definitely belonged on the American League All-Star team. His 15 complete games ranked second in the American league in 1987, and his 190 strikeouts were good enough for tenth place.

Asked about his strikeout prowess, the soft tossing Hurst responds, "I was never a power pitcher. My fastball might have been just about average. But my control got better as I gained experience. I would spot my fastball, and then come back with my split finger when I needed a strikeout. It worked out pretty well for me."

The 1988 season was the year of "Morgan Magic." After a lackluster first half, coach Joe Morgan replaced manager John McNamara. The team ended up winning its second Eastern

With batterymate Rich Gedman in 1988.

Division Championship in three years.

"Joe Morgan took over right after the All-Star game and we really caught fire. It was fun. We won 12 in a row, and Joe just let us go. In a lot of ways it was probably my best year in baseball. We really had a good time winning."

Hurst had his best outing of the season in an extra-inning game against the Detroit Tigers on August 7. Pitching in Tigers' Stadium, he held on for a 10-inning shutout and 3-0 Red Sox win.

The Oakland Athletics swept the Red Sox with four straight victories in the 1988 American League Championship Series. Hurst pitched well, putting together an era of 2.77 in two games, but he was matched up against Oakland ace Dave Stewart and took the losses in Games One and Four.

The 1988 season may have been Bruce Hurst's best year in the big leagues. He won a career-high 18 games, tying Roger Clemens for the team lead, and fourth best in the American League. His won-loss percentage of .750 ranked second in the league, and his 6.9 strikeouts per 9 innings pitched placed him sixth in the league standings. His outstanding pitching earned him fifth place in the Cy Young balloting for the American League.

NATIONAL LEAGUER

Bruce Hurst became a free agent after the 1988 season. And his outstanding season made him the most desirable pitcher among all free agents.

"I remember speaking with Dick Freeman of the San Diego Padres at 1 A.M. that December. We had asked the Padres for certain things and he told me they had agreed to all of them. I said, 'You've got yourselves a new left-hander.' I hung up the phone, sat down on the floor, and cried my eyes out.

"San Diego brought us a lot closer to our home in Utah. And family is the most important thing in our lives. But I already knew how much I would miss Boston."

Hurst pitched well for four years in San Diego. In 1989 he had 15 wins and led the National League in complete games. The following season he led the National League in shutouts. His combined ERA for 1989-90 was under 3.00. He won 15 games in 1991, and he followed up with 14 wins in 1992.

Asked if he had any second thoughts about the move to San Diego, Bruce responds, "Sure. Things didn't exactly work out the way we had hoped. When I signed, the Padres looked like a dynasty in the making. But things changed quickly and we didn't win anything. And I missed the intensity of the Boston fans. It just wasn't the same."

Bruce spent the 1993 season with the Colorado Rockies and moved on to the Texas Rangers in 1994. "My best memory with the Rangers is pitching and winning a game against the Red Sox in Fenway Park. I remember walking in from the bullpen to start the game and the cheers building as I got closer to the mound. Then they started a chant of 'MVP, MVP.' I was really moved by it. I'll never forget it."

LIFE AFTER BASEBALL

"I retired in June of 1994," Bruce recalls looking back on his major league career. "I probably could have pitched a little longer, but I realized that my family had been making sacrifices for me all those years, and it was time to stop being selfish."

At the time of our interview, Bruce Hurst was looking forward to returning to Boston in connection with the ceremonies marking the 100th anniversary of the Red Sox. "My wife Holly and I always loved Boston and New England. We lived in Wellesley during most of our time in Boston, and we loved it there. It's great to be a part of the celebration and to see so many old friends. And I love Fenway Park."

Bruce Hurst was inducted into the Boston Red Sox Hall of Fame in November 2004. His 88 wins ranks second to Mel Parnell among all-time Red Sox left-handers. And despite Fenway Park's reputation as a graveyard for left-handers, Bruce Hurst won over 60 percent (.629) of his decisions at home with the Red Sox.

Today Bruce Hurst and his family live in Gilbert, Arizona, about 10 miles south of Phoenix. Their old friend Danny Ainge and his family are near neighbors. Bruce and his wife Holly celebrated their 20th wedding anniversary in February 2001.

Bruce Hurst positively glows when he speaks about his family. "My son Ryan graduated from high school this May. He will go on a two-year Mormon mission when he turns 19 in October. My son Kyle is 15, my daughter Jordan is 13, and our youngest child, Mackenzie Marie, turns five on June 26th. They are all wonderful kids." Ten-year-old golden retrievers Mantle and Maris rounded out the Hurst household in 2001.

Red Sox fans will always consider Bruce Hurst to be an adopted son. But we understand that his heart will always belong to Utah.

Bruce Hurst's Rank in Red Sox History

CATEGORY	CAREER TOTALS	ALL-TIME BOSTON RED SOX RANK
10-K Games	13	4th
Strikeouts	1,043	6th
Games Started*	217	7th
Innings	1,459	15th
Wins	88	19th

* Tied

Source: 2004 *Boston Red Sox Media Guide*

38.
Rich Gedman Interview
March 1998

I interviewed Rich Gedman for a little over one hour at a skating rink in Marlborough, Massachusetts. While we talked, we watched one of his young sons play youth hockey. Rich gave me complete answers to all of my questions, but his eyes never left his youngster.

Rich expressed some concern about what direction my article would take. When I probed his concerns he said, "I know what I am trying to say to the fans, but it doesn't always come across the way I intend."

Asked for an example he cited a quote from his playing days. "I said, 'Red Sox fans are fickle.' I meant we are fickle, including myself in that comment. After all, I grew up sitting in the bleachers and I had been a Red Sox fan my whole life. But I understand why the fans reacted to my quote the way they did."

I wrote a draft of my article and sent it to Rich Gedman for his review. Then we sat at his kitchen table and went through his profile line-by-line. Rich struck me as a decent and sensitive guy who really cared about his message to Red Sox fans.

Rich Gedman was pleased with the way his profile turned out. I think that you, the reader, will be pleased as well.

RICH GEDMAN
NATIVE SON OF
NEW ENGLAND'S TEAM

Rich Gedman, a native of Worcester and a former Boston Red Sox All-Star catcher, loves baseball. "It's a great game. It enabled me to go places and to have experiences I never would have had. I think of my career as a dream come true."

LOCAL BOY

Gedman grew up in Worcester playing ball at Crompton Park, and listening to the Red Sox games on his transistor radio. "I was a little kid, but I still remember the '67 Sox, the Impossible Dream team. I would sneak the radio into bed and listen to them until I fell asleep. I thought I was really putting something over on my parents. But looking back, I'm sure they knew exactly what I was doing.

"I was 10 years old when I went to my first Red Sox game. My fifth grade teacher, Mr. Monfredo, took me, which was really nice of him. We sat right in the middle of the bleachers and I couldn't take my eyes off the field. I really could picture myself out there some day."

Ten years later, Gedman found himself standing on that same field in a Red Sox uniform. "I had been called up from Pawtucket in September of 1980, and I couldn't wait to get out on the field. I was just standing there, looking all around, taking in the sights. What an experience! Then some guy in the stands starts hollering 'Hey, Dave. Hey, Dave Schmidt.'

"I was the only player on the field, so I was pretty confused. Then it dawned on me. I was wearing the uniform they had assigned to someone else in spring training. Nobody even knew who I was," Gedman laughs reflecting on his big moment. "Things like that seemed to happen to me all through my career. It was kind of humbling, but it brought me back to reality pretty quickly."

Rich Gedman played baseball on the Worcester sandlots every chance he got. Like several thousand other New England teenagers, he chased windblown popups, and he remembers the sting of the bat on a cold March day.

"I went to St. Peter's Marian High School in Worcester where they had a good baseball program. My older brother, George Coleman, was in the Navy, and he used to send money home for my tuition payments," Gedman offers, obviously grateful for the generosity. "I played quite a bit as an undergraduate, but in my senior year we got a new coach, Bill Norkaitis, who challenged me to be a better player."

Gedman was a first baseman and a pitcher for the 1977 St. Peter's team, and he played a key role in their successful drive to the Massachusetts State Championship. One of his teammates on that championship team was J.P. Ricciardi, who is now the General Manager of the Toronto Blue Jays. But as a late-blooming New England kid, Gedman went unclaimed in the June Major League Draft.

At the time Gedman was 5'11" and close to 250 pounds. The major league scouts saw a young player who could hit for power, but who didn't project as a major leaguer at any position. The one scout who saw major league potential in Gedman was long-time Red Sox scout for New England, Bill Enos.

"I caught one game for our American Legion team that summer, and Bill Enos saw that I had some potential. He said, 'Rich, you'll never make it to the majors as a pitcher. You don't have enough power for the outfield or the corners, and you don't have the speed for the middle infield. What do you think that leaves?' I was happy to move to catcher, and it turned out to be the best thing I could have done."

Rich Gedman spent the summer learning to catch. While he adjusted to his new position, his weight dropped but he continued to hit with power. Bill Enos signed him for the Red Sox as an amateur free agent and Gedman went down to Pawtucket to practice with their players.

DOWN ON THE FARM

After spending the fall in the Instructional League, Gedman reported to the Red Sox farm team in Winter Haven, Florida. Rich Gedman has pleasant memories of his early days in the minors.

"We were bussed all over the state for away games, and a lot of the guys moaned and groaned about it. It never bothered me because my parents didn't own a car. It was kind of an adventure for me. I got along great with the Hispanic players because we were all happy just to have wheels," Rich recalls, smiling at the memory. "We had a great time looking out the windows and enjoying the scenery."

Gedman hit well in the Florida State League, and his .300+ average earned him a promotion to Double A Bristol, Connecticut, for the 1979 season. "I was pretty raw behind the plate. You don't get the game experience growing up in New England, and I hadn't been a catcher that long. But I busted my tail to improve. Having a good left-handed bat is a big advantage for a young catcher."

He continued to develop at Bristol, improving his handling of pitchers and batting a solid .278. Bristol manager Tony Torchia also taught him to put his bad games behind him and to focus that day's game. "That's a hard lesson for young players. You haven't played that much and you mostly have had success. But Tony was great with me."

Gedman's progress earned him a promotion to Pawtucket of the Triple A International League in 1980. Gedman's performance under PawSox manager Joe Morgan and his visible work ethic earned him his September 1980 call-up.

For every young boy who sits in the bleachers in Fenway Park and dreams of a career in a Red Sox uniform, possibly 1-in-100,000 sees his dream come true. If that young boy later signs a professional baseball contract as a non-drafted player, the odds drop to perhaps 100-1.

Asked what it takes to overcome these odds, Gedman answers, "In my case I had parents who encouraged us to go as far as we possibly could. They never put any ceilings on our ambitions. And they impressed on us the importance of hard work. Also," Gedman adds with emphasis, "I had the added motivation that each step in my baseball journey brought me closer to home."

Gedman managed to get into nine games that September. The highlight? "On my twenty-first birthday [September 26, 1980], I caught a Dennis Eckersley one-hitter. I just held my glove up, and he hit it every time. That was a memorable birthday," Rich recalls with a smile. "I'll never forget it."

When the 1981 season began, Gedman was back in Pawtucket as the PawSox starting catcher. His overall performance in Pawtucket earned him the honor of all-time PawSox catcher when that team held its twenty-fifth anniversary cele-

Geddy played in 62 games for Boston in 1981 hitting .288 and winning The Sporting News A.L. Rookie of the Year Award.

bration in 1997. And his outstanding play that season earned him a promotion to the major league club in Boston in June 1981.

BLEACHERS TO THE PLAYING FIELD

Gedman became the starting Red Sox catcher soon after he joined the team. He responded with a solid .288 batting average, and an eye-catching .434 slugging percentage. Although he only appeared in 62 games that season, *The Sporting News* selected him as their American League Rookie of the Year for 1981.

Rich Gedman was only 21 years old when the 1982 season began and he appeared to be the Red Sox catcher of the future. But his average tailed off to .249 in 1982, and his playing time declined. His offensive numbers improved in 1983, and he batted .294 in 204 at-bats, but he had lost his starting catcher's role to Gary Allenson. Clearly his career was at a crossroads.

"Walter Hriniak [former Red Sox hitting coach] really helped turn my career around. He told me that if I was willing to work, he would come out early every day and throw me batting practice. He went out of his way to help me, and I'll never forget it. He emphasized that I had to be ready when my chance came, and I started to make the most of my at-bats. Walter really worked hard with me.

"Then Walter asked around, and I got a spot in the Winter League in Caracas, Venezuela. The American players were heading home in droves that winter, but I stuck it out, and caught about 60 games down there. When I reported to Winter Haven for spring training in 1984, I went to our manager Ralph Houk and told him I was ready to be his everyday catcher."

Ralph Houk took Gedman at his word, and put him behind the plate for 133 games that season. Rich rewarded his manager with 24 home runs, and demonstrated an improved knack for handling pitchers. In addition to his impressive home run output, Rich contributed 72 RBI and produced a slugging average of .506.

Ralph Houk managed Rich Gedman from 1981 to 1984, and he has a lot of good things to say about him. "I really enjoyed watching Rich make himself into a major league catcher. He hadn't had a lot of playing time at catcher when he first came up, and it showed. But he really worked hard and showed me how serious he was. Watching him develop is one of my best memories from my time in Boston."

In 1985, new manager John McNamara recognized what he had in Gedman, and he penciled him into the lineup 144 times. McNamara's vote of confidence helped spur Rich to a batting average of .295 and 80 RBI. His performance earned him a spot on the American League All-Star team in July.

"What a thrill that was," Rich enthuses, looking back on his first All-Star selection. "Here I am, just a guy from Worcester, and I walk into the locker room in Minneapolis and there's Cal Ripken, Carlton Fisk, Don Mattingly, George Brett, and guys like that. I'll never forget it."

In September that season, Gedman had the biggest offensive day in his 13-season big league career. He hit for the cycle and drove in seven runs as the Red

Sox trounced the Blue Jays 13-1. He was only the sixth big league catcher since 1900 to hit for the cycle.

1986 SEASON

When the 1986 season began, Rich Gedman was 26 years old. He had spent at least a part of each of the six previous seasons in the major leagues, and he had achieved All-Star recognition. His baseball future appeared unlimited. But 1986 turned out be a mix of joy and sorrow for the Gedman family.

In late April he caught Roger Clemens' 20-strikeout game. Gedman set an American League record with 20 putouts in that contest. "What a memory that is," Rich says shaking his head in disbelief. In response to a question he answers, "Yes, my hand did hurt after that game. He's [Roger] throwing the ball 95 miles an hour and they're not cooperating by putting the ball in play. And everybody is cheering, knowing he's doing something special."

In May of 1986, Rich Gedman's father passed away. "He was my rock. His death was a terrible loss to all of us," Rich Gedman sadly reflects.

July of 1986 brought him All-Star honors for the second straight year. Playing in Houston's Astrodome for the first time, Rich had the challenge of catching Charlie Hough's knuckleball with the game on the line. But Gedman was equal to the task and the American League prevailed by a score of 3-2.

As the season progressed, he orchestrated the Red Sox pitching staff to 95 wins in their drive to the Eastern Division Title. But in September, Gedman lost his sister on the very day the team clinched its Eastern Division crown. "It was a time of real conflict for me. Family is the most important thing in my life, but the team needed me too," Gedman recalls with strong emotion in his voice.

The 1986 Red Sox went on to defeat the California Angles for the American League Championship. And Rich Gedman was right in the middle of the team's dramatic win over the Angels in Game Five.

"When I came up in the ninth inning we were down by a run and there were two outs," Gedman recalls. "They brought in a left-hander, Gary Lucas, who was tough on me. But his first pitch sailed inside and hit me. I was really startled but I was just happy to keep the inning alive."

The next hitter, Dave Henderson, drove a 2-2 pitch from Donnie Moore into the left-field bleachers for one of the most memorable home runs in Red Sox history. The Angels came back to tie the Red Sox in their half of the ninth, but Boston went on to win the game 7-6 in 11 innings.

The Red Sox swept the next two games in Boston and the Red Sox rode this storybook comeback into the World Series against the New York Mets. Gedman was a major factor in the Red Sox American League Championship Series victory, batting .357 and contributing six RBI.

The Red Sox had the heavily favored Mets down three games to two in the World Series, but failed to hold on to leads in Games Six and Seven. Gedman told sportswriters at the time, "Imagine being a kid from Worcester. I've been hearing all my life about how the Red Sox never win. I'd love to be a part of the team that ends that, and maybe have something to do with it. You don't know how excited I was after I hit that home run in the seventh game of the World Series. I really thought we had it won. It's still hard to believe we didn't win."

The loss of the World Series to the Mets clearly bothers Gedman many years later. "We wanted to win so badly. And we came so close. Looking back, I really did think we were going to win Game Seven. We really gave it everything we had."

LATER YEARS

During the off-season Gedman elected to test the free agent market to determine what the best young catcher in baseball might be worth. Unfortunately, he chose a time when baseball owners elected to hold the line on players' salaries. In a time period that was later ruled as collusion by the owners, no true market value offers were forthcoming from other clubs. Since he had not re-signed by January 1987, under Major League Baseball rules he could not go to spring training, and he could not rejoin the Red Sox until May 1.

"I don't even like to talk about those negotiations," Gedman offers many years later. "I just wanted to be paid what I was worth."

His shortened 1987 season resulted in a .205 batting average. "I couldn't even work out with the team before May 1. I got myself in shape, but I hadn't faced live major league pitching. The benefit of spring training is to get your timing down as a hitter. I never got on track in 1987."

Few baseball players maintain their offensive production at an All-Star level for an extended period of time. To do so requires an extraordinary combination of eye-hand coordination, physical reactions, and total concentration. Rich Gedman was unable to sustain his All-Star offensive production after the 1986 season.

In 1988, he batted .357 in the American League Championship Series with Oakland, but during the regular season his outstanding defensive play exceeded his offensive contribution. While Gedman caught 93 games for the 1989 team, his offensive production still lagged. In June of 1990, the Red Sox sold his contract to the Houston Astros. In 20 years the kid from Worcester had gone from the bleachers of Fenway Park, down to the playing field, and on to the National League.

Gedman finished out that season with Houston, and then moved on to the St. Louis Cardinals for 1991. He served as the backup catcher to the Cards' Tom Pagnozzi, and played under manager Joe Torre for two years. The 1992 season with the Cardinals would be Gedman's last in the major leagues.

"Once in a while a guy will say to me, 'Jeez, Rich, it's too bad how your career turned out.' I don't look at it that way at all. I'm just a regular guy from

In 1986 Gedman was named to his second All-Star team. His outstanding .357 ALCS batting average in '86 (10-28) was duplicated in '88 (5-14) when he led the Sox.

Worcester and I spent 13 seasons in the major leagues, 11 of them with the team I loved as a kid. I think of it as a terrific career."

TODAY

Today Rich Gedman's top priorities are his family, and his deeply felt spiritual beliefs. He lives with his wife, Sherry, two sons Michael and Matthew, and his daughter Marissa, in Framingham, Massachusetts. He actively participates in a number of charitable efforts in the Greater Boston area. He has also served as a member of the coaching staff at Belmont Hill.

Gedman has operated a baseball camp for youngsters for a number of years. He runs two sessions in Newton each summer. "I love to work with the kids to improve their skills. It would be terrific if some of them can enjoy the successful experiences I had as a player. And after all I've been through, I think I have a lot to offer some team as a coach."

Since our interview in 1998, the North Shore Spirit of the independent Northeast League has recognized that Gedman does indeed have a lot to offer as a coach. During the 2003 and 2004 seasons, Rich has been the bench coach for the Spirit. He serves under former Red Sox super sub, Manager John Kennedy.

Rich Gedman experienced the cheers of the Fenway Faithful and he felt the sting of their jeers during the later stages of his career. Asked if he ever wondered if it would have been easier in a different major league city, he responds with intensity, "Never. Nothing could ever begin to compare with the thrill of growing up rooting for the home team, and then going on to play for that team. It's a unique experience that few enjoy. I wouldn't change it at all. Not for a minute."

Take a good look at that young man sitting next to you at Fenway Park. It's a real long shot, but someday he may grow up to be an All-Star for the Boston Red Sox.

39.
Ralph Houk
March 2004

I interviewed Ralph Houk at his lovely home set on the outskirts of Winter Haven, Florida. Driving through Winter Haven on the way to Ralph's home brought back some great memories of past spring trainings. Winter Haven was the Red Sox spring training headquarters from 1966 to 1992, and the downtown area hasn't changed at all.

Ralph Houk has a lot of great baseball stories, but our focus was on the Red Sox-Yankee rivalry. He played against the Red Sox in a Yankee uniform in the late forties and early fifties. He managed the Yankees against the Red Sox in the sixties and seventies, and he managed the Red Sox against the Yankees in the early eighties. His is a unique perspective.

Houk sees the Red Sox-Yankee rivalry as the best sports rivalry of all. And he made some predictions that turned out to be prescient. In March 2004 he said, "These two teams are so evenly matched that I think it will come right down to the wire. I think this will be the best year ever for the rivalry."

Not only is he clairvoyant, but he is also completely up to date in his baseball theory. Forty years ago, he and his staff were manually tracking all the player match-ups that are computer-driven today. And he is quick to acknowledge that today's ballplayers are every bit as good as the ones he played against and managed.

Talking to Ralph Houk was a little bit like talking to an oracle. He celebrated his eighty-fifth birthday in August 2004. But to me, he sounded like he was capable of managing a major league ball club in 2005.

RALPH HOUK
ADOPTED SON OF
NEW ENGLAND'S TEAM

Former major league manager Ralph Houk is the only man alive who has managed both the Boston Red Sox and the New York Yankees. It comes as no surprise then that he has strong opinions on the ancient rivalry.

"I think it's the greatest rivalry in all of sports," Ralph Houk says with passion. "People talk about other rivalries, college football and the like, but I don't think anything else is even close. I can remember making appearances years ago in Connecticut, where the fans were pretty evenly split. That could get pretty intense.

"It's been such a great rivalry for so many years. And I think the two teams are so evenly matched that it will be bigger than ever this year. No other sports rivalry can top this one."

Houk managed the Boston Red Sox from 1981 to 1984. He had previously managed the Yankees from 1961 to 1963, winning three American League pennants and two World Series, before moving up to become their General Manager. He returned to the Yankees dugout as manager in 1966 and remained in that role through the 1973 season. He also managed the Detroit Tigers from 1974 to 1978.

When Ralph Houk retired after his 1984 season with the Red Sox, he had accumulated 1,619 wins during his 20 seasons as a major league manager. His win total places him 14th among all managers in the long history of major league baseball.

RED SOX FANS

"I loved my time in Boston. It's a great city and the fans are so loyal. There is so much history with the team and the fans are very aware of it. I think the Boston fans might have a better understanding of baseball than the New York fans," Houk emphasizes. "There is such a mix in the fans at a Yankee game, but just about everybody at Fenway Park is a serious fan.

"The fans in Boston took a little getting used to though. One inning they practically boo you off the field, and the next inning they're cheering you to the sky. They are so passionate about their team. Managing in Boston was very different, but it was a very enjoyable experience."

KANSAS FARM BOY

Ralph Houk was born in Lawrence, Kansas, on August 9, 1919. He grew up on the family farm during the Depression years. "We all had to pitch in," he remembers, "but I still found time to play sports. My brothers claimed I was playing ball all the time, but I really did work. I shucked corn and put up hay. I got up every morning and milked cows, and milked again in the evening."

Houk was an all-around athlete at Lawrence High School. He was best known for his prowess on the gridiron, but his high school yearbook included a poem about his basketball skills. "I was a pretty good player, very physical. Growing up on a farm, I was in better shape than most of the other kids.

"I didn't play a lot of baseball growing up. I played for the kid teams sponsored by the Rotary and Kiwanis, and later I played in the Ban Johnson League. That's where Bill Essick, the scout for the Yankees saw me.

"I had a chance to go to college on a football scholarship. I had offers from the University of Kansas and Oklahoma. But Bill Essick and the Yankees offered me $500 to sign a minor league contract, and $75 a month. That was a lot of money in 1939, so I took it. I thought I was a millionaire," Ralph laughs.

Houk began his career deep in the Yankees minor league system at Neosho, Missouri, where he played well and batted .286. He demonstrated an early streak of independence the following season, holding out for a raise before reporting to Joplin, Missouri, for a whopping $90 per month. The following season he was promoted to Augusta, Georgia, and he was clearly on route to the major leagues.

But shortly after the attack on Pearl Harbor the following December, he and his brother Harold decided to enlist in the Army. And the Army would be his employer for the next four years.

"THE MAJOR"

" 'The Major' was my baseball nickname. I think Gene Woodling pinned that on me when we were teammates on the Yankees and it stuck. My highest rank in the Army was captain. When I was discharged at the end of World War II, I was a captain. If I had remained in the Army Reserves I would have been promoted to major for time-in-grade, but the only place I was a major was in baseball."

Ralph Houk downplays his exploits during World War II, but the facts tell a different story. Shortly after enlisting, he applied for Officer's Candidate School and was accepted. He came out of OCS as a Second Lieutenant, and after additional training he was sent overseas. He was part of the D-Day invasion, and his unit served as an advance force checking roads and bridges as the Allies moved through northern France. He was wounded by shrapnel and became a company commander following his recovery. Later he was awarded the Silver Star for his actions during the Battle of the Bulge.

His closest call came near the end of the war when a sniper shot a bullet that went through the top of his helmet, perforated the helmet liner, and came out cleanly in the front. "I was sitting in my jeep, and the sniper was above us. All I heard was a 'tick.' I didn't even know what happened, but my driver saw it and thought I was dead. He pulled the jeep forward and was surprised when I asked him what happened."

Sixty years later Houk shows the helmet to a visitor at his Florida home, and remarks, "There have been many times when things weren't going well, that I thought of this helmet. And I've said, 'Hey, I'm lucky to be here.' "

YANKEE ROOKIE

Ralph Houk spent the 1946 season with Beaumont in the Texas League and he made the New York Yankee roster for the 1947 season. He played his first game for the Yankees in late April of 1947. In the early going he shared the catching duties with Aaron Robinson. "Robinson caught when there was a right-hander pitching for the other team and I took over when there was a lefty going. I was playing quite a bit.

"Early in the season Yogi Berra was playing out in right field. Later they brought him in to catch. After that, my main job was to break in Yogi's new mitts," Houk adds with a chuckle.

He also has an amusing story to tell about his near home run. "We were playing in Chicago in my rookie year and I hit a ball off the foul pole that landed in foul territory. In those days, that was considered a ground-rule double. I didn't think much of it. After all I was a young strong guy, and I figured I would get my share of home runs. But I never hit another one in my eight years in the big leagues," he laments. "And the following year they changed the rule so that anything off the foul pole was a home run."

One year he worked as a salesman for Ballantine Breweries in the off-season. "We all had to do something to make ends meet. I used to start off with a morning sales meeting where they would give us $25. We would give something to the bartender and buy a beer for the regular customers at each stop. But the regulars got to know my schedule, and when I got to the next stop they'd be there waiting for me."

RED SOX-YANKEES IN THE FORTIES

Ralph Houk remembers being conscious of the Yankee-Red Sox rivalry right from the beginning. "I couldn't tell you the exact day, but you just knew it was different from other teams. For one thing, there would always be a lot of Red Sox fans at the games in the Stadium. That didn't happen with other teams."

His most hotly contested play against the Red Sox occurred late in the 1947 season when both teams were in the thick of the pennant race. "The score was 6-6, and Johnny Pesky tried to score from third on a ground ball to first base. Tommy Henrich got the ball to me in plenty of time and I slapped the ball on Johnny. But the umpire called him safe. I couldn't believe it."

A review of a fine series of photos by UPI convinces even a Red Sox partisan that Ralph has a case. "Whenever I see Johnny, I tell him, 'You were out.' Johnny always says, 'No, Ralph, I got in there.' " Since this is Ralph Houk's article we'll give him the last word. "I think Johnny knows he was out," Houk states with confidence.

Ralph Houk is asked why the Yankees always seemed to finish just ahead of the Red Sox in the late 1940s and early 1950s. "That's a very good question. The two teams were so close it's hard to say who had the edge. Usually it comes down to pitching. And I think the Yankees had slightly better pitching during those years."

ROOKIE MANAGER ON THE HOTSEAT

Ralph Houk may have been Yogi Berra's backup catcher, but the Yankees understood his true value to the team. During the eight seasons he spent with the club, the Yankees won six American League pennants and six World Series. In 1955 the Yankees made him the manager of their Triple A franchise in Denver. Two years later they brought him back to the majors to serve as a coach under Casey Stengel. And when it came time to replace Casey as the Yankee manager, Ralph Houk was named his successor.

"That was quite a year to break in as manager. We had to go through the expansion draft right after I was named as manager, and we lost some good players. Then we were in a fight for the pennant for most of the season but all the writers wanted to talk about was Mantle and Maris chasing Babe Ruth's record. And we had a terrific team. I would put that team against anyone."

Billy Crystal produced a movie about that season, *61* and it was aired on HBO. Asked what he thought of the movie, Ralph offers, "It was alright. I thought they did a nice job with Roger Maris. The actor even looked like him. But I didn't like the way they portrayed Mickey. They spent too much time playing up his off-field activities. It wasn't like that. He couldn't have played if he was doing all that. His only problem was he couldn't say no."

With his tongue firmly implanted in his cheek, Ralph adds, "Besides, I think I was better looking than the guy [actor Bruce McGill] who played me."

The 1961 Yankees went on to defeat the Cincinnati Reds in the World Series. The following year Houk's Yankees won their second-straight American League pennant and followed up with a World Series win against the San Francisco Giants. In 1963 the Yankees finished first in the American League but were swept in the World Series by the Los Angeles Dodgers.

UPSTAIRS, DOWNSTAIRS

After the 1963 season Ralph Houk was asked to move upstairs and become the Yankees General Manager. "They asked me to take the job. Roy Hamey was retiring and they wanted me to fill his spot. Heck, I had been with the Yankees since I was 18 years old. I would have done anything they asked me to.

"But I didn't like that job much. I think it's different today, but then you spent more time on the business end than on the players. I would be negotiating contracts with groundskeepers, and worrying about stadium maintenance. I was glad to go back to managing in 1966."

Ralph Houk replaced Johnny Keane as the Yankees manager during the 1966 season, and remained in that role through 1973. But the Yankees farm system had failed to produce the endless supply of prospects that had powered the team for so many years, and his best showing was second place in 1970. Ralph Houk decided it was time to move on and he accepted the job as manager of the Detroit Tigers for the 1974 season.

"The Tigers organization had some good baseball men and they made me a nice offer. Detroit is a good baseball city. They have good fans, but they're different from the Boston and New York fans, more Midwestern.

"I had some good years in Detroit. But it was strange to go back to Yankee Stadium in a Tigers' uniform. It felt weird to go to the visitors clubhouse and the visitors dugout after all those years," recalls Houk shaking his head at the memory. "But the fans at the stadium were very nice to me. I appreciated it.

"After the 1978 season I decided I had had enough of managing. I was enjoying scouting for Detroit and being away from the grind, but Haywood Sullivan called and told me they wanted me to manage the Red Sox.

"I told him I really wasn't interested, but he kept after me. Told me he wanted me to fly down to talk to me. He was very persuasive and made me a very attractive offer," Houk recalls. "I accepted and I'm glad I did. Haywood Sullivan was as good a baseball man as I ever worked with."

MANAGER OF THE BOSTON RED SOX

Houk got an early baptism to the roller coaster that goes with managing the Boston Red Sox. Opening Day at Fenway Park in 1981 matched the Red Sox against the Chicago White Sox and Carlton Fisk, who was appearing for the first time in a visitors' uniform. Dennis Eckersley pitched brilliantly through the first seven innings, and reliever Bob Stanley was brought in for the eighth to protect a 3-0 lead. With two men on, Fisk golfed a Stanley sinker into the left-field screen, and the White Sox went on to win 5-3, spoiling Houk's Red Sox debut.

"When you play in Fenway Park you have to have a "lights out" closer. Bob Stanley did a wonderful job for me during the four years I was there. But no lead is safe in that ballpark. In other parks if you have a three-run lead going into the ninth, you feel pretty good about it. But in Fenway, with that wall in left field, anything can happen."

The 1981 season was marred by a player strike, which began on June 12. The Red Sox were four games behind the Eastern Division leading Yankees at the time. When play resumed in August, a "split season" matching the winner of the first half against the post-strike winner was adopted. The team enjoyed a good

A mound conference with Bruce Hurst and Rich Gedman.

second half, finishing only a game and a half behind the Milwaukee Brewers.

"We had a good team, but the strike was distracting for everybody. We made a nice run in the second half but it wasn't good enough. We had some good players on that team. Dennis Eckersley pitched well for me. Dave Stapleton played all the infield positions probably as well as anyone I've seen. Rich Gedman started to come along as a catcher," Houk remembers.

"And when I think back on that first year in Boston, I think about what a big help Carl Yastrzemski was to me. He was the leader of that team, a veteran, and all the players looked up to him. He showed me a lot of respect, and it helped me a great deal. It really meant a lot to me. As a new manager, you really need that support."

The 1982 Red Sox improved to 89 victories and were in contention in the American League East for most of the season. "Jim Rice had a big year. He was our big offensive threat all four years I was there. He was probably as strong as anyone I have ever seen. And Dwight Evans had a terrific season. He really came into his own that season.

"And we made some progress with our pitching. That was something we tried to work on. John Tudor pitched pretty well and Bruce Hurst showed promise. I felt we were really making progress."

The Red Sox slipped in 1983, finishing sixth in the American League East, but several players had outstanding seasons. Wade Boggs led the American League with a batting average of .361 and he topped the league in on-base percentage as well. Jim Rice led the American League in home runs and total bases. Bob Stanley's 33 saves ranked second in the league, and Bruce Hurst showed future promise with 12 wins.

YAZ

The emotional highlight of the 1983 season came on October 2 when Carl Yastrzemski was honored at Fenway Park for his 23 seasons with the team. At the conclusion of the pre-game ceremonies Yaz jogged around the perimeter of park, reaching out and touching as many fans as he could.

"Yaz worked as hard as any player I saw in all my years of baseball. He was the star of the team, but nobody worked harder. He took hours of batting practice and fielding practice. It was such a great example for the younger players. Jim Rice was another hard worker and I think it came from watching how hard Yaz worked.

"And he [Yaz] was a very smart ballplayer. He would have made a fine manager if he had the interest. I remember when we would come to Fenway and I was managing the Yankees, I would just give the third base coach a hand signal when I wanted to steal. But I noticed that every time we would go to steal the Red Sox would pitchout.

"I told Dick Howser, my third base coach, that I would flash him the steal sign but not to pass it on. Sure enough, they pitched out, so I knew the son-of-a-gun in left field was stealing my signs. I looked out at Yaz in left and I thumbed my nose at him. He gave me a hand signal right back."

The 1984 Red Sox won 86 games, but the Detroit Tigers got off to a torrid start and never looked back. Bright spots for the season included Tony Armas' league-leading 43 home runs, and Dwight Evans' 121 runs scored to top the league. In a sign of things to come, Dennis "Oil Can" Boyd won 12 games and 20-year-old Roger Clemens made his debut with the team. The highlight of Roger's 9-4 rookie season was an 11-1 win over Kansas City featuring 15 strike-outs and no walks.

At the end of the 1984 season, Ralph Houk decided it was time to retire. "I had managed for 20 years in the big leagues and I turned 65 during the season. It was time. Haywood Sullivan tried to change my mind. He felt we were making progress, and we were, but I was tired of the travel.

"It's not the games or the managing that gets to you. That's the fun part. It's the travel and everything else that goes with the job. It's leaving home and finding a new place to live every year. It finally wears you down.

"I really am grateful for my four years in Boston. It's a wonderful city and the fans are great. Haywood Sullivan was just a terrific fellow to work with. And Mrs. Yawkey was so good to us. I remember she gave my wife Betty a car. We have lots of nice memories of our time in Boston."

Asked if commanding soldiers in combat in his mid-twenties had helped make him a better manager, Houk agrees. "I really think it did. You learn a lot

about men in that situation. How they react, how much you can ask of them. I think a lot of what I learned during the war was helpful to me. And when you look back on that time, you realize things aren't as bad as they may seem."

MANAGERIAL THOUGHTS

Ralph Houk will be 85 years old next August, but he sounds as if he could put on a uniform and take over a big league club tomorrow. "If a general manager gave me a choice between an outstanding starting pitcher, even a 20-game winner, and an outstanding closer, I would take the closer every time. You get to use a starter 30-something games a year, but you get to use the closer 60 or more times a year, and always when it counts.

"He helps you not only in the game he saves, but it carries over to the next game you play. If you have a two- or three-run lead in the ninth inning and you end up losing, it's demoralizing and it stays with you."

Asked if he would have used computers if they had been available when he managed, Houk responds in the affirmative. "Absolutely, but maybe not for the reasons you think. We charted every pitch, and every ball that was put in play. We tracked the count and where the ball went. We had the information on every player we ever faced. I had all the information I could handle.

"But we did it all by hand and it took hours to record, tabulate, and summarize. The computer would have made that so much less time consuming. And it would have been a lot easier to get to the information when you need it. I can see how it would have been a big help."

And Ralph Houk has strong opinions on making pitching changes. "I always made my mind up on pitching changes based on what I had seen from the dugout. I never asked a pitcher how he was feeling because I knew what he was going to say. Every pitcher thinks he can get the next guy, and that's how you want them to feel.

"And I never asked the catcher how he thought the pitcher looked either. I was a catcher for years, and I was always closer to my pitchers than my managers. The catcher might be going out for dinner with the pitcher after the game, he's not going to disagree with him. I was usually signaling to the bullpen before I ever got to the mound and my pitchers knew that was how I operated. They knew they were gone before I ever got to the mound."

Ralph Houk thinks the ballplayers of today are as good as the players he played with and the players he managed. "The new ballparks have made some difference in how the game is played. But we had great players in the past and we have great players today. I think their equipment is a little better today and the training facilities are better."

Asked if he has any words of wisdom for rookie Red Sox manager Terry Francona, Ralph replies, "I would tell him to be sure to get along with the media. Keep them on your side. I'm sure he'll be a good manager."

RALPH HOUK TODAY

Today Ralph Houk and his wife Betty live in a lovely home set on a golf course outside of Winter Haven, Florida. The Houks celebrated their fifty-sixth wedding anniversary in June 2004.

"Donna is our oldest child, and she lives in Ohio. Dick is the next oldest and he lives in south Florida. Bobby is our youngest, and he lives in Seattle, Washington. He'll be coming in soon and we'll do some fishing together. We also have three grandchildren and five great grandchildren."

It seems a little unfair to ask Ralph Houk which team he would root for in a Red Sox-Yankees playoff series in October. After all, the man managed the Red Sox for only four years and he was associated with the Yankees for 35 years. But the question is asked anyway.

"I'm not even sure I can answer that. And remember, I've been gone so long that the only one on the Yankees who I really know is Mel Stottlemyre. Those are the two clubs to beat. Those two teams are so evenly matched this year, it's hard to answer that question. It's a toss-up. It's a long season. A lot can happen before then."

If you read his words closely, you can almost hear the voice of Houk's mentor, Casey Stengel, who was a master at handling tough questions. But if you read his words again, you will also notice that he didn't say that he would be rooting for the Yankees!

40.

Joe Morgan Interview

May 2001

I interviewed Joe Morgan at his home in Walpole, Massachusetts. When I arrived he was working in his garden, enjoying one of his favorite pastimes. We spent over an hour in his den while Joe reminisced about his 40 years in professional baseball.

Anyone who has ever heard Joe Morgan speak knows that he is a master storyteller. He has some wonderful stories about his long association with baseball, and he is also quite a baseball historian. At several points during our conversation he referred to a well-worn copy of The Baseball Encyclopedia, *complete with Joe's notes in the margins.*

Terry Francona may go on to win five World Championships and become the most highly regarded manager in Red Sox history. But Joe Morgan was one of us and "Morgan Magic" will always be part of our Red Sox lexicon. And Terry Francona will never plow our highways during a blizzard.

After I finish a one-on-one interview, I pop in the tape of our session and listen to it on the drive home. When I turned on Joe's tape, nothing happened. When I turned it over, there was still nothing. When I arrived home, I sat down and typed out every word I could remember.

Because I didn't have the tape, I sent a draft of the article to Joe for his review. He called me with a few minor corrections and told me that it "looked good." Best of all, I found out what "six, two, and even" means!

JOE MORGAN
NATIVE SON OF
NEW ENGLAND'S TEAM

If you are looking for the ideal next door neighbor, former Red Sox manager Joe Morgan would make an excellent choice. Joe is a great storyteller, he is a terrific family man and he is as honest as the day is long. But you had better plan on moving to Walpole, Massachusetts, because Joe has lived there all his life and he's not about to change that anytime soon.

"I grew up less than a mile from here," Joe states proudly in the study of his Walpole home, "and my wife Dottie lived about two miles away. We are both Townies."

When Joe Morgan succeeded John McNamara as the manager of the Boston Red Sox in the middle of the 1988 season, he became the first local man to hold that post since Shano Collins (of Charlestown, Massachusetts) managed the team in 1932. After the team won six straight games under Morgan, he went from "interim" to permanent manager. The win streak eventually reached 12 straight, and the team won 19 out of the first 20 games that he managed. About this time the phrase "Morgan Magic" entered the Red Sox vocabulary of terms for the ages.

The Red Sox had gone from nine games out of first place to a tie for the division lead during Morgan's first three weeks on the job. After spending 35 years in professional baseball toiling in relative anonymity, Joe Morgan had become one of the best-known public figures in New England.

THE PRIDE OF WALPOLE, MASSACHUSETTS

Joe Morgan was born in Walpole, Massachusetts, on November 19, 1930. Joe is a "Clareman." Both his mother and father were born in County Clare, Ireland. He grew up a Boston baseball fan like so many other New Englanders.

"I remember we would get on the bus in Walpole Center and it would drop us off on Huntington Avenue by Wentworth Institute. It cost us $1.04 for a round-trip. Then we would walk across the Fens to Fenway Park.

"My father worked weekends so he would take us to weekday doubleheaders, two for the price of one. He would always try to take us to see the Philadelphia Athletics when they were in town because their manager, Connie Mack, was an Irishman."

Joe starred in baseball and hockey at Walpole High School. "I loved baseball, but it seemed like you were more involved in the action in hockey. You could end up standing around a lot in baseball."

Joe's athletic prowess earned him a scholarship to Boston College. Legendary BC hockey coach Snooks Kelley offered him a scholarship and when they realized he was an all-scholastic baseball player as well, BC added free books to the offer. He commuted daily to BC from Walpole while playing center on the hockey team and shortstop on the baseball team. In 1952, the Boston Braves were looking for a shortstop and a catcher. Told that they could find both of them at Boston College, the Braves invited Morgan and Mike Roarke (who would also go on to a long career in professional baseball as a player and a major league coach) to Braves Field for a tryout.

"The Braves had a night game so they were all sitting around waiting to practice while we had the field. I had taken a lot of grounders from Braves manager Charlie Grimm, and one of the Braves said, 'They want to see what kind of arm you have. Throw the next one as far over the first baseman's head as you can.' With that I took the next grounder and threw it about 40 rows up into the stands behind first base. Charlie Grimm threw the bat up in the air and said, 'Sign him!' "

The Braves signed Morgan to a $22,500 bonus. "That was a lot of money in those days. I bought my parents a bunch of stuff for their house and I bought a car. It went pretty fast.

"I had a chance to sign with the Red Sox for a little less money but the Braves were struggling at the time, and I figured they were the faster route to the majors. Of course, about the time I was ready, the Braves were in the World Series every year and the Red Sox were down. But how could you know that at the time?"

THE REAL BULL DURHAM

Morgan's first stop on the road to the majors was Hartford, Connecticut, with the Braves' farm team in the Eastern

League. "Boy, was I overmatched at the plate. That was a pitcher's league. The next year they sent me to Evansville in the old Three-I League and I did much better there."

Joe earned his bachelors degree from BC in 1953, majoring in history and government. He spent the 1954 and 1955 seasons in the US Army, most of it at Fort Sill in Oklahoma. Although he lost two seasons in the prime of his career, he is not bitter. "It was my time to serve and I got to play a lot of baseball. It allowed me to experiment some at the plate and I came out a better hitter."

Morgan as Pawtucket Red Sox manager in 1975.

In 1956 Joe played for Jacksonville in the Sally League where he hit .301. More importantly, he married Dottie Glebus that year. "Dottie deserves all the credit in the world. Unless you've been a baseball wife, you have no idea what it is like."

In 1957 Joe hit .316 in Double A and the following season he played well in Triple A. That earned him a promotion to the big league team in Milwaukee. Joe began the 1959 season with the Milwaukee Braves and finished the year with the Kansas City A's in the American League. In 1960 he was back in the National League with the Philadelphia Phillies. In August, Phillies manager Gene Mauch called Joe into his office.

"I said, 'Well, Gene, is it back to Louisville or Buffalo?' And he said 'No, we've sold you to Cleveland.' I was bouncing all over Hell," Joe laughs in memory. "I played well in Cleveland. I hit .298 and I had a couple of home runs. That was my best year in the majors."

Joe started the 1961 season with Cleveland, but the

Indians traded him to the St. Louis Cardinals in May. The Cardinals told Morgan to report to their farm team in Charleston. The Morgans got in the family car and headed south. Joe stopped at a pay phone along the way to call the Cardinals to ask if it was Charleston, West Virginia, or Charleston, South Carolina.

It turned out to be Charleston, West Virginia, and Joe spent the better part of four seasons trying to find a route back to the big leagues. He finally made it to St. Louis in September of 1964, appearing in three games with the National League pennant winners. The Cardinals tried to add him to their World Series roster when their second baseman Julian Javier was injured, but since he was not on the Cardinal's roster on September 1, the Yankees exercised their right of refusal.

"It would have been nice to get to the World Series." Joe reflects. "I probably wouldn't have played but it would have been a great experience and a nice bonus."

ON THE ROAD AGAIN

That September call-up to the Cardinals would be Joe Morgan's last trip to the big leagues as a player. For Joe it was back to the minors and a new career as a manager. Managing in the Pittsburgh Pirates system, Joe made stops in Raleigh, North Carolina, York, Pennsylvania, Columbus, Ohio, and back to Charleston.

In addition to all of his major and minor league stops, Joe had also played winter ball in Puerto Rico, Venezuela, and the Dominican Republic. Wherever he went, his family came with him. "We always kept the family together. Dot deserves all of the credit for that. She drove all over the country with four kids in the car and a trailer hitched to the back. One time she took a wrong turn in Center City, Philadelphia, and she had to back the car up with the trailer on the back in the middle of all that traffic. She definitely earned her keep."

Joe made it back to the big leagues as a coach for the 1972 Eastern Division champion Pittsburgh Pirates. But in 1973 he was back in the minors managing in Charleston again.

In 1974 he heard that the Red Sox were looking for a manager for their Pawtucket farm club. "I called Dick O'Connell [Red Sox General Manager] at home. The first thing he said was 'How did you get this number?' Then he said, 'A lot of people have been asking about the job, and making a lot of calls, but you're the only one who has called *me*. I make the decisions around here, and I say you've got the job.' After 20-plus years of living all over the United States, I was with a team that was less than an hour's drive away. Finally we didn't have to move."

PAWSOX LEGACY

Joe Morgan's delight for Pawtucket was matched by the PawSox management's enthusiasm for him. Mike Tamburro, PawSox president, has always said, "Joe's a legacy in Pawtucket. He was the perfect man to have with us. He's a class act and he's an institution down here."

Joe Morgan was named the International League's Manager of the Year in 1977. Players who passed through Pawtucket on their way to making the 1975-1980 Boston Red Sox perennial contenders included Fred Lynn, Jim Rice, Rick Burleson and Butch Hobson. His next generation of future big league stars featured Wade Boggs, Bruce Hurst, Rich Gedman and Marty Barrett.

Joe has the distinction of managing in the longest game in professional baseball history. On April 18, 1981, the PawSox hosted the Rochester Red Wings in a game that began at 7:30 P.M. and was suspended after 32 innings at 4:09 A.M. on April 19th with the score tied 2-2. The game was finally resumed on June 23 and attracted worldwide attention. The PawSox ended the marathon contest with a 3-2 win in the 33rd inning.

"I wanted the game to go 40 innings," Morgan recalls today. "That way I figured no one would ever have a chance at breaking our record. Instead we won in the very first inning when they resumed the game."

Morgan managed the PawSox through the 1982 season, leaving to become a scout for the parent club in 1983. PawSox owner, Ben Mondor, remembers Joe Morgan fondly. "We'll always be beholden to Joe. He's a helpful, astute, cooperative man."

BACK TO THE BIG LEAGUES

In 1985 Joe Morgan returned to the big leagues as the first base coach for the Boston Red Sox under manager John McNamara. In 1986 he moved to the bullpen as the Red Sox fell just short of the World Championship. His World Series share allowed Joe the luxury of taking the winter off. For over 30 years Joe had worked at a variety of jobs to help balance the Morgan family budget.

"When I was working in the minors we were lucky if we broke even over the year. You did it for the love of the game. Let's see if I can remember all the jobs I had. I was a handyman, I delivered oil, and I was a bill collector. I did some substitute teaching and I coached hockey in the inner city. I was truck dispatcher and I took the census. But I ended up in the maintenance department for the Mass Turnpike and that was a good job.

"It seemed like you were always coming home with something you didn't need like 9-Lives cat food when a truck turned over. I'll never forget plowing during the blizzard of '78. You would be going along and all of a sudden you would hear 'clunk' and you would know you had run into another car buried in the drifts."

Morgan was the Red Sox third base coach when the 1988 season began. He took over as the interim manager of the team when John McNamara was fired right after the All-Star Game.

"I remember it happened just before the game. Haywood Sullivan and Lou Gorman came into the clubhouse, and Haywood went right into McNamara's office and Gorman came over and sat down beside me. Lou said that they were going to make a change and that I'd be taking over for the time being.

MORGAN MAGIC

"What I remember best was winning those first 12 games. I don't think anybody else will ever do that. First of all, when you take over a team during the season it is usually because they are going bad. Second, 12-game winning streaks aren't all that common to begin with. That 12-game streak is probably my best memory as a manager."

After winning 19 of their first 20 games with Morgan at the controls, the team cooled off somewhat but still managed to hang on to win the Eastern Division championship. The team played .600 ball (46-31) under Morgan and led the American League in runs and batting average for the year.

Unfortunately, the team ran into a red-hot Oakland A's team and they were swept four straight in the playoffs. "I thought we had a shot at taking them," Morgan remembers, "but when we lost that first game we were in trouble. Losing the first game of a series like that changes everything."

In 1989, Joe Morgan's first full year as manager of the team, the Red Sox never caught fire in the manner of his 1988 team. Former All-Star pitcher Bruce Hurst signed with the San Diego Padres as a free agent during the off-season and no one was signed to replace his 18 victories in 1988. The team led the American League in runs scored and batting average for the second year in a row, but the pitching just wasn't there. The team finished in third place with 83 victories, six games behind the division-winning Toronto Blue Jays.

Joe Morgan's 1990 Red Sox club added former National League All-Star catcher Tony Pena as a free agent, and outfielder Tom Brunansky in a trade with the St. Louis Cardinals. The team stayed in the hunt for the Eastern Division crown behind the 21-6 pitching of Roger Clemens. When Clemens came up lame with an inflamed shoulder tendon, the team struggled to hold on to their division lead.

The Sox went into the last game of the season against the Chicago White Sox at Fenway clinging to a one-game lead. In the top of the ninth Boston held a 3-1 lead. But with two outs, the White Sox had two base runners and Ozzie Guillen was at bat representing the lead run. Guillen lined a twisting shot in the direction of the right-field corner and Tom Brunansky was last seen diving desperately for the ball just as he went out of range of the TV cameras. Brunansky emerged with the ball, a division championship, and an assured place in every Red Sox highlight tape.

Unfortunately, the Brunansky catch was the last highlight of the 1990 season as the Sox were swept again in four straight by the Oakland A's in the American League Championship Series. The Red Sox had compiled the highest batting average in the American League for the third straight year, but could only manage four runs in four games against a strong Oakland pitching staff.

In 1991 the Morgan-led Red Sox dropped off in offensive production from the previous three years. The club's pitching was thin after Roger Clemens who registered 18 wins. The team stayed in contention for the most of the year but ended up tied for second with the Detroit Tigers, seven games behind the Toronto Blue Jays.

Following the 1991 season, Butch Hobson was named to replace Joe Morgan as the Red Sox manager. Joe Morgan managed the Red Sox in 563 games during his three and one-half years at the helm and his teams won 301 times. The fielding averages of each of his four teams rank among the 10 best in Red Sox history. And Joe Morgan was the first Red Sox manager since Bill Carrigan (1913-1916) to lead the Red Sox into postseason play twice.

SAFE AT HOME

Joe plays a lot of golf these days, something he really didn't get to do during his 40-year baseball career. "This is the year I'm going to break 90, if I'm ever going to do it," Joe states with resolve. Gardening is another passion, and an annual ritual for Joe and Dottie is a trip to the Kentucky Derby.

If you want to see Joe Morgan's Irish eyes light up, ask him about his kids and his grandchildren. He and Dottie see a lot of their four children, Joe, Jr., Billy, Cathy and Barbara Jean, and their five grandchildren. "They are all pretty close by, which makes it nice," Joe offers.

Joe is also active with the Boston Braves Historical Association, an organization devoted to preserving the history of the team that represented Boston in the National League from 1876 to 1952. He has served as master of ceremonies at their annual meeting, and he attends other functions honoring the Braves' proud history in Boston.

"When I was a kid, I rooted for the Red Sox and the Braves," Joe recalls. "A lot of kids followed one team and not the other, but I never understood that. They were both Boston teams, it was baseball."

Joe's best known saying is "six, two, and even." Asked for the story behind this saying, Morgan replies, "I had a minor league manager, Joe Schultz, who used to say it all the time. I finally asked him what it meant, and he said, 'Don't worry about it. It doesn't mean anything.' Then in 1992 somebody sent me an old racing program with a list of racing terms. And there it was, 'six, two, and even: a term used by bookmakers in the backstretch.' "

Pressed for his meaning when he used it in conversation with reporters, Joe laughs. "I was just trying to baffle them the way they were always trying to baffle me. You have to remember, I grew up around here!"

Joe Morgan is a baseball fan, just like the rest of us.

Index